Naked Lens

Beat Cinema

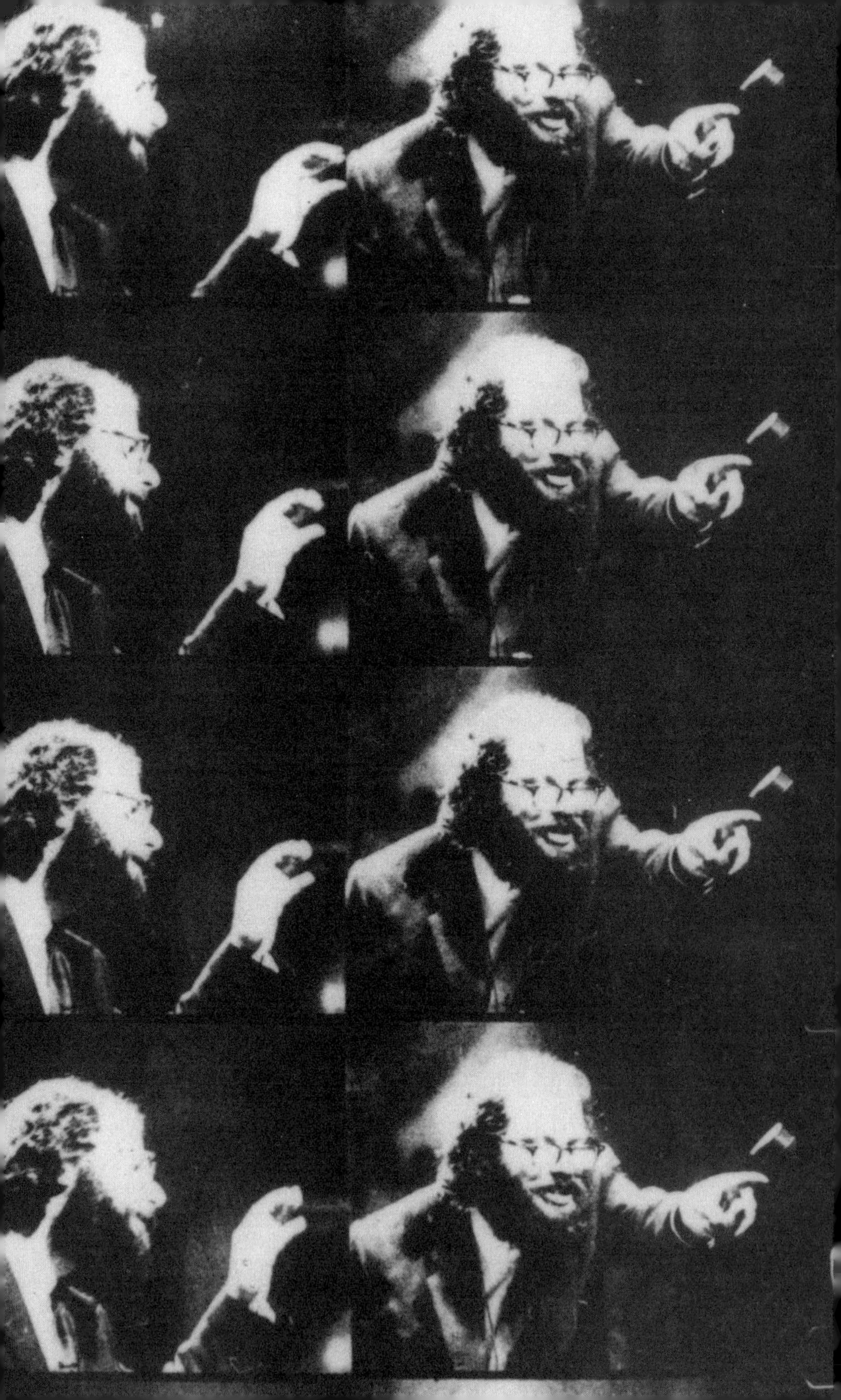

Naked Lens

Beat Cinema

Jack Sargeant

A Soft Skull ScreenPrint Book

Originally published by Creation Books, London, 1997, 2001

Library of Congress Cataloging-in-Publication Data has been applied for.

ISBN 10: 1-59376-220-8
ISBN 13: 978-1-59376-220-9

Cover design by Elinor McDonald
Interior design by Elinor McDonald

Printed in the United States of America

Soft Skull Press
An Imprint of Counterpoint LLC
2117 Fourth Street
Suite D
Berkeley, CA 94710

www.softskull.com
www.counterpointpress.com

Distributed by Publishers Group West

10 9 8 7 6 5 4 3 2 1

Many thanks to
the following individuals and organizations for their support while researching and writing this book: Joe Ambrose, Mark Bennett, Phillipa Berry, British Film Institute, Arthur and Corinne Cantrill & Cantrills Film Notes, Angus Carlyle, Stephen Drenham, Graham Duff, Robert Frank, Marisa Giorgi, Allen Ginsberg, the Harry Smith Archives, Tessa Hughes-Freeland, Jeff Keen, Richard King, David Larcher, Andrew Leavold, Alfred Leslie, Marian Luntz, Klaus Maeck, Gerard Malanga, Richard Marshall, Carlo McCormick, Taylor Mead, Jonas Mekas, Richard Nash, the New York Film-Makers Co-Operative, Kim Newman, Genesis P-Orridge, Donna Ranieri, Bob Rosenthal, Frank Rynne, MM Sara, Roslyn Sargeant, Rani Singh, Michael Sippings, Michael Spann, Stephanie Watson, Rob Whalley, Vanessa Winter, Casper Williams, James Williamson, Terry Wilson and Peter Whitehead.

Cover image
Allen Ginsberg from *Wholly Communion*
Courtesy Peter Whitehead.

This edition for MBS
with freedom, liberty and supreme love.

Contents

Foreword

All the obsessions start here. Completers — the academies, revenant psychogeographers, metaphysical panhandlers, norns — they have circled this book for years and now it comes back again to inseminate their tortured psyches. Wearied by the crank calls that have woken the hidden sleepers of this domain — recall Scorsese's *No Direction Home* playing at revelation whilst hiding Renaldo and Clara at the beginning of the new millennium — Sargeant takes us to the ur-texts, where Burroughs, Mekas, Kerouac, Frank, Gysin, Balch, Cassavetes et al improvise to their inner shadows and change the world into celluloid driftwood.

First time around there was gratitude for the book; second time, the parameters resist the wearisome arterial hardening of the theoretical mode. He hunkers down with the moot points like Pat Mezz McGillicuddy's horn playing in *Pull My Daisy* and if you don't get the atmosphere then the laconic thrills of the book'll be lost. More than that, though, he resists the tight sphincter of dotting every abstracted connection, crossing every theorized 'T'. It is writing with the Blakean signature, playful in its seriousness, needing little more than depth of perspective to reveal the whole underworld marvels of this junked-out cinema. To return to the book and read it again is not a chore but a fix brought about by the need for plenitude, for inspiration.

Because Sargeant is a more disinterested abstracted figure than a mere author. He works in the scholar's library, works his sources and references — interviews and essays, notes, rumours, asides, other books, other films — he takes them all out and makes them labour, react, do something, walk somewhere. Sargeant is out to revolve round a kind of wayward soul; he's working up a shrine to things maybe people think they know, think they've experienced — when you read this stuff you half remember conversations about some of the material — Kerouac's jazz '50s, Ginsberg's hippy '60s, Burroughs' punk '70s — and makes us mindful of what he calls "a cognitive mapping of this previously neglected area of cinema."

He's clear about what he is doing. Tracing a gesture is the romantic's dream of capturing the noumenal, the momentary blast of silver light in a mirror that spontaneously erupts into the eye and then is lost. Recall Kleist crouching by the mirror, trying to recall the strange image of his own abstracted body leaping through the air he's glimpsed in the glass, attempting to articulate something that could only be shown. Having moments that exist but only for a moment and then are lost in ever-impoverished memory is why these peculiar films engage Sargeant and his readers so deeply. It is the articulation of "a personal vision" that Sargeant is fetching up — and it's this notion of "personal vision" that Sargeant wants to say is Beat — those Wordsworthian "Thoughts that do often lie too deep for tears," and after reading the text you're able to find Sargeant as much as the people he discusses and engages with. His book is part of the project he describes. It's got a fluxy, engaged style. It's an example of Beat scholarship that's precise, critically alert and enthusiastic without being windy or asking for second chances. It's a book that knows the score. It's been there. It's done that. No special pleading.

What's fascinating about this book is the tension between the attempt to find out what this cinema was all worth — tracing the gesture but also making it accountable both in the sense of measuring its worth and also in the sense of making it utterable as narrative — and the counter ideal, which is to leave everything as messy, unmeasured, fluid, unstable — organs without a body — archiving the gesture, archiving it as just the haunted cinema it seemed to think it was at the time. In terms of style there's the feel and the mood of its subject matter — especially when reading the second section which revolves around Burroughs and his "war universe" — but throughout, especially when you read the transcribed interviews you pick up the 'to the moment', 'unmediated nowness' of the text. In a way it's about working out values without connecting up to any franchise.

The stories about the films — about how they were conceived, about how they were made, about how they were received — Sargeant has packed his detailed knowledge into this as into each of the stories he has to tell to give the reader a sense that everything's there and nothing vital is missing. These are organs of a fabled beast, scattered out for some alchemist to breathe life into them, to regenerate. Read them in the right order, find a way through and you'll restore the whole, complete it, bring it all back home. Perhaps memory will do this, or else an engagement at a level a notch above reality, explaining everything via a guilty conscience. Conscience is in the habit of clinging on to apparent consciousness and this Beat Cinema project was all about slinging out that habit. And Sargeant is writing it up to keep a certain kind of momentum going and break our lazy habit.

Once you've read this stuff, you want to get out and see the films he's investigated and test them out. You also want to get in on the projects, you want to do something yourself. This is the sign that the book works. Sargeant has done a job on the reader, he's made you feel lazy and stuck in a dumb habit and that you don't measure up to what is possible at a whole other level. Which is what good writing should do — cross a border and break things up.

Richard Marshall, 3:00AM

Introduction

To attempt a definition of the ontology of 'Beat' is necessarily problematic; by its very attitude 'Beat' continually re-negotiated and re-defined aesthetic, philosophical, sociopolitical and 'spiritual' perimeters. Exploring multiple possibilities which were antithetical to the homogeneity which dominated post-war American society and manifested itself most clearly in the paranoia of McCarthyism, 'the Red Scare' and the witch hunts undertaken by H.U.A.C. (the House Committee on Un-American Activities). The schizophrenic etymology of the term 'Beat' reflects this interest in potentialities: 'Beat' was a term which arose from street slang, as a phrase which referred to a state in which one was: exhausted, poor and homeless. The term was introduced into the vocabularies of William Burroughs, Jack Kerouac and Allen Ginsberg by street hustler storyteller Herbert Huncke[1] in 1946. But Allen Ginsberg articulates, this interpretation of 'Beat' does not only imply weary poverty or finality, but also implies a state in which one was open, a state that was "equivalent to humility"[2] and thus "receptive to vision".[3] In *On The Road* Jack Kerouac describes Dean Moriarty as "BEAT — the root, the soul of Beatific".[4] Kerouac thus draws attention to the idea that Beat is simultaneously Beatific, a state that is related to spiritual illumination, to an epiphany; to seeing the face of God. As Kerouac stated: "Beat means Beatitude, not beat up".[5] The wider term of Beat Generation is generally attributed to a 1948 conversation between Jack Kerouac and John Clellon Holmes.

Being BEAT and CREATION. 'Beat' means the absence of ambition directed towards obtaining money. Practically all the people spend their days in the active pursuit of Money. Those few who ignore this trend are given a special grace, the freedom of the mind which enables them to Create and receive the Joy.
Ron Rice

The entire Beat literary movement was based, to some extent, on Kerouac's estimate of be-bop as an improvised spontaneous form.
Allen Ginsberg

Jack Kerouac, Allen Ginsberg, William S. Burroughs, Herbert Huncke, Neal Cassady and later Gregory Corso[6] would become known as the Beats and/or the Beat Generation literary movement. This term would be expanded to describe the downtown New York literary and artistic scenes of the early '50s, which included the poets and writers: LeRoi Jones (who later changed his name to Imamu Amiri Baraka), Diane DiPrima and John Clellon Holmes. Following Allen Ginsberg's 1955 performance of 'Howl' at The Gallery Six in San Francisco, the phrase Beat was applied to/affiliated with the 'San Francisco Poetry Renaissance'. A loose-knit term for the North Beach scene, which included poets such as Lawrence Ferlinghetti, Gary Snyder, Bob Kaufman, Philip Lamantia, Michael McClure, Robert Duncan, Peter Orlovsky and Philip Whalen. In 1957 the Beat would be re-appropriated and re-mobilized by Gregory Corso to name Madame Rachou's cheap hotel at 9 rue Git-le-Coeur, Paris: the Beat Hotel. In the late '50s this Class 13, 42-room hotel, became the European residence of three of the 'original' Beat writers, Corso, Ginsberg and Burroughs, in addition to Peter Orlovsky and Brion Gysin.

The etymological duality of the word 'Beat' emphasized by Ginsberg and Kerouac may further be viewed as intrinsic to the Beat weltanschauung. The Beats lived a liberating philosophy which embraced the very limits of experience; simultaneously celebrating both the frequently harsh physicality of street life and the ecstatic state of varieties of psychical experience (ranging from the physiological effects of yage and LSD, to illumination via visionary experiences, madness, Buddhism and magick[7]). The Beats did not separate their art from lives, but saw the two as intimately connected; their articulations frequently crossed the traditional separation between art and life and they experienced both as unique celebrations. The Beats' reaction to the conservatism of '50s America was manifested through various radical actions: drug use, petty crime, sexual experimentation, religious exploration and travelling. A substantial portion of Beat literature was devoted to autobiographical and quasi-autobiographical material and this material was a guiltless affirmation of the Beats' lives at the margins of society[8] and recounts both their daily lives and routines, as well as their search for the holy and enlightening experience. As literature it pushed the boundaries of representation, demanding a poetics of freedom against the rigid straightjacket of censorship. This search for illumination, rather than being separated from the Beat writers' daily lives, was actually manifested both in and through, their lives.

Artistically the Beat writers had similar inspirations from literary outsiders such as Louis-Ferdinand Celine, Comte de Lautréamont, Jack Black, William Blake and Antonin Artaud. While the central Beat writers shared the belief in pursuing the very limits of experience and the philosophical view of the importance of retaining a marginal status in the face of American society, enthusiastically supporting each other's writing. They did not share a single overarching literary style or vision beyond the general belief in the importance of creating a new and uniquely personal form of writing; thus Ginsberg wrote poetry which described life in extreme candour, Kerouac attempted to create an unmediated prose which would flow from his 'soul' onto the page as he typed in ecstatic marathon sessions, trying to catch the authenticity of his personal voice and Burroughs would travel through various styles, until he came to experiment with the 'nature' of textuality by exploring the very limits of the role of the author via the processes of the cut-up and other related experiments such as the fold-in, the grid and the permutation.

There are as many differences between these writers as similarities. As Barry Miles observes in his biographical study *William Burroughs: El Hombre Invisible*, each of the three major Beat writers may be said to have had their own decade; Kerouac the jazz '50s, Ginsberg the hippie '60s and Burroughs the punk '70s and each contributed to the zeitgeist of their era. The time span suggested by this reflects the changing philosophical concerns of each decade, moving from the modernist literature of Jack Kerouac, with its emphasis on the existential quest and the author's voice within the text, to the post-modernism of the Burroughs' cut-up texts which bleed beyond every boundary traditionally ascribed to the novel, rejecting

Interviewer: 'The Beat generation has been described as a 'seeking' generation. What are you looking for?'

Kerouac: 'God. I want God to show me His face.

Kerouac television interview as recalled by John Clellon Holmes

Like the new poet, the new film-maker is not interested in public acceptance. The new artist knows that most of what's publicly said today is corrupt and distorted. He knows that the truth is somewhere else, not in *The New York Times* and not in Pravda. He feels that he must do something about it, for his own conscience, that he must rebel against the tightening web of lies.

Jonas Mekas

'plot', 'genre' and 'authorship', instead focusing on a vast de-territorialized intertext which circumnavigates and deconstructs any notion of organic wholeness.

The nature of the explorations undertaken by the Beats also varied: Jack Kerouac conducted his quest primarily in journeys across the American continent and among the various peoples that make up America, a country described in *On The Road* as "like an oyster for us to open".[9] In contrast to this, Allen Ginsberg, Peter Orlovsky and Gregory Corso were repeatedly drawn outside of America, travelling beyond the borders that physically, psychologically and legally constrained them, thirsting for experiences in South America, India, Tangier, Japan, Western and Eastern Europe. William Burroughs spent much of the period 1949–1974 living and travelling, in Mexico, Tangier, Paris and London, returning to America for only brief periods of time.

Simultaneous to the development of Beat literature, there was a growth in the American avant-garde, manifested across a variety of media: painting, music, performance and film. What these diverse artists, musicians, performers and filmmakers had in common with the Beats — indeed what made these artists Beat — was a sense of being outside of the vast bulk of American society. The work that these artists produced shared a similar desire to articulate and celebrate this feeling of otherness, to create artistic manifestations that were spontaneous, personal and visionary. One central facet of this work was that it was experimental, challenging the preconceptions of an audience and expanding beyond traditionally ascribed cultural boundaries. The work explored and existed at the social margins of: jazz, drugs, homosexuality and bisexuality, travelling, religion and magick and radical politics (these Beat artists espoused sexual freedom, Green issues and an anger towards the excesses manifested by the Western industrial war machine). The terminology Beat was thus also a name adopted (and misappropriated) by the media that described and defined all of these artists and their audiences as Beats or Beatniks (a fusion of Beat and nik, derived from the Russian Sputnik satellite which was launched in 1957, thus confusing the Beats with Communism in the popular psyche).

One of the central cultural boundaries transgressed by these artists was that of artistic homogeny. Against the totalising belief that an artist could only work in one field, these artists were willing to experiment across media. Thus, for example, the 'central' Beat Generation writers worked in various media; Allen Ginsberg in photography and music, William Burroughs in collage, painting, film and photography, while both Gregory Corso and Jack Kerouac painted. The Beat actor Taylor Mead was also a poet, writer, raconteur and filmmaker. This willingness to explore artistic practice across various mediums led to various collaborations between Beat writers and other artists and simultaneously expanded the concept of Beat culture from being 'merely' a literary phenomenon to being a wider cultural manifestation of artistic expression and socio-political discontent. Beats working predominantly in media outside of literature and poetry included filmmakers such as Harry Smith and Ron Rice, the photographer Robert Frank and the painter Alfred Leslie.

This emphasis on artistic experimentation across media inevitably led to links between the Beat generation writers and Beat generation filmmakers, or artists who were also willing to experiment with film. These links were most clearly developed between the Beats and various filmmakers, many of whom were associated with the New York independent/underground film scene of the late '50s. Several of these filmmakers espoused the same concerns and envisioned the same artistic experiments as the Beat writers and poets. This scene was primarily articulated via the journal *Film Culture*, founded in 1955; this publication was edited by the Lithuanian poet and filmmaker Jonas Mekas, and sought to articulate and disseminate histories and theories around the independent cinema. Initially the publication focused on the European avant-garde, but the journal soon began to document the increasing number of

American underground films. In 1959 *Film Culture* inaugurated the Independent Film Award, an annual prize awarded to films which were "original and unique American contributors to the cinema" — it is no surprise that, of the films and filmmakers that *Film Culture* chose to honour, several were made by Beats, or were Beat affiliated texts, including: *Shadows, Pull My Daisy, Flaming Creatures* and the films of Harry Smith.

The aim of *The Naked Lens* is to attempt a cognitive mapping of this previously neglected area of cinema and cinematic texts. This book is an inaugural attempt to trace this engagement across a wide variety of texts and authors — who share only the belief in expressing their personal vision/s — yet this tracing resists teleology, rather it seeks to explore these areas in specific essays which may be approached in any order.

The essays and interviews that form the first section of *The Naked Lens*, 'Searching For A Free Vision', detail the development of the 'Beat'-related underground film scene. These essays explore the desire to capture — or re-create — an apparently spontaneous cinema, to create a cinema which has a personal freedom analogous to that of Beat poetry and literature. These texts explore the development of this cinema from the apparently improvised texts of Cassavetes' *Shadows* and Frank's and Leslie's *Pull My Daisy*, through the freedom and (potentially limitless) play of Ron Rice's cinematic poems *The Flower Thief* and *The Queen Of Sheba Meets The Atom Man*, to the Dionysian celebrations of heterogeneous sexualities and the outsider lifestyle manifested in Jack Smith's films, the free-form representations of magick and music manifested in the transmogrifying images of Harry Smith and the personal poetic and diaristic films of Jonas Mekas. This section also includes essays on two filmmakers who are not associated with the New York Underground: Peter Whitehead, who directed *Wholly Communion*, the quasi-vérité documentary depicting the poetry performances of Ginsberg, Corso, Ferlinghetti, Trocchi et al at the Albert Hall; and Conrad Rooks, who directed the feature-length depiction of a man undergoing a cure for narcotic addiction, *Chappaqua*, which was cast with various Beat and underground figures. While neither of these films is fully underground, both offer further examples of the relationship between Beat culture and cinema.

The second section of this book — 'The War Universe Of William S. Burroughs' — deals exclusively with the work of William Burroughs, whose relationship vis-à-vis the Beat generation is by its nature a complex one. While Burroughs was a close friend of Ginsberg, Kerouac and Corso and is often described as a founding member of the Beat Generation literary movement, he also maintained a distance from the Beats. This distance existed both geographically — with Burroughs a willing exile from the conservatism of '50s and '60s America — but also philosophically. In *The Job* Burroughs states that he does not:

> "associate ... with [the Beat movement] at all and never have, either with their objectives or their literary style. I have some close personal friends among the Beat movement: Jack Kerouac and Allen Ginsberg and Gregory Corso are all close personal friends of many years standing, but were not doing at all the same thing, either in writing or in outlook".[10]

And:

> "Q: The Beat/Hip axis, notably in such figures as Ginsberg, want to transform the world by love and non-violence. Do you share this interest?
>
> A: Most emphatically no. The people in power will not disappear voluntarily, giving flowers to the cops just isn't going to work. This thinking is fostered by the establishment; they like nothing better than love and non-violence. The only way I like to see cops given flowers is in a flower pot from a high window".[11]

Not only is Burroughs thus distanced from the Beats, his collaborative film work, produced predominantly in Europe and North Africa in the '60s, with Antony Balch, Brion

Gysin and Ian Sommerville, exists as a direct extension of his literary explorations and his interests in the various manifestations and forms of authority. Burroughs' collaborative films are part of a massive experiment and exist in the same realm as his written texts, which throughout his career expanded beyond the printed page into scrapbooks, photographs, tape recordings, paintings and films. 'The War Universe Of William Burroughs' focuses on these collaborative films and on subsequent films which further explore the themes of Burroughs' work: Klaus Maeck's *Decoder* and David Cronenberg's *Naked Lunch*.

Finally, the appendix details the major intersections between the various manifestations of Beat culture and cinema. This includes a comprehensive overview of the various projects in which the Beat generation writers have appeared, as well as notes on the cinematic adaptations of Beat and 'post-Beat' novels and the misappropriation of Beatniks in exploitation movies. The appendix also include a detailed account of the quasi-Beat author Charles Bukowski and films based on his texts.

The Naked Lens does not simply articulate the production histories of these films, but also traces a gesture through these films, in which the filmmaker/s attempt to articulate a personal vision as film, to create a cinema which may be viewed as Beat.

---

1. Kerouac stated that Hunke borrowed the term 'beat', from either a "midwest carnival or junk cafeteria" and suggests the term 'beat' emerged from African American slang (cited in Park Honan's 'Introduction' to his book *The Beats: An Anthology Of 'Beat' Writing*, J. M. Dent & Sons Ltd, London/ Melbourne, 1987, p.ix–x.

2. Allen Ginsberg, 'Prologue', Lisa Phillips, ed, *Beat Culture And The New America, 1950–1965*, Whitney Museum of American Art, New York, Flammarion, Paris, 1995, p.18.

3. 'Prologue', p.18.

4. Jack Kerouac, *On The Road*, Penguin, London, 1991, (1957), p.195.

5. Jack Kerouac cited in John Clellon Holmes, 'The Philosophy Of The Beat Generation', in Park Honan, ed, *The Beats: An Anthology Of 'Beat' Writing*, p.147.

6. Gregory Corso met Ginsberg in 1950 at a lesbian bar called The Pony Stable; the rest of the original Beats became acquainted in 1944 through friendships developed around Columbia University.

7. As Allen Ginsberg has observed, all of the 'leading' figures of Beat literature had visionary experiences: Ginsberg had a vision of William Blake in 1948, while living in Harlem. Kerouac sat alone for 63 days in a cabin on Desolation Peak, in Washington State's North Cascades mountains, where he worked as a fire-watcher on the advice of fellow Buddhists Philip Whalen and Gary Snyder. On the mountain top Kerouac contemplated Buddhism, read the Prajnaparamita sutras, wrote a biography of Shakyamuni Buddha and experienced "The vision of the freedom of eternity" (Jack Kerouac, *The Dharma Bums*, Flamingo/Harper Collins, London 1994, [1950] p.203) and understood existence as "Noumena ... the immaterial golden ash..." (Jack Kerouac, *Desolation Angels*, Mayflower, London, 1968, [1960], p.57). Gregory Corso had a vision of light while in Crete in 1960. William Burroughs' work repeatedly engages with psychic phenomenon, via the use of drugs such as yage; he also understood the potentialities of 'magic' and — as his introduction to *Queer* makes clear — he believed in possession.

8. Jack Kerouac's books were autobiographical, although real names were masked by thinly-veiled false identities. Much of Allen Ginsberg's poetry is also autobiographical. Herbert Hunke's few published works are also broadly autobiographical. The exception to this apparently autobiographical nature of Beat literature is William Burroughs, whose most clearly apparent autobiographical works are *Junkie* and *Queer*, but, while various sequences in the *Naked Lunch* are loosely based on actual situations, much of Burroughs' work defies simple categorizations.

9. *On The Road*, p.138.

10. William Burroughs, in William S. Burroughs and Daniel Odier, *The Job: Topical Writings And Interviews*, John Calder, London, 1984, (1969), p.52.

11. *The Job: Topical Writings And Interviews*, p.74.

Part One

Searching For A Free Vision

Chapter One
Pull My Daisy

1. Notes On *Pull My Daisy*

One of the central aspects of Jack Kerouac's literature was the idea that the writer should attempt to achieve an authenticity in his work. For Kerouac writing was an act that would both describe and affirm his spiritual and existential quests for the 'truth' — and perhaps even 'soul' — of the human experience. Kerouac perceived himself as a "Recording Angel",[1] who — inspired, in part, by the rawness of Neal Cassady's letters[2] — realized that "you can write about life without changing anything".[3] Simultaneously Kerouac saw his work as functioning in a manner analogous to painting or jazz, as an unique and personal interpretation and presentation of experience, as he described it this personal intensity of vision was similar to when a sax player would "blow".[4] Kerouac's works were — famously — generally written in a matter of days, with the minimum of possible revisions made on the manuscripts.

Kerouac's books were — for the most part — autobiographical and the 'script' that formed the basis for the film *Pull My Daisy* was no exception. The events which inspired the text occurred in the Autumn of 1955, at the Los Gatos, California, home of Neal and Carolyn Cassady, where Kerouac was staying following a trip to Mexico. The Cassady's were — like Jack — interested in spiritual explorations and — at that time — would regularly see Bishop Romano, a Swiss Bishop ordained by the Liberal Catholic Church. The Bishop, according to Carolyn Cassady's autobiography *Off The Road*, "accepted reincarnation and the universality of all religious doctrines. An added curiosity was that his sermons were supposedly delivered by a higher being for whom the Bishop served as a 'channel'".[5] Both Neal and Carolyn were anxious for Jack and Allen Ginsberg (who at the time was living in Berkeley) to see the Bishop and organized a visit by the Bishop to their home following a service. Unfortunately neither Jack nor Allen were able to see the service, but both met the Bishop at the Cassady house. Also present was the Bishop's mother and aunt, as well as Peter Orlovsky and Pat Donovan. Kerouac — who was sitting on the floor — leant against the Bishop's leg, drunkenly proclaiming his love for the Bishop, while Neal asked the Bishop various questions comparing Eastern and Western religious beliefs. Allen Ginsberg sat between the Bishop's relatives and reportedly asked the Bishop "What about sex?" From *Off The Road:* "With this variety of nuts and with Jack's intermittent 'I love you's', to the Bishop, I was heartily glad when the ladies broke their silence by indicating decisively to their charge that it was time to go. When the trio had departed, we all breathed again and mirthful reflection took over".[6]

The first truly Beat film.
Jonas Mekas

My books are as it were poetry sheeted in narrative steel, a new kind of narrative which does not concern itself with discipline and dryness but aims at the flow of feeling unimpeded and uninterrupted by the calls of a dead craft, for I believe that the 'novel form' is dead the new prose literature of any originality and value will be cast in just that form, cf. Genet, Celine and the new work of William Burroughs.
Jack Kerouac

Two years later, following the publication of *On The Road* (1957) by the Viking Press and Kerouac's subsequent fame/notoriety on its publication,[7] Kerouac was approached by Leo Garin, an off-Broadway producer, to write a play. Kerouac wrote a play entitled *The Beat Generation Or The New Amaraean Church*, reportedly com-

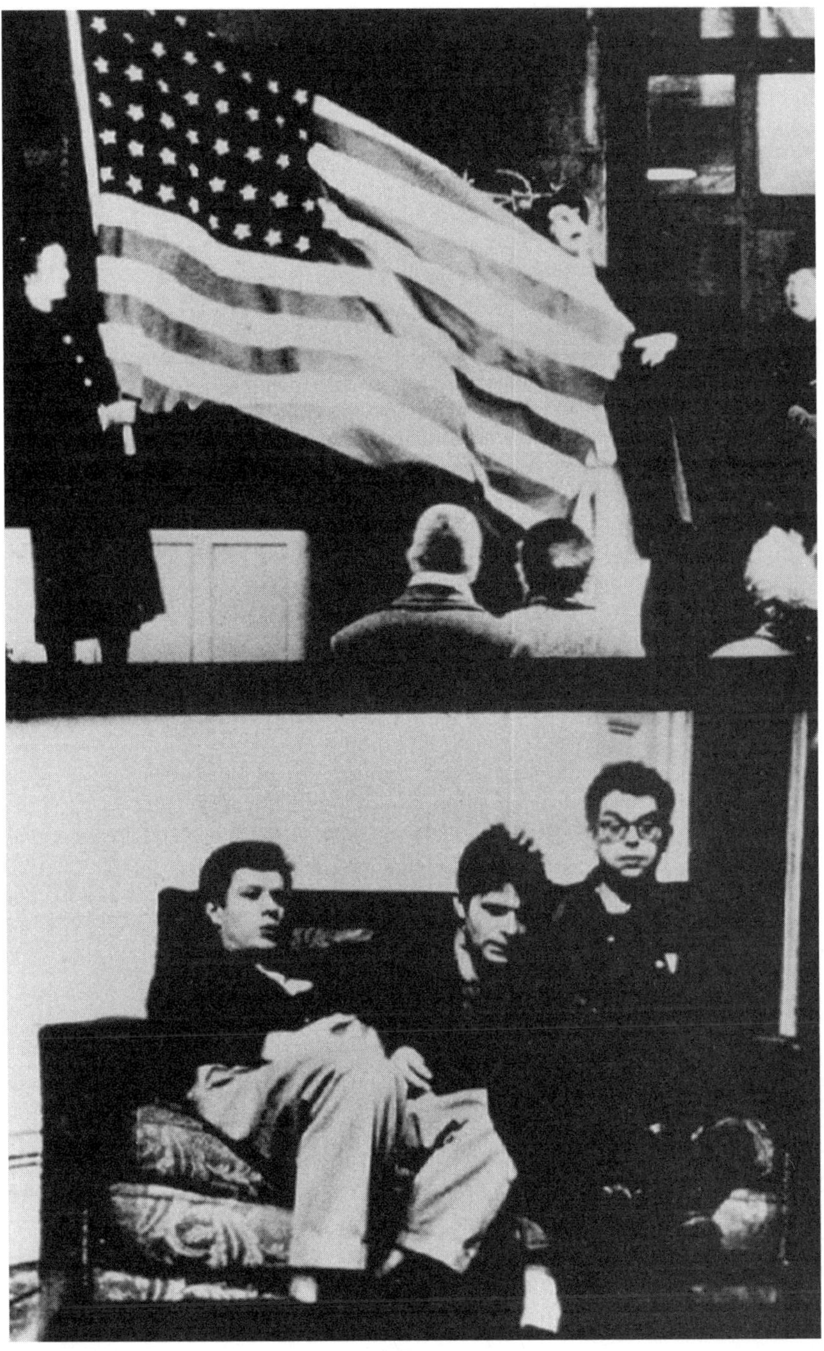

Pull My Daisy

pleting the project in one night. This play was composed of three acts, focusing primarily on the events that transpired during Kerouac's visit to Neal Cassady in California, during the Autumn of 1955. The first act was set in the apartment of a seaman, Al Sublette, with Neal, Al Hinkle and Charlie Mew, the second act followed Neal to the racetrack and the third act focused on the events that transpired when the Bishop visited the Cassady house. The play was never produced, however when Alfred Leslie, Robert Frank and Jack Kerouac began to discuss the possibility of making a film together it was the third act of this play which they eventually chose to form the basis for the film, which, unlike the play, was to be narrated by Kerouac, who would ad lib over the edited film.

Unfortunately for the filmmakers, the proposed title *The Beat Generation* had been copyrighted by MGM (who in 1959 released the B/exploitation movie of the same name). However a new title came from a poem written as part of a jazz styled jam session by Kerouac, Cassady and Ginsberg in the Autumn of 1949: 'Pull My Daisy'. This poem was itself loosely based on an earlier poem by Ginsberg entitled 'Fie My Fum', which, written in the Spring of 1949, is remarkably similar to 'Pull My Daisy', although is more restrained in its erotic imagery than the later group piece.[8] According to John G. Handartd's essay, 'A Movement Towards The Real', the title is a colloquial term for the removal of the stripper's G-string, this also serves to explain the reason that the film is a production of 'G-String Enterprises'. The poem, 'Pull My Daisy', was rewritten by Ginsberg and Kerouac and subsequently scored by the composer David Amram, the resultant piece became the theme song to the film,[9] which was sung by Anita Ellis. However — much to the chagrin of both Kerouac and Ginsberg — the words were changed for the recording, with the line "Hop my heart song" being used, as opposed to their lyric "Hop my heart on".

The central location of the film was Alfred Leslie's studio loft at Fourth Avenue and 12th Street, Manhattan, with the brief exterior scene shot outside an East River warehouse in Brooklyn. Shooting commenced on 2nd January 1959, with a cast which consisted predominantly of amateurs: both Allen Ginsberg and Peter Orlovsky played (versions of) themselves, although Allen is (mis)credited in the film's titles as 'Alan' (for the sake of clarity 'Alan' will be used when referring to the character in the film). The painter Larry Rivers played the role of the railroad brakeman Milo (another of Kerouac's portraits of Neal Cassady, alongside those found in the characters of Dean Moriarty and Cody Pomeroy), Gregory Corso appeared as 'himself', although the actions in which he engages throughout the film are predominantly those attributed to the character Jack in the play. According to Nicosia's biography of Kerouac, Corso was originally meant to play 'Jack', but Kerouac — on seeing Corso's awkwardness — reportedly told him to "be yourself".[10] The art dealer, Green Gallery employee, Richard Bellamy, under the pseudonym Mooney Peebles, played the role of the Bishop. Composer Dave Amram (who also scored the film) played a jazz musician called Pat Mezz McGillicuddy (called Pat McGillicuddy and described as "a real hep cat"[11] in the play). The Bishop's mother was portrayed by the artist Alice Neal, while the role of the Bishop's aunt in the play was changed to the role of his sister in the film, played by Sally Gross. A girl glimpsed briefly in bed and credited as such, was played by Denise Parker and Milo's son was played by Robert Frank's son; Pablo. Finally Milo's wife (who remains unnamed throughout the film, but is referred to as Caroline [sic] in the play[12]) was played by Beltiane, actually a pseudonym for the only professional thespian on the set, the actress Delphine Seyrig.[13] According to J. Hoberman's essay 'The Forest And The Trees', Seyrig was in New York to study the Method[14] and became involved in the production through her husband, Jack Youngerman, who was a painter friend of Alfred Leslie.

The film is deceptively simple; set in an apartment in downtown Manhattan, it opens with an establishing shot; tracking around an empty room. Kerouac's voice begins the narration which, save for a few short breaks, runs for the length of the film: "Early morning in the universe… "[15] A woman, whom the narration describes as a painter and the wife of a "railroad brakeman" enters the room. The wife walks to the windows and opens the curtains, letting the light stream in, her young son Pablo enters to eat his breakfast, before rushing off to school. Shortly before they leave for school Alan and Gregory enter, carrying bottles of beer.

Alan and Gregory sit down and begin to discuss poetry, the camera roving back and forth between them, in close up a joint is passed between the two poets. Alan and Gregory begin to argue about Apollinaire and in a long shot Alan stands up, in order to enact Apollinaire's collapse at the grave of Balzac. Gregory becomes frustrated with Alan's argument and this becomes emphasized by the rhythmic aggression of the narration, juxtaposing the velocity of Alan's frenetic speech patterns ("that's right/that's right/that's right/that's what I said/that's right/that's right/that's right" [the punctuation is mine]) with Gregory's sullen weariness at Alan's continued dancing movements. At the end of the argument, in established shot-reverse-shot style, Alan states: "The Lower East Side has produced all the strange gum chewing geniuses", to which Gregory replies, "Ah you make me — I could tell you poems that would make you weep with long hair, goodbye, goodbye…"

The scene is interrupted by the arrival of Milo and Peter, as Milo walks around the apartment the three poets follow him. Flute music plays on the soundtrack, switching from the (supposedly) diegetic sounds produced by Gregory's flute playing to the extra-diegetic music of Amram's score, the music serves to emphasize the almost childlike enthusiasm the poets have for the railway worker. Milo tells them that the Bishop is coming "you guys have gotta act a little better […] no flutes and no nonsense". A shot from the window looking down into the street depicts the Bishop's car arriving. The wife goes to welcome the Bishop and his entourage into the apartment while the three poets excitedly anticipate the Bishop's imminent arrival.

Milo dances around the apartment, a movement that is directly contrasted by the apparent stoicism of the Bishop. The Bishop and his family (mother and sister) are introduced and begin to settle down. Gregory begins questioning the Bishop about Buddhism, before rapidly sliding into 'nonsense' talk ("goofing […] playing around with words"), apologising and then asking more serious questions on Buddhism.

To a burst of the jazz soundtrack, Mezz McGillicuddy enters the apartment, shaking hands with everybody. Peter begins to talk to the Bishop, asking him "Have you ever played baseball and seen girls with tight dresses?" and then "Is baseball holy?" while swinging an imaginary bat.

The scene fades to an exterior shot, the soundtrack becomes more melancholic, while in long shot the Bishop preaches to a congregation of, predominantly, women and children. As he delivers his sermon an American flag, held by Milo's wife who is standing at the Bishop's side, blows over his face.[16] The camera tracks in medium close-up over the faces of the street congregation, all of whom are speaking, although, crucially, there is no narration at this point in the film.

Cutting back to the apartment the film continues to track across the faces of those around the Bishop (Alan, Gregory et al). Kerouac's narration: "The angel of silence hath flown over all their heads", the narration continues but begins to turn into 'music', no longer emphasizing 'real' sentences, but 'pure' word plays which seek to evoke the spirit of the evening. Not only is the silence of the apartment articulated by Kerouac's narration, it is also emphasized by the shots of the tightly shut lips of all in the apartment and contrasts the extra-diegetic silence of the animated congregation of the previous exterior scene with its images of speech.

Gregory slumps drunkenly while Milo's wife berates him for the Beats' behaviour. From the wife's seated position the camera flows around the room, to the mirrored door of the bathroom; "the Queen of Sheba takes a bath in this bathtub every day", then across the cooking surfaces, where Kerouac's narration describes the cockroaches that inhabit the apartment: "cockroaches, cockroaches, coffee cockroaches, stove cockroaches, city cockroaches, spot cockroaches, melted cheese cockroaches, Chaplin cockroaches, peanut butter cockroaches — cockroach cockroach — cockroach of the eyes — cockroach, mirror, boom, bang". The narrative rap is accompanied by the jazz soundtrack, along with a quick-fire montage of images of Alan dancing with gun-fingers pointed like a child playing cowboys. Then, as the rap ends, the film resumes its track around the room. As the bookcase comes into shot the narration states "Jung, Freud, Jung, Reich" as if reading the titles from the bookcase. Returning to long-shot the Bishop states "Strange thoughts you young, uh, people have." Gregory walks over to the Bishop and sits at his feet, simultaneously Peter walks to the table asking "Is everything holy, is alligators holy, Bishop? Is the world holy? Is the organ of man holy? [the narration continues] The Bishop says, What, holy, holy? He says, Oh my mother wants to play the organ."

Mezz McGillicuddy positions a chair in front of the pump organ so the old lady can play something "holy". Noticeably the music the mother plays is the same as that which was heard during the exterior scene depicting the street congregation. In a separate room of the apartment Gregory asks Milo, "When are we going to blow man, what are we going to do?" The soundtrack changes to jazz and the tempo increases, emphasized by the increased speed of the editing. In the bedroom McGillicuddy begins to play the French horn. A woman lying on the bed tosses and rolls away from him. While in the living room Alan has joined in the 'confrontation' with the Bishop, asking him, in quick fire questions, punctuating the jazz rhythms, "are holy flowers holy? Is the world holy? Is glasses holy? Is time holy? Is all the white moonlight holy? Empty rooms are holy? You holy? Come on Bishop tell us. Toy holy? Byzantine holy? Is mock holy? Izzamerican flag holy? Is girl holy? Is your sister holy? What is holy? Holy, holy, holy, holy, holy? And car holy and light holy? Is holy holy?" Each question is punctuated by the cutting of the film to illustrate it, which serves as an emphasis to the quick-fire Kerouac as Alan narration. The music becomes increasingly frenetic as Milo picks up a saxophone and begins to blow. The Bishop states that he should be leaving and Milo's wife sees the Bishop and his family out.

Pablo ambles into the room, where he is asked by Milo if he wants to play too. Returning from his bedroom clutching a horn he joins in the impromptu session. The soundtrack becomes punctuated with random blasts of out-of-key horn, emphasizing Pablo's playing.

Cutting to a long-shot of the table, with more relaxed music on the soundtrack, Milo picks up Pablo, the camera focuses on the action then moves to capture the smoke rising from the cigarettes in the ashtray on the table. Kerouac sings: "Up you go, little smoke. Up you go little smoke. Up you go, little smoke." Each line is higher in pitch. The smoke about which he is singing being both the actual smoke from the ashtray, but also — and more importantly — the child being lovingly carried on his father's shoulder from the room. Mezz plays alone while, outside, the wife waves goodbye to the Bishop.

Alan announces, "Wow, let's do something we've never done" and suggests that they "play cowboys". Milo — who has returned from his son's room — begins to tell a story about a cowboy. Milo's speech is delivered in Kerouac's driest quasi-William Burroughs-styled tones (indeed the story could almost be an homage to William Burroughs' blackly humoured routines). The story describes a cowboy who shoots a wino who is sitting at a preacher's feet (the story is a reference to Gregory's behaviour). Milo enacts the story while recounting it, finally — as the cowboy shoots the wino — Milo points his finger-gun at

Gregory's head. A close up of the finger-gun death shot to Gregory's head illustrates Gregory's anger at being the butt of the story; "What'd you do that for? — Pow!"

Milo's wife returns and once again berates him for his behaviour. The three poets — all sitting in line, wedged onto the sofa — appear like naughty schoolboys. Led by McGillicuddy the poets run from the apartment, calling for Milo to follow them "Come on down those steps. Let's go. We'll go somewhere, we'll find something. Maybe we'll play by fires in the Bowery." Milo argues with his wife, then angrily kicks the rocking chair, which rocks back and forth as he leaves the room. In a visual counterpoint to the movements of the rocking chair in the apartment, a ceiling rose in the dark entrance hall swings back and forth: "And the rose swings. She'll get over it. [Milo appears on the stairs to be greeted by the poets] Come on, Milo. Here comes sweet Milo, beautiful Milo. [In Milo's voice] Hello gang. Da da da da And they're going dada da da dada da da da" the narration becomes accelerated, in an affirmation of joy. The group run out, laughing, into the night.

Pull My Daisy was premiered on 11 November, 1959, at Amos Vogel's Cinema 16, on a bill alongside John Cassavetes' similarly groundbreaking feature *Shadows*. It has been suggested by the film critic J. Hoberman that this event was the moment at which "the Underground announced itself".[17] The filmmaker, writer and underground film proselytizer, Jonas Mekas became an immediate supporter of the film, which he perceived as "a free improvisation" and the first Beat film and suggested that Frank, Leslie and Kerouac were "the true independents, the conscious rebels, [who] reject any compromise";[18] part of the New American Cinema. On 26 April, 1960, the film won the Second Film Culture Independent Film Award (*Shadows* having won the first award the previous year) and Mekas stated that *Pull My Daisy* breathed "an immediacy that the cinema of today vitally needs if it is to be a living and contemporary art".[19]

Stylistically *Pull My Daisy* was initially viewed as a vérité portrait of the New York lives of the Beats: meeting in apartments, hanging out, discussing poetry, getting high, listening to jazz, etc. The camera work emphasizes this aspect of the film and several events within the film are presented to the camera/gaze so as to create the impression that the film's audience are assuming the gaze of another figure in the room, this is most clearly apparent when the Bishop's car pulls up and leaves and the events are shot from within the apartment looking down onto the street.

The vérité aspect of the text is heightened by the casting of the central Beat figures as 'themselves', or at least approximations of themselves and by the narrative's basis in actual events. *Pull My Daisy* further appears to have emerged as a document from the vérité strand in its apparent usage of improvisation. If part of Jack Kerouac's literature was to live and document life as poetry then this may also be viewed as part of the weltanschauung behind the production of the film, which appears to be a joyful cinematic affirmation of the Beat way of life. The 'improvised' nature of the 'acting' — with its boundless frenetic energy — similarly serves to separate the Beat characters from both the Bishop and his family and Milo's wife. The Beats are repeatedly presented as dancing, jumping or gesticulating, in contrast to the Bishop's family all of whom remain rigidly stoic and controlled in their movements throughout the film. Even during the sequence which depicts Alan and Peter sitting (nearly) motionless they are still exuding a wild, barely repressed energy, which becomes apparent by its containment; presented via their hands which are seen to be sandwiched tightly between their legs, as if in an attempt to contain their desire to explode into movement, this is immediately contrasted with shots depicting the Bishop's two female companions who sit in a state of complete stasis.

At the time of the film's initial screening Robert Frank and Alfred Leslie stated that the film was "an accumulation rather than a selection of images. It was made by nonprofessionals in search of that freer vision",[20] *Pull My Daisy* was similarly viewed by Jerry Tallmer who, in his introduction to the script suggests that it was an example of cinema's move "toward 'pure film', spontaneity, freedom".[21] Amos Vogel saw the film as a product from the "radical wing of the cinema vérité movement (which aims at leaving reality 'undisturbed')".[22] However not all critics and commentators perceived the film as a product of either a freedom of style or cinema vérité, Parker Tyler argued that the film was as "fresh as a frozen green pea".[23] These critical divisions were further built upon by the disintegration of the relationship between the film's two collaborators; Robert Frank and Alfred Leslie, both of whom would come to claim and/or be credited for directing *Pull My Daisy.*[24] Alfred Leslie would further state, in a *Village Voice* article (28/11/68) that the film was actually scripted and fully rehearsed.

Such debates which focus on the 'authenticity' (or conversely its lack) of *Pull My Daisy* ultimately become pointless, whether or not the film was 'planned' or 'spontaneous' is largely irrelevant. Firstly neither 'realism' nor 'spontaneity' are quantifiable and to view the film as either/or is to fail to recognize its importance as a catalyst and inspiration for other films and filmmakers (filmmakers such as Ron Rice and Taylor Mead were inspired by the film, as was Jonas Mekas). *Pull My Daisy* was, at least in part, a catalyst because people believed that it was improvized. By utilizing Ginsberg, Corso and Orlovsky to act/appear as 'themselves' the film also serves to deconstruct the division between 'reality' and 'fantasy', the meta-narratives around the lives of these members of the cast mean that the events could be read as appearing to be those that the poets would experience, they thus could appear to be authentic to an audience.

Further there is confusion between reading the film as vérité and perceiving it as improvised and 'real'. Vérité implies that the film is 'truth' and that these events are caught by the camera 'undisturbed'. Thus 'pure' vérité would imply that the role of the director/s is to capture the moment, yet simultaneously vanish into the ether. In vérité the director function exists only to vanish into invisibility, to leave 'reality' undisturbed. Yet *Pull My Daisy* does not deny that it is 'constructed', with its use of music, editing (including montage) and — most apparent of all — narration. The narration thus immediately grounds the film as an interpretation of reality rather than neutral depiction, yet one of the defining aspects of the American vérité aesthetic is a "stance of narrationless neutrality".[25] *Pull My Daisy* may be interpreted as an example of vérité, but to do so fails to recognize its romanticism, the film is personal in a manner which is antithetical to vérité. The director of vérité film must vanish for the work to succeed, in *Pull My Daisy* the directors' signatures are clearly apparent; in the camera work, editing and scoring. While the central philosophy behind vérité demands that the director denies any personal investment, *Pull My Daisy* emphasizes the personal. Indeed it is this aspect of the personal which makes the film succeed.

Importantly, Jack Kerouac's narration was delivered as an improvisation, albeit around the theme which was based loosely on recounting the night's events from 1955 and the subsequent play written two years later. Kerouac's narration frequently becomes the focal point of the film, such as when he takes on the voices of the poets (capturing the various nuances of each poet's spoken manner) and when he articulates an almost religious affirmation of the commonplace/everyday to a point where he begins to 'sing', his voice punctuating the various rhythms; from the melancholy and subdued tones as he describes Pat Mezz McGillicuddy's horn playing, to the rapping jazz epiphanies of the 'cockroach' sequence.

On several occasions Kerouac's narration loosely recalls *The Beat Generation Or The New Amaraean Church* play and certain events and lines occur in both this text and within the narration of *Pull My Daisy*. The play is set in a "Ranch Style House"[26] rather than a loft and the protagonists include Neal and Jack, rather than Milo and Gregory. In the play the 'confrontation' between the Bishop and the poets is far more 'intellectual', based around a discussion of the various spiritual beliefs of Jack, Caroline (sic), Allen, Neal and the Bishop. Although in the middle of the scene there is a long silence, in similarity to the film, which is broken by the line "This is what Chekhov called the Angel of Silence, it just flew over us didn't it!"[27] — although in the script it is spoken by Jack, whereas in *Pull My Daisy* it is voiced by the narrator. Following the departure of the Bishop and his family, in the play, the poets all play cowboys, each in turn describing a short routine, ending with Neal's story which is the same as that told by Milo in the film. Finally, at the end of the play each of the characters goes to bed, leaving Allen and Peter in the living room making up beds and listening to Jack playing flute in the garden, with Allen describing Jack's behaviour/philosophy; "because ... he's trying to figure out what all this is all about ... whatever it's all about, you know ... the world is what form is and that's all you can say about it huh?"[28] The noticeable difference between the two versions is that the play ends on a speculative spiritual note, whereas the film ends on an affirmation of male bonding and pleasure, as the characters run out into the street to play. Further in the play the role of the wife disappears into the background, rather than confronts the poets.

Kerouac's narration in *Pull My Daisy* becomes all the more powerful because he is not just recounting events and telling a story, but also observing and commentating on events transpiring within the film and simultaneously speaking for all the protagonists. Thus while the film may be viewed as 'real', the narration which makes up the entire spoken soundtrack is all based on the single authorial voice of Kerouac. This means that what the film's audience hear is only an interpretation of events, this becomes emphasized when the narration exceeds the boundaries of 'merely' speaking for the characters and offers opinions. This is most apparent when the narration assumes its focus around Milo's wife (a character who — it should be noted — exists as nameless in the phallic economy of the film) for example when the protagonists are seated during the Bishop's visit and the narration states: "They sit around the table, they're getting kinda congenial. By God, even the woman feels good" and later when she begins to nag: "Well it could have been better if Milo wasn't so silly and invited all these silly friends of his, we could have done some kind of impression for the Bishop" In part then, the narration must be seen as reflecting Kerouac's own bias.

While the narration does denigrate the role of the wife it is important to note that it also 'reveals' the tenderness Kerouac felt for the protagonists, not only in his impressions of their speech, but also in his descriptions of them, thus: Alan and Gregory are "bursting with poetry", Gregory is "the hero of stove and pipe butter", Peter is "Peter the saint" and Milo is "sweet" and "beautiful". Further, Kerouac describes the actual work of the poets, as Gregory and Alan argue about poetry Alan's notebook is glimpsed and Kerouac states: "Well, they turn over their little purple moonlight pages in which their secret naked doodlings do show. Secret scatological thought and that's why everybody wants to see it." When the poets are introduced to the Bishop, the narration describes them via their nationality: "the Italian poet [Corso], the Russian poet [Orlovsky], the Jewish poet [Ginsberg]", but Milo (Neal) is described as "the railroad poet". Milo is defined not by his nationality but by his 'travelling', by his transience.[29] For Kerouac, Neal Cassady represented (or came to represent in Kerouac's texts) something of the essence of his America, a land to be explored and — more importantly — experienced. Kerouac describes Cassady (as manifested via the character Dean Moriarty) in *On The Road*, as being "schooled in the raw road night, Dean was come into the world to see it";[30] and travel was not a choice so much as his raison d'être, "'...this road drives me!!'"[31]

Kerouac's narration also reveals his observation of children's speech, firstly he raises his voice to a higher pitch and speeds up, as he speaks (for) Pablo, talking about his breakfast:

"Do I have to eat that stuff all over again, that farina? I ain't gonna say that I'm gonna live a hundred years but I been eating farina for about a hundred years". Then, as Pablo prepares for school Kerouac recites a childlike list of school subjects which Pablo is studying: "geography and astromology and pipliology and all them oligies and poetology and [as Pablo leaves for school] goodbyeology". Of course this list of childlike terms is a list spontaneously devised by a poet and Kerouac's delivery emphasizes the joy of being able to create the words which inform the uncomplicated language of the child. When Corso first talks to the Bishop he states: "is it true that all the ignus that come falling inside the magic beer bottle magian candle stick?" Then, when the Bishop appears puzzled, Corso states "awfully sorry, I'm goofing there [...] playing around with words", it is this very affirmation of playing with language, of spontaneous poetry, which Kerouac's narration both excels in and reveals. *Pull My Daisy* thus demands to be understood as Kerouac's singular cinematic poesy, as the only film to be produced by/with the 'central' Beat writers during the time at which their work was first being recognized, yet was still largely a product of the underground.

2. An Interview With Alfred Leslie

Alfred Leslie was born in the Bronx, New York, 1927 and has worked in a number of disciplines, including painting, photography and film. His abstract expressionist paintings of the late '40s and early '50s were exhibited alongside Franz Kline at the New Talent 1950 at the Kootz Gallery and the Ninth Street Show in 1951 alongside Jackson Pollock, Willem de Kooning, Kline et al. In the early '60s Leslie exhibited with Jasper Johns and Robert Rauschenberg, as part of the 4 Americans exhibition. In his book *Lonesome Traveller*, Jack Kerouac described Leslie's paintings as "his giant feet canvases" and declare that "Al Leslie's giant is sleeping in the Paramount building".[32]

From 1953 to 1955, Leslie also worked as a theatrical set designer, designing sets for the Artists Theatre production of Lorca's *The Love Of Don Perlimplin For Belisa In Their Garden*, amongst others. As well as working as a painter and set designer, Leslie also edited *The Hasty Papers*.[33] This was a literary magazine which was published in 1960 and featured contributions from Frank O'Hara, Jean Paul Sartre, et al.

Leslie's film credits include *Directions: A Walk After The War Games* (1946), *The Last Clean Shirt* (1964), *Alfred Leslie's A Birth Of A Nation* (1965), *Philosophy In A Bedroom* (1965) and *Act And Portrait* (1965). Following the seizure of footage from *Act And Portrait* by the LAPD Vice Squad, in 1965, Leslie shot footage with cinema vérité director Al Maysles which detailed the seizure.

In 1966 Alfred Leslie's studio was destroyed by a fire, which also caused the deaths of twelve firemen. The fire also resulted in the destruction of many paintings, as well as the loss of more than 3,000 copies of *The Hasty Papers*, in addition to the loss of unused footage from *Pull My Daisy*, (including footage of the Beats in costume as cowboys) and the complete destruction of many of Leslie's other films.

Leslie describes the meta-narrative around the production of *Pull My Daisy* as one which is characterized by "greed and betrayal" and states that "it was innocence that made it possible for the film to be made". Following the completion of the film the relationship between Robert Frank and Alfred Leslie broke down irreparably, subsequently Leslie has been, "in litigation with him [Robert Frank] legally for over thirty years" and states that "the problems I've had with him are legitimate." According to Alfred Leslie, Robert Frank "says what he wants to say [about the production of *Pull My Daisy*]" and "has acted more than badly".

Since the '60s Leslie has continued to paint, write and produce films and he is currently working on an autobiographical film *Cool Man In A Golden Age*. Alfred Leslie was interviewed in his studio in New York's East Village.

How did you get to meet Jack Kerouac?

I met him years and years ago I ran into him the first time in 1949, actually at a party where this guy — I've forgotten his name now — I hate to remember him by the fact that he stuck his head out of the window … got his head knocked of on the subway.[34] But it was about 1949, he had a loft on 21st Street or something like that, he was an interesting guy, he was a lawyer as I remember, tremendous energy but he was fearfully self-destructive and was always doing wild, wild things. He used to give parties and when I went to this one party I remember Jack was there, I think it was 1949/1950 — something like that and Anatolle Broyard and Jack were standing over there and I knew a number of people there at the time. I think I went with this girl Liz Lehrman and that is where I met him.

A couple of years later I met Allen, this was about 1952 I think and I met him because Allen was trying to be a straight man at the time and he was — I think — trying to get in bed with my wife who was working with him at a market research corporation and I had a loft at the time in Hoboken, in New Jersey, a great loft and so she said "can I invite him over for dinner he's a nice guy" and I said "sure absolutely". So he came over and he was delightful, I mean really witty and energetic and entertaining, but he wouldn't leave and it only took about … the subway which was directly in front of our door. We were on the waterfront, the Hudson tubes was directly across the street you walked out of the door and walked down. It's clean, operates on schedule: every fucking ten minutes, bang! It comes in and you are in New York, at Christopher Street in like three minutes, or something like that. And he wouldn't leave. So Esta — which was my wife's name at the time — was exhausted [because] she had to go to work, he kept talking and he wouldn't go … Kept talking about poetry talking about … just drove me crazy, finally I said "you just gotta leave" and he says "can't I just sleep here, on the floor?" It drives me out of my fucking head: "you can't do it!" He was very upset, or maybe he wasn't very upset — but whatever it was, he left. Then I didn't have too much to do with them, until 1956 maybe 1957, I think it was after Allen had his great success, it was after he had the reading in San Francisco of 'Howl', tell me the date, '56 or '57?

Well, '56, I think…[35]

Now at the same time friends of mine, a sculptor David Smith and a painter Herman Cherry had discovered a small bar across the street from Cherry's loft called the Five Spot, well at that time the Five Spot was as we know it today … shall I tell you the history of it? It became a famous jazz club and artists' bar. The Five Spot was owned and run by Joe and Ignatious Termini, the Termini brothers, it was a family bar, it served eye-openers. What we called at the time the bums — the Bowery alcoholics — needed a drink in the morning when they got up and so for 25 cents, 15 cents, ten cents they could wander along to any of these places and get a couple of drinks to wake up. So it was basically that kind of place. Apparently there was a musician named Dale Wales — who played, I think it was, the bass trumpet — was renting a room on top of the bar and he said to Joe and Iggy one day "hey listen, let me bring some friends in here, put in a piano and we'll play and we'll have a jazz club". And they figured there was nothing to lose.

On the night they opened, David Smith was having a drink with Herman Cherry in Cherry's studio, when they heard this music and they could look out of the window of this little two storey building … they could look out of the window and into the Five Spot, right across the street. So they heard this music and said "hey" and so they went across the street and saw Dale Wales and a couple of guys playing, so they sat there and had a drink, it was 15 cents at that time — or a quarter — for a beer. There was no cover or anything like that and there was nobody there, it was empty. And it must have been like a Thursday night or a Friday night, because those were really big nights — or a Saturday night — at the Cedar Bar. So they came over to the Cedar, which was packed, to see if they could get a crowd to The Five Spot and at that time I had a model A Ford pick-up truck, which just happened to be parked right in front of the bar and David came in and told me about this great empty jazz club and the Cedar was jammed — you could barely move in the fucking place — people were spilling out like the scene you see at the clubs now. So I grabbed about fifty people — not all at once — little by little and I brought them over to the Five Spot. And at about five o'clock in the morning — we were still at the Five Spot — and the bartender, Joe, one of the bartenders came over from the Cedar and wanted to know why we were taking all his fucking customers [laughs]. So that was actually the first time the Five Spot and painters began to make a

Flag painting by Alfred Leslie

linkage, it was actually David Smith and Herman who brought it to us.

Then after that, because Dale was a real musician and Joe and Iggy were such remarkable guys and they trusted musicians to guide them, they were responsible … Dale would suggest people, so soon Cecil Taylor was playing there. Ornette Coleman played his very first date when he came to New York and stunned everybody and the place was jammed. And the very famous poem that Frank — Frank O'Hara wrote — about Billie Holiday took place around that time, '56 or '57. Anyway linking this back with Allen, at that point Allen had been living all the time on the West Coast and I don't know how long he'd been there because I know he'd traveled a great deal. And he came in and was there I think with Frank O'Hara and some of the New York poets and then I got to see Allen again. At the same time a very old friend of mine, Dody Mueller, who had been married to the painter Jan Mueller who had died a couple of years before started to go around with … maybe this is a little later now, but this is how everything became interwoven … Dody started to go around with Jack, so then I came into contact with all of those people I would see them every night, every other night. You know, just on the scene, simply because it wasn't my nature in terms of the work I did to call people up, none of us basically did that, we'd simply hang out at the Five Spot, or the Cedar, or the Ninth Circle, or San Remo's, or any of the various bars and whoever was there you'd talk to them. It wasn't codified or any way made into any kind of formal thing or anything like that. So that's how I came back in touch with Jack, Allen, Peter, Gregory, the four of them at that time.

How did you meet Robert Frank?

I met Robert in '50/'51. He and Mary was living at the time on 23rd Street, over Wynns Chemical Supply Store ... they sold beakers, test tubes. A nice little loft and he and Mary were living there and I guess Pablo and Andre were born at the time — they must have been very, very little at that time. I am trying to remember how I got there ... Mary had made a party and my wife at the time — the one I had met Allen through — somehow we got invited through ... I'm not exactly sure. My wife at the time was a painter but she was also interested in pre-Bach music, early music and seriously played the recorder and I think the guy she was studying with — there was some kind of connection between them I think — anyway we found ourselves at the Frank's house and we all connected. I regarded them both as European, even though Robert was the only European person there, Mary's father — I think, if I remember — was a composer [and] I think she had lived some time in England. They appeared to me at the time — even though I liked them — I had my little suspicions. We came from very, very, very different backgrounds, I regarded them as people who were privileged financially and who were sort of playing house, slumming in a way. Where as I had no money and if I didn't get money from some place I would just sink: period, I had no resources and they did.

Were you painting at this time?

Yeah, I have been painting, making films and taking photographs and writing, just like one of those kids. I have three children. You understand that some kids generate their own energy; their own enthusiasm; they create themselves. So I have been doing all that since I was a kid.

I've always been hard of hearing, as a child I had the same hearing disability, but it wasn't caught. People just thought I was preoccupied and I was. Because I was talented I was left alone and I learnt a lot from the movies, from things that I read, actually sort of like an autodidact. At any rate, I began ... I had a little formal knowledge of the art world. I went into service in the summer of 1945. The war ended while I was in boot camp. It was fortunate that I happened to have enlisted in the Coast Guard, which during World War II was part of the Navy. So when the war ended all of a sudden the Coast Guard had these swollen ranks so they said, if you don't want to be a regular in the Coast Guard we're going to give you an early discharge. So I was discharged after being in the service for nine months and sixteen days, that gave me one year, nine months and sixteen days of Veteran's benefits. Early 1946 until early 1947 I had a year in which I set up my first studio right around the corner from here. And I carried on this practice of making films, taking pictures ... doing all of this stuff at once; I was very, very talented. Since I didn't really listen to anybody, I just did what I wanted to do.

By 1949 I already had a small reputation as a painter. And people knew of my films simply because I used to show them at rent parties. We would have a party, like Larry Rivers would have a party around the corner to raise the rent, Rudy Burkhardt and myself would show films, people would pay a dollar to come in and then we would all take a little share of the proceeds. At that time I would show films that I made, notably this one film which was the longest and the best, it was called *Directions: A Walk After The War Games.* In 1949 which was a watershed year, there was a crisis in my work as an artist. What had happened was I had been selected by Clement Greenberg and Meyer Schapiro for an exhibition, an 'important' exhibition because they were important critics it was an important show called *New Talent* at the Sam Kootz Gallery. At the same time I showed *Directions* at the Museum Of Modern Art in the main auditorium as part of an educational conference. And I gave some classes in making photographs and at that time ... suddenly I began to realize I was carrying on two major dialogues. I was, like, 22 years old [and had] a serious dialogue as a filmmaker and equally committed as a painter. And then I had my so-called writing, well this was pretty bananas and remember I was still working as a floor waxer and artists model to support myself. I realized that I could not develop carrying on public dialogues in more than one area, it seemed impossible. As well as turning into some kind of aesthete: a little bit of this, a little bit of that. But I had no way to seriously commit myself to a body of work. Basically I decided to stop making films, stop taking photographs, stop writing and only paint. And I sold all my film and motion picture equipment. But with in a year of getting rid of all of my equipment I found himself taking photos, without admitting to myself I was doing it. I would know actors and take pictures of them, I would borrow a camera, borrow a darkroom. My best friend at the time Tom Guarino came and set up a darkroom in my studio in 1951 and in 1952 when Allen came and visited me in Hoboken I had a darkroom. I realized that I was beginning to do the same thing again, but I was not carrying on as a public dialogue. Just kept public profile as painter.

In 1955, about six years later, it suddenly occurred to me that if I was going to mature as an artist that what I had to do was let all of these things happen at the same time. It was great risk-taking, that is to say it might destroy my development as a painter. But being a painter and being an artist are too separate things. I didn't know yet what was going to happen to me. So the so called x-factor that we all have, that was in me, I had to look towards them seriously. So I started to write again, I brought a camera, a friend gave me one of the first Polaroid cameras ever made and I began taking photographs with the Polaroid, with another camera and I began writing and I began planning to make films again.

Then somewhere in 1956, I was living at 36 Third Avenue, Robert was living next door, Robert and Mary. Anyway one day I was listening to the radio and this guy started talking about the break-up from the Hollywood system and the inroads of television and that the movie theatres were all closing down. Empty moving theatres because the studios didn't own them anymore. I know it's an old fashioned word but in this flash I thought, "all of those empty fucking screens. That means that if I make a film now, if I do it right at this minute, there is a screen that I could get hold of. Get into an empty theatre, rent it for a week", just the idea of the empty screen. I had already written something called *The Chekov Cha Cha,* which I called a multipurpose work (part play, part film, part everything), it was autobiographical, written about the art world. I had already written a play called *The Cedar Bar* years earlier. And I began to think what it was I would cast as a film. And the first person I thought of was this guy Tom Guarino, my partner in making *Directions.* And I tried to reach Tom, because he also had the print of *Directions,* I'd given it to him because I kept moving so many times and I didn't want anything to happen to it, so I gave it to him for storage. Unbeknown to me he had died of cancer; he was a year younger than I was. So Tom had died and I kept on trying to get in touch with him, so we could work together. I had no idea that Robert was in anyway interested in film; I admired him as a photographer. In 1954, when I split up with the wife I mentioned before — Esta — the one who was living with me in Hoboken, I went to Province Town with Franz Kline. Franz went there to visit a girlfriend of his and I was sleeping in the back of my truck. And at that time Mary and a whole group of people I knew from New York, were living in P.Town, they took me in. Robert at that time was, I guess, on one of his last trips shooting *The Americans*. I think that was the summer of '54. Anyway we all became closer friends and it was just an accident that we found ourselves next door to each other, 36 Third Avenue, it was a complete, when I moved there I did not know that they were neighbors, I guy that I knew [that] had the place had left it and gave it to me and then I though maybe Robert would be interested.

So this is where we get to *Pull My Daisy*. I went to Robert when I couldn't locate Tom Guarino and I said "how about it, do you want to work with me on the film?" At first he hesitated — I didn't exactly know why — then apparently he talked it over with Mary and he agreed, I would be the director, he would be the cameraman. I then tried to locate my print of *Directions* I called Tom's father, his father told me Tom was dead, I then located his wife — his widow — and she told me that before Tom had died he went crazy and he had cut the picture up into pieces and it was in a cardboard box in the basement next to the oil burner. I figured "well, this is going to be a difficult thing to deal with, to try to show around and try and raise some money". I still had no idea of what it was that I was going to make.

Now, from this point here you will always hear me referring to it as "I" because I am telling you what went on with me. When Robert becomes a part of it I will tell you, okay. So I just want you to know that.

I thought "what can I show?" and I realized I did not have *Directions* to show. So I went to Robert and said "blah blah blah" and he said "well you know two summers ago" ... I guess maybe even the summer I was there with everybody in Province Town, he and Ivan Karp had shot a film together, it had never been edited. Ivan was the writer and director and Robert was the cameraman. So Robert gave me the footage and looked at it and thought that I would cut it and maybe perhaps use it to show that the two of us together could actually produce something.

So I did my best and made a cut of it. The footage I thought was terrible; it was poorly photographed, didn't look good, it was to me a ... satire on the early silent film. I guess if you wanted to extend it you could say that it was an absurdist film, but it was more like an amateur picture of people jumping in and out of the water. Nothing much that interested me. I wasn't able to make a good cut of it and I made a cut of it the best that I could, from the material I had. I showed it to Rudy Burkhardt, he was completely silent and anyway I said "this is gonna be hard to raise any fucking money" because Robert was basically an unknown photographer and I was an unknown painter, even though we both had people who knew our names, he had not yet published *The Americans*. And I thought "this is gonna be a difficult fucking thing". But ... this was a very, very energetic time, a lot of people were trying to do things, not only myself, not only Robert and Mary and all of the rest of us. So at one point Robert and I went around and tried to raise money and it really came down to what we were going to use as what we were going to say we were going to make. And there was a story I had read in the *Parisian Review* in the '40s by Isaac Babel, who was one of my favourite writers, called *The Sin Of Jesus* and I thought this could be a great film, a great story and I had worked in the theatre with the translator Miriam Goldina, in 1954 when I did *The Dybbuk* and I loved Babel. And I had, by this time, decided that what should be done was a triptych, a three-part film should be made. This way you could make up ninety minutes by making three thirty-minute films, which would mean you could perhaps raise money for thirty minutes, make the picture, show that and then get the money for the remaining hour. I was very, very optimistic. So what happened, I wrote a screenplay of the Isaac Babel story. And at that time both I and Robert knew Zero

Directions: A Walk After The War Games

Mostel[36] and I had always loved Zero's work and I thought "gee, it would really be fantastic to be able make a film of Zero". So Mary, or Robert, had remembered an article in the French newspapers about a guy who was living with a mannequin, now this was a story that was a familiar story, John Collier was a writer [who] had written a story, a sort of surrealist story, about a man living with a doll, that is how I think we got to be talking about this thing. And of course the painter Kokoschka, who had been living with Alma Mahler, when he and Alma separated and went to live with some architect, he carried around a doll, a full sized doll wherever he went. I didn't really like the idea of the story, but I thought if you had a way to treat it, if I could write it for Zero then it could be made to work, then it wouldn't just be some kind of sentimental, erotic piece of gobbledy gook. So anyway I wrote a screen treatment of this called *Mr. Z*, for Zero and I called Zero up and Robert and I went to see him. We had a very, very funny meeting and I gave him the script to read. He said he was going to show it to Dorothy Thompson ... or maybe it was Dorothy Parker ... I don't remember which and the minute he said he was going to show it to either one of them I thought "this is not going to work" because this was not a literary screenplay, one had to understand it in terms of who I was as a 'writer' at that time, this was primitive, as primitive as you could imagine.

Anyway Dody at that time had been going around with Jack and I had been seeing him from time to time, at one point Dody was trying to persuade Jack, Robert and I to get together and make a film of *On The Road*. Now, I didn't want to do that, mainly because I didn't want to shoot outside of a confined environment. I liked the idea of having control over my setting, much in the way that Hitchcock liked them to be in a particular place, be on a set, have control over everything. I didn't want to shoot outside; I wasn't exactly sure why but

I thought that by shooting outside, going on the road, there would be a kind of looseness to the texture of work itself that I did not want. But I really wasn't quite sure. So I read everything that Jack wrote, every fucking thing that he wrote and I could not — in my mind — find any idea. In the meantime, while I was reading these things I thought "Ah! Okay, we'll make a film of Alain Robbe-Grillet's *The Voyeur."* Okay, I tried to get the rights to it but I couldn't. Then I thought "Ah! We'll make a film of Horace McCoy's *They Shoot Horses, Don't They*", I had already written a screenplay of that. That was suggested to me by Frank O'Hara but I didn't know the work at the time. Then I called the guy who was the executor of the McCoy estate in Paris and he refused me, then three years later it appeared in Hollywood, then I thought of a story that I had written called *The Flag*, but it was sentimental, social realist 1940s style, very heavy-handed story, about an Italian immigrant and the American flag. At any rate I couldn't put my fingers on what I wanted to do with Jack. So finally he gave me a play called *The Bishop Of The New Amaraean Church, The Beat Generation*, a three act play. His agent, Sterling Lord, had shown it to Lillian Hellman; anyway she thought it was a terrible play. Anyway what was interesting about it was that there was nothing dramatic about it, there was no real story to tell, it was the depiction of an event that took place in Los Gatos.

At Neal and Carolyn Cassady's...

At Neal Cassady's house. The third act of the play attracted me the most, it had some kind of stuff in it. What I liked about it was that it was just in one place and was about nothing. And I thought in order for something to be about something it had to be about nothing and in order to create what I wanted to do was create a new cinema, a theatre in which ideas could come out, you really had to give the audiences very, very little and be nuanced in a way the greatest innocence and simplicity.

So, I still couldn't pick anything up from this play, finally Dody was ready for a conjugal visit with Jack. Jack, you know, when he wasn't living with other people was living with his mother. So Robert and I drove Dody out to sleep with Jack and to tell Jack that in fact, nothing doing. I couldn't figure out what the fuck to do with any of these things he had written.

So we got there and Dody and Jack went of to a motel or something, Jack left a tape to play. And he said "listen to this, it's me reading the play". You know the story? So he was reading and in the background was Symphony Sid. Now I had heard Jack read before, he was a phenomenal reader, he had the sweetest delivery ... he had a sweetness that none of the other poets had. I mean sweetness is, I think, the right word, a kind of genuineness. A kind of longing, I think that everything he did, a kind of humanity that was really extraordinary and he was great, a great voice ,a great delivery, nuance of speech. Nobody, I mean nobody, can deliver language like poets. Actors can't do it. So all of a sudden I hear him reading this play, why I can't think of making this play because actors can't play these roles because everything that Jack has written is still a whole poem, it is all about him. All the characters are aspects of Jack. So when he was speaking their voices it had to me a measure of authenticity and so immediately I had another one of my visitations and I thought "this is the way I can make the film with Jack".

What I was going to do, I decided, was to Mickey Mouse the picture track to the sound track. I would take this tape, just the way [he] had done it and Mickey Mouse the image to it and see if I could get all of the lip-sync on all the actors in relationship to Jack's voice.

So, you know, you only normally do this in animated films. It's very, very difficult to do with live people. I didn't know how successful I could be but I figured I could make it work, I knew I could make it work. One problem of course, for me, was what do you do about all that music in the background. It's all different musicians, he's listening to Symphony Sid and Symphony Sid was playing all of these different musicians, all of these songs. So anyway, Dody decides to stay the night with Jack and Robert and I drive back. The whole way back I tried to persuade Robert this is what we should do, he was totally uninterested, he thought it wouldn't work, he had no concept of what I wanted to do. But he was my best friend and I knew that I was right and what had to be done was that I wanted to bring him into this, it was very important to me that he be brought into it. So finally, I expect out of sheer exhaustion from the amount of energy and persuasiveness I was putting out, he agreed. I figured that he agreed because he had nothing to lose, right? In other words he was going to photograph it, if it's good photography ... beautiful photography, badly written and poorly directed, so that is all he needed, right?

So when I got back I tried to set everything in motion, I took the soundtrack to Earl Brown, who was a composer and also an A&R arranger. And he said the track was terrible, it was so poorly recorded that it would be an abomination, you'd never be able to get releases of the songs. I then took it to the great listener Tony Schwartz, who was a great sound-man, that's all he did was sound. He had an extraordinary ear and he shuddered he could not even bear to listen to it. So I realize, well I knew I was right and what had to be done, I had to figure out another strategy. While I was trying to figure out a strategy a fantastic stroke of luck occurred, the Swiss ... Swedish curator Pontus Hulten who was the director of the Moderena Museet in Stockholm, he was the man who created the big museum at Beauberg, he was the man who made that ... the Pompidou Centre possible. Pontus became a friend of mine, he brought in some rich Swiss collectors, this particular woman, a Mrs Geigy, was part of a collector's consortium, she came to my studio 108 Forth Avenue in a Limousine and came up with three guys and brought a painting. And when she left she gave me a check for $1,000, now I had no money. I had no teeth. No hearing aid. I had N.O.T.H.I.N.G. So I called Robert up and said "I've got a thousand fucking dollars. What we'll do is I'll take this $1,000 dollars, we'll go out rent a camera, we'll buy film, I know exactly who I want to have in the cast, we'll write them all letters and we can shoot, we can get $1,000 of something done and that is how the film started.

Right.

The minute that happened Robert and I got together, we figured out what to do, I established — I called this friend of mine John and I put together a crew. Besides making films in the early '50s I had worked as a set designer. I had worked in the theatre and all the guys who I had met at this time; John Robertson was the theatre manager, the stage manager, he was my best friend, he was working at the Early Public Theatre when it was uptown at 108th Street, something like that. Shakespeare in the Park. And I would help John, so I had a crew, I brought together John, the lighting people, an electrician, all of those people together and then laid out the people who I thought should be in the cast.

About a week later Robert called up and said, he had just gotten paid $1,000 for a debt that he had never thought would be paid, he'd like to contribute $1,000 also. I thought that was beautiful, because then we could be equal partners, which I thought was great. Now we had been asking a friend we had in common, Walter Gutman. He had been an art critic when he was young, he was kind of a nice guy. He had refused to give us any money at all, but when he found out that both Robert and I had put in $1,000 apiece Walter said exactly "if you guys are willing to lose your own money I'll put in $1,500." So now we had $3,500. And then I went to lawyer friend of mine and I said "what kind of organization can we make of this so that it can work legally?" So he suggested creating a limited partnership. A self-dissolving partnership which would be financially attractive to people giving money, so at that time you could put in money and if you lost it, in three years you got the whole deduction. Walter went to his office and got seven other people to donate $750 apiece, before you know it we had like $7,000 and production began on the film.

And you shot in your studio ...

Yeah. We shot it ... what happened was that Jack's story took place in a little house, a suburban type house. I switched it all around, what I actually did was rewrite it and made it into the film that you know now. You can read Jack's script and you can see how faithful I was to what it was he wrote and also at the same time how much I departed from it. I did what a director does, what I did was I changed the location, I made it into a film.

Apparently you shot thirty hours' worth of footage...

Well I don't know where that number came about, I might have said that, but I don't think we did. Mainly because I shoot very, very economically. And the way the shooting progressed was very simple. I would block out ... I mean one of the first things that a director has to understand is the space that they're in, where things are going to take place. So I lived here. I knew it was ... the place was hardly much wider than this, but also had a fourteen-foot ceiling, so there was a lot of height, but very, very shallow, which isn't that much room to move around in. So what I did was that I cut out a little piece of cardboard, made it into a viewer and laid out everything in terms of shots and I figured that there would have to be two periods of principal filming. The first period of principal filming would be to attend to some kind of chronological development of what Jack had written. With some changes that I had made. And then I would make a rough cut of that material and see what it felt like and then after that rough cut I could do a second stage of principal shooting to see what else was necessary. So I wanted for example, the script I added the girl on the bed, I added Pablo and ... at one point in the beginning of the film I had written an introduction in which the girl in the bed is lying in bed and instead of the camera seeing the room empty the way it is, the camera sees the room empty then cuts to the girl who is in bed and she has a toy car and she is able to manage the car with a remote control and the car spins around the room then goes crashing into the wall. Robert and I shot that scene and it looked terrible. Really looked terrible. And I realized that what looked terrible about it, is that after Robert, John Robertson and I and Chuck Hayden, who was the electrician, had lit the place ... anyway after it was shot I realized I didn't like the attitude of the camera, I didn't the attitude of the picture. And what it was, if you really know Robert's early work, there was a whole period of his work in which the pictures were sort of like the pictorials of the '30s. There is a certain kind of astonishing beauty, great, great, printmaker — he's a great printmaker, like that shot of those kids in the street in Dublin, or England, or wherever it is. They were very, very beautiful and the image that was coming up was too pictorial, it wasn't loose enough. There has to be a way in which the camera has to be positioned on a tripod, everything under control, no random shooting, everything rehearsed, yet at the same time it has to look more informal. And so I took my clues in creating an informal look for the picture basically from Orson Welles, you know the *War Of The Worlds*, that famous broadcast of his and also from the idea that already entered into mainstream studio cinema of what like in *Citizen Kane* he had the fake documentary, you know, introducing the life of Kane. So I thought the thing to do is there a way where one can in this situation like make with all our control and skill make it in a way look like it is improvised, look like it's a snapshot. And what I noticed, that what I had to be careful was simply by — you know where you have to position the camera like whose talking, where is the camera positioned — that was too close in laying out the shots so that when they really fell into place it looked too artificial, so that I had to leave in long shots that looked a little unfocused, not technically unfocused, but unfocused in terms of point of view. And by having unfocused point of views it could look like what was then becoming known as cinema vérité.

See I never believed in the conditions of the cinema vérité because it's … it's basically what we were doing, except they were saying they just walk in and take the picture, when they'd arranged everybody.

Okay, let's talk about Jack on the set …

Jack came very infrequently. I tried to keep him off the set, I've been quoted before telling the same story …

The bringing drunks in and such?

Now I found that personally not offensive, because he was bringing a drunk up into my studio who is a stranger, no. But I felt that it was humiliating for the person being brought up. It's like a friend of mine who once brought a prostitute to a dinner party and she was very, very uncomfortable, because the people did not know and she was an outsider. And so he would bring these guys up and, you know, they are human beings and they felt uncomfortable. I didn't mind them drinking on the street but they were coming into my life. Plus the fact that all of these fucking guys smoked and here I have these open cans of volatile fluids all over the place: turpentine, these various things that were very flammable. So I didn't want him coming. So he only could come when there were a lot of people, in this instance he came, this one [instance] in which I was shooting these scenes and that's when John Cohen took those photographs during the shooting.

Right. What is interesting now looking at the film is looking at the way women are represented, because they are marginalised so much in the film. They are just…

Hey man, that was the scene. That was the scene of their lives, they were marginal to their lives. They were treated … that was the basis of the story and I just followed the line. And it was like part of a gay subculture at the time, only they were all bisexuals, you know. So this was the thing, it was like the boy's club. That was very truthful to the period. And the play that I wrote in the Cedar Bar, woman are totally marginal, not that they were not there but they were marginalised because they were marginalised in society as a whole and you had to be an exceedingly strong woman to stand forward and make your voice heard, like Jo Mitchell, Grace Harding, you really had to push yourself forward and a lot of them couldn't do that. So I don't think it was anything except reflecting exactly what the culture of that group was about.

Okay, so how did your disagreements with Robert Frank come about, do you want to talk about those, or are you unable to?

No. I'm able to talk about it, sure. The disagreement is very, very simple, [it] was that when the film was completed and I was putting the titles on Robert came to me and asked if he could be given a share of the director's credit with me and I was shocked that he wanted to do that. Then I realized one of the reasons that he wanted to do it, because he had become very, very uncomfortable with his name always used synonymously with my name, it was always; 'Alfred and Robert', 'Alfred and Robert', 'Alfred and Robert', 'Alfred and Robert' and he didn't want that and he was eager to try and separate himself from me. Where as when I had created this unit, to me the unit was a production company, like the Mercury Theatre, that's how I envisioned it. That's why so many things happened. So, Robert wanted to share the credits and I was unwilling at first, then I thought about it and I said he was my best friend and we had just done this thing together, that had become an instant classic, this was before it was titled, this was still in the editing room. And people knew about it, I had shown enough people clips of it and everything in the editing room. And so I agreed and I said "I agree if we set some kind of boundaries and terms on this. I'll give you a credit and in fact I'll even favour the credits so it seems as if I have taken a secondary position, but it's got to be for a period of ten years. And at the end of ten years the credits go back to the way they should have been really." And he agreed. Plus that I said "besides I share in the credits we then, if we do it, have to share credits in everything including photography. So if you want to be co-director and co-adapter, then I have to be also the co-photographer," And then he agreed. But immediately apparent after agreeing he worked assiduously from that day on to this very moment to cut me out, to never admit and acknowledge what the understanding was and what the true circumstances in making the film were. And I have here a copy of *Pull My Daisy*, when the book came out in 1961, in it — I was ill, I had pneumonia at the time — so Robert was interviewed by this guy Jerry Tallmer and Robert was talking to Jerry and he is quoted as referring to me as the director and his being photographer. And the minute he says it he corrects himself and says that Alfred actually did his directing in the editing room. So by 1961 he had demoted me to being the editor and then in the book itself it says "photos: Robert Frank".

So this is the ... and then the next stage of it was when my studio burnt down in 1966, it was a real disaster, twelve firemen were killed and I was out on the street with a five-year-old child and a woman who was just about to put herself into hospital for ten years, you know, plunging electrodes into her brains and living with cold baths, you know. It was a very hard time. While I was in this state of shock Robert went to the lab where the film was stored and took the film out and re-deposited it under his name. And for the past thirty years I have been trying to effect some kind of reasonable reconciliation, in order to have access to the film. That's why I'm struggling with him now. And the fact is that at that time, when he did this, I was the sole copyright owner to the film. Because the film had been copyrighted in the name of 'G-String Enterprises and Alfred Leslie'. Nobody else's name appeared on the copyright up till 1975 or so, whenever it was. G-String Enterprises ceased to exist in 1962, it was only three years until 1962 then it was over. So the only person technically, who owned it legally, was me. But I still have been involved in and figuring, because he had a hard time personally, that it could be worked through but it was never able to be worked through and finally when it came time for the copyright to be renewed he was unable to renew the copyright because his name wasn't on it. I was the only person to be able to renew the copyright and because he had kept the film and I was unable to get it without taking him to court, great legal expense and people lie, the whole fucking thing is insanity when you get into that machine. And I thought I would give him legally half the copyright, hoping he would see that was a conciliatory gesture he will give me my rights to the film which he had seized and was holding, he refused and he still has. And in the meantime I had given him half of the copyright and the guy who was helping me with the copyright told me "this is stupid, just simply copyright it in your name and share the proceeds with him."So, that's what I'll do. So you've heard the whole story.

The last thing is just to ask about how Kerouac's narration came about in the studio?
You know there was a tape that had been made, the very first one I had heard of Jack reading. Now when the time came in order to put Jack's voice on, by that time I realized I could not cut the picture to the sound — Mickey Mouse it. I then had to do some kind of traditional movie. Okay, I thought, Jack will not be able to go into the sound room and deliver what he has to deliver to give that continuity and that flow just the way a

jazz musician would if he only watches something — the same thing going over again- and has to say a couple of lines. And then he has to repeat the lines that are there, but there are no lines that are there, since I had created a whole new object, a picture. I went out again with Robert to where Jack was living with his mother. I brought a projector, I brought a copy of the film and I played the film for him and he had his tape recorder and I said what I want you to try and do is become familiar with this and improvise and get some kind of feeling, you know, what is happening. Because what he was seeing was a whole new work. So he did it. He wasn't too comfortable with it and of course it was like the first feel, he would sit talk into it then we would rewind it and play it back, we'd play the tape and go back and forth — that's a very crude way to do it. Er ... but I wasn't interested in him understanding what I was doing, because you don't make films like that. What I was interested in doing was getting him to give out his best and when he gave me his best then I'd figure out — you know — how to draw these collaborations. Then what I did, I rented the sound studio of this guy Jerry Newman, who was a friend of Jack's and arranged for Jack to come and we'd bring the film, set everything up and he could do the 'narration' at the time. Now, when [we] set this up every scene in the film had been photographed three times. The night before I would rehearse and lay out what I figured about one minute of film, I figured could be shot in a day, so I would lay out the actors, where they were going to be, where the camera could be positioned, people would come in and I would rehearse and then we would photograph them three times. Each scene was photographed three times, slowly, clank! like that, even though there was not a sound sync on it, it was all slated. So with Jack what I determined was that I would get three lead-ins from him — don't ask me why two wouldn't have done, but I always do things in threes like that, it seems that the third number allows you a kind of matching of stuff which in terms of making gives you a lot of options. So we got to the studio, this is how we set it up: David Amram sat in a sound booth at a piano, he had talked to Jack, who had told him the various songs he liked and David could hear Jack talking and Jack had earphones on to watch the film and listen to David play, okay. I had earphones on and I could hear David play and Jack talk and I could watch the film. Then David played.

Now I had told Jerry Newman, "the minute Jack was on, the minute Jack got there and he got near the microphone never turn it off. In-between takes never turn it off." What I wanted was every fucking sound that he made. Figuring that in-between there would be some little pieces of richness that could come through. So we did three takes of the film and we showed it in ten minute segments, so that would have been three takes: ninety minutes. And they all had different qualities, one of them I knew would be like — let's say — the master and then I would be able to go into the others and bring stuff out and fit stuff in. Like one of them he did in sort of a Chinese accent. His voice was rich, as you know [doing] this like this is very demanding and very difficult thing to do, there was a whole roomful of people who were there at the time. And he was brilliant and he delivered these three takes plus I had all the sound in-between.

When I got back into the editing room I laid in the take which I thought was the best; the thirty minutes which I thought was the best and stretched almost from beginning to end, remember there was no music or anything like that. So then I started to cut it up and then re-splice in other segments, so, for example in the part the end when the musicians are leaving and Pablo is going to be put to sleep and Larry Rivers bends down and picks him up, Jack says "up you go little smoke, up you go, up you go little smoke" and Pablo — I love the scene — he reaches over and hits the wind chimes and his head falls down on Larry's shoulder, carries him out. That was Jack [during] an 'in-between-er', he was sitting while rewinding the film and getting ready for the next reel, he's smoking and he puts his cigarettes down and, while watching the smoke curl, says "up you go little smoke, up you go, up you go", brilliant. Then for example in the 'holies', when he is saying "is light holy/is man holy/is the car holy/is holy holy, Bishop? Holy/holy/holy/holy" and you notice if you listen very carefully there are strange [high voice] "holy/holy [deep voice] holy/holy" They are from 'holies' I lifted from other tracks to expand the 'holies' because I didn't have enough 'holies', so in that what the actual 'narration' was, was the three tracks being edited together. So, for example, things had to be spliced out in order to be made … the voice sync when Gregory said "what did you do that for?" and Jack's voice is in a perfect sync with Gregory's lips and it is a great line, it's a very sweet moment.

So you see the whole film, since it has been made, has been misread and misinterpreted partially because Robert would tell people "we just all sat around and I just pointed the camera" and partially because hardly anyone who ever looked at the film and wrote about it could get past what they wanted to believe and the merchandising of Kerouac's myth. Personal agendas and ambition were far more important to them than what was actually happening on film and only since I decided to try and set the record straight has there been a change.

3. An Interview With Robert Frank

Robert Frank was born in Switzerland and moved to America in 1948. In 1955/56, thanks to a grant from the John Simon Guggenheim Foundation, Frank began to devote himself to photography, shooting with a Leica that could fit into his pocket. Frank travelled throughout America with his family in his newly purchased second-hand Ford, taking the photographs that would come to form the bulk of his book *The Americans*. The book was initially condemned as being anti-American and was first published by Robert Delpire, in 1958, in Paris and Rome, under the title *Les Américains*, before being published the following year in America by Grove Press. The American edition of the book included an introduction written by Jack Kerouac, who wrote "Anybody doesnt like these pitchers dont like potry, see?"[37] The photographs that make up *The Americans* show an outsider's viewpoint of America, as a multicultural country, in which various communities live together, under a shared — yet paradoxically different — belief in America, an image repeatedly symbolized by Frank's use of the American flag. Through these photographs the viewer is aware that the journey Frank undertook in order to take the photographs was not just a journey through America but also a journey into himself.

The majority of Frank's films are intensely personal, revealing a deep kinship with the Beat emphasis on the broadly auto/biographical thematic that informs art. These 'autobiographical' based films include: *Conversation In Vermont* (1969), *Life Dances On ...* (1980) and *Home Improvements* (1985), as well as *Moving Pictures* (1994), a short silent collection of footage of several of Frank's collaborators, including Harry Smith and Allen Ginsberg.

Between 1965 and 1968 Frank worked with Sam Shepard, Allen Ginsberg and Julius and Peter Orlovsky on *Me And My Brother*, a 35mm feature length film that primarily focused on the complex nature of the relationship between Peter Orlovsky and his institutionalized brother Julius. Several of Frank's subsequent films feature appearances from Ginsberg and Orlovsky, including: *About Me; A Musical* (1971) and *C'est Vrai! (One Hour)* (1990). In 1983 Frank shot *This Song For Jack*, a black and white half-hour 'homage' to Kerouac, filmed primarily on the porch of the Columbia Lodge, in Chautauqua Park and featuring appearances from Ginsberg, Burroughs, Corso and David Amram.

In 1972 Frank directed the legendary Rolling Stones feature length tour-movie/documentary *Cocksucker Blues*, which remains largely unseen due to its depiction of the Rolling Stones' notorious rock-and-roll excesses, added to which, as Frank states, "There was a misunderstanding that ... when the film was finished Keith left a copy lying around in London and some guy picked it up and showed it and they thought it was me ... so it was unfortunate ... but, you know, so long ago."

Frank has also co-directed three films with Rudy Wurlitzer; two 16mm shorts: *Keep Busy* (1975) and *Energy And How To Get It* (1981), which features a brief cameo by William Burroughs in a scene which Frank describes as being "very good ... done in Nevada", the film also features appearances from New York downtown poet John Giorno and New Orleans' voodoo-jazz man Dr John. The last film to be co-directed by Frank and Wurlitzer was the road movie *Candy Mountain* (1987).

> **Robert Frank, swiss, unobtrusive, nice, with that little camera that he raises and snaps with one hand he sucked a sad poem right out of America onto film, taking rank among the tragic poets of the world. To Robert Frank I now give this message: You got eyes.**
> Jack Kerouac.

You began as photographer, you did *The Americans* book ...
I started to use a movie camera in '58 I think, after I finished the book.

What motivated the move from photography to film?
It is the question everybody asks me; I can answer in many different ways. It is a natural thing to look in the viewfinder, sometimes it is a more interesting to think of what is between the frames as a photographer. It is just more challenging too, you have to deal with people too, you have to explain sometimes, as a photographer you don't need any you just go around capturing that moment. I think it is a very natural development.

Let's start off by talking about the influence of naturalism in *Pull My Daisy*, because it's a film which aimed to be naturalistic, or realistic. it wanted to capture what was going on, 'the natural', and I was interested in that because of the concept of editing. Editing is something which immediately 'loses' naturalism, because you start controlling the natural. With this in mind do you find it difficult to go back to it now?
Well you learn. But maybe when you start film and this was the first film — the second film, that I worked on — there is a purity in what you are trying to do. So, I think that purity was, it was ... kept in the picture and was certainly kept alive in the words of Kerouac which were spontaneous, you know. It went together with some of the acting [which] was spontaneous, some of it was controlled and all of it certainly, the picture was controlled in the editing. You select, cut and so on. It is a very big difference. Today I finished I video piece, I liked it a lot because, for the first time, I was able to ... to preserve a spontaneity and not interfere with the editing, I let them run. I just did short pieces and people talk. It was not edited and it worked out well, maybe video is the best way to do it. Anyhow the way it [*Pull My Daisy*] was shot there was a tremendous amount of footage and so the film was essentially made in the editing and after the picture was put together Kerouac came and spontaneously recorded.

Didn't you edit together three versions of Kerouac's speech in the end, though?
He did it in three sections, roughly ten minutes each and I think only one reel he did twice. And I remember having big fights with Alfred about that, he wanted to edit the voice, he took out a couple of sentences but that was all. It was unnecessary to edit it ... it was done so...

The kind of free-form jazz poetry that Kerouac did.
Yeah. And for me the best part of the picture is Kerouac's voice.

It is part of history as well. What was Kerouac like to work with, because he was drinking a lot at that point...
Yeah. Yeah. One of my regrets is that I said I don't want him on the set when filming, I was afraid of the destructiveness that he could bring about and it is one of my great regrets. I was afraid of him that way. He was just ... he was ... he really was a model of spontaneity, he knew what it was: it was life! That is what he talked about.

What made you cast Corso in the Kerouac role? I mean given that the film is 'based' on real events and Corso is in the role that Kerouac was in...
Well it was a group. You know. They were friends; Allen and Rivers and Orlovsky and Corso and so forth. Corso very much wanted to be in it and he was a young poet and he wanted to be in a film, you know, it was natural to use him. It was very difficult [because] Allen wrote a little outline of the film, what it would be. Kerouac didn't want to write, I mean he said "you

can use my piece, this piece where the Bishop comes to visit". So Allen wrote a little outline, about two pages and in it he ... three times he used the word "fuck" or something like this. We had actors coming and saying "what kind of film is it?" and we gave them this outline — and two or three — they would just walk out they were so insulted, by the language. It was very difficult, I knew an actress I liked a lot and she said she would do it, she thought it was a good project, but anyhow the agent then read it and he said "absolutely not", he could not allow this, she was fairly well known. And I got Delphine Seyrig, who was at that time ... I had photographed her as a model ... This was the problem about the women, it was definitely a film that dealt with the life of these men. Now 'beatnik' it has become such a word ... you know, they were my friends, you know. I mean one is a painter, a poet. I mean I never considered myself a beatnik and neither, I think, would Alfred. But now everything is, you know ... pin a label on it and it's neatly categorized and then you look back. Then people like you come and investigate [laughs]. It's kind of boring.

One thing that stands out, is the way that women are represented in the film, because they are all nagging or pissed off, or whatever. For example there is the girl on the bed who just moans when David Amram comes in and plays and the wife who starts moaning at them for going out and for ruining the Bishop's visit. How do you feel about that in retrospect, because obviously the representation of women has changed so much since then?
Yeah. Well I think it represented the general view of that group of people, you know, that did not want to be responsible for a family, didn't want to ... you know. I mean Kerouac lived with his mother and was very kind to her, but as a rule they [women] would interfere with that kind of life that group of men would have or want to have. So a woman was there in the bed, I think it was ... I forgot now how it was ... but I think, Alfred, a friend of Alfred ... a painter's wife, I forgot the name, but he said "it's a good-looking woman, we should be able to use her", well let's just put her on the bed and not give her a role. Just ... she'd be there. Some kind of a symbol. You do a lot of things at that time, when you are young, they are intuition, they are not — you know — conceptual art. You do not have a concept, your intuition is right.

One thing I found very interesting was the way the film divided in the middle, around the exterior shot of the Bishop, that scene ... it is almost like the film divides into two halves...
I wanted to go outside, I felt it would be good to have a scene outside, the scene with the flag and the preacher. It was sort of made up as we started shooting the film. The ... I think it was the pan around the table, I like that it was like some kind of dream or some kind of memory, as opposed to the present of that room at that time. [pause] Yeah, sometimes I think it would have been better without but ... you know.

I think it's important, the way in which it divides the film...
I remember very well when we shot it and the flag and Bellamy — who played the preacher — he ... I would say "well you are the preacher, you talk about your beliefs and your religion, you know preach" and he would only repeat this one word, you know, "bastards, bastards" [laughs]. It's very good, you know you can read the lips.

I'm also interested in how it comes out of that [exterior] and back into the scene in the room and Kerouac just starts rapping, about "cockroach".
There is a good video out, that I made (Alfred made his own so...) and that has the original printing where the scene around the table is very dark, dream like, when he

says "cockroach" and all that and then it gets lighter, you know. So I did that very carefully it was very important for me then to make that pan around the table and intercutting these scenes.

What I found interesting about that is the way that the duality of 'beat philosophy' where on one hand it is reflecting reality and about life and on the other hand the concern with the spiritual, the mystical. And that seems interesting to me in the way in which that scene goes into the magical and mystical, when you see the Bishop outside preaching and then back into the reality of the apartment, but the narration kind of continues the mystical, firstly with the cockroach stuff, then with the use of the repetition of 'holy'; "holy, holy, holy, is Allen holy, is man holy" and so on. I thought that was interesting the breakdown between the quite cold 'realism' at the beginning, where you have them coming in with the beers and talking and then with the more 'mystical' part at the end, which gets higher and higher, with the jazz music playing and stuff. How do you feel about that, was that an intention at the time, or is that retrospective?
Well see it got much stronger with the words, because for me at that time it was just to get the image right and I had the idea of making this room darker and come in with all the reality, so uh ... I don't think that much about it. I just went out and did that scene, it was an easy scene to do and we wanted the other world to be there, the people who listen to the preacher, I mean my wife was in it, my grandmother and oh ... So I thought it was important to see that, then go back into the room. The rest, I really think Kerouac in his narration brought out that mysticism and that poetry and to me it is more poetry...

Yes it is poetry, but it is also the personal mysticism that Kerouac was involved in. His own kind of Buddhism and such. His relationship with the holy experience of life itself...
I didn't know him that way so much, you know...

Well, it is something you get more from his books, when he is talking about...
Yeah, you get it from the books and, I wasn't inclined at that time really to even listen to it much, I mean I was too pushy...

Yeah. You shot thirty hours of film or something like that, how did you choose what to edit?
Well, it was a big crisis, because we didn't really know how to edit. We got help then; you have to classify the stuff and a lot got lost, unfortunately ... There were some absolutely wonderful scenes; with cowboys and cowboy uniforms, so ... You know when you make a work you leave it alone afterwards. And that was my big thing with Alfred, that he took it out of the lab and everything burnt, all the stuff burnt. He had no right to take it out. It was unfortunate. And so — I just remember then — I think you just leave it alone, what has been done, not try to change it.

You have to move on.
Yeah.

How did you come to meet David Amram, what was his relationship with the film?
Because I got that singer, that sings that song ['The Crazy Daisy'], Anita Ellis and she said get David Amram. Then he came in. I think that's how it was. Yeah. And I didn't really know him that well, before or after, I mean we still see each other sometimes, but there's

no ... I think he played not a good role when they wanted to bring out the record. Once the film was finished I sort of turned away, I wasn't really interested in ... And he made a big deal, the record and a lot of money and he was not quite there I think, I think he was not ... already he felt he should get an enormous some of money although the film was, you know, just a small film. So I think his role in that was not good.

When he actually scored the film, did he score it afterwards, or beforehand? Did you have music by him that you wanted to use, or did he actually watch the film when it was finished and then play to it?
He ... I forget exactly. He played while Kerouac ... Kerouac listened to his music on earphones and then he made up the words. But then he scored it afterwards. It was afterwards.

I thought it was interesting that the soundtrack seems to represent the character's thoughts, but also seems to go beyond the language, that spoken language so the narration breaks down: into the "cockroach" section, then at the end when Kerouac says let's go out into the street and starts clicking his fingers and humming and stuff. I thought it was very interesting the way that it goes beyond language. I mean film is a visual medium and I thought it was interesting that you were breaking away from the whole narration, the whole spoken language by the end of it, into just the music, until even the voice became music.
Yeah, "ta-da-da-da-ta" [singing]. Yeah, well he [Kerouac] had a wonderful feeling. It was really, there was not so much depth as you see in it. It was just about life, you know: you run out from the nagging woman, go down with your friends and go and play on the Bowery. Actually we had some footage then, going out into the dark street and all that.

But you've said since, haven't you, that words get "kinda boring"[38] in films.
Yeah.

I just wondered how that related, because I thought that was important. The silencing of...
Well, the film was at an end then, I mean the story was told, you know, the evening was over. So for me that was a clear thing to do, go out and play. I forgot now, was there music there at the end, no it just "da-da-da-da"?

It's the actual language ... when that becomes music, that is what I thought was so interesting, because there is that wild scene, where they are all playing together in the apartment and the Bishop is going and then they argue, before going downstairs and Kerouac's voice becomes like a repetition of the jazz that was playing before. When you opened the film it was with Cassavetes' film *Shadows*.
The first time it was shown, I think it was shown in Cinema 16,[39] with Amos Vogel who runs it and they showed it in a fairly big place together, yeah, with lots of people there, yeah I remember that.

Because in 1961, Parker Tyler wrote about how the film wasn't as good as *Shadows*, how *Shadows* was better and stuff,[40] but Cassavetes' apparently said that part of what inspired *Shadows* was your photographs in the book *The Americans*. I just wondered what you felt about that?
I didn't know that. I knew the actor [Ben Carruthers], whom I liked a lot, from *Shadows*. I thought the films were very different really, they were made at the same time but...

I got the feeling that they both had the same, or similar, ideas, but were radically different in their methods of approach, but I wondered how you felt about the criticism you got from Parker Tyler?
I can't remember it. [Pause] I remember when we showed *Pull My Daisy* to the people who gave us money, four, five or six people. And they looked at it and one or two left before the finish, they didn't understand anything about it. It seemed strange to me that intelligent people, who had money and work on Wall Street ... I liked the man very much who gave most of the money, Walter Gutman, who was responsible for it.

He was the art dealer? He worked on the stock market, but also collected art...
Yeah, he worked on the stock market. But he was a very, very special man, so far ahead. He was way ahead of his time. He liked all artists. He got a lot from artists, they inspired him and he wrote about them in his stock market letters. But Dwight MacDonald liked it, he wrote for *Esquire*. You know, I'm always interested to go on. It's very important to finish something and go on.

You also cast your son, as Pablo in the film, that was quite interesting, the counterbalance of the child and the men acting as kids, especially when he comes out and plays jazz with them. The way Kerouac takes on the kid's voice ...
You make all these connections and, you know, it's uhn ... Kerouac knew my son then, we had traveled together, it was a natural thing to put him in that. Actually my favourite line of the whole film and I really felt that, when he lifts up the little child and he takes him up and he says "go up little smoke". That is a wonderful line.

Yes and he sings it as well. Kerouac sings that line, because he says it three times and each time it gets higher.
Yeah, yeah. "Up little smoke."

That is really beautiful, where the camera follows the smoke up. That is really interesting, one of the best Kerouac lines, that is a moving scene...
Yeah. He had another line that always excited me, which Alfred absolutely wanted to get rid off that line and finally I gave in. It was at the end, when the people come down the staircase and they say "come on Milo, come on" and then, above the ceiling there was a rose hanging down and Peter holds out his hand and makes the rose so it wouldn't swing anymore and then Kerouac just very calmly says "And a rose for Mary". Mary that was my wife then. I thought it was a very ... it was almost as if he had made peace with the woman up there, that didn't understand the beatniks. And I remember that I had such fights with Alfred, completely ... He's a real asshole. I'm sorry to say that, but I mean ... we made the film together, but he is really the pits. I mean he developed that ... I don't know when ... when an artist's ambitions are not fulfilled the way he thinks they should be, then they get very difficult and I mean he got absolutely impossible but, it's you know ... There's a strangeness in it, it was forty years ago, you should just drop the fucking thing, you know. It's good the film is out, it's not going to make a million dollars with it. It's not *Gone With The Wind* or what, but that is the disappointing part of the film, because with all of the other — the ones that are around — I see them and ... you know, I'm still good friends with Orlovsky and people ... We have worked on other things together. But often a film can destroy a friendship, you know.

It's so much work, you spend so much time arguing over small things...
Squeezing out the last drop of something. But a critic like you can see much more in it

than I see now. It's a personal thing, like when my daughter recites the lines "Humpty Dumpty fell off the horse", but I tell everybody, the piece of Kerouac, I mean his narration is absolutely a masterpiece for me, somebody being able to sit there and watch that film and talk that. But the idea came from that. I went up to wherever he lived in Long Island and he said "Well, we could make a film and I will take all the voices and Symphony Sid will play," you know. Then he read me a piece in his house — I forgot what it was now — and he took on all these characters and I though it was very good. You know at that time it didn't go on a tape recorder, it was too bad, it would have been...

I think that hearing the narration and hearing Kerouac talk, it's far better than reading it, than reading his work, because of the tones of his voice and the rhythms which come out so strongly in it.
He had a ... he was a real good guy. I didn't realize it, I mean, we were friends, but I didn't see the incredible talent he had. I knew that something with his memory was outstanding; I mean he would be lying on the floor drunk and he would go up the next day, or two or three weeks later, he would show me something he wrote and there was every word that we said at that party. He was like a sponge, he would just be there.

After you finished *Pull My Daisy*, did you see anything in common with other filmmakers working at that time, because Jonas Mekas starting talking about the New American Cinema. Did you see any movement, any new aesthetic developing, or collective, or do you think it was just Jonas Mekas 'marketing' his journalism?
I think, in a way, the strongest connection to me was *Flaming Creatures*, although when I saw it I really didn't like it, I was sort of amused by it but I thought it had a certain freedom, in making films I mean there were no rules which, you know, I am too ordered, I am too square to have ... so that film meant a lot to me that way, although it's not my world and I didn't particularly like it but I do ... Then I saw pieces that he [Jack Smith] did — little theatre [pieces] and so on — and I could really see that he was an important artist and he had a vision that was completely original and singular and ... quite sad, [and] in a way, poetic. Much more than [Jonas] Mekas as a filmmaker, much more than Shirley Clarke[41] ... and actually, what interests me always are outsiders, not so much the people who push towards the middle.

After you finished *Pull My Daisy* you began to work on *Me And My Brother*...
No, I made another film then, in-between, called *The Sin Of Jesus*,[42] which was not very good. Well, it was an Isaac Babel story and the mistake was to take a story and try and make a film of it, but I was learning, you know, because there was no film schools, you had to learn by making the stuff.

You get a greater freedom through learning as you do it, than you do sitting in a school...
But you pay.

When did you start making *Me And My Brother*?
I started '63, '64, something like that.

Wasn't Sam Shepard[43] involved at some point?
Yeah, he wrote a couple of scenes and then Antonioni came and he left, he went to make *Zabriskie Point* (1970) with Antonioni.[44]

Right. ***Me And My Brother*** **was about the Orlovsky brothers, about Peter and Julius.**
Yeah, who was a catatonic and he gets lost and comes back. It was a very difficult and complicated film to make. It's too long, but it has very good ideas in it, very good scenes in it...

How long did it take to make that film?
Two or three years really. Also the story is Julius disappearing when he travels with them, once or twice I went with them to California, but then he wasn't available — he got lost — and they found him, it was two months later in a hospital in California. And then, I needed more money and the guy who gave me money said "we have to make something in colour and take an actor, I want some actors in it" and I did it because I needed the money, so it took away something, it gave a little bit. That's when I used Joseph Chakin you know him? He collaborated on many things with Sam Shepard, he was an actor, there was a book out by him that was very good just his thoughts. I would show it to you, but I don't have it anymore, all these things ... he was very good, very influential, tremendous influence on Sam Shepard, called the Open Theatre.

The other thing you became involved with at this time was ***Chappaqua,*** **on which you did the cinematography...**
Most of it, yeah.

That is a really interesting film...
Because the guy [Conrad Rooks] was interesting, he was a real nut. Yeah, he was a real ... But at least he was ... he was completely out of everything, he had so much money to spend. It could have been a good film, a really strong film, but he wouldn't use the footage that I shot of him and he was the story.

Is any of your footage in the finished film...?
Oh yeah...

But you shot more stuff as well...
But he took out, you know, really strong scenes with him, which showed him as a this extraordinary, insane man that he really was...

He lives somewhere in the Pacific now?
He lives in Thailand. I just got a letter from him, a weird letter. I just got it two days ago. That was an experience, I remember when I was shooting in Paris, in a cafe and [Jean Luc] Godard[45] was there and he watched it for a little while and he said "you ought to make a film on him", you know. It's a funny thing.

How do you feel when you are working on somebody else's film, as opposed to directing your own films, do you feel that it compromises you too much?
Well that was easy because I had, really, freedom to do what I wanted to do. I mean he just said "let's go and rent a château and get women in there and ice that steams up and makes smoke" you know, pretty free. He would go [laughs] every time after it was over, he would go to Jamaica or India and he would always say afterwards "okay" and take out his big fountain pen and he'd write me a check and say: "You're a bastard! I'll never work with you again!" [laughs]. Then he'd call me after a month and he'd show up in India and say "let's go to Ceylon", something like that.

He was a very unhappy man, he couldn't concentrate and pursue a thought. He'd open up a magazine and start to say "oh, let's go to Oregon, where the big trees are and get a bambi running around the trees" ... he had this ... he was an interesting guy ... many people like that movie, I don't know.

I think it's very interesting that in the six or seven years between *Pull My Daisy* and *Chappaqua* the entire aesthetic changes, in *Pull My Daisy* it is like 'real life' and 'real people' and *Chappaqua* is totally psychedelic.
Yeah, yeah that was very different.

Like all the double exposure photography, of the man walking along through the flat landscape, Nebraska or whatever and the double exposure of all the mad lights from Times Square or whatever.
Yeah, he had wonderful ideas. I mean he would say "I want to go to a Peyote Ceremony" you know and he had some connection in Montana and so he said "you — with your little camera — and I and Ornette [Coleman] will go there and we'll give the guy a gun and he'll let us photograph it." And then the same day, or the day before, we walked by and there was Moondog — the blind beggar — on the street and he just looked at him and went up to him and said "I want to take you to Montana with Ornette Coleman, I'm making a film", the guy had no idea and he just wrote him a cheque and said "come with us".

So he would just be picking people up and flying them to different places...
Yeah, yeah. And that was a wonderful quality. So we went there. And it was an absolutely singular thing, that you could not remake ... you could remake *Pull My Daisy* in some way. But this complete insanity and psychedelic ideas would be hard to duplicate, but that's too bad, there were wonderful scenes with him and women ... well, it is hard to rebuild the truth in films about oneself.

That's quite interesting, that whole idea of showing the 'truth' in films, how important is that to you, that idea of showing the truth in film?
Well, if it is a personal film, which I often make, that dealt with my life, it was important to get as much truth in there as possible, so I know how difficult it is. It is a trap you don't want to get caught in.

That kind of aesthetic demands a certain intensity of vision...
It demands courage and you risk something. You actually risk every thing.

Something else that struck me as quite interesting is the whole on the road thing of the Beats and then the whole kind of on the road thing in your movies, in *Chappaqua* to an extent, in *Cocksucker Blues*, then later in *Candy Mountain* ... how important is travelling, the whole question of travelling to you ... as a way of finding about yourself...
Well, coming from Europe, from a small country like Switzerland and I come to America, you realize the tremendous space there is here and naturally the normal thing is to travel, you get a car and you travel, you look, you see more when you travel, when you stay you have to look more inside, when you travel landscape goes by and ... so its easier to outside. Even now I travel a lot between Canada and here, the film I have just made — the video — has a lot to do with just moving from one place to another, at the end you don't even know which place you are in, it's just the same guy struggling, struggling, trying to make

something. When you are travelling, you go from Minneapolis to Dakota and Dakota to San Francisco. It's laid out for you.

But obviously Kerouac and Ginsberg, spent a lot of time travelling. There is that whole idea of learning about yourself, of developing your aesthetic, on the road. It's like the developments in Ginsberg's poetry after he went to India, or Kerouac's whole thing ... his whole vision ... the most important, most influential, part of his work, came from traveling. And also the question of your being Swiss, of being an outsider and you said earlier about admiring outsiders, when you have a vision that is outside something and also the idea of exploring internally, as well as externally and geographically.

I like a lot the diaries of Ginsberg in India, I remember when I went to India with Rooks, there was not much footage travelling, it was such a beautiful country but I was so occupied trying to make footage that wasn't a travelogue. I have forgotten what there was in there about India, but we went there twice, the second time we went there he was to make *Siddhartha*. The temptation is that it is going to be a sort of road movie, I never liked *Candy Mountain* that much. Not because of the travel, but it is too controlled...

You co-directed that film didn't you?

Yeah, with Rudy Wurlitzer. I think he is a wonderful writer, but it is very difficult to co-direct, that friendship is gone after that film. But to me it was just too controlled, we had too much money to do it and too many demands to satisfy the money and the rules were too strict, you couldn't be spontaneous.

Do you think that it is easy to be spontaneous as a filmmaker? Shooting on film as opposed to video.

Very difficult. It is the clear thing, video and anyhow it ends up in the little box, so it's there and now you can transfer it to film, very little difference.

You also made *This Song For Jack* at the...

I forgot what that conference was called, it was the anniversary of Kerouac's death, or publication of *On The Road*, or something like that.[46]

How much is it a companion piece to *Pull My Daisy*?

I don't think it's ... I haven't seen it in a long time. I made it in a hurry. I put it together in a hurry. All these people are in it, you know, Corso and ... Kerouac is there by ... I think they read *On The Road* there, the whole thing, they read it outside, on the porch there. So it's nice to see. And Ginsberg and Orlovsky and Kesey were there ... all the figures of that time were there. I think I tried to ... it was more like interviews, like trying to talk to them. Carl Soloman was there.

That was all filmed on the porch there?

Yeah, I shot it mostly on the porch. I had an operation then and I couldn't move very much, that's right. I had to take it easy.

What was it shot on?

It was shot on film. I never think too much about that film, I never remember really. I think Allen gave me some money to do it and the Naropa Foundation gave me some money. It's a film really that I have no voice in it, it was the other people that talked.

It's almost like a documentary.
Yeah. Yeah. Yeah.

You didn't edit it that much then?
No. No. Each one that I got on film ... the one thing I do remember was a reading by that poet Jack Michelin ... a wonderful reading of a poem, I only used a small part, but even that small part was very good. Uhm. So I don't have that much to say about that film. Allen was in it and Gregory and Burroughs.

Are you still shooting in film, or is it more video work now?
Mostly video; I've finished a film I liked a lot, it's called *The Present*[47] and it was the first time I was able to have a spontaneity that isn't false, that doesn't ... I had to do ... because every time I picked up the camera I did talk behind the camera, the reason that I picked up the camera is that I wanted to say something. More what I had to say, about what I'm trying to do, than what I looked at. I looked out of this window and just started talking and that — I just showed it — that was pretty good, it's also quicker and has many different scenes in it, I like that kind of film. And I think that it is because I had the courage to reveal more, in a way and also it was ... the shooting was very sparse, it was a film I started, maybe, three years ago, on video and I didn't shoot much. There was only two hours of video, which ... er ... I only picked up the camera when I felt that this was the right time to do it; when I see somebody I liked, there are not many people in it. So it's, uhm ... quite good. I don't know how that will be shown. I made another movie, much earlier, which was called *Home Improvements* and it's like the suite of it, the continuation and I like this one better, because it's not too heavy and it deals with my life and it tells it only like you could tell it; in that way with a video and your voice ... it's not a narration. And I find you have to be very sure of what you are doing and here I had the help of a young editor, from here and she really understood it. I can't stand to look at video more than twice in an editing room, it's very easy to edit on a computer, so I would just explain what I want and I don't want to have it manipulated, just leave it as it is and put it together and she was very understanding ... she did a very good job, very good.

Anything else you would like to add?
I just think it is important at my age to go on. That is what I tell everybody, to keep on your feet, be able to get up and still have the wish — the desire — to express something. You know, I wouldn't care anymore what it would be to bring up that energy to do that. Yeah it makes your life better if you can do that. And I tell all the young people to use the video, this is clearly the thing to start and not go into big films right away and have to spend money on that and get an idea and do it on video and go onto films later. It is a wonderful tool to use. Sometimes I go and lecture in some school and so on and they are mostly people who do videos and have gone away from photography, or who do the two, but it is clear that the video is pushing photography back. And video can be poetic too, it can reveal — sometimes — more than a film and the big film machinery like Hollywood, there is so much money, there are so many people involved, so many compromises to be made, that you might as well go into it in a big way and do it right if you have the talent, or work as a small wheel in these productions.

Finally, how do you feel about *On The Road* being made as a big Hollywood film?
[pause] The way business is run here ... [pause] you are lucky if you can keep your individuality, your voice and you recognize that voice and it is not somebody else's. You still

recognize your own voice. With all the possibilities it is easy to lose it. I can see it with video, with computer editing, it makes it so easy to do anything you want; turn it upside down, backwards, inside out, the temptation is very great to lose whatever vision or voice you have. That is why I like my last film, because it is kept together, no attempt is made to make something that isn't there. It is very hard to ... I am surprised that it took me so long to accept that. I always tried to put the class in, so it keeps together, tell a little story. So one is happy when it works ... something that before you weren't able to achieve. Making films, I think that every film is different, there is always new mistakes you make, in photography it wouldn't be like that. It is my name anyway so they'd say it's great anyhow, it's good enough. In films you have to make a tremendous effort, you have to know, I learnt a lot making my own films.

---

1. This was how Kerouac described his role as author of *The Subterraneans,* cited in Gerald Nicosia *Memory Babe: A Critical Biography of Jack Kerouac,* Grove Press Inc, New York, 1983, p.445.

2. The most famous of Neal Cassady's letters being his description of a bus journey seduction, dated 7 March, 1947. Reprinted in Cassady's book *The First Third & Other Writings: Revised & Expanded Edition,* City Lights Books, San Francisco, 1991 (1971).

3. *Memory Babe,* p.338.

4. Kerouac in a letter to Ed White, 6 August, 1953, cited in *Memory Babe,* p.447.

5. Carolyn Cassady, *Off The Road: My Years with Cassady, Kerouac and Ginsberg,* Penguin Books, 1991 (1990), p.264.

6. *Off The Road,* p.266.

7. Kerouac's *On The Road* was published on 5 September, 1957 and climbed to number seven in the bestseller list.

8.'Fie My Fum' was published in the Spring 1950 issue of the journal *Neurotica,* edited by Jay Landesman, the poem was the first work by Allen Ginsberg to be published outside of either college or local newspapers.

9. This song has been variously referred to as both 'Pull My Daisy' and 'The Crazy Daisy'. According to Alfred Leslie the original poem was composed on the Brooklyn Bridge "while he [Allen] and Jack were jerking each other off." (Alfred Leslie, personal correspondence)

10. Cited in *Memory Babe,* p.584.

11. Jack Kerouac, *The Beat Generation Or The New Amaraean Church,* Act Three, unpublished.

12. In the book *Pull My Daisy* (*Pull My Daisy,* text ad-libbed by Jack Kerouac, for the film by Robert Frank and Alfred Leslie. Introduction by Jerry Tallmer, Grove Press, Inc: New York, Evergreen Books Ltd: London, 1961) — which contains a transcript of Kerouac's improvised narration of the film — the wife is named as Carolyn in the credits. However in the film's credits (at least on the versions I have seen) she is referred to simply as "the wife".

13. Delphine Seyrig also appeared in Alain Resnais' *L'Anéee Dernière A Marienbad* (*Last Year At Marienbad,* 1961), Joseph Losey's *Accident* (1967) and Harry Kumel's *Daughters Of Darkness* (1971), amongst others.

14. The Method was a technique of acting that was based on the actors' complete identification with the role.

15. All subsequent script quotations from the film *Pull My Daisy* are taken from the book *Pull My Daisy.* Where I have felt it necessary I have altered the punctuation of a sentence, any alterations are noted within the text.

16. The American flag is recurring motif in Robert Frank's book *The Americans,* where it was used to simultaneously symbolize both identity and lack of identity; belonging to a national culture and being excluded from it, for many Americans the flag also functions as a visual signifier of their own freedom.

The American flag is also a 'thematic' of Alfred Leslie's paintings from the early '50s, 'abstract' works such as *Spots And Stripes Painting'* (1952) and *'Hoboken Oval* (1953) are characterized via the repeated use of stripes (both vertical and horizontal) which are visually contrasted with painted areas of circular shapes.

17. J. Hoberman Introduction, in Parker Tyler *Underground Film: A Critical History,* Da Capo Press, New York 1995 (1969), p.vi.

18. Jonas Mekas 'New York Letter: Towards A Spontaneous Cinema', in *Sight and Sound*, V.28, no 3 & 4 (double issue), Summer/Autumn, 1959, p.119.

19. Jonas Mekas 'Appendix: The Independent Film Award', in P. Adams Sitney, ed., *Film Culture Reader*, Praeger Publishers, New York, 1970.

20. Robert Frank and Alfred Leslie cited in 'New York Letter: Towards A Spontaneous Cinema', p.120.

21. Jerry Tallmer, 'Introduction' in *Pull My Daisy*, p.19.

22. Amos Vogel, *Film As Subversive Art*, Weindenfold & Nicolson: London, 1974, p.92.

23. Parker Tyler, 'For *Shadows*, Against *Pull My Daisy*', in *Film Culture*, n.24, Spring '62, p.29.

24. The nature of the cinematic relationship between the two directors/ producers during the making of *Pull My Daisy* varies according to different reports, thus, for example, in *The Underground Film*, Sheldon Renan (Studio Vista: London, 1968 [1967]) states "Alfred Leslie wrote and directed and Robert Frank photographed" (p.100), in the Introduction to the script Jerry Tallmer writes "cameraman Robert Frank and director Alfred Leslie" (p.17) then, on the same page, quotes Robert Frank stating that "Alfred did the directing in his editing"(p.17). While Parker Tyler, who disliked the film, saw it as a collaboration between "the painter Alfred Leslie, the novelist Jack Kerouac and the filmmaker Robert Frank" (*Underground Film: A Critical History*, p.89). The exact nature of the creative relationship between the Frank and Leslie remains a mystery, what is certain is that the film benefits from the input of the various contributors.

25. Michael Renov, 'Towards A Poetics of Documentary', in Michael Renov, ed, *Theorizing Documentary*, AFI/ Routledge: NYC, London: 1993, p.201.

26. *The Beat Generation Or The New Amaraean Church*, Act Three (unpublished).

27. *The Beat Generation Or The New Amaraean Church*, Act Three.

28. *The Beat Generation Or The New Amaraean Church*, Act Three.

29. Stephen Dwoskin suggests, in a strange interpretation of the term 'railroad poet', that the term is actually a euphemism for "ex-drug addict" (*Film Is ... The International Free Cinema*, Peter Owen: London, 1975, p.), despite the fact that at the opening of the film the narration makes it apparent that Milo works on the railroad as a "brakeman".

30. Jack Kerouac, *On The Road*, Penguin Books, London, 1991, (1957), p.278.

31. *On The Road*, p.279.

32. Jack Kerouac, *Lonesome Traveller*, Granada Publishing Ltd, London, 1982, (1962), p.114. According to Leslie "the Paramount building Jack refers to is a movie theatre of the grand palace variety — the Paramount theatre on 42nd Street."

33. *The Hasty Papers* was reprinted in 1999, with an additional fifty-page supplement and new introduction.

34. Bill Cannastra, who was killed on 12 October, 1950, in an accident while leaning from a subway train window as it pulled out from the Bleeker Street Station.

35. Allen Ginsberg initially performed 'Howl' in October, 1955, in San Francisco; the reading was so successful that Lawrence Ferlingetti asked to publish the poem in his Pocket Poet Series. This reading is considered by many to be the inauguration of the San Francisco Poetry Renaissance. It was, however, the performance of 'Howl' in Los Angeles the following year which gained most notoriety, primarily due to Ginsberg's impromptu strip during the reading in response to hecklers in the audience, literally "The poet stands naked before the world" (attributed to Ginsberg in *Ginsberg: A Biography*, by Barry Miles, Viking, 1990, p.215)

36. Zero Mostel (Samuel Joel Mostel) was an actor, of both stage and screen, who was blacklisted by the notorious H.U.A.C. He theatrical appearances include *A Funny Thing Happened On The Way To The Forum* (1963) and *Fiddler On The Roof* (1964), while his film appearances include Mel Brooks' *The Producers* (1967).

37. Jack Kerouac, Introduction, Robert Frank, *The Americans*, Cornerhouse, Manchester, 1993, p.9.

38. Marlaine Glicksman, "Highway 61 Revisited: Robert Frank Interviewed", in *Film Comment*, v.23, #4, p.35.

39. The film opened at Cinema 16 on 11 November, 1959. Cinema 16 was founded in 1949 by Amos Vogel and Marcia Vogel and ran until 1963. Its film distribution service was taken up by Grove Press.

40. 'For *Shadows*, Against *Pull My Daisy*', in *Film Culture*, #24, Spring '62, p.28-33.

41. Shirley Clarke directed several short films: *Dance In The Sun* (1953), *Bullfight* (1955), *Moment In Love*

(1959) and *Bridges-Go-Round* (1958). She also directed the feature film *The Connection* (1961), focusing on the downtown drugs scene of the late '50s, cast with members of the Living Theatre and based on Jack Gilbert's play. Her following film was *The Cool World* (1963), which dealt with life in the ghetto. This was followed by the acclaimed *Portrait Of Jason* (1967), a film in which the homosexual Jason Holliday describes his life; as the film progresses he reveals more about his lifestyle as a gay hustler. The film is frequently noted for its engagement with vérité, primarily because of its straight to camera monologue and use of 'real' time.

42. *The Sin Of Jesus* (1961), was a black and white, 35mm, 40 minute-long adaptation of Babel's story, featuring Julie Bovasso, John Coe, Robert Blossom, St. George Brian and Telly Savalas.

43. Sam Shepard is a writer and actor; his credits include the stage plays *Cowboys* (first performed on 16/10/64) and *Cowboy Mouth* (12/4/71) co-authored with Patti Smith and the screenplay of *Paris, Texas,* for Wim Wenders. As an actor he has appeared in Malick's *Days Of Heaven* (1978), Kaufman's *The Right Stuff* (1983) and Altman's *Fool For Love* (1985), amongst others.

44. Amongst other films, Michelangelo Antonioni directed *Blow Up* (1966) and *The Passenger* (1975).

45. Alongside Francois Truffaut, Godard was one of the pioneers of French New Wave Cinema (Nouvelle Vague, generally considered to have been at its creative peak between 1959–64); his works include *A Bout De Souffle* (*Breathless,* 1959), *Bande A Part* (1964) and *Une Femme Mariée* (1964).

46. The film documents the 1982 *On The Road,* Jack Kerouac Conference, which transpired in Boulder, Colorado and celebrated the 25th anniversary of the book's publication.

47. *The Present* (1996) was shot by Frank on video and transferred to 35mm by Ruth Waldburger of Vega Film in Zurich.

Chapter Two

Spontaneous Cinema? In The Shadows With John Cassavetes

By Stephanie Watson

Born in New York City in 1929, the son of Greek immigrants, actor/filmmaker John Cassavetes studied at the American Academy of Dramatic Arts, New York, before embarking on a career in television and film. Often cast as the 'outsider', he appeared as a juvenile delinquent in *Crime In The Streets*[1] (Don Siegel, 1956) and an army deserter in *Edge Of The City* (Martin Ritt, 1957). Cassavetes also starred in and directed five episodes of the *Johnny Staccato* television series with NBC in 1960. Throughout his career Cassavetes used his position as a mainstream actor to finance his independent filmmaking; Cassavetes also appeared in *Rosemary's Baby* (Roman Polanski, 1968) and *The Dirty Dozen* (Robert Aldrich, 1967), for which he was Oscar-nominated.

As an independent filmmaker Cassavetes directed eleven films of which *Shadows* (filmed 1957–59) was the first.[2] *Shadows* can be included in a discussion on Beat film because both its subject matter and cinematic expression broke away from mainstream Hollywood film in an attempt to portray the lives of those who were living in and exploring the margins of, mainstream society, such as artists. *Shadows* focuses on the day-to-day lives of an African-American family, of two brothers and their sister, who are sharing an apartment in Manhattan. The brothers are jazz musicians. Hugh (Hugh Hurd) the older brother is a singer and supports the family by travelling to nightclub gigs in different cities. His younger brother Ben (Ben Carruthers) is a trumpeter who spends his time hanging out with groups of young white males, primarily in cafes, clubs and on the street. Lelia (Lelia Goldoni), their sister, is seen in the context of her relationships with black and white males. A general atmosphere of existential angst pervades the narrative whereby social conventions and myths are shown to be meaningless and life exists as a series of near-identical repetitions. For example, the myth of the American Dream with its goal of success and the American Declaration of Independence which declares all 'men' equal does not apply to either African-Americans or women; Hugh is discriminated against because of his ethnicity whilst Lelia and Ben, who have what was termed as a 'passing complexion', are shown to be unable to find either easy acceptance or a sense of belonging in either black or white society. A basic narrative takes place over a few days whereby the members of the family are seen to meet up from time to time in cafés, a dance studio, Grand Central Station and collectively at their Manhattan apartment.

> **Since John Cassavetes' film *Shadows*, independently produced by Maurice McEndree and Seymour Cassel, more than any other recent American film, presents contemporary reality in a fresh and unconventional manner, it rightly deserves the first Independent Film Award. Cassavetes in *Shadows* was able to break out of conventional moulds and traps and retain original freshness. The improvisation, spontaneity and free inspiration that are almost entirely lost in most films from an excess of professionalism are fully used in this film.**
> Jonas Mekas

The narrative of *Shadows* gives fairly equal attention to these three characters and their narratives are interspersed. Hugh's narrative focuses on the difficulties of his music career and his relationship with his manager Rupert (Rupert Crosse). Ben's narrative centres on his alienation and the antics of his 'white' gang as they try to pick up girls and eventually get beaten up in a street fight. Lelia is viewed alongside her relationships with men. She is initially with David (David Pokitillo), an older writer who takes her to literary events who educates her and with whom she puts on a 'lady-like'

Shadows

act. She then has a one-night stand with Tony (Anthony Ray) who rejects her when he realizes that Hugh is her brother and that she has an African-American heritage. Finally she is seen with Davey (Davey Jones), an African-American that she derides until he tells her to stop being "masculine", in other words to drop the mask of invulnerability which Tony's rejection has forced her to wear.

Shadows can be seen as an independent film in terms of its production and cinematic expression, yet Cassavetes was not totally opposed to using the advantages and money of mainstream cinema, or in favour of following the rigid production and aesthetic ideals, of independent cinema laid down by individuals and groups such as the filmmaker/promoter Jonas Mekas and the New American Cinema Group[3] (formed in 1960, just after the release of a revised version of *Shadows*). Cassavetes' dispute with Mekas is well documented; after awarding *Shadows* The First Independent Film Award in Film Culture (Jan 26, 1959), Mekas revised his opinion when he saw a second, revised version of *Shadows* on November 11th, 1959 at Amos and Marcia Vogel's Cinema 16 Film Club alongside *Pull My Daisy*[4] which was being premiered. Mekas attacked the remake in the *Village Voice* (18 November, 1959) and later suggested that Cassavetes had been forced to re-shoot for commercial reasons and that

Shadows had subsequently lost its spontaneity. A debate then took place through the letters page of the *Village Voice*; Cassavetes and Amos Vogel both wrote in to defend the revised version, while Ben Carruthers agreed with Mekas. Finally, before the debate was closed, Parker Tyler supported Cassavetes in his essay 'For *Shadows*, Against *Pull My Daisy*'. Mekas' influential *Sight And Sound* article of 1959 praised both the first version of *Shadows*, *Pull My Daisy* and other films by filmmakers who he saw as being both creatively and financially independent of Hollywood, such as Stan Brakhage, for having "an open ear and an open eye for timely contemporary reality ... their disrespect for plots and written scripts; their use of improvisation. And since their most passionate obsession is to capture life in its most free and spontaneous flight ... these films could be described as a spontaneous cinema".[5] Mekas' diary entry for the night of 11 November, 1959, reads:

> "At this fateful night I realized that what I have to say, if I have anything to say, I'll be able to say it only as an anarchist ... My realization that I was betrayed by the second version of *Shadows* was the last stone [sic]. It helped me realize that what I was talking about, what I really saw in the first version of *Shadows*, nobody else really saw: I was pursuing my own ideal, my own dream. They didn't know what they had: a blind man's improvisation which depended on chance accidents."[6]

Cassavetes' relationship with mainstream film was equally problematic, although the initial critical success of *Shadows* appeared to be a good omen. *Shadows* won the Critics Award at the 1960 Venice Film Festival, it also received many positive reviews; this led to Paramount funding Cassavetes' second film, *Too Late Blues*. When this film 'flopped', Cassavetes was released from his contract with Paramount. His future relationships with mainstream studios remained problematic.

Cassavetes was acutely aware of the compromises, yet advantages, that working with Hollywood and mainstream studios entailed. Cassavetes chose to go with Paramount for *Too Late Blues* although he had enough money from potential investors ($375,000), to make the film, his investors were not convinced of its commercial appeal. Cassavetes stated at the time:

> "If I had the opportunity to make what amounts to an art film in a major studio it would be foolish of me not to. However, when you work in a major studio, when the studio owns the story (as they do now), you have to be very clear in your own mind why you are here. If you are here primarily to make money, the compromise is alright, in fact it becomes obligatory. In my case, I have to know when to quit at any time. If I am prepared to quit rather than give in to changes, then I am safe."[7]

Cassavetes' position of uneasy compromise between independent and mainstream film and his relationship to Beat film, can be explained by looking at the production of *Shadows* from first to final version and by comparing it to Beat films such as *Pull My Daisy*. This will reveal why Cassavetes as filmmaker has been pushed to the margins in terms of popular and critical acclaim (with the almost exclusive exception of Ray Carney). It is ironic that the criticisms levelled at Cassavetes (selling out, ambiguity in terms of narrative and cinematic expression, incomplete use of cinema vérité and failure to be use pure improvisation) are in fact those qualities which allow Cassavetes to stand out as a filmmaker who both embraced 'Beat sensibilities', yet also modified them to fit his expressive agenda.

By Beat sensibilities I am referring to a desire/disposition whereby a person explores/transgresses social conventions and boundaries, expressing the lack of order and stability that lies beneath social definitions of reality. Such transgression reveals that there is no absolute order to living; absolute definitions are discovered/found to be in a state of flux. As Ginsberg states: "If it's either/or, it is an old Aristotelian stupidity: it's both! And neither! And no contradiction either!"[8]

This is the arena of ambiguity, multiplicity, spontaneity, process and exploration which can have a different emphasis in each person's lifestyle and work — there is no single or correct form of expressing this transgression because it defies a single authoritative/ objective voice (it is interesting to observe that *Pull My Daisy*, unlike *Shadows*, draws attention to a very subjective central narrative voice, Jack Kerouac, which incorporates the speech and thoughts of the other characters in a sing-song poetry form). The varied expressions of transgression explain the very different styles of work produced, the frequent crossover between creative roles both between different artists and within an artist's own work (for example Cassavetes directed, edited, photographed and also wrote the screenplay of *Shadows*). These crossovers created a move towards multimedia and recognition that elements 'found' yet ignored in everyday life, were not divorced from art either in terms of the process of their production, or the process of their exclusion from such 'higher' ideals.

Beat transgression arose in a post-war, nuclear, cold war, ethnically divided United States, which was expanding and prosperous in terms of economics and technological advances, yet also very conservative in terms of moral climate. To an extent this society opened itself up to disruption, to disbelief in its authenticity; it was fertile ground for personal expansion, for the introduction of a sense of play (as critique, or an end in itself) and the desire to find a new form of emotional or spiritual transcendence. Those involved were trying to communicate a perception of living which generally remains hidden when a society appears to embody the beliefs that it holds; 'gaps' in a society's 'logic' indicate that the definition of reality and order that it holds needs to undergo a new consensus. Potential disruption is always present, but is suppressed until a particular socio-historical 'crisis' such as war or extreme and rapid social change brings it to the surface where it is then transformed into various expressions such as film, literature, music, philosophy and so on. The United States has a 'melting pot' history, it also has a 'frontier' or 'pioneer' tradition and incorporates the 'self-made man', the American Dream, as a cultural goal. Each of these characteristics creates a society that is particularly open to a self-conscious awareness that reality can be transformed, that reality can have plural interpretations and also appear to be a state of process.

A central theme of Beat work[9] was that the definition of what was art and what was life became blurred; this is reflected in both their work and their lifestyles. For example Kerouac went on the road in terms of a spiritual, physical and creative movement embodying a fluidity and spontaneity which was taken as a prime motivation. Travel is a prime metaphor for crossing boundaries, for refusing to stay still for long enough to be defined. Like many Beat artists, Kerouac held a belief that spontaneity and the creative process, rather than final result, were the 'true' and 'real' forms of living. The continuous, or present 'moment' became the goal of Beat expression and can be seen in their work and lives, within a diverse continuum of modernist/post-modernist expression. For example, Kerouac tried to follow and endorse a 'first thought, best thought' approach to his writing. The shift from emphasizing the creative object, or end-result, to the creative process is an attempt to reveal that there is no given or definitive way of viewing 'reality', 'revelation' offers a seductive vision of both dissolution of old accepted patterns and the possibility of new creations; personal, political, spiritual and so on. The difficulty that many Beat works faced in trying to mirror the present 'moment' in their work, was that representation of any form, including that which offers a sense of process (such as music and film), is secondary to the 'original moment', it is always a re-presentation, a copy or repetition which cannot capture the spontaneity of its origin. The difficulty was in trying to avoid presenting the spontaneous 'moment' in static and/or repetitious forms. For many this precipitated a transcendental movement into certain forms of spirituality, or a desire to escape from representational forms which particularly emphasize stasis and finite interpretations, such as traditional modes of narrative writing, in favour of an Antonin Artaud-style veneration of music (particularly improvisational jazz) and live performance (although arguably the 'spoken word', whilst coming from an original source, tends to close interpretation and is more authoritative than the written word). Burroughs in particular expresses an obsession with the controlling force of language, he tries to expose and deplete this control via representing process in his texts and by his cut-up technique. Film has an advantage over other forms of representation (although it repeats its action when shown and can be repeatedly copied, shown and distorted), because it is a moving medium, like music.

Cassavetes realized that neither a deceptively unmediated cinema vérité or self-conscious/postmodern approach to film — Shirley Clarke's *The Connection* (1961) made reference to the place of the camera in filming — would be able to effectively show his own view of reality in a form which could reveal underlying tensions without appearing contrived or 'unreal'. The objective style of cinema vérité fails to recognise the camera's mediation in viewing and influencing events; also, like *Shadows*, its documentary style was partly based on its 'unrealistic' use of black and white film, which was a visual convention denoting verisimilitude, but also sublimely communicates the camera's presence. Cassavetes was searching for a mode of representation that could expose 'hidden' feelings and thoughts that inform, yet are sometimes in conflict with, outer appearances. In other words Cassavetes was attempting to represent the process of functioning as a person, the process of identity gaps, ambiguities, indirection, spontaneity and movement. Cassavetes was attempting to adopt a midway position between exposing subjective reality in an objective form. He did not want to create a detached work of art which might show the surface of the way we live yet fail to communicate any of the accompanying everyday experience of having feelings, thoughts and a physically individual perspective on viewing ourselves and the world around us, which undergoes continual change.

Cassavetes wanted to express his belief that "Life is stranger than it is in the movies. In life, something is happening all the time".[10] As Cassavetes discovered with the first version of *Shadows*, which was largely unscripted, life can only be seen as being an experience of process and improvisation in re-presentational/re-produced form, if the filmmaking process is planned out in such a way as to 'appear' to have not taken place. This meant that the impact and function of the filming process had to be acknowledged and then deliberately disguised through creating the 'appearance' of verisimilitude, whereby events are manipulated/constructed to appear as they might do in everyday life without the presence of actors, film equipment and so on. This approach differs from cinema vérité and postmodernist film aesthetics, yet also bridges the gap between their aspirations which are trying to show/communicate life as it 'really' is; Cassavetes' films inadvertently acknowledge that the camera's detachment from an event can also be a formative part of that event, blurring the boundaries between the camera as an agency of re-presentation and the camera as a representative of its own presence. Our sense of what is real, demands that the division between subjective/objective vision is blurred

At some points in the filming you really want to take the camera and break it for no reason except that it's just an interference and you don't know what to do with it.
John Cassavetes

If we had had a writer we would have used a script.
John Cassavetes on *Shadows*

Shadows

and that this process of blurring is undetectable. It is not coincidental that many Beat figures believed that the 'personal is political'.

Shadows observes the transformative nature of identity, in the context of social constructions and hierarchies of ethnicity. The mid to late '50s saw an intensification of the American civil rights movement, with frequent violent clashes in the Southern states. *Shadows* reveals how racism in society in general was also present in the jazz and Beat subcultures cultures in New York. *Shadows* shows us that social appearances and definitions, such as ethnicity, condition our lives yet cannot fully capture, or define us, because life does not have a pre-ordained master plan and people exhibit a spontaneity which, unlike *Pull My Daisy*, is shown to be internal as well as external, shown through play, performance, etc. *Shadows* also reveals that we cannot be totally free of social definitions, our acts of spontaneity occur alongside our social roles, not independently of them.

The first version of *Shadows* was conceived on 14 January, 1957, in a loft on 46th Street, New York, by Cassavetes and a group of actors who were improvising on the theme of an African-American family living in New York. The actors were from and acting school that Cassavetes had formed a few years previously with Bert Layne. By the next evening the stage had become an apartment scene, with the actors providing furniture and equipment. Erich Kollmar (a skilled cameraman), arrived with a 16mm Arriflex camera, tripod and sound equipment. Kollmar trained some of the actors in technical skills such as using the boom and basic use of the camera, although the group still lacked the necessary technical skill and finance. On 13 February, 1957, Cassavetes was interviewed on Jean Shepherd's 'Night People' radio show to publicize *Edge Of The City*. Cassavetes stated that he could make a better movie than the one he was promoting, "a movie about people"[11] if each of the listeners sent in a few dollars. To Cassavetes' surprise, approximately $2,500 arrived over the next few days. Of the total amount raised for the first version — $20,000 — $1,000 was given to Cassavetes by supporters such as Josh Logan, José Quintero, Wyler, Feldman, Robert Rossen, Sol Siegel and Hedda Hopper; the remainder was borrowed. Cassavetes stated:

> "*Shadows* from beginning to end was a creative accident. We got the things we did because we had nothing to begin with and had to create it, had to improvise it. If we had had a writer, we would have used a script. I invented, or conceived the characters of *Shadows*, rather than a story line. A lot was written down about the characters and before shooting began the actors went out to do life study on these characters. The boy who plays the part of the singer [Hugh Hurd] went around trying to get a job and finally got one in Philadelphia in a third-rate night club [...]. The script, as such, did not exist until after the film was over. Then we made one up just for copyright reasons."[12]

According to Cassavetes, "*Shadows* shot ten weeks the first time around and to make the second version we shot again for ten days and replaced about three-quarters of it".[13] Cassavetes also gives four months as the time taken to shoot the first version in a different interview and goes on to add that the second version, of one hour and twenty-seven minutes, is "much deeper. I think the greatest things in the film, I mean the best things in the film, were shot in the reshooting".[14] The first one-hour version of *Shadows*, took four months to shoot and the final version of one hour and twenty-seven minutes took ten days to shoot and replaced about three-quarters of the first version. Ray Carney states that what remained was "mainly transitional, establishing, or action footage (street and sidewalk shots of characters racing for trains in Grand Central Station, a fight scene). Most of the important dramatic interactions between the characters were from the new scripted parts".[15] According to Carney, technical problems meant that the original soundtrack was inaudible and at one stage lip readers had to be brought in to allow new dialogue to be dubbed onto the original soundtrack, because no-one had thought to write down the dialogue. The editing was done by Len Appelson, a film editor who offered his services to Cassavetes and Maurice McEndree (who also edited and co-produced *Shadows*, with Nikos Papatakis and associate producer Seymour Cassel). The editing took a year to finish. The soundtrack was written by Charles Mingus and later expanded by Shafi Hadi (aka Cole Porter).

The first version of *Shadows* was shown at the Paris Theater, New York, in late 1958. Jonas Mekas and Gideon Brachmann then ran it at the Young Men's Hebrew Association, 92nd Street, New York, for about six packed-house performances. However Carney states that Cassavetes screened the original version only three times in late 1958.[16] Cassavetes said of the original version:

"The first version was filled with what you might call 'cinematic virtuosity' — for its own sake; with angles and fancy cutting and a lot of jazz going on in the background. But the one thing that came at all alive to me after I had laid it aside a few weeks was that just now and then the actors had survived all my tricks. But this did not often happen. They barely came to life. That's why the first version was a mess. When it was shown at the Paris Theater in New York the audience was helped along by a large group of my friends — but I guarantee that 90% of them didn't like it."[17]

In response to the criticism of commercial sell-out thrown at the second version, Cassavetes responded; "This is very insulting of course because as I think you will discover when you see the film, it is not a 'commercial' film in the usual sense. And I just did not think the first version was very good".[18]

The final production costs for *Shadows* totalled $40,000. This included $2,000 which Nikos Papadakis gave and $13,000 which Cassavetes raised for the completion of the final version. The confusion over the improvisational status of *Shadows* is, alongside its spontaneous appearance, partly due to Cassavetes' retention of the original version's end-title which reads: "The film you have just seen was an improvisation".

Shadows was shot from restaurant and car windows, disguised dustbins, subway entrances and the backs of trucks. Cassavetes liked authentic locations but his films focused on people so he was prepared to use studio sets. Other Beat films such as *Pull My Daisy*, are more expressionist and tend to focus more on external appearance as authentic experience, creating a sense of artifice, subjectivity and personal expression with a reliance on surface actions and behaviour, for example, the singular narrative of Jack Kerouac and the playful antics of the male protagonists. *Shadows* appears more objective; while both films were pushing the boundary between subjective/objective reality, their expressions were very different.

Both films focus on Beat lifestyles, on literature, play, music and philosophy. Although *Shadows* had the added theme of racism and identity crisis, it could be said that *Pull My Daisy* expressed an equal exploration of reality in its cinematic aesthetics. Both films blur the line between art/life, both in their productive processes and the end result. For example, *Shadows* matches the names of the actors with those of their characters and utilize the actors' real-life experiences. Actors names are also partly matched in *Pull My Daisy* and the characters and events portrayed, have some basis in the actors' past and present experiences. *Shadows* also draws on the 'failed' real-life romantic relationship of actors Lelia Goldoni and Anthony Ray to create an 'authentic' screen portrayal of a problematic relationship. It is notable that *Pull My Daisy* emphasizes performance, while *Shadows* tries to naturalize performance by downplaying it in a semi-Method acting style. The actors in *Pull My Daisy* probably did not perform in this way all the time in real life, while the actors in *Shadows* had similar experiences, yet very different histories from those they portrayed. Both films had to devise their aesthetics on pre-lived experience in order to create the appearance of spontaneity.

When Cassavetes attended the American Academy of Dramatic Arts, Stanislavskian/Method acting was fashionable; it informed the acting style of many 1950s actors, such as Marlon Brando and James Dean. It influenced Cassavetes' directing and acting styles to an extent because it involved a process-orientated attitude towards character that can open up an expressive space between internal thoughts and feelings and external, surface behavioural gestures. This can reveal a character's ambiguity of motivation, a device which Cassavetes exploited beyond the systematic use of Method acting by playing games or 'tricks' on the actors. A favourite 'trick' was to withhold the narrative script and character information from the actor (although he did provide very brief notes focusing on the dilemmas that each character faced). Ben Carruthers' short character script is the only one that survives:

"BENNY. He is driven by the uncertainty of his colour, to beg acceptance in this white man's world. Unlike his brother Hugh, or Janet [changed later to Lelia], he has no outlet for his emotions. He has been spending his life trying to decide what colour he is. Now he has chosen the white race as his people, his problem remains acceptance. This is difficult, knowing that he is in sense betraying his own. His life is an aimless struggle to prove something abstract, his everyday living has no outlet and so he moves with... (Here the script ends.)"[19]

Acting is itself a role, an 'act' and Cassavetes' 'tricks' sought to break down the boundary between role-playing as art and role-playing in life. Cassavetes felt, according to Carney,[20] that all modes of behaviour are formulaic; imitative rather than spontaneous. Cassavetes shows how Method acting suffers from mimicry and cliché in the over-emphasized Beat postures of Ben and Tony. It would be far too simplified and easy, to say that Cassavetes' films exhibit bad acting, because identity is itself performative and becomes obvious as such when we 'fail' to act out our roles with ease. *Shadows* reveals that bad acting is a sign that we are not acting out the roles we would like to project. For example Ben 'fluffs' his lines in a scene where he is bragging to Lelia about his plans for having a big car with lots of status. When Ben realizes that Lelia is not listening but crying — she has in fact just been rejected by Tony because of her ethnicity — Ben loses his confidence and verbal direction. It does not matter whether this is deliberate or unintentional on Ben Carruthers' part, because it serves to show that Ben's cool, macho exterior is a role he plays to hide the confusion of his own identity.

Another device that Cassavetes used to upset the actors' sense of character direction was to withhold the script from some actors until right before their scenes. This also encouraged interactive, rather than solo or star-centred, acting, unlike the carefully scripted exchanges of Hollywood acting. For example, Carney notes, in one scene prior to their romantic involvement, Tony appears to be manipulating Lelia by pushing for certain responses from her which critique David in Tony's favour. Lelia in turn, appears as hesitant but willing to be led. Cassavetes created this scenario by withholding Lelia Goldoni's script until just before the scene; Anthony Ray had received his script some time before and did actually have to 'feed' Lelia her lines and responses.

Cassavetes does not provide the sense that there is an overall direction or plan to life, unlike *Pull My Daisy* which seems to offer an alternative 'escapist' reality where play and music can override certain aspects of social reality. Cassavetes' desire to show identity to consist process and indirection, is the desire to fragment easy interpretations and definitions, to show that a person, or event, cannot be reduced to a single static definition, or meaning, interpreted in the same way by everyone. This does not mean that events cannot appear predictable in retrospect, but shows how the present moment allows for transformation.

Shadows rejects an overall framing of character or event, explaining Cassavetes' lack of popularity with critics who formulate interpretations and categories. Cassavetes does not allow the audience the security to interpret and predict the narrative; *Shadows* tries to function like a spontaneous jazz performance, resisting repeated or pre-ordained forms, existing in a continuous movement of the present which cannot be repeated. *Shadows* shows that identity and events are 'found' rather than predetermined and laid out in a neat pattern that we can interpret. Cassavetes encourages a cinematic technique whereby actors, cameras and audience all strive to follow, or capture, the narrative without having the promise of a neat resolution. *Shadows* shows how a person's social role is always being exceeded, their identity cannot be contained by a single definition. One device for showing this is to allow the camera to linger on a character beyond that required for narrative function, to the point where they appear out of place/role. People are shown to be the locus both of flux and of the roles which they incorporate. Similarly, the camera follows the protagonists and sometimes arrives too late to observe events and provide comprehension of the narrative.

This withholding of visual/narrative focus, does not allow meaning to be located in one place, instead it becomes a continuous process of piecing things together. For example in a scene where Lelia is shown at an intellectual, literary party with David, other people walk in front of the camera and obscure them and at one point the camera moves away from them and focuses on a group of people where two women are arguing about existential philosophy. Some scenes have an almost film noir quality where people talking are shown in angular poses and in differing relationships to the light source and shadow. However the framing and focus is not conventional; speakers do not emerge from shadow and characters' heads and limbs are severed by the film frame, implying that action can never be truly caught or finalized. The sound also adds to this sense through echoing cinema vérité's use of 'unmediated' sound, noises are heard which are out of shot of the main action, or seem true to context such as traffic sounds in street scenes.

However this 'improvised' feel is constructed, like the jazz soundtrack which emphasizes parts of the action. Cassavetes' direction allowed for ensemble acting but this too was engineered. Spontaneity and improvisation were encouraged as long as they did not interfere with presenting a film that is ultimately coherent; *Shadows* presents a portrayal of life as random, it is not random in itself. This explains Cassavetes' desire to make a second version and the techniques, which he devised to create the impression of spontaneity, such as beginning the action in mid-flow. For example, *Shadows'* title sequence shows us a scene of people dancing prior to the title acknowledgements. According to Carney:

> "His original screenplays (for *Shadows*, Faces and Love Streams, for example) reveal that in many cases he originally wrote and shot beginnings to films that now lack them, but then cut out the beginnings or transposed the material during the editing process. In short, the abruptness and elipticalness of Cassavetes' narratives was not the result of sloppy scripting or editing. It was a conscious, chosen strategy of presentation. During editing, Cassavetes punched black holes in scripts that originally didn't have them. It was if he deliberately wanted to frustrate a viewer's quest for simplifying origins [...] He wanted us to be kept in the dark as long as possible, so that there would be no release from the stimulating uncertainties of an eternal present."[21]

Carney goes on to say that:

> "Cassavetes limits our point of view. The audience's perception of a scene (optically as well as intellectually) is usually no more accurate or better informed than that of a character within it. In fact, it is often the case in Cassavetes' work that the audience's view of a scene or a character (again, in both the visual and the imaginative senses of the word) is not only no more authoritative than, but no different from that of another character in the scene. As viewers, we frequently find ourselves in almost the exact optical and imaginative stance as one of Cassavetes' supporting characters."[22]

Shadows shows life to be a series of repetitious actions where the places and people alter to some degree and dramatic events take place but are soon replaced by more mundane concerns. The central focus of the film does not particularly concern a specific person or event, but the general recognition that essential identity exists as a process, which is both within and exceeds social roles. Ray Carney has noted that; "There is one extended metaphor in *Shadows* ... It involves a comparison of the 'masks' we wear in public with the 'faces' that we hide beneath them ... It is typical of the film's rhetorical tact that it surfaces as an explicit visual image at only two points".[23] Visual attention is not focused on the mask to a great extent because overt metaphors both fix interpretation and artificially stand out from the narrative. The first visual reference occurs when Ben and his gang — Tom (Tom Allen) and Dennis (Dennis Sallas) — are walking/running through the Museum of Modern Art's sculpture garden. Ben refers to a piece of sculpture as a "mask". Ben admires the mask but Tom is irreverent, he criticizes its static form and the segment of society which endorses such art such as his college professors, authority figures who Tom in his present, macho, childlike play, is obviously rebelling against. Tom refers to the museum in typically macho and bitter terms as "a place for sexless women who have no love in their lives". Tom 'touches-up' the sculpture of a woman's torso and refers to it in crude terms, Ben objects, but Tom is bitter and resentful because he has seen that the hierarchical ideals of femininity and culture are masks hiding an empty and false authority. For Tom, these ideals are desires which have become debased and perverted by being suppressed and removed from everyday life. Ben's position is slightly different, he may mock Lelia's aspirations and reject David's patronage, alongside the social invitations of Hugh's African-American friends, yet he cannot totally reject either culture without confusion. Ben is himself, wearing a 'dramatic' and visual mask in terms of his Beat posturing, complete with black leather jacket and sunglasses.

The second visual reference to masks prefigures a post-coital scene between Lelia and Tony. The mask is African and seen in shadow on Tony's bedroom wall. When Lelia realizes that Tony is not particularly interested in a relationship (prior to their reconciliation and Tony's later discovery of her ethnic identity), the camera closes in on her face and cuts to various angles. This subtly prefigures Tony's later rejection of her because of his racism. It indicates that Tony can only see the social mask or label of identity and the narratives that surround it and not Lelia's actual identity, which he had not 'seen' because he took it for granted that she was white. Shifting camera angles on the close-up of Lelia's face indicate the multiplicity of thoughts and feelings that underlie the masks which she wears or which are imposed on her.

Ray Carney states that Cassavetes only liked one essay on the film because it focused on "the film's human problems"[24] rather than the racial angle. Carney also suggests that Cassavetes' *Too Late Blues* (which also expresses Beat sensibilities) is effectively a remake of *Shadows* with white characters;[25] 'Ghost' Wakefield is a white musician who encounters similar expressive difficulties to those of Hugh and Ben. The theme of 'miscegenation' has been frequently used to question the inequality and constructed hierarchies of racism upon which America built much of its wealth as a founding nation. It can provide an obvious site of ambiguity in terms of ethnic identity and naturalisation of social hierarchies. *Shadows'* use of the theme of ethnicity makes the 'human problems' such as facing conflict with social roles more obvious, because arguably these 'human problems' are intensified in a position of exaggerated alienation and discrimination.

Perhaps *Shadows'* greatest achievement is its ability to blur the line between spontaneity and convention; like *Pull My Daisy*, it was ultimately a scripted rather than an improvised film (it should be noted that Kerouac improvised from a script outline — he had to record his reading four times and the final version was pieced together from three of these readings — Kerouac objected to this process). Yet unlike *Pull My Daisy* or many of the acclaimed independent and mainstream films that influenced/were influenced by Beat aesthetics and themes, *Shadows* retains a sense of independence in its refusal to be neatly pigeonholed, by showing us that acting and actuality are not in opposition. For the same reason, it has an openness of expression and vision which provides a fresh and timeless communication on the spontaneous nature of life. *Shadows* questions what it means to have identity, in a way that involves our own active participation in watching and relates to our own experience of perceiving ourselves and others, particularly in shadowy areas where definition is 'lacking'.

---

1. Also starring Sal Mineo who appeared in *Rebel Without A Cause* (Nicholas Ray, 1954, released '55). Note that Nicholas Ray was the father of Anthony Ray who plays the character Tony in *Shadows.*

2. *Shadows* (1957–9, released '59), *Too Late Blues* (1961, released '62), *A Child Is Waiting* (1962, released '63), *Faces* (1965, released '68), *Husbands* (1969, released '70), *Minnie And Moskowitz,* 1971, released '71), *A Woman Under The Influence* (1972, released '74), *The Killing Of A Chinese Bookie* (1976, released '76 and again in '78 as a re-edited print), *Opening Night* (1977, released '78, withdrawn and re-released in '91), *Gloria* (1980, released '80) and *Love Streams* (1983, released '84).

3. Alongside Mekas, this group included stage/film producer, Lewis Allen; filmmakers Lionel Rogosin, Peter Bogdanovich, Robert Frank, Alfred Leslie, Shirley Clarke, Gregory Markopoulos and Edward Bland; actors Argus Speare Juilliard, Ben Carruthers ('Ben' in *Shadows*); distributors and producers Emile de Antonio, Lewis Allen, Daniel Talbot, Walter Gutman and David Stone. Their 'First Statement' issued in Mekas' magazine, *Film Culture, 22–23,* 1961, gave their ideal of cinema as "a personal expression" (quoted in David E. James, ed, *To Free the Cinema: Jonas Mekas And The New York Underground,* Princeton University Press, 1992, p10.). This group continued from the work of Maya Deren, a filmmaker who had done much to organize and promote funding for the independent film community in New York. Deren created the Film Artists Society in 1953 (later renamed as the Independent Film Makers Association), which met monthly until 1956. Deren also founded the Creative Film Foundation (1955–61) to attempt to secure grants for independent filmmakers.

4. *Pull My Daisy* became the next film that Mekas championed, awarding it the Second Independent Film Award (April 26, 1960). Mekas even applied, word-for-word, some of the former praise of "immediacy" that he had levelled at *Shadows,* with the added praise of "honesty". Mekas did not realize that *Pull My Daisy* was, according to Alfred Leslie, a scripted and rehearsed film.

5. Quoted in Jonas Mekas 'New York Letter: Towards A Spontaneous Cinema', *Sight And Sound,* vol.28, #3 & 4, Summer/Autumn 1959, p119.

6. Mekas quoted in J. Hoberman 'The Forest and the Trees' in David E. James, ed, *To Free The Cinema: Jonas Mekas And The New York Underground,* p101.

7. Cassavetes quoted in Colin Young & Gideon Brachmann 'New Wave — Or Gesture?', *Film Quarterly,* vol.14, #3, Spring 1961, p.8.

8. Ginsberg quoted from an interview in this volume.

9. The artists and work I am exemplifying, was primarily produced by the leading names in Beat literature. Personal expression by others in the Beat movement of different ethnicity and gender was very influential but tended to be marginalized both at the time and since, not by well-known Beat figures, but by the society around them which places authority on subjective expression in accordance with other hierarchies in society. These hierarchies forward 'objective' representational forms, such as documentary, as 'real' and male and 'subjective' representational forms, which are trying to show a reality which is contrary to this 'objective' vision, such as abstraction, as female and 'artificial'.

10. Cassavetes quoted in Ray Carney, 'Seven Program Notes From The American Tour Of The Complete Films: Minnie And Moskowitz, A Woman Under The Influence, The Killing Of A Chinese Bookie, Opening Night and Love Streams', *Post Script, Vol.11, #2,* Winter 1992, p.84.

11. Cassavetes quoted in Ray Carney, *The Films Of John Cassavetes: Pragmatism, Modernism and The Movies,* Cambridge University Press, 1994, p.29.

12. Cassavetes quoted in 'New Wave — Or Gesture?', p.7.

13. Cassavetes quoted in 'New Wave — Or Gesture?, p.7.

14. Cassavetes quoted in Ray Carney, 'No Exit; John Cassavetes' *Shadows*', in Lisa Phillips, ed, *Beat Culture And The New America: 1950-1965,* Whitney Museum of Modern Art, New York, in association with Flammarion, Paris-New York, 1995, p.235.

15.'No Exit: John Cassavetes' *Shadows*', p.236.

16.'No Exit: John Cassavetes' *Shadows*', p.236.

17. Cassavetes quoted in 'New Wave — Or Gesture?', p.7.

18. 'New Wave — Or Gesture?', p.7.

19. Quoted in 'New York Letter: Towards A Spontaneous Cinema', p.119.

20. Carney discusses this at some length in *The Films Of John Cassavetes: Pragmatism, Modernism and The Movies*, p.44–50.

21. 'Seven Program Notes From The American Tour Of The Complete Films... ', p.40–41.

22. 'Seven Program Notes From the American Tour Of The Complete Films... ' p.41.

23. *The Films Of John Cassavetes: Pragmatism, Modernism and The Movies*, p.36.

24. *The Films Of John Cassavetes: Pragmatism, Modernism and The Movies*, p.35.

25. *The Films Of John Cassavetes: Pragmatism, Modernism and The Movies*, p.286.

Chapter Three

Wild Men & Outcast Visionaries

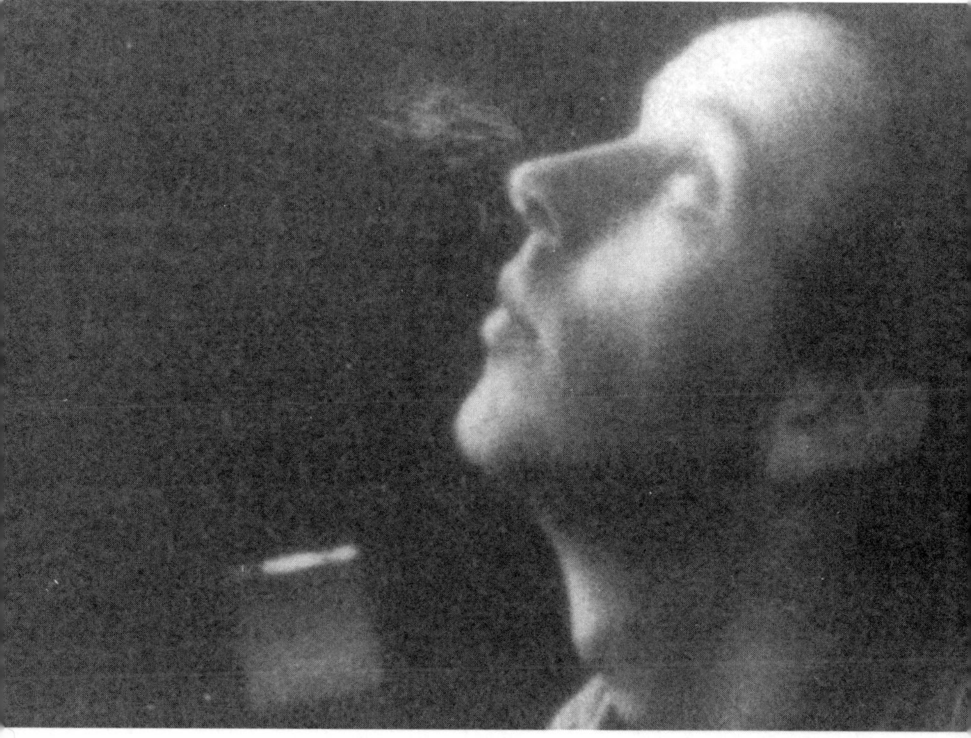

1. Notes On The San Francisco Renaissance

San Francisco had an avant-garde and bohemian artistic tradition which could be traced at least back to the 1940s, with poets such as Kenneth Rexroth, Robert Duncan and Philip Lamantia settling in the city and its environs. Allen Ginsberg would later state: "The panoply of tolerances and understandings and gnostic (mystic, psychedelic) awarenesses, as well as social hopes and humors, were already fully developed in the 1940s and that continued right on through in San Francisco".[1] By the early 1950s various artists and writers who would become affiliated with the Beats had made their homes on the West Coast in — or near — the city. They included Neal and Carolyn Cassady, the filmmaker Harry Smith and the poets Philip Whalen, Michael McClure and Gary Snyder. In 1953 Lawrence Ferlinghetti and Peter Martin founded the City Lights Bookstore, from which Ferlinghetti would begin publishing Beat poetry via City Lights Books in 1955. The artistic community of San Francisco was additionally supported by galleries such as the Gallery Six (formally the King Ubu Gallery) and legendary North Beach hangouts such as The Place, the Black Cat Cafe, the Coexistence Bagel Shop, The Cellar and the Coffee Gallery, all of which would become valuable artistic spaces in which poetry performances and, later, 'Happenings', would transpire.

They were really outsiders.
Robert Frank on
Ron Rice and Taylor Mead

The world-weariness of Antonioni is strictly European and however interesting and beautiful can not satisfy America. Besides, it's not beat. It's not mongrel, wild, uncouth, naive, heartless, heartful, pornographic, licentious, insane, bold, bald, fat, monstrous, square enough for America — strong enough to release the monolithic freeze which periodically grips this land and is settling in again this year along with the weather. America's great movements are too little — we must have the screen. The enormous 12,800 mile SCREEN! He says, falling all 500 stories to the cement. America, loosen up or strangle.
Taylor Mead,
The Movies Are A Revolution

In 1954, following a trip to Mexico, Allen Ginsberg moved to San Francisco and it was while living in San Francisco that he met his lifelong friend and lover Peter Orlovsky. "Allen saw a painting of me [by Robert LaVigne] ... and fell in love with me through the painting".[2] Immediately after viewing the painting at the apartment at 1403 Gough Street, which LaVigne shared with Orlovsky (and Cassady's girlfriend Natalie Jackson), Allen met Orlovsky. Ginsberg decided to stay in California to begin a Master of English degree at the University of Berkeley and became friends with many of the West Coast poets.

On 7 October, 1955, at the Gallery Six on Fillmore Street, Ginsberg participated in an evening of poetry readings, performing alongside Michael McClure, Philip Lamantia, Gary Snyder, Philip Whalen and Kenneth Rexroth. It was here that Ginsberg gave his first, legendary, public reading of 'Howl', an event that for many crystallized the Beat movement and the San Francisco Renaissance. Jack Kerouac described the event in his book *The Dharma Bums*, as "a great night, a historic night".[3] According to the account in *The Dharma Bums*, Kerouac:

"followed the whole gang of howling poets to the reading at Gallery Six that night, which was, among other important things, the night of the birth of the San Francisco Poetry Renaissance. Everyone was there. It was a mad night. And I was the one that got things jumping by going around collecting dimes and quarters from the rather stiff audience standing around in the gallery and coming back with three huge gallon jugs of Californian Burgundy and getting them all piffed so that by eleven o'clock when Alvah Goldbook was reading his, wailing his poem 'Wail' drunk with arms outspread everybody was yelling 'Go! Go! Go!' (like a jam session) and old Rheinhold Cacoethes the father of the Frisco poetry scene was wiping his tears in gladness".[4]

However, as Rebecca Solnit has noted:

"The Beats who were to become so famous were largely strangers to the crowd who supported the Six; they lacked a community that maintained cultural spaces, resources and connections that would make such readings possible. If Ginsberg had broken new ground, the Six had made it possible. The reading was modeled after one Robert Duncan had given at the Gallery Six earlier that year, with his lover Jess and friends Larry Jordan and McClure among the participants. And it was McClure who had invited Ginsberg into the community and Ginsberg who brought Kerouac, a complete unknown in these circles".[5]

The North Beach scene also led to the publication of various magazines, including *Ark II —Moby I* (1956) edited by James Harmon and Michael McClure and, later, *Beatitude* (1959) edited by Ginsberg, Orlovsky, Bob Kaufman, John Kelly and William Margolis. *Beatitude* ceased publication in 1960 and its fall has been cited as marking the end of the San Francisco Renaissance. As Steven Watson notes in his Beat 'Chronology', by 1960 many of the artists and poets who had inhabited North Beach had left, an event which coincided with "tourist fascination with North Beach reach[ing] a new height of popularity".[6]

2. Ron Rice & Taylor Mead: Flower Thieves & Dharma Bums

Poet, writer, actor, filmmaker and traveller Taylor Mead was staying in San Francisco in 1960, having hitched there in late 1959 and, while staying in North Beach, Mead met New Yorker Ron Rice "circa 1960",[7] who, according to Mead's account of their relationship, had just completed a "year, or something"[8] studying film at Cooper Union, "and [was] very fresh too".[9] Ron Rice had recently moved to San Francisco and Mead was drawn to his spontaneous creative energy, as Mead states in the autobiographical *Son Of Andy Warhol*: "[Rice] didn't sit around theorizing on a 'project' or how to make a movie. He made the movie. He believed in 'pushing the button'. The passion of the idea was the catalyst, not the intellectual rational and 'worry' or organization, or even the financing."[10]

Rice and Mead were both aware of the "death-knell of the 'Beat' scene in North Beach"[11] and began to collaborate on a film depicting Taylor and "the last 20 or so genuine intellectual wastrels of the area".[12] The subsequent film was titled *The Flower Thief* (1960) and has been described by P. Adams Sitney as "the purest expression of the Beat sensibility in cinema".[13] *The Flower Thief* was shot on outdated 16mm black and white military film and the soundtrack, which was made from a combination of 'found noises', contrasting pieces of music and wildly stoned poetics, was added afterwards. The film's title emerges from a scene in which Mead steals a flower from outside a florist; more importantly, however, the title may also be viewed as a direct reference to Leslie's and Frank's *Pull My Daisy*, which greatly influenced both Ron Rice and Taylor Mead.

In a statement on the film's release Ron Rice wrote:

"The central character Taylor Meade a poet moves through a sequence of events. He steals a flower he enters The Bagle Shop, returns to his home, (an abandoned powerhouse), discovers a man hidden in the cellar with a child's teddy bear. He washes the teddy bear in the bathroom then discovers the room full of people, and is chased. He destroys a bullshitting radio. The Beatniks carry on with spontaneous antics, reinacting the crucifistion and changing the graphic meaning to the flag plainting at Iwo Jima. Telephone, pits, beats in lockers making love; a woman climbing monkey bars to reach her lover.

"The poet is searching, but he never finds love. The ending of the film suggests he finds something, but we do not know for he disappears into the sea. The audience must discover the 'message' if one is demanded. Elements of Franz Kafka and Russian Humanism are there." [14] [The spelling and punctuation are Rice's.]

While Rice's statement describes the general flow of *The Flower Thief*, it misses out on various key elements within the film. The first of these is the character portrayed by Taylor Mead (described by Rice as the 'The [P]oet' and as 'the Wild Man' — see below). Taylor Mead's character maintains an outsider status throughout the entire film, a status that — in part — is manifested through what some commentators on the film have described as "childlike"[15] behaviour. For example during his exploration of San Francisco at the film's opening, Taylor walks past a group of children and smiles at them and briefly hangs out with them. Later in the film he gives a petal, from a stolen flower, to an infant. When Mead finds the gigantic child's teddy bear he scrubs it clean with a toilet brush; after cleaning it he holds a mirror up to the bear's face, as if allowing the toy to examine its own clean visage. Taylor takes the bear with him and carries it for much of the rest of the film and in one sequence even introduces the toy to his pet cat. This 'childlike' behaviour is further manifested via Taylor using an old trolley as a go-cart and 'racing' down one of San Francisco's steep streets, while holding the bear.

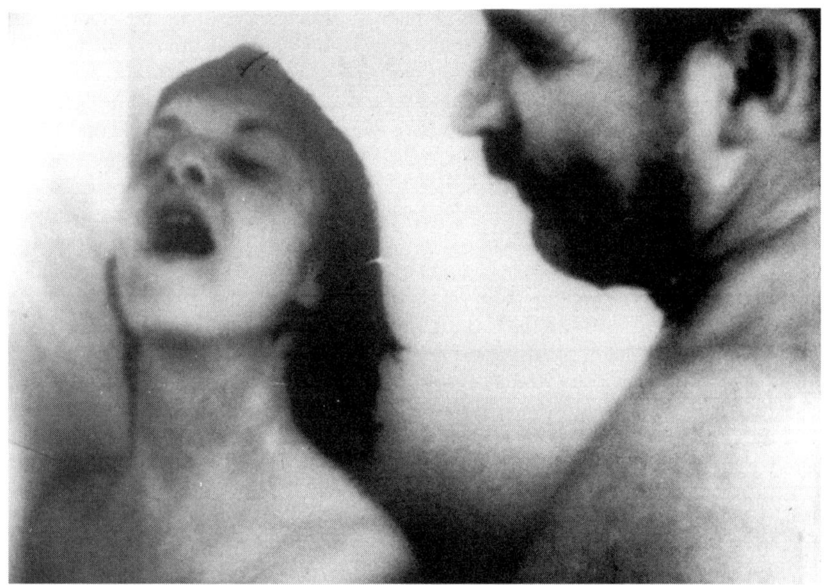

The Flower Thief

It has also been suggested that Mead's outsider status belongs to the tradition of silent movie clowns such as Charlie Chaplin (and also, as the writer Ray Carney suggests, the more infantile Harry Langdon)[16] and Mead's behaviour in *The Flower Thief* evokes Chaplin's performance from *City Lights* (1931). This 'clowning' 'comic' element also occurs in various scenes, such as when Mead climbs over a fence and his trousers fall down and he moons the audience; when a fire-engine stops and he climbs onto the running board; and also when he walks along behind a policeman, mimicking the cop's gestures behind his back. This silent movie comedic element also occurs in the sequences involving the gang of beatniks, who chase Taylor in absurd fake slow motion and in scenes in which Taylor is poked and tickled by a woman in a bathing costume.

Ray Carney suggests that Mead's character in *The Flower Thief* and other characters played by Taylor during this period,[17] are "not adults ... They are eternal children, divine fools, pure-hearted simpletons detached from the world and innocent of its machinations. They illustrate what Kerouac might have had in mind when he defined Beatness as Beatitude",[18] but Carney notes that Mead's character in *The Flower Thief* (like the male leads in *Pull My Daisy*) emphasizes "boyish charm",[19] at the expense of "mature sexual or social relationships".[20] Yet, while these scenes are reminiscent of silent comedies and while Mead can be read as childlike, or clown-like, there are other elements to the film. Mead's character is superficially innocent and is on occasion shot looking at events (the demolishing of the building, for example) with a gaze which may be categorized as both 'naive' and 'magical'; however the character he portrays also has other functions within the film. In one scene Taylor parodies the beatniks; the sequence depicts a hand knocking on a door, which opens to reveal an incredibly small cupboard in which a beatnik couple are making love, the hand then knocks on a second door, on an adjoining cupboard, which opens to reveal Taylor Mead making love to the gigantic stuffed toy bear. This positions Mead as 'childlike', but also simultaneously positions him as anarchically sexual.

Further, not all of Mead's behaviour is childlike, as events in the last segment of the film illustrate. This opens with Taylor entering a building on the seafront, in the building he sees a young man and — via a standard shot-reverse-shot edit — their mutual gaze at each other is established. The young man exits and Mead follows him. Following a brief fairground ride the two talk, although there is silence on the soundtrack and as they speak the young man rubs his abdomen. Taylor gestures behind the camera/audience's gaze and the two walk together out of shot. A brief edit of fairground shots follows, firstly depicting Taylor riding on a horse on a merry-go-round, then riding with the young man in a carriage on the ride. A superimposition shot merges a shot of a stone lion, next to which Mead's character was seen sleeping in a previous sequence, with the youth's head replacing the lion's head. The youth and Taylor walk over an empty lot. On the way across the lot Taylor falls out of step with the man and slows down slightly, allowing him to sneak a glance at the young man's body. The two men walk down to the beach together. The film cuts to a brief shot of the fairground, followed by the image of exploding fireworks. This then cuts to a shot of the sun rising, with Mead wandering alone on the beach.

This scene clearly depicts Mead picking up the youth. Although no sexual encounter is depicted in the film — and Rice's notes only ambiguously state that "he finds something" — the image of the fireworks is clearly sexual. Not only within the context of metaphors of exploding desires and passions, but also as a reference to Kenneth Anger's underground film *Fireworks* (1947), which utilized the image of an exploding firework to symbolize male ejaculation. Likewise the superimposition of the youth's head onto the lion's body emphasizes a fantasy in which the youth is sexualized as a powerful beast. Such images can hardly be read as purely 'childlike' nor as mere 'clowning' but rather as articulations of sexual desire. A further, brief, scene which depicts a beatnik couple making love in a shower, also serves to emphasize and articulate a 'mature', rather than infantile, sexuality.

The tension in *The Flower Thief*'s presentation of Taylor Mead, which contrasts his sexuality against his 'innocence', suggests that the text is utilizing 'play' rather than childishness. To read Mead's character as 'childlike' is to reduce the character to a state of imagined essential purity and to remove agency from the character's motivations and replace it with innocence. Rather, the character portrayed by Mead and the various beatniks in the film, are utilizing 'play'. Play is manifested as a potentially liberating force, as a response to the mundanity of the commonplace and as an affirmation of existence; "To laugh is to affirm life, even the suffering in life. To play is to affirm chance and the necessity of chance".[21] Play must be seen as a Beat weapon against totalizing dogma, as a spontaneous manifestation and affirmation of the 'individual', like the bebop jazz musicians that inspired Kerouac with their desire to challenge the boundaries: "There's always more, a little further — it never ends".[22] As Ron Rice wrote: "In the old Hollywood days movie studios would keep a man on the set who, when all other sources of ideas failed (writers, directors), was called upon to 'cook up' something for filming. He was called the Wild Man. *The Flower Thief* has been put together in memory of all dead wild men who died unnoticed in the field of stunt".[23] Rice emphasizes the spontaneity of the characters and Mead's character is best viewed as embodying spontaneous craziness.

Further, among all the images of clowning — articulated by both Mead's character and the group of beatniks — are explorations of American identity in relation to the Beat generation. In many ways the beatniks were intrinsically American, following an American tradition of dissent from "Emerson and Thoreau and Whitman to the pioneer-outlaw — a tradition of the individual forging an independent way against the majority ... the Beat spirit can be traced back to the old pioneer and cowboy notion of the excitable, intense and independent personality exemplified by frontier America".[24]

The Flower Thief

When the beatniks depicted in *The Flower Thief* mimic the raising of the flag at Iwo Jima, they are satirizing the homogenising phallocentric aspect of America as a cold war power; the America which ostracized the beatniks was an enemy, but the America of possibilities was not. This ambivalent relationship with America is also illustrated in a sequence which initially appears to depict Taylor pissing in a public park, but the camera reveals that rather than pissing he is holding a ribbon at groin level and the motion of the ribbon moving in the breeze only appears as piss. Unfortunately two cowboys carry Taylor away, presumably believing that he has just urinated in public. Taylor is held up before a gigantic cardboard box, on which the word 'Justice' is written. A 'door' on the box opens and a man can be seen inside and Taylor is 'judged' before the two cowboys. A shot of an eagle and Taylor reaching through a barred fence emphasize the fact that he is being judged by America. The cardboard box falls over, signifying the collapse of justice and Taylor is tied to a flag-pole, an American flag tied around his neck. Taylor Mead slumps down onto the floor. While this appears as a critique of America, the collapse of 'cardboard justice' implies that it is possible to have a better form of justice, rather than advocate the complete destruction of the concept of justice; the scene emphasizes only the stupidity and ignorance of a certain manifestation of justice. This critique of America is also articulated by a voice on the soundtrack that states:

"Peruvian civilization based on cocaine, America on Coca-Cola."

Visually *The Flower Thief* embraces a spontaneous filmmaking style, with wildly varied lighting and occasional chaotic camera work, which is manifested via styles such as faked slow motion, montage sequences, speeded up footage and double exposures. This draws attention to the belief in film as Beat poetry, as a way in which to get things down with as much immediacy as possible and unmediated by the planning and technical work generally considered necessary before producing a film; as Hoberman observes, the film is "genuinely haphazard, [and is] filled with goofy non sequiturs".[25]

The soundtrack also emphasizes this approach, with various noises edited together; thus for example in the cafe scene there is a schizophrenic combination ranging from jazz, to purely percussive sounds, to backwards-voices, to what appears to be a narration taken from the Cheshire Cat's speech in Lewis Caroll's novel *Alice In Wonderland.* At one point — in a clear reference both to Ginsberg's 'Howl' and to *Pull My Daisy* — a voice states: "holy, holy, holy, everything ... holy, holy, holy methadone". Like the repetition and distortion of the word 'holy' in Jack Kerouac's narration for *Pull My Daisy*, the word 'holy' is similarly manipulated during this sequence with echoes and what sounds like multiple voices repeating the phrase; this device serves to emphasize the usage of the word. This emphasis on the word briefly spills from the soundtrack onto the screen, where words that have been torn from a newspaper are held up to the camera, one of which reads: 'violence'. During another sequence a voice states: "Junkie profits, Christ on opium, marijuana used in the past, hook me into the Orgone Accumulator spouting steam ... what is the ultimate pleasure?" At other points the soundtrack is made up from children's records, such as Serge Prokofiev's musical interpretation of *Peter And The Wolf* (1936), while Mead walks through the park picking flowers.

The apparently haphazard nature of the film's production, with the emphasis on spontaneous creative freedom, similarly reflects the nature of 'play' and spontaneous creation; the visual 'play' of Mead in *The Flower Thief* is echoed within the very 'play' around the film's style. As Jonas Mekas has commented, *The Flower Thief* (and Zimmerman's *Lemon Hearts*[26]): "combine the spontaneous cinema of *Pull My Daisy*, the freedom of the image of Brakhage,[27] the 'uncleanness' of action painting, the theatre of Happenings ... and the sense of humour of Zen. Their imagination, coming from deeply 'deranged' and liberated senses, is boundless. Nothing is forced in these films. They rediscover the poetry and wisdom of the irrational, of nonsense, of the absurd ... Nevertheless, the materials with which they create are embedded in reality".[28]

On its New York release *The Flower Thief* was described by Jonas Mekas in the *Village Voice* as "the craziest film ever made, a peak of spontaneous cinema and one of the five landmarks of the new American cinema"[29] (these other landmark films included *Shadows* and *Pull My Daisy*). According to *Popism: The Warhol '60s*, Ron Rice and Taylor Mead gave the film to Jonas Mekas to release in New York and, whilst Mead and Rice wanted the film to open on Madison Avenue, to their (temporary) chagrin Mekas opened it "Way down at the Charles Theatre on the Lower East Side!"[30] The Charles Theatre was located on the corner of Avenue B and 12th Street and the screenings organized by Mekas of *The Flower Thief* at the venue broke the attendance records and the film was a summer 'hit', as Mead remembers: "between [Jack Smith's] *Flaming Creatures* and *The Flower Thief* we sort of kept it [the Charles Theatre] alive".[31] Not only was *The Flower Thief* successful, it was also one of the first underground films to introduce the concept of the underground film superstar; as Warhol would write in *Popism*, Taylor Mead was "one of the first underground film stars".[32] When Rice made *Chumlum*, four years later, he worked with Jack Smith, one of the other original underground superstars; like Mead, Smith left his unique stamp on any film on which he collaborated.

Following the success of *The Flower Thief*, Ron Rice travelled to Mexico and produced *Senseless* (1962). *Senseless* was shot throughout Rice's travels in and around Mexico and the 'cast' is made up of the group of travelling friends and companions. *Senseless* consists of a combination of quasi home-movie footage and short improvised non-narrative scenarios, onto which a soundtrack featuring Mexican folk music and Bartok, amongst others, was dubbed. Several of the non-narrative parts of *Senseless* are reminiscent of the depictions of the beatnik group in *The Flower Thief*, with a similar emphasis on creating parodic tableau

The Flower Thief

that luxuriate in a combination of absurdity and play. For example: two people — one of whom is wearing a gas mask — in an auto dump unravel an American flag and pretend to drive in a junked car and later an old train engine becomes a set on which the group chase one another, whilst a woman sitting on the locomotive, holding a parasol, is serenaded by a guitarist. Another tableau appears to depict a marriage between a bare-chested man and a pregnant woman in front of a pumping oil derrick. Where *Senseless* differs from *The Flower Thief*, is in its editing (by Howard Everngam), which is far more rhythmic and more powerful in its usage of montage. For example, one lengthy sequence juxtaposes footage of a bullfight with footage of a water fountain, a couple kissing and marijuana smoking, amongst other images and, as the bull is killed, a figure with material over his face is smothered.

Senseless also has a more overt 'political' element, with occasional images depicting various members of the group holding peace protest banners, which read; "war is murder and hell on earth is the consequence" and "world wide strike for peace". Although non-narrative, the film is structured around the actual journey, with the first section of the film intercutting footage of a car journey and the last part of the film intercutting footage of a train journey; notably both sequences are punctuated with the previously mentioned car and train tableaux. According to the film's credits it was shot in "super anti-realism" and, because at the time of the film's production Jonas Mekas was writing about the importance of the plotless film, the credits attribute the nonexistent script to Mekas. The word: "Dadazendada" (Dadaists of Zen — echoing Jonas Mekas's description of *The Flower Thief*'s anarchistic humour as Zen-like) also makes up the titles. When *Senseless* was screened at the Charles Theatre Filmmakers Festival, in July 1962, it won the festival award.

Having returned to New York, Rice embarked on a new film, a proposed three-hour epic called *The Queen Of Sheba Meets The Atom Man* (1963/1982), again starring Taylor Mead, this time cast alongside Winifred Bryan, "a six-foot formidable black woman who was famous for taking off her clothes at unexpected moments. She once climbed on a bus in the nude and the apocryphal story is that the driver took her in the bus to Bellevue Hospital, but Winifred said he simply called the police".[33] Mead's account of the film's production illustrates the spontaneous approach to filmmaking embraced by Rice:

"Ron Rice was a man of action in those days and the idea was put into motion before my doubts could formulate. We were in a taxi within minutes, off to borrow a camera and then travel Manhattan looking for locations. On Park Avenue around 46th Street we saw a building with a dramatic escalator in the lobby. The guard refused to let us use it. We went next door to the Union Carbide building and rather than ask permission we went ahead and took shots of their escalator with me ascending and descending it. It actually became the ending of the film. There was an 'Atomic Exhibit' going on in the building with huge replicas of atoms and panorama photographs of New York buildings. I related in a slightly insane mad-scientist way to the atoms and buildings. We decided then and there to call the film *The Queen Of Sheba Meets The Atom Man*. We then rooted out Winifred Bryan and in various apartments and outdoor venues constructed what I think is one of the most beautiful films ever made".[34]

During the production of *The Queen Of Sheba Meets The Atom Man*, Ron Rice filmed a short colour film, *Chumlum* (1964). The film was named after the musical instrument which musician, poet and Buddhist, Angus MacLise (an original member of The Velvet Underground) played for the film's soundtrack. The filmmaker Tony Conrad, who scored *Flaming Creatures*, assisted with the sound recording. The film is different from the others produced by Rice, not only because of its use of colour but also because of the repeated use of double exposure footage. Chumlum is almost entirely set in one room, which is decorated in an Arabesque style, with draping pieces of patterned colourful translucent material hanging from the ceiling and walls and a hammock in one corner. The film's protagonists, festooned in brightly coloured costumes varying from drag to a Hollywood-style Sultan's outfit, dance, smoke and make love. Chumlum was clearly influenced by Jack Smith's *Flaming Creatures* [35] and the cast includes, amongst others, Smith, Beverly Grant, Mario Montez and Frances Francine (the latter two also appeared in *Flaming Creatures*), alongside poet and Warhol associate, Gerard Malanga. Notably, despite the number of underground personalities cast in the film, *Chumlum* recognizes only the plasticity of film as a star, drawing attention to the multiple exposures, colour, sound and superimposed footage, rather than the actors.

Ron Rice was always broke and in order to finish *The Queen Of Sheba Meets The Atom Man* various benefit screenings were organized. The version of the film screened at these benefits was described by Rice in a director's note as: "a wild man rough cut like no Hollywood director would dare show the public for fear of having his ideas stolen. We defy anyone to cop our style. This is only 70 minutes of a protracted 3 hour epic by the director of *The Flower Thief*. This is your opportunity to help challenge the Hollywood stranglehold on morals, expression and art and what have you. Dig us."[36] [The spelling and punctuation are Rice's.]

> Taylor Mead: "I cashed [in] a life insurance policy and got a couple of thousand dollars in order to finish that film, then we had a big show at Cooper Union, [which] sold out. And I had literally spent my last dime on the film and after that I said 'now we have a lot of money I need some money, we had the fifty-fifty agreement and everything' and Ron said 'oh we put it in a night deposit, for safe keeping' … [that night Ron Rice and his girlfriend] took off for Mexico with all the money, I had literally one dime in my pocket!
>
> "I went and told everybody what had happened. When he came back, some months later, I don't know how long later and I told my landlady not to let him in the building or anything, but he could persuade anybody anything. He was incredible that

way. And he got up to my place on the top floor, a little room and he came in and I said 'Out! Out!' and he said 'No, I have this great new movie, a great new movie!' [laughs]. Then he went to try to borrow money and he said 'Taylor, why did you tell everybody that I ran off with all that money, now I can't borrow a dime?' And I said 'and you think it's on my conscience? Of course I told everybody.' He said 'I have to go back to Mexico, I can't afford to live in New York, no one will give me any money.' So I exiled him back to Mexico and death".[37]

In 1964, shortly after Ron Rice returned to Mexico, he became ill and died of 'bronchial pneumonia' in December. He was 28 years old.[38]

Following Rice's death, Howard Everngam edited *The Queen Of Sheba Meets The Atom Man* footage "according to his best knowledge of the filmmaker's intentions"[39] into a version of the film which was distributed until 1982, when, guided "by memory and notes made during the shooting, Taylor Mead prepared the present, definitive version of the film and the soundtrack".[40]

Ron Rice's few films are a testimony to his vision and to his desire to create an improvised, spontaneous art using chaos and play.

3. An Interview With Taylor Mead

Following brief periods of university education, from which he would repeatedly drop out due to the restrictive nature of formal study, Taylor Mead gained employment at Merrill, Lynch, Pierce, Fenner and Beane as a broker-in-training. Here he 'played' the markets for nine months until, bored with both his pompous future-occupation and the dull surroundings of Detroit, Mead hit the road.

Mead crossed America five times, hitching lifts and, on one occasion, by stealing a car. Taylor survived by the meagre income generated by casual work and — when absolutely necessary — begging. "Kerouac's *On The Road* put me on the road ... and Allen's *Howl*, which had just come out, had a big effect on me."[41] While staying in New York, Mead painted, wrote and performed poetry alongside Allen Ginsberg, Gregory Corso, Bob Dylan and Ed Sanders, amongst others, at various hangouts including the Gaslight and Epitome. At the end of the '50s Mead hitched across the country to San Francisco, in time to enjoy the last year of the North Beach scene and appear in *The Flower Thief* and *Lemon Hearts*. After travelling to Southern California and Mexico, Taylor returned to New York and the subsequent critical and counter-cultural success of *The Flower Thief*.

Taylor's reputation as a traveller and increasing cult status as an underground actor and poet, led to a meeting with Andy Warhol in 1963. Mead was subsequently asked to drive across country with Warhol, Gerard Malanga and Wynn Chamberlain to Los Angeles, where Warhol's Elvis Presley screen-prints were being exhibited at Irving Blum's Ferus Gallery on North La Cienega Boulevard. While in Los Angeles, Mead acted in (and subsequently edited) Warhol's *Tarzan And Jane Regained ... Sort Of* (1963) alongside Dennis Hopper and Naomi Levine. This was the first of several Warhol film appearances in the early '60s; others include *Couch* (1964) and *Taylor Mead's Ass* (1964).

Mead also acted in various off-Broadway productions, including Frank O'Hara's *The General Returns From One Place To Another*, for which Mead won an OBIE (an Off-Broadway acting award) in 1964 and LeRoi Jones' *The Baptism*. Unfortunately, due to 'vanishing' door receipts and LeRoi Jones' withdrawal of support for *The Baptism*, both plays were cancelled. Mead was further frustrated by Warhol's lack of enthusiasm for screening *Tarzan And Jane Regained ... Sort Of;* Mead states that "he refused to show it more than once or twice".[42] In frustration at "the fake promises of Andy Warhol and LeRoi Jones",[43] Mead left America for Europe.

In 1967, following a screening of Andy Warhol's and Paul Morrissey's *Chelsea Girls* (1966) in Paris, which emptied the cinema, Mead returned to America to renew his relationship with Warhol, stating "the US has the worst and the best".[44] He subsequently appeared in *Nude Restaurant* (1967), *Lonesome Cowboys* (1967) and *San Diego Surf* (1968) amongst others. Settling in New York, Taylor currently divides his time between acting, both in theatre and film, painting and writing. Mead's three-volume book *Anonymous Diary Of A New York Youth*, won the acclaim of Allen Ginsberg, who stated that Mead's "Prose/Poesy is instantaneous, honest, fan-

That's what Taylor used to love to do all day — drift all over town in that way he had that people called pixieish or elfin or wistful. He always had a slight smile on his face and in his eyes — one of them drooped and that was a little trademark. He looked so chronically relaxed you felt that if you lifted him up by the back of the neck, his limbs would just dangle.
Andy Warhol and Pat Hackett

tastic as Manhattan Consciousness is fantastic, intimate and awkward enough to make Poe giggle, flat and campy enough to be real and more embarrassing than that of any other modern politician movie star in the West. Original soul!"[45]

How did you come to meet Ron Rice?

Well I was reading poetry in the Village since the late '50s, so both he and Andy [Warhol] — oh, there's that name again — a lot of people picked up on me reading poetry. And he, especially, saw me in San Francisco as I guess I arrived there in 1960, which was, I guess, after the height of Allen Ginsberg's 'Howl' reading and Kerouac's ... But I had been there in the mid-'50s hitchhiking across the United States. But they threw me out of North Beach, this awful cop went around in this big black Mariah booking up people. Just a round up of people who did not look like they belonged, or looked like they might be beatniks or something. And he told me, he said "where are you staying?" and I said "well over in the Mission District" and he said "I think you better go back there". And it's like he's going to throw me in jail. Sergeant Bigarini [was his name] and he spooked me. It scared me. Because I can't stand jail, even though I have been in twelve times. The big city jails are so claustrophobic I just can't take it for more than a few hours. So he split me out of the scene at its ultimate, its poetic height.

So when I went back in the '60s, it was still going on but they sort of resented any new poets coming in. And so I got up on a bar, at the Bagel Shop in North Beach and all these drunks [adopts slurred voice] "arwww, shud-up" and I gave them my dirtiest poem, I was like "cocksucker, fucked by queer policemen with big..."[46] Just hit it out at them and they accept me, if I hadn't really attacked them, you know ... And from then on it was ... Well Ron had someone else chosen for *The Flower Thief*, but the person disappeared. I had him thrown into the ocean [laughs]. So he picked me to follow around San Francisco. And it was a film, it was really ... Ron and I were both inspired by *Pull My Daisy*,[47] but in a way that was a professional film compared to ours, that had a crew and everything.

What inspired you about *Pull My Daisy*?

Just the spontaneity of it. And the picaresque or non-plot thing of Allen and Gregory and everybody wandering around. And we thought it was wonderful and that's all you had to do to make a film. So he got the hand held 16mm, no crew, nothing and people could realize that, which I think really encouraged people to do their hand-held camera things. Of course Bolex should have given Ron a million bucks.

Yeah. Was that the first film that you had been in?

Oh no. In New York I was in a film called *Too Young, Too Immoral* by Ray Phelan. I played a deaf-mute drug pusher. And at one point I get pushed off of the subway platform onto the tracks; fortunately his [Phelan's] uncle was on the transit board or something. And one time on the street somebody came up to me and said "I thought you were dead, I saw you pushed in front of the subway". And I thought "wow! This is the great American public, they are so naive they will believe anything!" It's so easy. It's beautiful. In a way it can be dangerous too. But I thought "how beautiful". Then I walked by — it played for months on Times Square, at a place on the corner of Seventh and Forty-Second Street at a place called the Rivoli — and one day I was walking by the Rivoli and the manager of the theatre came out and said [slowly] "do ... you ... want..." and mute gestures, "do ... you ... want ... to ... see ... the ... film?" And I wasn't even thinking about that, "Oh I've seen it many times!" And he practically fell off into traffic, off the curb. So I thought "Gee! I got it" you know? So then ... it made a lot of money, but by being right at the theatre practically every day counting the house he managed to make a great deal more than the movie cost him, I got like a hundred, couple of hundred bucks or something.

Then my cousin was a famous Broadway musical star, Richard Kiley, married to my first cousin, he offered me his lawyer to get some money out of this guy. The lawyer said "I'll call him up and talk to him" and I said "well, well, oh, er, well he's promised me another movie" you know, the whole chicken-out thing. So I got sort of stung financially. But it was still wonderful the way the public reacted, even though the picture was a real grade B piece of shit.

Was this an underground movie, or a...?
No, no it was trying to be ... it was like an Ed Wood[48] movie [laughs]. Of course Ron Rice used to say to people, they'd say "Ron. How do you make the...? What is your theory of movie making? How do you approach the theory of...?" and Ron would say "Oh, push the button" [laughs]. Which is the secret of filmmaking; push the button. And show it.

How much did it cost to make *The Flower Thief*?
Oh *The Flower Thief* cost us, well it cost me ... because I had a small, tiny income so I'd contribute some money to it. And then Ron's girlfriend, he was writing phoney cheques on her, I had to spend a whole day with her persuading her not to go to the police. But we used World War Two film, machine-gun film, that he got in LA for almost nothing. So the movie may have cost $500 maybe a thousand at most. I'd say a couple of thousand according to this inflationary standard.

When you were actually making that film was there anybody else involved, or was it just you and Ron?
Yeah, essentially. Maybe Ron would have an assistant and that was it. Then there were a dozen of us who were leftover drinkers and so he recruited all these wonderful people — and then there was this great old firehouse being torn down which we used as sort of like a factory, we had a wild party there and everything. And this came all together. And it was really sort of the last — because many of those people disappeared soon after — the last of the Beat scene. Then two years later came Haight Ashbury in another part of town.

How did the tableaux evolve, with all the beatniks acting out Iwo Jima and all the other scenes?
Ron Rice just picked locations and let us do whatever we wanted to, just spontaneous ideas came to us, but it was just various people just discussing what to do at the moment, we didn't plan anything.

Was that the same with all the slow-motion stuff?
Yeah, well that's sort of Ron also, experimenting with the camera. As this was only about the second film he ever made.

At the end of *The Flower Thief*, when you pick up the guy on the beach, to the modern viewer it is obvious that is what is going on, but was this so apparent at the time?
Oh yeah. Oh no, they would have understood that, especially in Southern California. No, no, everyone got that.

I'm also interested in the soundtrack, on the soundtrack there is a poet saying "holy, holy methedrine" and things like that. Who was the poet?
That's from Allen Ginsberg, when he had the poem about [how] everything is holy and I think everything was improvised on that...

But you don't remember who it was who actually wrote and said it?
No. I think it was an old guy with a moustache, but I can't remember his name at all now.

Who chose the music for the film and edited all those different pieces together?
Well, I did a lot of the music, I did as much as possible. I [also] did the soundtrack for *The Queen Of Sheba Meets The Atom Man* as well as *The Flower Thief*, but it's also collaboration with other people.

***The Flower Thief* stands out as a Beat film, but it is very different from say, *Pull My Daisy*, which, when you watch it today, appears as contrived; edited and calculated...**
I still love it.

Oh yeah.
But it had the feeling of first shot, like with Allen or ... I don't know ... first shot best shot. So I think they, I don't think any scenes were re-shot, but I'd have to ask ... oh who was the director? I've made several movies with him myself. Robert Frank, I've made two or three movies with him.[49]

After you had made *The Flower Thief* didn't Ron Rice want to dye the film blue?
He wanted to put a blue wash over it. Then he wanted to announce to the LA paper that printed news about us ... I forget what it is called, it's still there, the big major paper, he wanted to tell them he was going to burn it. And he would really say "I'm going to burn this film", because all the time he was defying Hollywood, at the same time he resented the fact that Hollywood didn't discover him and I had to fight with him like crazy, it took all my energy too, I said "this is the last of the Scene, you've got the last of the Scene, you have got to leave it alone" and I said "there is sort of continuity there", stuff like that. I just fought with him tooth and nail. Then we showed it at the Coffee Gallery and the response was so great he decided to keep it the way it was.

Did you premiere it there then, in San Francisco, or did you bring it over to New York?
Well, it just showed at the Coffee Gallery a few times, which was an exciting place, because we had poetry contests there and everything. In fact, Bob Kaufman,[50] the famous black poet who was in *The Flower Thief*, he and I won first prize at a poetry contest, which was Kenneth Tynan and Nancy Mitford, or her sister, were the judges and they gave us both first prize, a bottle of champagne or something. So that was great, it was an exciting place, it was about as big as this [gestures around bar].

You were doing poetry at the same time as *The Flower Thief*? Were you still working as a 'poet', or were you 'becoming an actor'?
Oh no. I had nothing to do with it. I had been at the Pasadena Playhouse [Theatre School][51] and I had studied with Herbert Berkov in New York, but otherwise I wouldn't go to auditions or anything. I was too shy. So I just drifted into movies, films. But I am a compulsive writer, I've got thousands of unpublished pages and I published my first

three books ... The guy who runs the Gotham Bookstore said he'd print my first three books, but when I reminded him, he said "I've got too many manuscripts". See I've got such great blurbs.

Ron Rice said that *The Flower Thief* was an homage to "the wild man"...
That's it. That is stuff he wrote years later.

What do you think he meant by that?
Well, he meant that we just thought up stuff off the cuff, on the set.

Because a lot of people have written about Charlie Chaplin in relation to you...
I'm much better than Charlie Chaplin. Charlie Chaplin to me was mechanical, repetitious ... I've made a film[52] with his daughter Geraldine and Rebecca Horn, in Portugal and I spoke to her and I said my favourite film was *City Lights*. And she said "Well that's mine too," she said it was her favourite film also, but other than that I find him rather boring.

The other thing that interested me was the fact that people talked about your acting in *The Flower Thief* as 'childlike' and 'direct from nature', that's what Parker Tyler said.
'Childlike'. Well every actor is a child. If they're any good they have to be. they have to believe like a child in what they are doing, or link to their surroundings or something. But I don't know, every critic has a different thing.

Were you aware, when *The Flower Thief* came out, that you were this underground superstar?
I always knew that. I was always a star from the fifth grade on [laughs].

***The Queen Of Sheba Meets The Atom Man* was 'unfinished' and you had to finish it?**
Well I thought it was finished, what I put together [for] *The Flower Thief* and *The Queen Of Sheba Meets The Atom Man*, was to put it into some remote continuity. They really had no plot, either one. We really didn't bother with plots, just locations that's all Ron was interested in. And he was right, he was a great. Wonderful locations and people and to me that's about everything a director can do. It [*The Queen Of Sheba Meets The Atom Man*] was really finished. There was no more to show. There's no plot anyway. I think he had other ideas but he would have gone on for ever anyway. Except his budget really ... it used to be like a nine by ten piece of paper, the budget would be for the film three-quarters and then a quarter for drugs and other stuff. And that went to three-quarters for drugs and one-quarter for filming. You could see it all written out, because he would write out these lists of expenses. He literally went heavily into drug stuff.

What about Rice's movie *Senseless*?
It came from part of his Mexican trip. But actually he made most of that at a funny little loft in Tribeca. Oh that was in-between, I edited *The Queen Of Sheba Meets The Atom Man* there, before he went back to Mexico.

What about that film, *Chumlum*...
That was mostly Mexico wasn't it?

No, it was mostly in an apartment...
Oh. *Senseless* was Mexico. *Chumlum* was ... well he had a Mexican hammock in his apart-

ment and everything and all this sort of cloth, some of it I guess he must have brought from Mexico and it was a beautiful film. I think when he was filming that, I was editing the fucking Queen Of Sheba, putting it together. But like with the Museum of Modern Art with Andy [Warhol] and things, everything that was shot, practically everything that was shot, 90% is in the films, we never threw away anything.

I was interested because *Chumlum* is almost like a Jack Smith film...
Oh, well they both admired each other tremendously. I was supposed to be in *Flaming Creatures*, but I already had my *Flower Thief* image so I thought ... and I heard there was nudity in *Flaming Creatures*, so I thought "well, I have this image" I was like a young actor "I have this image I must maintain", you know. So I goofed on not being in *Flaming Creatures*, which was such a great film, but Jack did once have me playing the violin in front of the screen until the audience began objecting.

That seems to be a real difference to me, between the Beat stuff, like *The Flower Thief*, where it is like kind of a Beat film following a 'real' person around and *Flaming Creatures* which, I'm not sure if I would consider it to be Beat, because it is more concerned with masks and is all camp and there are few authentic characters there ... it's all masks, games and stuff. There seems to me to be a real move within that three or four years from 'reality' to camp and stuff...
We weren't camping, we were just living our fucking lives.

Yeah. But it all kind of changed.
In *Lemon Hearts* there is a little bit of camp, but otherwise it's me tramping around these old mansions and pretending to be various characters, but it's acting also [laughs].

So what do you think changed then and made it become more camp-oriented?
Well it was just Jack's nature. It was then also everybody was on speed and into colours [laughs] and fabrics and weaving stuff and beads and jewels and everything. I think in San Francisco speed hadn't really come on the scene, it was just pot and drinking. And speed came on later in New York, then heroin, then crack...[laughs].

Ron described all of his actors as "dadazendadaists".
In our lifestyle yeah, we were just going day to day. We were totally against the establishment, we knew the war in Vietnam sucked. And ... was it that early the war in Vietnam, 1962?

Well, I'm not sure, but I think it was starting then.
Starting then. And coming from the '50s with that white-bread bullshit middle-class stuff and all the TV programs, whatever and movies or whatever, *The Partridge Family*, or some other family ... and I knew from boarding school, boarding schools are just to brainwash the children of the rich. I used to just hit my head against the wall and everything and I should have quit school in the ninth or tenth grade, because I was already reading tremendously. But when I was forced to read Shakespeare before I was ready for him I had a great rebellion, it's like George Bernard Shaw said — he turned down a huge money contract that they offered to have his books published for schools — "I don't want kids hating me as much as they hate Shakespeare" — and he's right, he's absolutely right. When I read Shaw, when I went to [the Pasadena] Playhouse, I had picked up Shaw, I heard *Pygmalion* was a terrific movie and I couldn't see it. So I went to the library and got Shaw and the

first thing was a preface called 'Parents And Children'. It did a number on the class boarding schools, it was just right to the point, so I did nothing for the next couple of years but read Shaw. I forgot about acting school and everything, I read Shaw. I used to quote him to death to my family [laughs].[53]

You were talking about having fun and such, hating the war...
We just despised the [war]. Many of us were from wealthy families, my father was 'Boss of Michigan'. Very powerful family. Although I lived with my mother, my father was a miser, wouldn't give her enough to live on. But she was from high society and they dropped a lot of money during the Depression, but she insisted on living at Rose Point among the richest people who were her best friends. But I was always broke. And since we weren't members of the country club I always had to get people to sign my checks for food and everything. Then I really found myself not on the other side of the tracks, but on the middle of the tracks, you know. I have views at ... I often wish we lived in the poorer section of Detroit.

You always felt that sense of being an outsider then?
Yeah. That's very much in my book [*Son Of Andy Warhol*]. It's like the book *Edie*,[54] which I thought was a terrific book, the whole background of this supposedly chivalrous respectable New England family and uhm ... ours was similarly scandalous, although there was no incest, I wouldn't even go to bed with my cousins [laughs]. No I felt a tremendous thing about incest, anyone blood-related I felt was just repellent to me, no matter how attractive they were.

After he completed *Senseless*, Ron Rice went back to Mexico City again?
Oh yeah, he had to go back ... Acapulco.

And that is where he died?
His wife Amy, she said she walked him to the hospital, but it is a notorious cliché, Americans going to Mexican hospitals to die. (And I wound up in one once, with an ice bag leaking all over the bed and it was the American-English hospital in Mexico City, it's supposed to be the best, they didn't know what they were doing.) But she walked him to the hospital and he had — probably because he had terrible hepatitis and the people at the hospital in San Francisco thought he'd never recover and he recovered and they were amazed, he recovered in a few weeks or a month. He was built very powerfully — and he walked into the hospital and I'd swear they gave him a shot of something totally wrong for his system otherwise he would have survived, but supposedly it was pneumonia or something, God knows, mixed with drugs. But if she walked him to the hospital then he should still be alive, it was something they did at the hospital.

Didn't he used to live really madly; editing and filming, but never sleeping...
Well the problem is ... one problem was getting the film away from him, because if he had nothing to do, no new film to make, or anything, he'd start working or making silly ideas like putting blue washes on it, stuff like that.

He was always totally obsessed by his work then?
For a long time, until the dope got him, I think, mostly. But, see, it was still always in the back of his mind. To me he was so refreshing, compared to the filmmakers ... so many filmmakers now can't make a film in less a year or two or something. And we just churned them out and showed them, that's the fun of it, we got a feedback you know. But to me

making films is horrendous then to have some kind of fancy editing come in, oh! And also if you film a scene and you know you are doing your best and it is spontaneous and wonderful, but somehow the lighting person thinks the lighting wasn't quite right, so we re-shoot that and re-shoot and re-shoot and re-shoot until all the technical stuff is right and the human element is practically dead.

And you believe that the human element is the most important then, just doing it once off...
Infinitely, infinitely, infinitely. But now there are so many good films that obviously have been terribly professionally done like *Welcome To The Doll House*, or this thing with Steve Buscemi, where he plays ... they are making a low-budget film...

***Living In Oblivion* (1995)?**
Exactly.

You hooked up with Andy Warhol after Ron Rice?
Well Andy saw what we were doing and of course with Andy nothing got by him. As Andy would say "well timing is everything" and he picked up on it and he had known me from poetry readings and stuff and he bought his first Bolex, I guess here in New York. And we drove across the country to California, where he had a show of Elvis Presley paintings. That was the film ... supposedly the first movie he made was John Giorno sleeping, but the first movie with any kind of plot or any kind of events happening was *Tarzan*, which has never been shown.

Right. *Tarzan and Jane Regained ... Sort Of.*
Which is a wonderful movie and I've been helping at the Whitney [Museum of American Art] check it out and I edited *Tarzan* in the first place and put music to it and they [the Whitney] left it just as it was 33 years ago which is very refreshing, but whether they'll ever show it I don't know. They're treating them like works of art ... there is huge audience for them. I found that out in Helsinki and Japan.

There is obviously a stylistic change between Ron Rice and Warhol, but did you see a kind of philosophical change in the way they approached their films?
They were both awfully easy to work with, although Ron liked to move around with his camera a little more than Andy did [laughs].

Well, I mean I am interested specifically in the Beat idea, Ron Rice was very clearly a Beat filmmaker, but...
A few years before Andy died I said "Oh Andy we are just about the last of the beatniks." And he said "Oh Taylor I was never a beatnik" [laughs]. Andy was heading for the country club [laughs].

Andy actually made a film of you, Ginsberg, Corso and Kerouac, sitting on the couch...
Oh yeah. And that day he was filming from behind everybody. And I said "Andy, these people Gregory, Jack, Allen ... they will probably never be together again" — I was absolutely right because Jack died a few years later. I said "can't you move the camera?" "Nah. Nah. Nah. It's stationary today, it's from this [angle] ..." [laughs]. And Jack — he was so magnificent, even in real life he was like a poem — and he's all over ... and it would have been a great study of movement, if he had the camera out in front of the couch.

You were actually good friends with Corso, Ginsberg and Kerouac?
Oh yeah. Forever, sure. Kerouac used to say we were husband and wife in the 16th century in London. And to someone else he said I was the greatest comedian who ever lived. He admired me tremendously, but I only remember being with him a few times in San Francisco and New York. I was supposed to go to bed with him, he and his girlfriend, who was a black girl and we were on 9th Street, or 10th Street, in an apartment right up here, I think. Some fancy apartment. And he wanted to go home and I lived on Stuyvesant Street and he said "Taylor can we go to your place?" And I thought "gee" and I said "yeah." And I was hoping it wouldn't happen, because nothing could have happened with me regarding the woman but I thought "it's my tiny room, absolutely nuts" but the time we got near my house the girl wanted to go to Brooklyn to Jack's place, or her place, or something, thank goodness. But he was very drunk and just wonderful and that was about one year before he died.

---

1. Allen Ginsberg in Allen Young, *Allen Ginsberg Gay Sunshine Interview,* Grey Fox Press, Bolinas, 1974, p.42.

2. Peter Orlovsky, quoted in James McKenzie, 'An Interview With Allen Ginsberg', in Arthur Winfield Knight and Kit Knight, eds, *The Beat Journey, volume #8* of "the unspeakable visions of the individual", 1978, p.28.

3. Jack Kerouac, *The Dharma Bums,* Flamingo/Harper Collins, London, 1994 (1958) p.13.

4. *The Dharma Bums,* p.15.

5. Rebecca Solnit, 'Heretical Constellations: Notes On California, 1946–61', in Lisa Phillips, ed, *Beat Culture And The New America: 1950–1965,* Whitney Museum of American Art, New York, Flammarion, Paris, 1995, p.73. In Barry Miles' book, *Ginsberg: A Biography* (Viking, London, 1990), the author emphasizes the fact that not all of the San Francisco poets wished to be identified as members of a larger school and certainly not a school fronted by Ginsberg and the East Coast Beats. Miles goes on to suggest that both Robert Duncan and Michael McClure were keen to retain their individuality, even refusing to pose for group photographs (p.212/213).

6. Steven Watson, 'Chronology', in Lisa Phillips, ed, *Beat Culture And The New America: 1950–1965,* Whitney Museum of American Art, New York, Flammarion, Paris, 1995, p.256.

7. Taylor Mead, *Son Of Andy Warhol,* (unpublished), p.61.

8. Personal conversation.

9. *Son Of Andy Warhol,* p.61.

10. *Son Of Andy Warhol,* p.61.

11. *Son Of Andy Warhol,* p.61.

12. *Son Of Andy Warhol,* p.61.

13. P. Adams Sitney, *Visionary Film: The American Avant-Garde,* Oxford University Press, NYC, 1974, p.351.

14. Ron Rice quoted in *Visionary Film: The American Avant-Garde,* p. 352

15. Parker Tyler, *Underground Film: A Critical History,* DaCapo Press, New York, 1995, (1969), p.88. Mead's character was also described as "wistfully infantile" by J. Hoberman, in the *Village Voice,* 14 November, 1995, p.37.

16. Harry Langdon started as a vaudeville comedian, before appearing in various Mack Sennett comedies in the 1920s. His stage persona combined childish innocence with somnambulism, and he would appear as a passive figure around whom chaos whirled.

17. For example Mead's roles in both Vernon Zimmerman's *Lemon Hearts* (1960) and in Rice's *The Queen Of Sheba Meets The Atom Man* (1963, re-edited/completed 1982).

18. Ray Carney, 'Escape Velocity: Notes On Beat Film' in Lisa Phillips, ed, *Beat Culture And The New America: 1950–1965,* Whitney Museum of American Art, New York, Flammarion, Paris, 1995, p.202.

19. 'Escape Velocity', p.202.

20. 'Escape Velocity', p.202.

21. Gilles Deleuze, *Nietzsche And Philosophy*, trans. Hugh Tomlinson, Columbia University Press, New York, 1983 (1962), p.170.

22. Jack Kerouac, *On The Road*, Penguin, London, 1991 (1957), p.241.

23. Ron Rice quoted in *Visionary Film: The American Avant-Garde*, p. 352

24. Lisa Philips, 'Beat Culture: America Revisited', in Lisa Phillips, ed, *Beat Culture And The New America: 1950–1965*, Whitney Museum of American Art, New York, Flammarion, Paris, 1995, p.29. This view is reiterated by the poet Ed Sanders in the same volume: Ed Sanders, 'The Legacy Of The Beats': "The Beats in their sense of public spectacle drew from a long & complex tradition … …and the concept that there was oodles of freedom guaranteed by the United States Constitution that was not being used" (p.244). (See also the Mead quote that opens this essay.)

25. J. Hoberman, in the *Village Voice*, 14 November, 1995, p.37.

26. Vernon Zimmerman assisted Ron Rice during the production of *The Flower Thief* and his film *Lemon Hearts* (1960) was shot with Taylor Mead in San Francisco following the completion of *The Flower Thief*. The black and white 16mm short *Lemon Hearts*, featured Taylor Mead who improvised all the characters in the film, which wove a series of vignettes based "around the old mansions that were being torn down in a part of San Francisco" (*Son Of Andy Warhol*, p.62). The film was financed by Mead's cousin's husband Richard Kiley who gave Mead and Zimmerman the necessary $50 budget. According to Mead's autobiography: "Since I was not seeing much or any of the money *The Flower Thief* was taking at local showings I made Vernon promise to give me 50% of all income from future showings — he laughed at me, but I insisted we shake hands on it. He apparently didn't have much faith that it would earn anything. I did. Later, the following year or two, The Museum of Modern Art in New York gave him $1,000 prize, the Rosenthal Award. He gave me $100 and I've never seen a dime since from future showings." (*Son Of Andy Warhol*, p.62).

27. Stan Brakhage, director of such movies as *Flesh Of Morning* (1956–57), *Sirius Remembered* (1959) and *Dogstar Man* (1959-64)

28. Jonas Mekas, 'Notes On New American Cinema', in P. Adams Sitney, ed, *Film Culture, An Anthology*, Secker and Warburg, London, 1971 (1970), p.101.

29. Jonas Mekas 'Movie Journal', *Village Voice*, 14 October, 1961, cited in J.Hoberman, 'The Forest And The Trees', in David E. Williams, ed, *To Free The Cinema: Jonas Mekas And The New York Underground*, Princetown University Press, Princetown/Oxford, 1992, p.117.

30. Taylor Mead, quoted in Andy Warhol and Pat Hackett, *Popism: The Warhol '60s*, Hutchinson & Co Ltd, London, p.39.

31. Personal conversation

32. *Popism: The Warhol '60s*, p.35. Jack Stevenson similarly observes the evolution of these underground superstars, adding Mike and George Kuchar's stars' Donna Kerness and Larry & Francis Leibowitz, to this list. (*Desperate Visions #1: Camp America*, Creation Books, London, 1996, p.172/3.)

33. *Son Of Andy Warhol*, p.70.

34. *Son Of Andy Warhol*, p.70.

35. The depth of this influence can be seen in Rice's use of Arab and 'Eastern' style costume in this film, while his other films use chaotic oddments (a figure wearing a gas-mask in *Senseless*, a man dressed in '20s clothes in *The Flower Thief*). The lavish coloured materials and '50s B-movie Hollywood Maria Montez-style Arabian abundance are pure Jack Smith.

36. Ron Rice mimeographed note, quoted in *Film-maker's Cooperative Catalogue no.7*, New York, 1989, p.407.

37. Personal conversation.

38. Following Rice's death a dozen rolls of exposed footage (colour and monochrome) were found in Mexico; a ten-minute selection of this footage has subsequently been made available under the title *The Mexican Footage*.

39. Jonas Mekas, cited in *Film-makers Cooperative Catalogue* #7, p.407.

40. *Film-makers Cooperative Catalogue* #7, p.407.

41. Taylor Mead, quoted in *Popism: The Warhol '60s*, Hutchinson & Co Ltd, London, 1980, p.38

42. *Son Of Andy Warhol*, p.88.

43. *Son Of Andy Warhol*, p.90.

44. *Popism: The Warhol '60s*, p.241.

45. Allen Ginsberg, press/cover blurb, Taylor Mead, *Taylor Mead On Amphetamine And In Europe, Excerpts From The Anonymous Diary Of A New York Youth, Volume 3*.

46. The complete poem that Taylor Mead recited read:

"I was a cock sucker in Arcady
And was fucked by queers
And football players with big rears,
And policemen with syphilis
And huge erections that tore me apartment,
And sailors and marine captains
And sergeants on board other people's troop ships
And negroe chauffeurs
And children age God knows what
And a Utah sheriff
And a Pennsylvania farmer
And a truck driver
And many other truck drivers but not as great
And the world." (*Son Of Andy Warhol,* p.58)

47. Ron Rice and Taylor Mead saw *Pull My Daisy* together in San Francisco shortly after its release.

48. Ed Wood Jr. was the aesthetic mastermind behind such classic Z-grade movies as *Glen Or Glenda* aka *I Led Two Lives* (1953) and *Plan 9 From Outer Space* (1959). Part genius and part 'naive' artist, Wood's early life was celebrated in the biopic *Ed Wood* (Tim Burton, 1995).

49. Taylor Mead has appeared in Robert Frank's films *C'est Vrai!* (*One Hour*) (1990) and *Last Supper* (1992).

50. Bob Kaufman began performing in the North Beach clubs with jazz musicians in 1953 and was friends with eminent musicians such as Billie Holiday and Charlie Parker. His publications include *Abomunist Manifesto* and *Second April* (both City Lights Books, San Francisco, 1959). His books include the collection *The Ancient Rain: Poems 1956–1978* (New Directions Publishing Corp, New York, 1981).

51. According to his autobiography Mead "didn't like it. The curriculum was just a continuation of boarding school, with required this and that and 3 or 4 hours of homework on the history of the theatre and the history of costuming etc. The few acting classes I had I made a great impression on the teachers, but they couldn't let me out of the other curriculum" (*Son Of Andy Warhol,* p.33).

52. *Buster's Bedroom* (1990) directed by Rebecca Horn and featuring Mead, Geraldine Chaplin and Donald Sutherland.

53. According to *Son Of Andy Warhol,* reading Shaw liberated Mead: "It peeled away years of oppression from my brain and I spent most of the following months in Pasadena skipping 'homework' and reading Shaw." (p.34)

54. Jean Stein, edited with George Plimpton, *Edie, An American Biography,* Jonathan Cape, London, 1982. This book focuses on the life of socialite, Warhol superstar, model and actress Edie Sedgewick (she appeared in many of Warhol's movies in 1965, including *Vinyl, Face, Afternoon, Poor Little Rich Girl, Beauty #2, Bitch* and *Kitchen,* amongst others).

Chapter Four

Eyeball Head Poem: The Animated Worlds Of Harry Smith

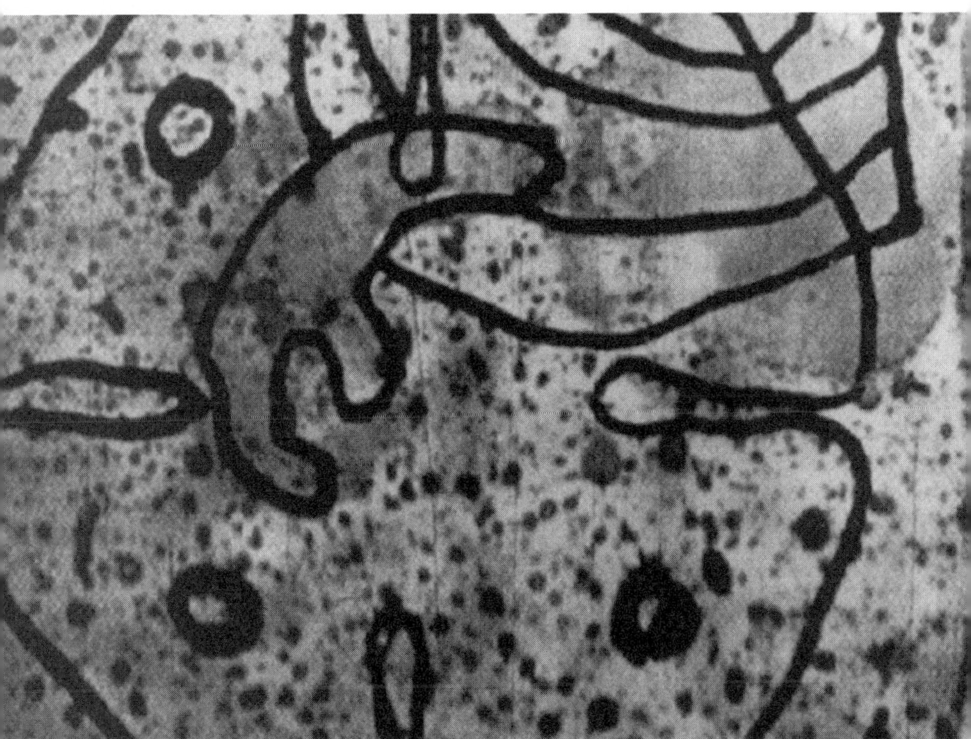

Filmmaker, painter, folklore expert, anthropologist, musicologist and occultist Harry Smith would repeatedly re-invent his origins and age, suggesting — at times — that he was the "probably"[1] the son of Aleister Crowley, who, Smith stated, had seduced his mother when "he was in this country in about 1918, while he was living on some islands in Puget Sound north of Seattle".[2] Alternatively Smith would state that his mother was Princess Anastasia and he was born "on a Russian gunboat off the coast of Alaska".[3] His origins finally emerged when Jonas Mekas and the Staff of the Anthology Film Archives assisted Smith in his application for a grant and it was necessary to obtain Smith's birth certificate and Social Security number: Harry Smith was born in Portland, Oregon, on 29 May, 1923.

Harry Smith's family were steeped in occultism; in an interview with P. Adams Sitney, Smith stated that "the Knights Templar were refounded by my great-grandfather",[4] while his parents were Theosophists. Occult and magickal literature was always available throughout his childhood. According to Smith, on his twelfth birthday his father gave him a blacksmith's workshop and told him to transform lead into gold (the archetypal alchemical process). Smith also stated that his father taught him how to draw the cabalistic Tree of Life. Smith maintained an active interest in the 'occult' throughout his life and studied, among other areas, the philosophy and magick of Aleister Crowley, the Cabala and Enochian. In addition he was an affiliate of the O.T.O (Ordo Templi Orientis) and was consecrated as a Gnostic bishop in the Ecclesia Gnostica Catholica.

My cinematic excreta is of four varieties: batiked abstractions made directly on film between 1939 and 1946; optically printed non-objective studies composed around 1950; semi-realistic animated collages made as part of my alchemical labors of 1957 to 1962; and chronologically superimposed photographs of actualities formed since the latter year. All these works have been organized in specific patterns derived from the interlocking beats of the respiration, the heart and the EEG Alpha component and should be observed together in order, or not at all, for they are valuable works, works that will live forever — they made me gray.
Harry Smith.

Smith's father would also encourage him in making various historical models, including the Bell telephone and Edison's light bulb and "very early my parents got me interested in projecting things".[5] Smith's mother worked as a teacher on the Lummi Indian Reservation and Harry became interested in documenting the songs, dances and rituals of the indigenous peoples. This would lead to a lifelong interest in Native American culture, anthropology, ethnomusicology and folklore and cumulated in Smith's compiling and editing the immensely influential Folkways Records albums of American Folk Music,[6] as well as a recording of the Kiowa Peyote Meeting, which documented the peyote songs of the Kiowa. He also recorded Allen Ginsberg's *First Blues: Rags, Ballads And Harmonium Songs* and countless other pieces by musicians, writers and poets, including Gregory Corso and Peter Orlovsky, as well as various ambient noises and sounds.

Following a brief period spent studying anthropology at the University of Washington, Smith relocated to bohemian California, living in Berkeley and later in San Francisco's Fillmore district. While living on the West Coast Smith became involved with Frank Stauffacher's and Richard Foster's Art In Cinema Society (1947–1955) at the San Francisco Museum of Art, where he attended screenings of films by avant-garde and experimental

Harry Smith in front of a mural

filmmakers, such as Jean Cocteau and Maya Deren. In 1948 Smith coordinated one of the first screenings of Kenneth Anger's *Fireworks* (1947) at the 'Art In Cinema Society'. It was while living in Berkeley that Smith's work garnered attention from Hilla Rebay, from the Museum of Non-Objective Painting (subsequently the Guggenheim Museum of Modern Art). Rebay arranged for Smith and fellow filmmaker and magus Jordan Belson[7] to travel to New York. While Belson returned to San Francisco, Smith remained

— for the most part — in New York, where he lived at a small apartment at 300½ East 75th Street, before moving to various legendary/notorious hotels (including the Chelsea, the Breslin and the Earle). In 1985, following his departure from the Hotel Breslin, Smith spent several months living as Allen Ginsberg's house guest. In 1988 Ginsberg and Smith travelled to the Naropa Institute, in Boulder, Colorado, where Smith was made Philosopher-in-Residence, although he was also known as the Shaman-in-Residence. Harry Smith died on 27 November, 1991.

Harry Smith's first eleven films, produced between 1939 and 1956, are commonly referred to as his *Early Abstractions*. All of these films are numerically titled, except for *No. 5*, which is also known as *Circular Tensions Homage To Oskar Fischinger*; as Smith stated: "You can tell how much I admire Fischinger: the only film of mine that I ever gave a real title to was *Homage To Oskar Fischinger Film No. 5*. ... I learned concentration from him".[8] The first three *Early Abstractions: No. 1* (1939), *No. 2* (1940–42) and *No. 3* (1942–47),[9] were produced by Smith physically manipulating the plasticity of celluloid without the use of a camera (notably when Smith did begin to use a camera he would regularly borrow cameras, then pawn them following the completion of shooting). *No. 1* was produced by drawing, with a crow-quill pen, "taking impressions of various things, like ... the lid of a Higgins Ink bottle"[10] and painting directly onto 35mm film stock.[11] This was described by Smith in the Film-Makers' Cooperative Catalogue as an "animation of dirty shapes — the history of the geologic period reduced to orgasm length".[12] The film depicts a series of shapes, which dance, play and transform as the film progresses. The transmutations which the shapes undergo are multiple: geometric, as they change from squares to triangles; spatial, as they increase and decrease in size; and spectral, as they change from colour to colour.

No. 2 was described by Smith as "Batiked animation, etc., etc. The action takes place either inside the sun or in Zurich, Switzerland".[13] As Sitney observes in his essay on Smith, Zurich, at the time the film was produced, was the home of Carl Gustav Jung and Smith's note suggested that "the film might also take place in the mind of Carl Jung".[14]

No. 3 was described by Smith as "Batiked animation made of dead squares, the most complex hand-drawn film imaginable".[15] *No. 2* and *No. 3* were produced by Harry Smith using his 'batik' technique; this consisted of Smith starting with a piece of film (normally about six foot in length) on which there would be a thin coat of emulsion. Smith would then stick gummed labels cut into various geometric shapes onto the film, carefully positioning them according to the label in the previous frame in order to animate them correctly. Once this was finished he would use a perfume atomizer containing ink and spray the film with it. Smith would then put a petroleum jelly over the entire strip of film, before removing the gummed labels using a needle, revealing geometric, 'clean' areas on the film. He would then re-spray the film, before 'washing off' the jelly. Because the jelly acted as a mask, the original colour would remain on the strip of film and the second colour would only be in the designated areas. The more colours Smith used in a film, the more times the process had to be repeated (some sequences in these films use up to ten colours).

These first three films were originally silent, but in the late '40s Smith heard Dizzy Gillespie play, an experience which Smith would come to describe as an epiphany; "I had a really great illumination the first time I heard Dizzy Gillespie play. I had gone there very high and I literally saw all kinds of coloured flashes".[16] Following this, *No. 2* was edited down from its original half-hour length to approximately five minutes in order to allow it to be scored by Dizzy Gillespie's 'Guacha Guero'. This was to be one of several pieces of music subsequently used by Smith to accompany his films. Smith would also take his films to clubs, such as Jimbo's Bop City, where bebop jazz musicians would improvise to the projected images, 'reading' the shifting colours and transforming shapes as music. He would also project the films at different speeds, allowing for the potential of further improvisations by the assembled musicians.

Although working as a filmmaker, Smith would always describe himself as a painter — "The films are minor accessories to my paintings; it just happened that I had the films with me when everything else was destroyed"[17] — having executed a series of paintings based upon his interpretations of Dizzy Gillespie recordings, such as 'Algo Bueno', or 'Manteca', a jerky hand-held shot of which opens film *No. 4* (1950). The brightly coloured forms of Smith's 'Manteca' painting are notably organic in structure and exist in direct contrast to the rigid shapes of dots, circles, squares and grilles which make up the rest of the short film, which is shot in black and white. However, the blurring visual patterns formed by the speed of the dancing 'white' images are less about black and white than about the relationship between light and dark. The film is a disorientating, hypnotic exploration of light and movement.

No. 5, aka *Circular Tensions Homage To Oskar Fischinger* (1950) is similar to *No. 4*, but is shot in colour. The film depicts dancing red grids and spinning blue and red gyres.

No. 6 (1951) is thought to have been lost; Smith described this film as a "Three-Dimensional, optically printed, abstraction using glasses the color of Heaven and Earth"[18]. The film was originally twenty minutes long.

Smith's film *No. 7* (1951) is an "optically printed Pythagoreanism in four movements supported on squares, circles, grille-work and triangles with an interlude concerning an experiment"[19] and was funded, in part, by a grant from the Solomon Guggenheim Foundation. Sitney suggests that the film is analogous to an animation of the geometric abstract paintings by the expressionist artist Wassily Kandinsky and notes that the Guggenheim Museum was specializing in collecting Kandinsky's work during this period. Notably, Smith shared with Kandinsky an interest in creating a visual language to represent music in pictorial form. The film depicts various shapes and forms transmuting and transforming, circles into squares, triangles and so on. *No. 7* maintains an illusion of depth via the use of hypnotic images radiating 'outwards', 'towards' the audience's gaze.

Harry Smith's next two films, *No. 8* (1954) and *No. 9* (1954), were collage animations produced following his move to New York. Smith described *No. 8* as "made up of clippings from 19th century ladies wear catalogues and elocution books",[20] while *No. 9* is a "collage of biology books and 19th century temperance posters. An attempt to reconstruct Capt. Cook's Tapa collection".[21] Neither of these films survives.

No. 10 (1956) is "an exposition of Buddhism and the Kaballa in the form of collage. The final scene shows agaric mushrooms ... growing on the moon while the Hero and Heroine row by on a cerebrum".[22] The film is the earliest surviving collage animation by Smith and depicts various magickal transformations: it opens with geometric snowflake shapes 'falling' down the image, a single flake expands outwards into a series of geometric shapes and finally into the cabalistic Tree of Life. A bird lands on Kether (the zenith of the Tree of Life) and Kether transforms from a circle into a human skull. The tree explodes into a collection of human bones and demonic heads. These heads then transform into eyeballs. The bones form a human skeleton, which becomes garbed in a ritual costume ... etc. These transformations continue throughout the film, as collaged objects emerge and metamorphose into a variety of patterns, shapes and objects. The film — while not fully cyclic — emphasises a repetition of images and, at the film's end, dancing figures are transformed into the Tree of Life. The film is clearly an occult text; among the images utilized in its structure is Eliphas Levi's illustration 'The Sabbatic Goat' (Lucifer), as well as several demonic forms. The film also contains symbolic magical images, such as the moon and the agaric mushroom, both of which represent the alchemical state of self-reflection. While the film is primarily constructed by collage it also utilizes various optical devices reminiscent of Smith's previous films, such as radiating shapes of colours and a brief sequence in which the entire visual field is momentarily transformed into quasi-pointillist coloured dots.

No. 11 (1957; 1962–76) was described by Smith as an exposition of *No. 10,* but was synchronized to Thelonious Monk's 'Mysterioso'. Notably both *No. 10* and *No. 11* are also known under the title *Mirror Animations.*

The Early Abstractions (films *No. 1–No. 5, No. 7* and *No. 10*) were screened with various soundtracks. Originally projected in silence, they were then either edited to jazz (such as *No. 2*), or utilized in performances by jazz musicians. The films were later scored by Lower East Side post-Beat band The Fugs. Unfortunately the tapes of the soundtrack were destroyed during an altercation between Harry Smith and a member of the audience at a screening. Following this the films had a soundtrack taken from the first album by the Beatles, although for copyright reasons these prints are no longer distributed. The American video releases of the *Early Abstractions* includes a soundtrack by Maya Deren's husband Teiji Ito.

Heaven And Earth Magic, aka *The Magic Feature,* aka *The Heaven And Earth Magic Feature,* aka *No. 12* (1962)[23] is Smith's longest collage film and originally lasted six hours, before being cut, initially to two hours and then to its current 66 minutes.[24] The film was — according to Smith — an expanded version of the lost *No. 8.* Smith's notes in the Film-Makers' Cooperative Catalogue describe the film as having two parts: "the first ... depicts the heroine's toothache consequent to the loss of a very valuable watermelon, her dentistry and transportation to heaven. Next follows an elaborate exposition of the heavenly land in terms of Israel, Montreal and the second part depicts the return to earth from being eaten by Max Muller on the day Edward the Seventh dedicated the Great Sewer of London".[25] The film is made up from a variety of different images, culled from books and catalogues. These include images of people, various animals[26] and birds, skeletons (both human and equine), a melon, Egyptian sarcophagi, various pharmaceutical tools and arcane technologies (cogs, a lift, an insanely mechanized dentist's chair). Many of the images are juxtaposed with the absurdity of a dream, for example: a house with legs walks across the screen, a cat carries a watermelon, a mechanical contraption operated by a skeleton juggles a baby and two characters appear to be a constructed from spoons. Several of these images are also reminiscent of Victorian engravings and the surrealistic juxtaposition of images evokes the artwork of Dadaist and Surrealist artist Max Ernst, in his collage novels *Une Semaine De Bonté — A Surrealistic Novel In Collage* and *The Hundred Headless Women.*

The soundtrack of *Heaven And Earth Magic* is a juxtaposition of various noises recorded by Smith on the streets of New York and includes: bird song, dogs barking and

Q: Why did you start making films back then in the early 1940s?

A: Because an old woman with a bullroarer that had a snake drawn on it, swung it and I heard it.

Arthur & Corinne Cantrill, *Harry Smith Interview*

For those who are interested in such things: No. 1 to 5 were made under pot; No. 6 with schmeck (...it made the sun shine) and ups; No. 7 with cocaine and ups; Nos. 8 to 12 with almost anything, but mainly deprivation, and 13 with green pills from Max Jacobson, pink pills from Tim Leary, and vodka; No. 14 with Vodka and Italian swiss white port.

Harry Smith

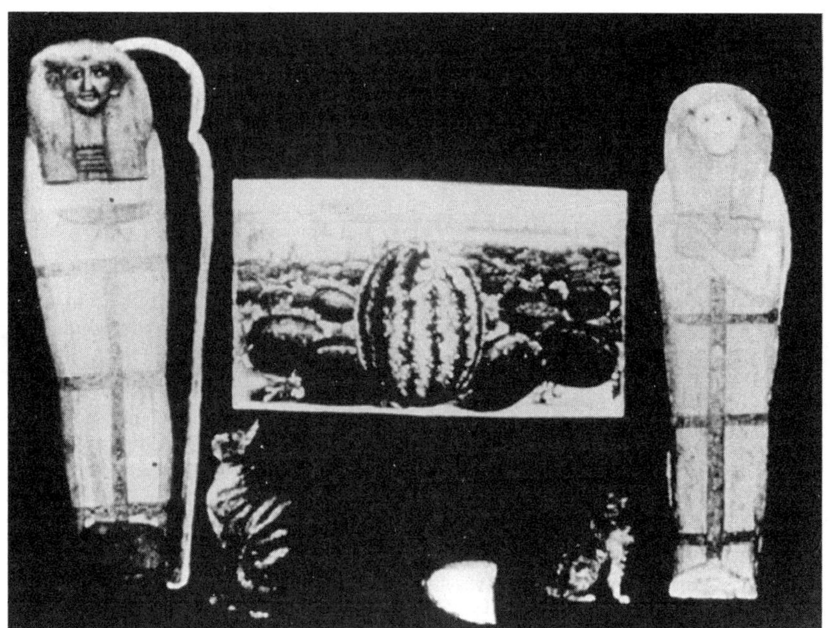

Heaven And Earth Magic

howling, cats, the chatter of voices, babies wailing, traffic, sirens, glass breaking, wind, water splashing, trains and carny sideshow barkers. The soundtrack mirrors the cut-up style of the images, cutting between one series of noise, to the next, in a manner analogous to "musique concrete",[27] although in some sequences the sound becomes diegetic (for example when the dog appears the soundtrack features barking).

Heaven And Earth Magic depicts images that frequently suggest alchemical experimentation (fluids are mixed, various syringes, teats and so forth are employed by protagonists). Like *No. 10* the film also contains various allegorical references to alchemy and alchemical philosophy, manifested via its use of Hermetic symbolism, for example: the meditative journey inwards is depicted via the journey the film takes, through various metaphysical plains, from Earth to Heaven and finally returning to Earth, echoing the "circular nature of the Hermetic contemplative process";[28] while the images of events transpiring within silhouettes of human heads symbolize inner reflection.

Harry Smith constructed the film in a process analogous to the permutations and cut-up experiments suggested by William Burroughs and Brion Gysin:[29] "All the permutations possible were built up: say, there's a hammer in it and there's a vase and there's a woman and there's a dog. Various things could then be done — hammer hits dog; woman hits dog; dog jumps into vase; so forth. It was possible to build up an enormous number of cross references".[30] The film's images of magick and transformation are thus constructed in part via permutation and the act of creating permutations is, in some Cabalistic traditions, viewed an act of magick: "the way of Permutations is the closest way to truly know God".[31]

Smith also tried to make the juxtaposition of images automatic and attempted to remove logical thought processes from the production of the film. This focus on the automatic process of film was, Smith stated, stimulated by Allen Ginsberg, "though [he] denies having said it, [but] about the time I started making those films he told me that William Burroughs made a change in the Surrealistic process — because ... all that stuff comes from the Surrealists — that business of folding a piece of paper: One person draws the head and then folds it over and somebody else draws the body. What do they call it? The Exquisite Corpse. Somebody later, perhaps Burroughs, realized that something was directing it, that it wasn't arbitrary and that there was some kind of what you might call God. It wasn't just chance. Some kind of universal process was directing these so called arbitrary processes: and so I proceeded on that basis: try to remove things as much as possible from the consciousness".[32]

Heaven And Earth Magic was designed to be screened on a specially made projector. Smith constructed this projector, which utilized various masking slides and colour filters, to transform the image of the film as it was projected. Smith also "projected — around the film itself — other images and designs and used also color filters here and there. So it was like every time it was slightly different".[33] Unfortunately Smith — who, according to Sitney, was "notoriously self-destructive"[34] — destroyed this projector in a fit of peak in the early '60s, when he threw it from a window and into the street. Smith also destroyed several films and sequences of film and art in various acts of anger and frustration.

Harry Smith's tempestuous nature, combined with his hectic lifestyle, including a period of heavy drinking between 1962 and 1966, meant that much of his work has been either lost or destroyed. This is especially so in the case of his films following *Heaven And Earth Magic*; as Smith told Sitney: "All of my later films were never quite completed".[35] *No. 13* aka *Oz* (1962) was an attempt at creating an animated feature based on L. Frank Baum's Oz novels, although Smith would also describe the film as being an exposition of both shamanism and Buddhism. The film had a producer and received backing and Smith — who was assisted by a crew of twelve — filmed six hours of test shots. Unfortunately, following the death of the film's backer, the project was never completed, although one short segment (approx. 15 minutes), subsequently entitled and reworked as *The Tin Woodsman's Dream* (aka *No. 16*, 1967), survives.

No. 14 aka *Late Superimpositions* (1964–5) is made from unedited 100-foot reels of superimposed footage, including footage of the Kiowa, shot in Oklahoma, possibly when Smith was assisting Conrad Rooks with *Chappaqua* (1966). *No. 15* (1966) and *No. 17* (196?) are lost, although, according to Sheldon Renan, *No. 15* featured patterns based on the art of the Seminole Indians. *No. 18* aka *Mahagonny* (1970–1980) was a four-screen color film, shot on 16mm. The film was shot at various hotels in which Smith lived throughout the '70s — including the Chelsea — and depicted footage of various associates and friends, amongst scenes of New York. Allen Ginsberg — who appears in the film — described it as "an image bank".[36] Alongside its portraits and cityscapes the film also utilizes both superimposition and animation. The film was also designed to be screened through special frames "beautiful Moorish or Greek outlines",[37] which once again were damaged by Smith in a fit of anger.

Much of Harry Smith's work can be clearly viewed as Beat. His films are characterized by a singular poetic vision and were integral to his life, in a manner similar to that of the Beat writers, who attempted to break down false the division between life and art. Smith's films describe his researches into the nature of existence, exploring spiritual and existential questions via devices such as metaphor and allegorical motifs. His jazz-derived cinematic phraseology compares closely to Kerouac's avowed bebop book syntax.

There is a tension in the films of Harry Smith, between the film's ability to create the illusion of movement (and therefore transformation) and the importance of the individual frame. Smith was aware of the necessity to consider every single frame of film in its own right: "you shouldn't be looking at this as a continuity. Film frames are hieroglyphs, even when they look like actuality. You should think of the individual film frame, always, as a glyph and then you'll understand what cinema is about".[38] Amongst his multiple talents, Smith was also a painter, animator and magickian. An as animator Smith was attuned to the illusionary nature of film as a medium, with its ontological emphasis on making many static images appear to be in motion and subsequently aware of the importance of every single frame of film. While as a magus he was aware from his magickal and cabalistic studies, of the importance of minutiae and the powerful resonant symbolism of even the smallest detail. This is especially important in the collage films, in which the images present in every frame can be read as symbolic. The films show that process/movement and static/fixed definitions are interdependent.

Further, the projected cinematic image maintains the contradictory state of being present, yet is simultaneously absent, it appears to be visibly extant yet always remains intangible, thus the projected image seems recognizable, yet removed from the commonplace. The transformations depicted in these films and Smith's avowed interest in the processes of alchemy and the occult, mirror and are mirrored by, the processes of cinema. In Smith's work, film itself becomes an act of pure visual magick.

---

1. Harry Smith cited in P. Adams Sitney, 'Harry Smith Interview' in P. Adams Sitney, ed, *Film Culture: An Anthology,* Secker & Warburg, London, (1970), 1971, p.264.

2. 'Harry Smith Interview', p.264.

3. Bill Breeze, 'In Memorium, Harry Smith', in Paola Igliori, ed, *American Magus Harry Smith: A Modern Alchemist,* Inanout Press, New York, 1996, p.7.

4. 'Harry Smith Interview', p.263.

5. 'Harry Smith Interview', p.263.

6. This was a three volume, six-record set of American folk music (volume one: *Ballads,* volume two: *Social Music* and volume three: *Songs*), released in 1953. Allen Ginsberg has suggested that "it was largely responsible for the '50s folk music revival wave in America. Peter, Paul and Mary ... the Almanac Singers, New Lost City Ramblers. But one of the people who studied it most closely was Bob Dylan." (Ginsberg, in Paola Igliori, ed, *American Magus,* p.110). Smith was awarded a Grammy, in 1991, for this contribution to music.

7. Jordan Belson met Harry Smith in 1946 and the two shared an interest in "the genre of the non-objective movement of Kandinsky, Bauer and Franz Marc. Studying the correspondence between image and color, they concentrated on space, rhythm and movement in a given plane, in regards to one-, two- and three-dimensional space" (Rani Singh in *American Magus,* p.15). Jordan Belson began working as a painter until 1946 when he saw the animated films of Oskar Fischinger and the Whitney brothers. Belson subsequently became interested in animation and produced the films *Bop-Scotch* (1952), *Mambo* (1952), *Caravan* (1952) and *Mandala* (1953). Between 1957–1959 Belson collaborated with the composer Henry Jacobs on the *Vortex Concerts,* a combination of electronic music and projected visual abstractions (filmed imagery and non-filmic geometric and polymorphous light). These transpired at the San Francisco Morrison Planetarium and the Brussels' World Fair in 1959. Belson's experiments in "creating visual phenomena in ... real time, by life manipulation of pure light ... has been the technological basis for ... more than 20 films from *Allures* (1961) to *Northern Lights* (1985)" (William Moritz, in *American Magus,* p.269). Belson was also interested in Zen Buddhism and was involved in the North Beach scene in the '50s. His interest in Eastern philosophy is reflected in the themes of his films, such as *Re-Entry* (1964), which focuses on rebirth. Belson described his films as "not to be seen but to be experienced [and] not as creations, but as recognitions" (Jordan Belson cited in Sheldon Renan, *The Underground Film: An Introduction To Its Development In America,* Studio Vista, London, (1967), 1968, p.116). Unable to control the conditions in which his films are screened Belson all but refuses to distribute them, although a video of selected images, plays of light and form entitled *Samadhi,* has been released by Mystic Fire Video.

8. Harry Smith quoted in *American Magus,* p.30.

9. These dates are from Sheldon Renan's book *The Underground Film.* Harry Smith does not specifically date his work. When interviewed by P. Adams Sitney, Smith states that he made his first film between 1939 and 1942, "at the latest" ('Harry Smith Interview', p.260).

Note also that, because many of Harry Smith's films — and other additional artworks — have frequently been either misplaced, lost or destroyed, several sources have been used to form the basis for details of unavailable films: Renan's *Underground Film,* Sitney's *Visionary Film* and the two catalogues reproduced in Paola Igliori's *American Magus*: the *1965 Film-makers' Cooperative Catalogue No. 3* — which contains Smith's complete details of films *No. 1–No. 14* (the current catalogue excludes *No. 6, No. 8, No. 9* and *No. 13*) and the 'Articulated Light' program from Harvard, 1995, which includes very brief details (including titles) on films *No. 1–No. 7, No. 10–No. 12, No. 14, No. 16* and *No. 18*. The 'Articulated Light' program excludes *No. 13 (Oz)*.

10. 'Harry Smith Interview', p.261.

11. Smith states that he worked directly onto 35mm film stock in his interview with P. Adams Sitney (p.261).

12. Harry Smith, in *New American Cinema Group, Inc, Film-maker's Cooperative Catalogue No. 7,* New York, 1989, p.449.

13. *Film-maker's Cooperative Catalogue No. 7,* p.449.

14. P. Adams Sitney, *Visionary Film: The American Avant-Garde,* Oxford University Press, NYC, 1974, p.276.

15. *Film-maker's Cooperative Catalogue No. 7,* p.449.

16. 'Harry Smith Interview', p.270.

17.'Harry Smith Interview', p.267.

18. Harry Smith, quoted in *American Magus,* p.30.

19. *Film-maker's Cooperative Catalogue No. 7,* p.449.

20. Harry Smith, quoted in *American Magus,* p.31.

21. Harry Smith, quoted in *American Magus,* p.31.

22. *Film-maker's Cooperative Catalogue No. 7,* p.449–450.

23. The origins of the film's title are unclear, although Allen Ginsberg's journals for March 1961, reveal that he assisted in the naming of the film: "Suggested Titles for What Later Became *Heaven And Earth Magic* Feature: Eyeball Head Poem, Asshole Homunculus Eyeball, Mandala Watermelon, Hammer Dog, Eyeball Vomit, The Vomiting Lesson ... Reptile Consciousness Of Machines" (Ginsberg, *Journals: Early Fifties, Early Sixties,* Grove Press, Inc, New York, 1978, p.185–186).

24. According to Smith: "There was ... an enormous amount of material made for that picture. None of the really good material that was constructed for that film was ever photographed. ...I started out with the poorer stuff. The really good things were supposed to be toward the end of the film, but being as the end of the film was never made..." ('Harry Smith Interview', p.269).

25. *Film-maker's Cooperative Catalogue No. 7,* p.450. According to P. Adams Sitney, Harry Smith's reference to Israel in his notes on the film is a reference to the cabala, whilst Montreal is a reference to the neurosurgeon Dr. Wildner Penfield. Sitney recounts Smith's interest in the hallucinations of the patient undergoing brain surgery.

26. The film features recurring images of a cat and a dog, both of which first appeared in *No. 8.*

27. 'In Memorium, Harry Smith', p.8.

28. Kenneth Rayner Johnson, 'The Secret Language Of Alchemy', in Simon Dwyer, ed, *Rapid Eye, No. 1,* Annihilation Press, London, 1993 (1989), p.328.

29. See "Image Hoard" in this volume for further information on permutations and cut-ups.

30. 'Harry Smith Interview', p.272.

31. Abraham Abulafia, cited in Paul Cecil, 'Inside Out The Mysticism Of Dream Machines' in Paul Cecil, ed, *Flickers Of The Dreamachine,* Codex, Hove, 1996. p.74.

32. 'Harry Smith Interview', p.272.

33. Jonas Mekas in *American Magus,* p.80.

34. *Visionary Film: The American Avant-Garde,* p.280.

35. 'Harry Smith Interview', p.269.

36. Allen Ginsberg quoted in *American Magus,* p.112.

37. Allen Ginsberg quoted in *American Magus,* p.112.

38. Harry Smith, cited in *Visionary Film: The American Avant-Garde,* p.299.

Chapter Five

Low-Rent Hollywood & Cobra Camp: Jack Smith's *Flaming Creatures*

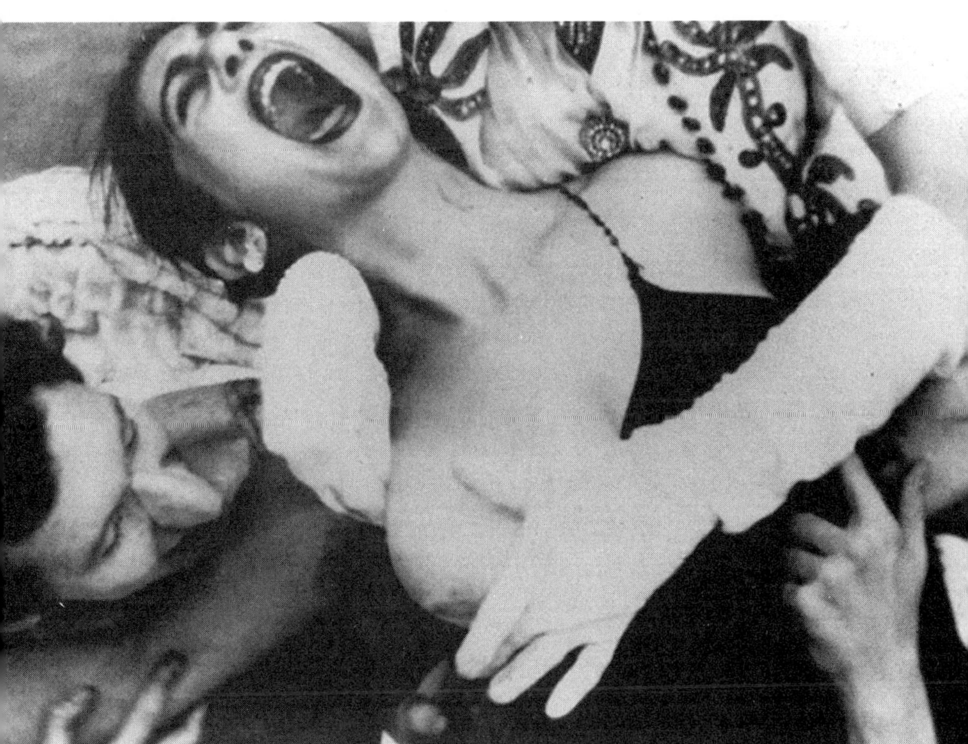

Born in Columbus, Ohio in 1932, to a family he would claim were hillbillies, Jack Smith moved to New York in the '50s. Here he became interested in experimental theatre and studied dance with Ruth St. Denis and direction with Lee Strasberg. Jack Smith spent his entire life working in theatre and film, in a variety of functions including director, set designer, actor and writer. In his role as an actor Jack Smith initially emerged in the underground films of Ken Jacobs, appearing in *Little Cobra Dance* (1956), *Saturday Afternoon Blood Sacrifice* (1956), *Little Stabs At Happiness* (1958–63) and *Blonde Cobra* (1959–63). A film Jacobs described as "a look in on an exploding life, on a man of imagination suffering pre-fashionable lower East Side deprivation and consumed with American '50s, '40s, '30s disgust",[1] while Parker Tyler compared Smith's performance to Taylor Mead's in *The Flower Thief* (1960) and suggested that both stars shared a common "bohemian ... eccentricity".[2]

In addition to appearing in Ken Jacobs' films, Smith also acted in films such as: Andy Warhol's *Dracula* (aka *Batman Dracula* aka *Silver Dracula*, 1964) in which he appeared as Dracula; *Hedy* (aka *The Fourteen Year Old Girl*, aka *The Most Beautiful Woman In The World* aka *The Shoplifter*, 1965); *Camp* (1965); Ron Rice's *Chumlum* (1964) and *The Queen Of Sheba Meets The Atom Man* (1963/1982); George and Mike Kuchar's 8mm camp classic *The Lovers Of Eternity* (1963); Gregory Markopoulos' *The Illiac Passion* (1964–66); Bill Vehr's *Brothel* (1966); and Piero Heliczer's *Dirt* (1967), in which Smith appeared as God. In the '80s he appeared in films such as Beth and Scott B's *The Trap Door* (1980) and Ela Troyano's *The Bubble People* (1983). His final film appearance, before his death from AIDS-related diseases in 1989, was as the Spirit of Death in Ari Roussimoff's feature-length underground movie *Shadows In The City* (1990).

In addition to appearing in film, Jack Smith also wrote and acted in, theatrical performances/happenings. These performances included a collaboration with Ken Jacobs entitled *The Human Wreckage Review* (1961), which was shut down by the police, although two rolls of film shot for the performance formed the basis of Jacobs' *The Death Of P'Town* (1961) in which Smith appears as the Fairy Vampire. Smith's play *Rehearsal For The Destruction Of Atlantis* was presented at the Filmmakers' Cinematheque on 7th and 8th November, 1965. In 1968 Jack Smith appeared in Bill Vehr's play *Whores Of Babylon*. In the '70s Smith's performances included *Withdrawal From Orchid Lagoon* (1970), *Claptailism Of Palmola Christmas Spectacle* and *Gas Stations Of The Cross Religious Spectacle* (1971), all of which transpired at his loft — aka the Plaster Foundation — at 36 Greene Street, to a small but dedicated audience. Later performances, augmented with slide shows, were presented at a variety of venues in addition to Smith's loft. These included *Horror Of The Rented World* (1975),

Jack Smith doesn't care.
Joan Adler

He has attained for the first time in motion pictures a high level of art that is absolutely lacking in decorum; and a treatment of sex that makes us aware of the restraint of all previous film-makers.
Jonas Mekas

L: You mean your film was some sort of parody of Hollywood?

S: It has a lot to do with it, yes. It took place in a haunted movie studio. That's why those people were coming and going like that.

L: Was Hollywood really on your mind when you made the film?

S: Of course. My mind was filled with it...
Jack Smith interviewed by Sylvère Lotringer

Flaming Creatures

How Can Uncle Fishhook Have A Free Bicentennial Zombie Underground? (1976), *The Secret Of Rented Island* (1977) and *Clash Of The Brassiere Goddesses: Boiled Lobster Colored Light Bath Of Jingola* (1984). These theatrical events were vastly influential, primarily on the ridiculous theatre of the late '60s and early '70s, the director Charles Ludlam and the writer/director John Vaccaro.[3]

As a filmmaker Jack Smith directed *Buzzards Over Baghdad* (1951–56, unfinished), *Overstimulated* (1960) and *Scotch Tape* (1961), in which "various faggots cavort in a dense, three-dimensional lattice of curving, namely bent and twisted steel girders...".[4] However it was Smith's following film that was to be his masterpiece: *Flaming Creatures* (1963). This was shot on the roof of the unused Windsor Theatre (renamed the Wonder Theatre in the film's credits), Grand Street, New York City, in bright sunlight on outdated black and white film stock.

The quality of the film stock, combined with the various materials and gauzes through which the film is occasionally shot, give *Flaming Creatures* a hypnagogic, dreamlike quality, with the images transforming and fading into shades of gray and periodically burning into overexposure. Stylistically the film benefits from the same "wilful technical crudity"[5] as *The Flower Thief*; the emphasis is on a spontaneous creativity emerging from chaos and this is mirrored in the film's central images.

Flaming Creatures is a film of Dionysian affirmation, manifested as a celebration of multiple, heterogeneous sexualities. The film has no linear narrative, but rather depicts a group of 'creatures',[6] both male and female, dressed in various forms of exotic costumes, which hint at a combination of influences from Arabian to thrift-store. These creatures play games, put on make-up, grope, expose their genitals (in brief flashes at the camera), pose and dance, to a soundtrack ranging from Latino pop records ('Amapola' and 'Siboney') and rock and roll to Chinese music. As the creatures apply lipstick the soundtrack switches to an advertiser's voice promoting an indelible "heart-shaped lipstick", this then cuts to

Jack Smith's voice as he asks "is there a lipstick that doesn't come off when you suck cocks?". A woman — "a hermaphrodite" according to Smith[7] — in a black dress is chased across the set and is 'raped'[8]/groped by the creatures. This leads to an orgy and then an earthquake, symbolized by shaking camera work and "the set falling all over them".[9] The scene was shot while the cast were all "high as kites, Jack pouring ceiling plaster all over them (a large chunk bruised Frankie [Frances Francine[10]], who got mad telling about those sufferings too)".[11] After the earthquake a gaunt vampiric Monroe-style transvestite rises from a coffin, finally Dolores Flores (aka Mario Montez[12]) appears as the Spanish Girl and, with a rose locked between her teeth, begins to dance the fandango.[13]

Through its use of mise-en-scène and transformations of various cast members via thrift store 'drag' and quasi-Arabic/Hollywood sultan costume, *Flaming Creatures* creates a gender ambiguity amongst the protagonists. The film creates a poetry and eroticism through this ambiguity. The central themes of *Flaming Creatures* are those that would come to define much of Jack Smith's work: re-enacting themes from Hollywood B-movies and especially the films of Maria Montez (1920–1951, aka 'The Queen of Technicolor'). Born in the Dominican Republic, Montez's early films made her a star and she moved to Paris and became a theatrical actress. On stage, however, Montez was a critical failure and she returned to her film career. In order to lose weight Montez began to bathe in scalding hot salt water and eventually died as the result of a heart attack caused by the extremity of this treatment. Maria Montez was the star of various movies, including *Arabian Nights* (1942), *Cobra Woman* (1944), *Gypsy Wildcat* (1944), *Sudan* (aka *Queen Of The Nile*, 1945), *Siren Of Atlantis* (1947), *Pirates Of Monterey* (1947), *Wicked City* (1949) and *The Thief Of Venice* (1949). These films were characterized by a visual and narrative thematic of magical exotica and alongside Montez's stardom, had a profound influence on Jack Smith. The presentation in *Flaming Creatures* of such exotica positions Smith as one of the key figures in the formation of 'New York camp'. As Susan Sontag observed, "the texture of *Flaming Creatures* is made up of a rich collage of 'camp' lore".[14]

The film recognizes the dissonant pleasure of the star, whose performance maintains an intensity, rather than authenticity, of character; this is most clearly apparent in Dolores' performance, with his/her sensuous/evocative appearance and exotic Spanish dance. It is notable that, soon after the film was completed, Dolores 'transformed' fully into the figure Mario Montez, based on Maria Montez, because, as Mario stated, "she's one of my favourite screen sirens. I adopted my name from her. She does everything with such fire … nothing is pretended".[15] In many ways Maria Montez's entire life could be viewed as an extended performance; as Joan Adler observed, Smith "thought Maria Montez was like that all the time".[16] Irving Rosenthal's book, *Sheeper*, recounts Jack Smith describing the importance of Maria Montez's films and stardom on his own subsequent work:

"It's good for an artist to fall in love with the mediocre. How I adore Maria Montez with her stunning 1935 padded shoulders, that marvellous creature, that sheer gossamer goddess, I have seen *Cobra Woman* twelve times in my life. All during my childhood she was my ideal of raging pasty glamour and all I want my photographs to do is recapture what she exuded".[17]

Flaming Creatures joyfully plays with Maria Montez's films (and similar lush and exotically-themed B-movies) with its emphasis on a combination of Persian arabesque and wonderfully trashy sets. At the film's opening Smith appropriates a sound bite from some (nameless) Arabian Nights movie and a voice states "Today Ali Baba comes! Ali Baba comes today!" The film's camp aesthetic thus emerges, in part, from its interpretation and re-negotiation, of Hollywood mythology; the star Montez and her films.

Flaming Creatures' camp aesthetic is further manifested in its emphasis on the theatrical, on gender and sexual identity as performance. This is clearly manifested in Mario Montez's

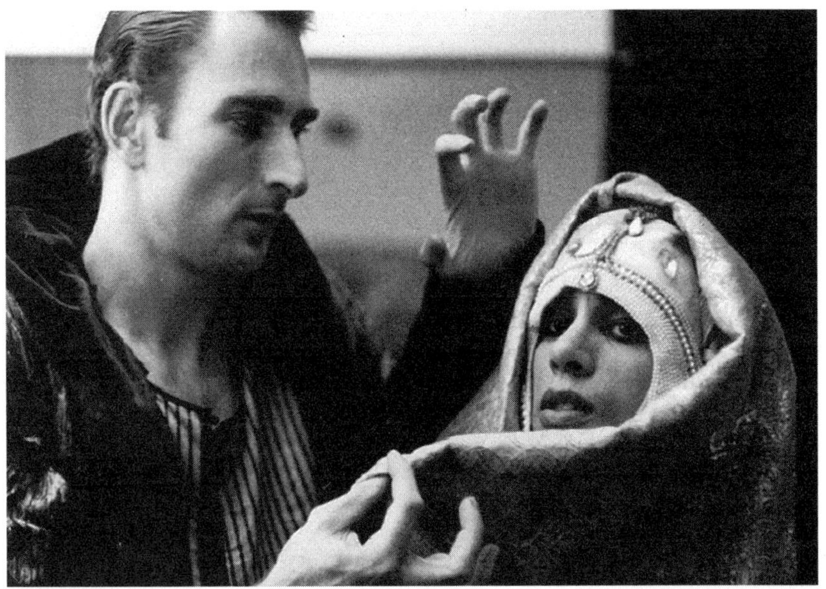

Top: Jack Smith; below: protesting censorship of **Flaming Creatures**

statement that "I don't like the use of the word 'drag' because it has other meanings ... it means something bad. I'll wear costumes for films or plays — but not at home — because *I'm creating something for art.*"[18] (My emphasis). Mario Montez thus 'becomes' 'female' and identifies as such only at certain times and in certain situations.[19] Costume and the accompanying performance necessary to create the illusion of being 'other', thus draws attention to the constructed nature of identity. Identity is not fixed, but in a continual morphogenic flux and is best understood as fluid, able to transform, to be in a continual state of 'becoming', rather than static 'being'. Jack Smith's casting of Mario Montez and his own aesthetic which was characterized via an apparently random structure with forays into costume/drag, has led Smith to be described as a "highly artificial performer".[20] Smith spent much of his life creating and re-creating, his own "fantasy world"[21] based on the Hollywood version of the Arabian Nights:

"He lived in a tiny sixth floor walk-up jammed with garbage and decorated to look like a kindergarten version of Baghdad. The bathroom was a lagoon filled with plastic vines. His bathtub was filled with moss. ...The doorframes were modified with spackle to resemble Arabian arches and the place was crawling with roaches ... Jack wanted to change his name to Sinbad Glick, the Pink Pirate, but then decided it might offend 'anti-semitic pressure groups' so he changed it to Sinbad Rodriguez".[22]

With its emphasis on the theatrical and the surface, the camp aesthetic manifested in *Flaming Creatures* is, in many ways, antithetical to Beat philosophy. Jack Babuscio has observed: "camp is often exaggerated...[and]...it signifies performance rather than existence".[23] As an aesthetic strategy camp can be said to function as undermining "the depth model of identity from inside, being a kind of parody and mimicry which hollows out from within, making depth recede into its surfaces. Rather than a direct repudiation of depth, there is a performance of it to excess: depth is undermined by being taken to and beyond its own limits".[24] Camp thus draws attention to the constructed status of ontological identity (and, by implication, 'morality', 'normality', etc.) using a strategy that embraces parody, pastiche and exaggeration. In *Flaming Creatures* (and other Jack Smith texts, across a variety of media) an aesthetic of camp manifested via the use of lavishly costumed, ambiguously gendered creatures implicitly acts as a challenge to the 'norms' and 'certainties' of dominant culture.

Beat culture would also appear to differ from camp in the Beat interest in the questions of the spirit, spiritual and transcendence. As Jack Kerouac observed, "The Beat Generation ... is basically a religious generation".[25] The Beat philosophy also embraces the concept of the existential individual, partly as a result of its emphasis on autobiographical material; as Park Honan notes, the Beats believed that "the self, the soul of each person must be heard"[26] and they also had a the romantic investment of belief in the (anti) hero, manifested via figures such as Neal Cassady. In contrast camp does not recognize the existential sufferings of the individual, rather, as Dollimore suggests, camp "mocks the Angst-ridden spiritual emptiness which characterizes the existential lament"[27] and takes its stars from the glamorous, exaggerated figures of stage and screen.

Camp and Beat culture share a belief in combining the commonplace, daily life, with the aesthetic; both see a link between art and the everyday. For the Beats the everyday was one of the foundations for their literature and poetry: much Beat writing emerges from autobiographical material and personal, everyday experience informed their work. In camp the link between art and the everyday functions antithetically to this, rather than life informing art, art informs life, thus, a key element of Jack Smith's camp aesthetic was the desire to make and live, the everyday as art and his home was at various times both a film set and a theatre (the Plaster Foundation).[28]

Allen Ginsberg has suggested that camp and Beat culture are related, both through their shared political dissidence and because of their shared investment in the 'homosexual community'. Ginsberg also suggests that to separate Beat culture and camp is to create an artificial and dehumanizing binarism.[29] While camp is primarily viewed as investing in the surface and superficial, as opposed to depth and the authentic, Ginsberg suggested a very

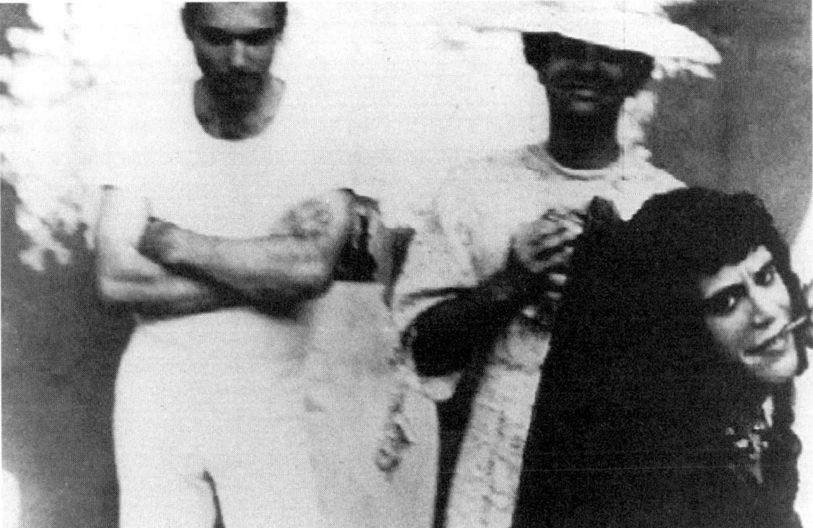

Top: **Normal Love;** ***below:*** **Flaming Creatures**

different ontology of camp in his *Gay Sunshine Interview*:

"Of course, there's nothing more ancient or and in a sense honourable than the old shamanistic transvestite that we see running up and down Greenwich Avenue or, among American Indians, a shaman who dresses himself up like a woman and even takes a husband. The screaming young queen — *there's something very ancient and charming about that; great company, total individuality and expressiveness.*"[30]

This concept was echoed, in part, by Jack Smith who, when asked why he used transvestites in his films, replied "There is no reason other than ancient dramatic reasons".[31]

What the Beats and Jack Smith's camp did have in common, was a belief in the right to free artistic expression, against all forms of censorship and forces of control[32]. Further, the camp vision of *Flaming Creatures* shared with the Beats the desire to openly articulate and affirm homosexual and dissident heterogeneous sexual desires, despite any and all risks (*Flaming Creatures* was made six years before the Stonewall riot and the 'birth' of the gay liberation movement). *Flaming Creatures* also shares with the Beat aesthetic the desire for spontaneous creation and affirmation of the creative imagination: "his movie beats with total life ... it is a realized vision".[33]

This interpretation of *Flaming Creatures* was echoed when, in 1963 the film won the Fifth Independent Film Award and Smith was praised by Jonas Mekas for showing: "how the poet's license includes all things, not only of spirit, but also of flesh; not only of dreams and of symbol, but also of solid reality".[34]

Flaming Creatures, despite its immediate critical acclaim, was also condemned for its 'explicit' depictions of sexuality. The initial screenings of the film transpired in lofts, in an attempt to avoid police raids. However, according to Paul Arthur's 'Routines Of Emancipation', in 1964, the New York City Government, anxious to maintain a good image of the city for the World Fair, began to close down coffee houses, clubs and porn theatres. As a result of this 'cleaning up' the police seized both *Flaming Creatures* and Genet's 1950 homoerotic prison masterpiece *Un Chant D'Amour*. Following the seizure and arrest of Jonas Mekas, at the Film-Makers' Cooperative in St Mark's Place, New York, *Flaming Creatures* was prosecuted. The defence of the film was undertaken by Jonas Mekas, who elicited the support of Allen Ginsberg, Susan Sontag and Shirley Clarke, amongst others. However, the film was branded as "obscene" by the New York Criminal Court in June 1964.

Following the completion of *Flaming Creatures,* Jack Smith began working on *Normal Love* (1963, unfinished). The film was never fully completed, although Smith would occasionally screen the rushes in various combinations. In many ways a continuation of the revelry of *Flaming Creatures* (although shot on Ektachrome colour), the film included scenes of chorus girls/creatures (including Frances Francine, John Vaccaro and a very pregnant Diane diPrima) dancing on a cake (constructed by Claes Oldenburg) in a field near Wyn Chamberlain's rented summerhouse in Old Lyme. Mario Montez appeared in the film as a mermaid bathing in milk, while Beverly Grant was cast as the Cobra Woman (once again in homage to Maria Montez). According to Joan Adler's account of the production of *Normal Love,* Smith "shot [a] ... sequence in a yellow-painted wrecked car lot with Tiny Tim".[35] Other footage included quasi-horror film scenes depicting an Egyptian mummy and a werewolf.

During the shooting of *Normal Love,* several members of the cast and Smith, spent time at Ron and Amy Rice's loft, located just off Canal Street, New York, where they appeared in Rice's Jack Smith-style short, *Chumlum*. In addition to this, *Normal Love* was also the basis for Andy Warhol's second movie,[36] a newsreel film depicting Jack Smith and the cast of *Normal Love,* called *Andy Warhol Films Jack Smith Filming 'Normal Love'* (1963). The film was shot on one roll of 16mm stock and lasted just under three minutes. Unfortunately, Warhol's newsreel film was mistaken for *Flaming Creatures* by the police, who seized it in March 1964. *Andy Warhol Films Jack Smith Filming 'Normal Love'* was subsequently 'lost' and is now presumed to have been destroyed.

Normal Love was never completed, but for Jack Smith the final screening of the film was perhaps less important than the pleasure of making it. The actual making of the film was a performance in which all the cast, crew and collaborators were, whether they wanted to or not, participating. As Andy Warhol would later write about the *Normal Love* shoot at Old Lyme: "Jack Smith was filming a lot out there and I picked something up from him for my own movies — the way he used anybody who happened to be around that day and also how he just kept shooting until the actors got bored."[37] This emphasis on performance, on the performance/process of shooting both *Flaming Creatures* and *Normal Love*, once again positions Jack Smith — at least partly — within the Beat milieu, with its emphasis on spontaneous creation and performance. Yet Smith's work cannot be viewed as purely Beat; with its emphasis on the surface and the superficial glamor and appeal of the Hollywood star, it also invested equally in the growing Pop Art and Queer Theatre, scenes.[38]

---

1. Ken Jacobs, 'Blond Cobra Notes' in The New American Cinema Group, Inc, *The Film-makers Cooperative Catalogue No 7*, New York, 1989, p.269.

2. Parker Tyler, *Underground Film, A Critical History*, Da Capo Press, New York, 1995 (1969), p.86.

3. Andy Warhol's 'script writer'/collaborator Ronald Tavel was also an influence on this style of '70s camp theatre. Tavel's work with Warhol included providing the 'scenarios' for *Vinyl, Suicide, Screentest #1, Screentest #2, Drunk, Horse* and *Kitchen* (all 1965) and sections of *The Chelsea Girls* (1966). Tavel wrote various plays including: *Vinyl Visits An FM Station* (1970); *Arse Long — Life Short* (1972); and *Playbirth* (1976). Charles Ludlam founded the Playhouse of the Theatre of the Ridiculous and his plays were cast with various Warhol and post-Warhol, drag artists. John Vaccaro worked with Ludlam and became known for his use of glitter (his work is occasionally referred to as Glitter Theatre) and a confrontational style with its emphasis on the pleasures of shock.

4. Stefan Brecht, *Queer Theatre: The Original Theatre Of The City Of New York. From The Mid-60s To The Mid-70s*, Suhrkamp Verlag Frankfurt am Main, p.23.

5. Susan Sontag, 'Jack Smith's *Flaming Creatures*', in Battock, Gregory, ed, *The New American Cinema: A Critical Anthology*, E.P. Dutton & Co, Inc, New York, 1967, p.207.

6. The term 'creature ' emerged from Smith's personal vocabulary: "Well, we are all creatures. Number one, you see. And the part of a person that is the same as everybody else is his creature self. ...But this has soulful extensions too because in a lot of respects all humans have the same imagination and so forth and they have — and this is all I meant by the term 'creatures'"(Jack Smith, quoted in Gerard Malanga 'Interview With Jack Smith', in *Film Culture, #45*, Summer, 1967).

7. Jack Smith cited in Ken Kelman 'Smith Myth' in P. Adams Sitney, ed, *Film Culture, An Anthology*, Martin Secker and Warburg, Ltd, London, 1971 (1970), p.282.

8. Stefan Brecht suggests that the rape is actually a mock-rape: "That ... is made clear: by the metronomic, loose swinging of the girl's free right arm, a visually invalidated gesture of helpless warding off."(*Queer Theatre*, p.25)

9. Joan Adler, 'On Location' in Stephen Dwoskin, *Film Is ... The International Free Cinema*, Peter Owen, London, 1975, p.12.

10. Francis Francine appeared in various underground films, including Warhol's *Lonesome Cowboys* (1967), Beverly Grant Conrad and Tony Conrad's *Coming Attractions* (1970) and the Play-House of the Ridiculous production of *Conquest Of The Universe* (1967).

11. 'On Location' p.12.

12. According to Sheldon Renan's *The Underground Film*, Jack Smith 'discovered' the transvestite star Dolores Flores/Mario Montez in a subway station. Montez would go on to become one of the leading stars of underground film, appearing in Warhol's *Mario Banana, Harlot* (both 1964), *Camp* (1965), *Screentest #2, Hedy* aka *The Fourteen Year Old Girl* aka *The Most Beautiful Woman In The World* aka *The Shoplifter* (1965), *More Milk Yvette* aka *Lana Turner* (1965) and *The Chelsea Girls*, as well as Rice's *Chumlum* and José Rodriguez-Soltero's *Lupita* (aka *Lupe*), amongst others. Mario Montez also appeared in off-off-Broadway theatrical productions such as Ronald Tavel's *The Life Of Lady Godiva* (1966) and Tavel and John Vaccaro's *Screentest* and *Indira Gandhi's Daring Device* (1967). Mario Montez did not like the term 'drag', stating that he preferred the term "going into costume" (Warhol and Hackett, *Popism: The Warhol '60s*, Hutchinson & Co, Ltd, London, 1981, (1980), p.91).

13. Jack Smith makes a similar appearance — as a dancing senorita — in Jacobs' *Little Cobra Dance* (1957).

14. 'Jack Smith's Flaming Creatures', p.210.

15. Mario Montez, quoted in Gary McColgen, 'The Superstar: An Interview With Mario Montez', in *Film Culture, #45*, Summer 1967.

16. 'On Location', p.11.

17. Jack Smith cited in Irving Rosenthal, *Sheeper,* Grove Press, Inc; New York, 1968, p.204.

18. Mario Montez, quoted in 'The Superstar: An Interview With Mario Montez'.

19. That Mario desired to be seen as 'female' and identified as such (when in costume) is apparent in Warhol's description of Mario viewing *The Fourteen-Year-Old Girl*: "When he [Mario] saw that I'd zoomed in and gotten a close-up of his arm with all the thick, dark masculine hair and veins showing, he got very upset and hurt and accused me in a proud Latin way, 'I can see you were trying to bring out the worst in me.'" (*Popism: The Warhol '60s,* p.91). A similar event occurs during Warhol's film *Screen Test,* during which an off-camera Tavel interviews Montez, eventually forcing him — almost brutally — to admit to being a male. These two films both serve to emphasis the 'putting on' of identity that accompanies the putting on of a specific costume.

20. Richard Dyer, 'Believing In Fairies: The Author And The Homosexual', in Diana Fuss, ed, *Inside/Out: Lesbian Theories, Gay Theories,* Routledge, London, 1991, p.199.

21. Nick Zedd, *Bleed: Part One,* Hanuman Books, Madras & New York, 1992, p.64.

22. *Bleed,* p.51–58.

23. Jack Babuscio, 'Camp And The Gay Sensibility' in Richard Dyer, ed, *Gays And Film,* BFI, 1977, p.44–45.

24. Jonathan Dollimore, *Sexual Dissidence: Augustine To Wilde, Freud To Foucault,* Clarendon Press, Oxford, 1992, (1991), p.310–311.

25. Jack Kerouac, cited in John Clellon Holmes, 'The Philosophy Of The Beat Generation' in Park Honan, ed, *The Beats: An Anthology Of 'Beat' Writing,* J.M Dent & Sons, Ltd, London, 1987, p.147.

26. Park Honan, 'Introduction' in Park Honan, ed, *The Beats: An Anthology Of 'Beat' Writing,* p.xxii.

27. *Sexual Dissidence,* p.311.

28. In *Queer Theatre,* Stefan Brecht describes Smith's apartment cum theatre: "The loft was not too large for a loft, perhaps 15 by 50 foot, with the stage at one end, stove, refrigerator, table at the other. It is double height, the ceiling has been broken through to another loft, with a balcony left above the kitchen for sleeping, storage..." (p.10).

29. See the interview with Ginsberg in this volume.

30. Allen Ginsberg, in Allen Young and Allen Ginsberg, *Gay Sunshine Interview,* Grey Fox Press, Bolinas, 1974, p.19.

31. 'Interview With Jack Smith'.

32. Among his various stands against control, Smith was arrested in 1965 (alongside jazz musician Jack Martin and filmmaker Piero Heliczer) for assaulting an undercover narcotics cop who tried to stop a bail-raising benefit poetry reading. According to Heliczer's account of the arrest, once the group were taken to the police station Jack Smith was "seated in a chair and offering no resistance brutally beaten by a man I later learned to be a Detective Imp of the fifth precinct, he gave him continuous body blows with both of his elbows and forearms from behind which looked like some kind of karate or judo..." (Piero Heliczer, 'The United States Of America Versus Piero Heliczer' in Ross Firestone, ed, *Getting Busted,* Penguin Books, Harmondsworth, 1972 (1970), p.44).

33. 'Smith Myth'.

34. Jonas Mekas, 'Fifth Independent Film Award', in P. Adams Sitney, ed, *Film Culture: An Anthology,* Martin Secker & Warburg Ltd, London, 1971, (1970), p.426.

35. 'On Location', p.12.

36. Warhol wrote in *Popism: The Warhol '60s* that this film was the "second thing I ever shot with a 16mm camera" (p.32), however in the 'Filmography' in Michael O'Pray's book *Andy Warhol Film Factory,* BFI, 1989, the film is listed as his fourth in 16mm, following *Tarzan And Jane Regained, Sort Of* (1963), *Sleep* (1963) and *Kiss* (1963).

37. Andy Warhol, *Popism: The Warhol '60s,* p.31.

38. Jack Smith shot various other films, none of which were ever fully completed, instead they were used as fragments with which to punctuate his performances. One such film was the 16mm black and white *No President* (1967/68), which evolved through various incarnations (including *The Kidnapping and Auctioning Of Wendell Willkie By The Love Bandit*). The film focuses on the kidnapping of the president by a pirate and his subsequent auctioning as a slave. These themes of piracy and slavery are references to the lush exotica of Maria Montez's movies. *No President* would be screened alongside performances by Smith, often accompanied by music sourced from his collection of Martin Denny records. The film has recently been restored by Jerry Tartaglia.

Chapter Six

An Interview With Jonas Mekas

By Tessa Hughes-Freeland

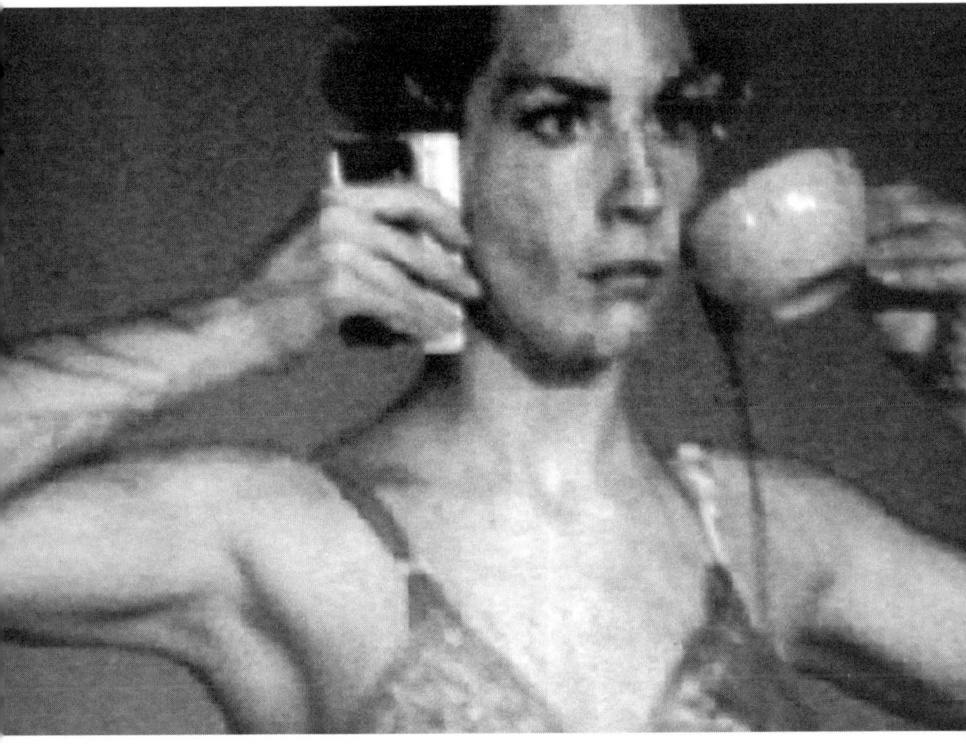

Jonas Mekas is a seminal figure in the history of the American avant-garde. His work involves not only film and poetry, but also a dedication to film as an art, pronounced both through his writing on film and his commitment to screening and to preserving film.

Born in Lithuania in 1922, Mekas was displaced from there by World War II and in 1949 landed in New York. In 1950 he bought a Bolex and began filming the Lithuanian immigrant community in his Williamsburg environment. He attended film classes taught by Hans Richter and in 1953, moved to Orchard Street in Manhattan. He also started to screen avant-garde films at Gallery East, on Avenue A and two years later, with his brother Adolfas Mekas, he began publishing *Film Culture* magazine which became a prime tool for voicing his opinions on the current state of film. Criticism of the current avant-garde in the first issues raised the ire of filmmakers, to whom Mekas, a couple of years later, turned over magazine space for the publication of their own articles. Around this time, Mekas became integrated into a bohemian community of artists, writers, musicians and performers. His ideas became more widespread after 1958 when he began writing a regular 'Movie Journal' column for the *Village Voice*, whose circulation became national in the early '60s.

In 1959, John Cassavetes' film *Shadows* was awarded the first Independent Film Award by Film Culture. The following year's award was given to Robert Frank and Alfred Leslie's *Pull My Daisy*. Although these films are notable for their suggested influence on Mekas' *Guns Of The Trees* (1961), it may eventually be, in the case of *Shadows*, that the material which was cut out of the first version in favor of a more commercial re-edited version, had a more pervasive and subtle influence on Mekas in the development of his "personal cinema".[1]

Jonas Mekas and *Film Culture* contributor Eduard de Laurot started to shoot *Guns Of The Trees* in 1960. The film itself opens and closes with Mekas himself reading from *Prometheus Unbound*. Essentially narrative, the main part of the film is centred around two couples who are friends: one white, depressed and pessimistic (Adolfas Mekas and Frances Stillman), the other black, optimistic and in tune (Ben Carruthers and Argus Speare Julliard), in spite of the fact that they are both living in New York in 1960 under the shadow of the atom bomb. Frances' constant battle against her eventual suicide, is at odds with Argus' pregnancy in an ultimate human dilemma.

An ironic yet intentional interdependence existed between the actors and their characters. Frances, in real life, was in fact a depressive and Carruthers and Julliard, as in the film, were later married. Despite staging, the interior scenes have a realistic quality of self-aware young people living in their beat pads. Complementing this is the outdoor footage of Fulton Street fish market, city dumps etc., real documentation of police violence in Washington Square and "US out of Cuba" protests. Incorporating protest footage was, at that time, innovative and not yet commonplace. Intermittently, the whole scenario is interrupted by two white-faced Felliniesque mime characters playing around in a field.

Shot entirely in black and white, *Guns Of The Trees* is simultaneously lyrical and jarring. Sequences of sound and image mesh, then stand opposed, rub off against each other, then reunite. The soundtrack is a mixture of folk songs, news reportage, experimental jazz and a poetic narration by Allen Ginsberg which fuses "Beat notions of pacifism, existentialism and Zen".

Guns Of The Trees was premiered at the New American Cinema Exposition in Spoleto, Italy and in 1962 won first prize at Porretta Terme, Italy.

As champion of the New American Cinema, in September 1960, Jonas Mekas called the first meeting of the New American Cinema Group. The most significant development to come out of that meeting was the sixth point of the manifesto, which stated the need for their own cooperative distribution centre. Initially, Emilio de Antonio tried to distribute a number of 35mm features and shorts. In 1962 Mekas took over the distribution project. Although some

From left to right: Ken Kelman, James Broughton, P. Adam Sitney, Jonas Mekas and Peter Kubelka

filmmakers who had hoped for a change in the production and distribution of feature films were experiencing disappointment, Mekas saw the invaluable possibility for the distribution of films by filmmakers like Stan Brakhage, Gregory Markopoulos, Marie Menken, Ken Jacobs, Jack Smith and others. This distribution project transformed into the Film-Makers' Cooperative, which remains the largest distributor of avant-garde films in the US.[2]

For the previous two years he had been running one-man shows of avant-garde filmmakers as well as open screenings at the Charles Theatre on Avenue B. It was here that Mekas first encountered Jacobs' *Little Stabs At Happiness*. During this time too, he saw Brakhage's films for the first time. Films which Cinema 16 refused to distribute or screen. It was making discoveries such as these which gave Mekas the determination to have them available for further screening. These Film-Makers' Showcases, which later became The Film-Makers' Cinematheque, continued at the Charles Theatre until 1963. Mekas then organized midnight screenings on Saturdays at The Bleeker Street Cinema, then moved to the Gramercy Arts Theatre. They were thrown out of there eventually in 1964 for showing unlicensed and obscene films.

Although Mekas experienced harassment on the street when he filmed *Guns Of The Trees*, shooting *The Brig* was more of a pressured situation.[3] *The Brig* (1963) was a record of brutality in military prisons recreated by The Living Theatre's off-off-Broadway production of Kenneth Brown's play. *The Brig* was shot illegally after the FBI had closed The Living Theatre on the grounds of some tax loophole. Mekas, his assistants Ed Emshwiller and Louis Brigante and the actors climbed into the theatre through a coal chute. They shot quickly during the night, rotating three single system Auricon cameras in ten-minute takes, whilst the guards stood outside watching the padlocked doors. In 1964 *The Brig* won first prize in the documentary section at the Venice Film Festival and was also shown at The New York Film Festival. In 1963 Mekas also filmed a short newsreel type documentary on the arts for *Show* magazine, called *Film Magazine For The Arts*.

Award Presentation To Andy Warhol (1964), documents Warhol receiving the Independent Film Award in 1964. The Award consisted of a basket of fruit and vegetables. This was also the year that Mekas was arrested for screening *Flaming Creatures* by Jack Smith and Jean Genet's *Un Chant D'Amour* at different venues, within the same week. From 1965 to 1968 Film-Makers' Cinematheque continued to move around, a few months here and a few months there. In 1968 Mekas became the film curator at the Jewish Museum. In 1969 he began to work with P. Adams Sitney and Jerome Hill on the foundation of the Anthology Film Archives at 425 Lafayette Street, of which he became the official director when it opened in December 1970.[4]

In terms of Jonas Mekas' filmmaking, the only film which he 'made', is his only created narrative, *Guns Of The Trees*. Mekas had been continuously filming since soon after his arrival in New York. This recording took the form of a film diary, which amounted to a huge, personal resource of impressions and reflections. He started to release his records of events, as with *Report From Millbrook* (1965–1966), a visual record of a weekend spent with Timothy Leary, accompanied by a soundtrack of an interview *The East Village Other* did with the local sheriff who raided Millbrook in 1966. *Report From Millbrook*, as with many of Mekas' short film records, became integrated into his longer diary films, either in full or in different forms.

The three main, epic diary films of Jonas Mekas to date are *Diaries, Notes & Sketches* (also called *Walden*, 1968–9); *Lost, Lost, Lost* (1976); and *He Stands In A Desert Counting The Seconds Of His Life* (1985).

Diaries, Notes & Sketches (Walden), is divided up into four reels, each between 40 and 50 minutes in length. Containing material from 1964–1968, the material is entirely in camera-edited and in chronological order. The reels include portraits of and impressions of: Tony Conrad, P. Adams Sitney, Stan Brakhage, Carl Theodore Dreyer, Timothy Leary, Marie Menken, Allen Ginsberg, Ed Sanders andy Warhol, Barbara Rubin, The Velvet Underground, Ken Jacobs, Hans Richter, Yoko Ono and John Lennon. These are people in intimate and commonplace human situations, visits with friends, celebrations and different varieties of activities. Spontaneous in essence, Mekas' erratic hand-held camera style, sometimes staccato, sometimes soft, conveys a poeticism whose tone and rhythm is evocative of music. This is Mekas' "personal cinema", his own, intensely subjective, home-movie-making which rejects conventional dramatic narrative.

Lost, Lost, Lost consists of material that basically precedes *Notes, Diaries & Sketches*. It is made up of six reels of film from the years 1949–1963, yet was not edited until 1975. The first two reels depict Mekas' early years in New York, a displaced person in a Lithuanian Community in Brooklyn. The middle two reels focus on his first years in Manhattan and his contact with poetry and filmmaking communities; Robert Frank shooting *The Sin Of Jesus*, LeRoi Jones, Ginsberg and Frank O'Hara reading at the Living Theatre. These also contain records of political protests and peace marches. The last two reels deal with the world of his friends and fellow artists. These include *Rat Shit Haikus*, a series of haikus filmed during the making of Adolfas Mekas' *Hallelujah The Hills* (1962); scenes at the Film-Makers' Cooperative; a visit to the Flaherty Seminar; and visits to the countryside from two points of view including the footage shot by Ken Jacobs on this occasion. The imagery is intercut with sporadic intertitles that are not descriptive, so much as verbal indicators, which complement both the images and the soundtrack. The soundtrack is made up of a number of elements; folk tunes, classical music, natural wild sound and Jonas' own comments, observations, memories and sentiments. In spite of a certain lightness, *Lost, Lost, Lost* maintains a level of tension with an undertow of angst, which only towards the end transforms into a sense of joy.

He Stands In A Desert Counting The Seconds Of His Life is a continuation of the film diaries dating from 1969–1984. Mekas considers this to include mostly impersonal footage, or scenes viewed from a distance, balanced with more personal footage. It consists of "124 sketches of people, places, seasons".[5]

Eclipsing *Walden* in time is *In Between* (1978). Edited in 1978 and containing material from 1964–1968, it consists mainly of friends in the city as well as some travel footage. Actually made up of footage not included in *Walden*, the sounds were all recorded at the same time.

Jonas Mekas' films are by nature personal. They all ultimately reveal a part of his inner self. The two films which focus on his family are *Reminiscences Of A Journey To Lithuania* (1971–2) and *Paradise Not Yet Lost* (1979). *Reminiscences Of A Journey To Lithuania* is a film in three parts. The first concentrates on Mekas' early life in New York, specifically on gatherings of Lithuanian exiles in Williamsburg where he and Adolfas lived. The second part deals with his first visit to Lithuania since 1942, a reunion with his family in the village of Semeniskiai, where he was born. In the middle part the commentary disappears as if to emphasise an irreconcilability of past and present. The last part begins with a short parenthesis in Elmshorn, where Jonas and Adolfas Mekas visit the site of a forced labour camp, where they spent a year during the war. Thereafter, the film celebrates the present, time spent with Peter Kubelka and Annette Michelson and Hermann Nitsch on a return trip via Vienna. There is a similarity in theme between *Reminiscences Of A Journey To Lithuania* and *Lost, Lost, Lost* in that they both contain the sentiment of the loss of a homeland and adapting to and discovering, a new aesthetic family and home. *Paradise Not Yet Lost* lies in emotional opposition to these, being a joyful and celebratory film for and about Jonas' three-year-old daughter Oona.

Three other films of performers shot in the '60s which were edited in the '80s are: *Street Songs* (1966/1983), a documentation of a segment of the Living Theatre's *Mysteries And Smaller Pieces; Cup/Saucer/Two Dancers/Radio* (1965/1983), a recording of Kenneth King's postmodern dance, performed by Phoebe Neville and Kenneth King; and *Erick Hawkins: Excerpts From "Here And Now With Watchers"/Lucia Dlugoszweski Performs* (1983), which was filmed as part of Mekas' film on the arts for *Show* magazine.

Notes For Jerome (1978) and the more recent *Scenes From The Life Of Andy Warhol* (1990) and *Zefiro Torna Or Scenes From The Life Of George Maciunas* (1991) were all made as if in memory of each individual. Portraying them, their lives and their friends, the only conscious elegy is that for George Maciunas, dedicated "to the wind of Lithuania".[6]

Jonas Mekas, to this day, continues to record life in images as it goes on around him, as well as put together parts from his past. He continues to be active in his position as Director at the Anthology Film Archives. A book of his written diaries, *Nowhere To Go*, was published in 1991; he is also the author of five books of poems.

2. Jonas Mekas: 6 February, 1997

What do you think about the different roles that you have as filmmaker, writer, poet and archivist?
Frankly, I don't think about it. I have no time to think about it. All those different activities are not planned or something that I even want to do. In general people do too much. Ideally, I would really prefer not to do anything. But I have no choice.

What prompted you to start the Film-Makers' Cooperative and the Anthology Film Archives?
I got involved in screening what was known as experimental, avant-garde, independent film, only because nobody else was showing them. When I see something that I like, something that gives me great pleasure, sends me into ecstasies, I want to share it with others. I wanted to share those films with others and I had no choice but to start screenings myself. When I started, in 1953 there were some other organizations, like Cinema 16, who did not like the films I liked. For instance, with Stan Brakhage, Cinema 16 accepted some of his earlier works, but after 1957 they didn't want to distribute or show his films. So I had no choice but to start our own film distribution centre, the Film-Makers' Cooperative, from inescapable necessity. Then, in 1970, when we created Anthology Film Archives and we began looking for the best possible prints, we discovered that nobody knew where the originals were, or the originals had fallen to pieces, we had no choice but to go into film preservation. So we inaugurated a film preservation program in 1971.

Was that your reason for starting the Archives?
No. The reason was that we thought it would be great fun. "We'll just show films," we thought. But again you see, Anthology was not created for fun. It was created from inescapable desperate necessity. In 1960 in the US there were only about a dozen universities and colleges with film departments. In 1970 when the AFI brought out its first catalogue of universities and colleges with film departments and courses there were 1,200. In one decade it jumped that much and why? Because independent filmmakers kept travelling and pushing and showing their films across the country. Film education and film culture just grew. As the number of film departments increased, each of them wanted to show examples of various styles of filmmaking. Of course they mostly taught Hollywood film, but from necessity they also had to show one or two or three programs of avant-garde film. This was because the students demanded them and there was a need to expose them to something else. Most of them were not in San Francisco or New York. If you were in either of those places you could've seen those films and would know what to choose from and what to show. How did those who taught film in Arizona and New Mexico know what to show? Now in New York there was Jonas and there was P. Adams Sitney, so they would call me and they kept calling me saying "We have money for two or three programs, what could we show that would be okay? There are all kinds of filmmakers and we don't know where they are and we need your advice." So I prepared programs for them one time, ten times, twenty times and the same happened for P. Adams Sitney, he was in the same situation. So we said, "Enough! Why don't four or five of us get together, look at all of these films from the '40s, '50s, '60s, '70s and prepare a list and if anybody calls and asks for advice we will send them that list saying that any film on the list is okay. It may not be a masterpiece, but it has something that adds to the movement, to the style content wise and technique wise." So that is how Anthology Film Archives began. Five of us created a film selection commit-

Top: Ken Jacobs in Lost, Lost, Lost; *below:* Scenes From The Life Of Andy Warhol

tee because we agreed that one person should not decide. In other words, when we created Anthology, it was so that we could escape from all of those calls and repeating ourselves. The list was prepared and that became a guideline for the universities and colleges. The only thing is that that list, the Essential Cinema Collection, was supposed to be something in progress, a continuous process and evaluation of what's been done. But in 1973, Jerome Hill, who sponsored the collection and all the trips of the members of the committee, died. We continued for a while, but in 1975 we had to abort it, so nothing made after that date is included. Still it represents very well what was done until 1973/4.

Were most of the films generated in San Francisco and New York City?
No, we didn't stick to any location. It was international. We included early French avant-garde, the Germans and of course San Francisco and New York City.

Did you go looking for them or did people find you?
No. For some we made trips to Brussels and Paris and Switzerland to check some of the films that we could not get prints of here. Most of those made in the US we could get a hold of through the Film-Makers' Cooperative. There were some discoveries. For instance we only knew Dwinell Grant by name. Nobody had seen any of his work. They only knew that in the '40s he did something. When we located him and looked at his work, we discovered that he did very advanced work and we saved his work and brought it to the public. It became part of the repertory cinema and there were other such discoveries that nobody knew anything about.

So in those days the definition of avant-garde would be quite simply something that wasn't made in Hollywood because there was such a wide gap. How would you define avant-garde nowadays?
We did not go by any definition. The attitude was more that we had an interest in cinema and this is cinema. There is the usual narrative film, such as Hitchcock. Then there is a more complex narrative film such as *Citizen Kane*. But the films of Bresson are really more abstract and more intense and more condensed and therefore less popular. Bresson was never shown in the US across the country, only in some spots, in art theatres. Then you go one step further to, let's say Gregory Markopoulos' *Twice A Man*, which is already much more abstract than Bresson, therefore it's even more limited, but still a narrative. Then you can go still further and then you have Stan Brakhage's *Dog Star Man*. There is a protagonist, very abstract, going through life's struggle. It's an epic poem and epic poems are narratives, only the language is more condensed. Epic poem is not a lyrical poem. So there are these different varieties of narrative cinema. Still, a film is a film. The terms avant-garde, experimental, personal, they come and go but sometimes in conversation it helps to use these terms to indicate which area of cinema you are working in. When a young filmmaker comes to me and says, "I'm interested in cinema and I want to make films," I ask, "who are your favorite filmmakers?" "Godard, Bresson, Truffaut," they answer. I immediately know that this filmmaker's interested in the usual narrative art. Another comes to me and I ask the same question. "Maya Deren, Brakhage, Duchamp," they reply. Then you'll know into which area this person is going. That is into less commercial, non-industrial, more personal cinema, defined by the works of those filmmakers that are named. The different branches are defined less by the terms avant-garde etc., but more by the names, by the authors themselves and their works on this big tree called cinema.

You describe some films as poems, epic poems.
Yes and some are very little poems like the little films of Marie Menken, where there is maybe one moment, or a little teeny stream, barely visible, one motion. Maya Deren described it once in a famous conversation between Arthur Miller, Dylan Thomas and Amos Vogel. She was discussing horizontal and vertical cinema. But they sort of laughed, they

did not understand what she was talking about. They made fun of her actually. Horizontal is where there is a future, a past and a present and is more narrative. I think Godard said, "It doesn't have to be in that order". It could be mixed up as in Joyce. Then a little poem, like Marie Menken's, let's say, is vertical like a song. You sing. It mounts, another detail, another detail [Mekas demonstrates by raising his hand in increments higher and higher off the table], another note and then it ends. It reaches the point where it exhausts itself and that's it.

So it has its own organic end?
The films of Marie Menken are such and some of Maya Deren's films.

So the horizontal she was describing is not the difference between linear and lateral. It's more a combination of those and a saturation.
Yes, then there are combinations. Like Dovzhenko's *Earth*, it is a narrative, obviously, but it is like an epic poem. The story goes on and is sort of very literal and then suddenly it stops and there is a vertical moment when it is practically like a song. Those moments are throughout that director's films. There are moments that don't progress the narrative plot directly. But he does it indirectly. There are moments that have nothing to do with the story but they add something that then throws light and mood on the rest and how we perceive it.

In terms of your work, how do you think the power of words and the power of sound and image compare? Or do you consider them interrelated and without comparison?
Most of my films are diaries. I react to the situation and suddenly I have to film. I have to pick up some images from this situation. I have to react with my camera. Interact and react. Maybe I'll pick up one or two minutes or just a few seconds of film from that situation. These are then individual little songs and then I string them all together. Each one is complete in itself because the next day or next time I'll be somewhere else, in a completely different mood, different rhythm, which has nothing to do with what I filmed the other day. So one can look at them like a series of little poems, or songs as I go through life. I'm not interested in recording depressing or morbid subjects. I leave them to others. The songs are little celebrations and explosions of joy and reactions. If you look through *He Stands In A Desert Counting The Seconds Of His Life*, there are 150 such moments. All the structuring and editing is done during the shooting. It's all in camera because you cannot remember and re-create a situation in the editing room; you cannot re-create the feeling, the rhythms of the frames and lighting. You either get it during the filming or you don't.

So is your shooting ratio 1:1?
I make some corrections. It's like when you write a poem. You may take a comma out, you may have to correct a letter, or maybe even change one word.

So you accumulate all these parts?
Yes, over years and years and years. What I'm editing now is already 25 years old. I haven't touched practically any of the material in the last 25 years.

Do you shoot the intertitles at the time you film, or do you shoot them later?
No, later. I take notes of when and where I film. If I have no notes then I'll improvise. Last summer I started going through all my past footage.

What is the time bracket of the footage you're going to be using?
From 1973. Twenty and some years' material.

Sometimes you repeat the parts. There are some parts from *He Stands In A Desert Counting The Seconds Of His Life* that reappear in *Scenes From The Life Of Andy Warhol.*
Only when I make those portrait films. Then if there is material in other completed films that relates to that person I repeat it. Like I did with George Maciunas and Andy Warhol.

The manner in which you describe using your camera is as recording...
To me it's musical. To me it's like I'm playing jazz.

Where do you get that drive to record images?
I don't know. Obsession. I just have to do it.

This diarist method that you use predates and pre-empts the existence of video cameras. When they became available?
I have one. I do a lot of video work now also, especially when I travel, or carry too many things. I have done a lot of video during the last ten years, but I also keep using my Bolex.

Is the Bolex your favorite rig?
Yes. I would like to say that I'm a filmmaker but I don't make films. I don't go out and make films. I don't make films, I'm filming. I'm a filmer. I'm obsessed with filming not making films. I don't make films.

Do you shoot in reversal or negative?
Reversal only, so that I can look at it immediately. Also it's cheaper.

At what point do you decide you're going to assemble something or edit something together?
What I'm facing now is actually another case of that desperation, or an inescapable need to something. About a year ago when I was looking at some of my material I discovered that it is going. It is fading, shrinking. I really have a year or so to complete or use what I have so that it won't disappear. I cannot delay any more. I have to do it. That is why last summer I began working quite intensively and I have a lot of material. I discovered that I had many practically finished films from as far back as 1966 which I really have to finish. So I finished five films last year. I wanted to do one for every month but I failed because it just became too busy at Anthology,

What are those films called?
In 1966 I filmed Living Theatre production of *Frankenstein* in Cassis, France. That was 30 years ago. I did not release it then or finish it because I was unhappy with the results. Now when I looked at it I decided that there very little documentation from the '60s theatre. Also that this is a very important production and document and I should release it. So I finished it and the title now is *Memories Of Frankenstein*. It's my memory; it's not exactly what it was. Like *The Brig* was not exactly what it was, it was my reaction to it. In 1972, I filmed John Lennon's birthday. I have to check the exact date. Again, the material is fading, so I put that together with one of his last concerts that I filmed and this film is called *Happy Birthday To John Lennon*. Then I finished one that has to do with

the early years of my daughter Oona, when she was three or four years old. That's from 1974, '75, '76, '77 — *The Song Of Salamander*. It's a little film of 7 minutes. *Memories Of Frankenstein* is eighty minutes and *Happy Birthday To John Lennon* is 18 minutes. I went to Japan four times and every time I went there I filmed. So I put all that footage together and the title is *On My Way To Fujiyama I Saw* ... That's like 25 minutes. Then I finished another one called *Birth Of A Nation*. It's about 75 minutes. It's not printed yet because I ran out of money. I cannot take it to the lab. It is about 160 portraits of avant-garde independent filmmakers from all around the world between 1960 and now. Some are very short and some are longer.

When did you start shooting film?
Filming. When did I start filming? As soon as I came to New York from post-war Europe in late 1949. Practically the next week after I landed here I borrowed, rented a Bolex camera and began filming. That was in the Fall of 1949.

Was that something you always wanted to do?
Yes. Already in 1948/49 in Germany I became interested in cinema. I didn't know what I wanted to do, but I wanted to film. I was preparing myself for Hollywood or something. Then I discovered that what I was doing was collecting notes of real life. That early material appears in my film *Lost, Lost, Lost*.

When you came to the US was there a reason, or was it out of choice?
No, I was dropped here, I did not immigrate. During the war I was in a forced labour camp, then after the war I spent four years in a displaced person camp. The United Nations Refugee Organization helped displaced persons to find a new countries. Somebody in Chicago made arrangements for me and my brother to work in a bakery in Chicago. One day we received a notice from the refugee organization that the boat was leaving to go to Chicago. So we thought "Okay, what's the difference?" Before that we had signed up to work on a ship that cruised between Le Havre, France and Sydney. While we were waiting for that, this came up so "Okay, it makes no difference." So we came to New York where we had to pick up the train after coming by boat and go to Chicago. We looked at the skyline of New York and said. "We are in New York. We would be crazy to go to Chicago." So we didn't go. If we would have gone, we would probably be very good bakers now.

Instead you went to Williamsburg, Brooklyn?
Yes. We had a friend who had come half a year earlier and he had a little apartment with his family on Meserole Street in Williamsburg. That was the beginning of our life in New York. So we never went much further than that. So that I would say that I'm not an American, I'm a New Yorker and this is my new home. I don't know America and I'm not sure I even want to know it. I like New York and here I am and this is where my new home is.

Do you travel?
Oh yes, but not much.

Do you think that the emergence of a global culture through telecommunications provides a real possibility for equal voices to be heard?
I don't quite understand what is meant by equal voices. I'm not sure I'm interested in it. I'm only interested in people who are doing something with passion from real need. I don't

understand why people are so busy and always doing something. So I'm interested only in some individual people who are doing something that they really believe in. So, of course, they are not equals because, if they really believe in something, each one is something else. So all these people that interest me are very different. For all the different filmmakers or different musicians there is no equality. So I don't know what we're talking about. I don't understand the necessity to want to be equal at all. Do I really want my films being shown across the country like *Star Wars*? That would be idiotic. It's like this: when we created Film-Makers' Cooperative, some of the principles were that there should be no advertising. Every film should be listed equally and in alphabetical order, so as to not push one against the other. If anybody wants to see those films, they will firstly have to have a need and then they will come, they will find and they will search. Nobody told me to read Rimbaud etc. The time came when I found him. The same with avant-garde film, the cinema we believe in. If it's only seen by 1,000 people, then that's what it's for. It's for that 1,000 people not for one thousand million, because they need something else. They need cabbage and potato and this is neither potato nor cabbage. It's for a limited few. There are things that are for millions and there are things that are for a very few. The media is helping to spread some things that shouldn't be spread at all. There is bohemia in Paris, New York etc. That is usually a few dozen people. The artistic sensibilities there, their work, what they do, requires a completely different style of living and relationships. They lead a different life. This is then thrown on television; then someone in Texas and someone else somewhere else there responds, "Oh, un hun, drugs etc, this is the thing to do." But in reality these styles and practices are a question of survival for those few who need all that for their work. Whether they be jazz musicians or whatever. Suddenly, that style of life is adopted as a fashion by thousands and millions in various places and then we have drug problems and all kinds of real problems going on because they're trying to imitate the life that is really not their own style of life. They don't need it and then it becomes destructive. In any case, I have very strong opinions about media.

Do you think that film possesses magical properties?
I think that you get as much magic from anything as you put into it. Nothing that has never been touched by humans has any magic. They're just things. What is magic? Magic is a very complicated thing. Something that you put in, that you do yourself. There is a need. It's our needs that determine what we throw of ourselves into. Where we really jump and what affects us are very deep needs. Otherwise reality is very passive and innocent. So you ask about the magic of cinema. I don't think anybody knows why one paints or makes music. Greeks of course knew there are gods of music, of dance and you have no choice because they make you do it. There are the seven Muses. Those are the needs that we have and as humanity progresses some other subtle needs develop. Cinema came at a certain time and nobody can explain really why. There is no magic. It just came from some deep necessity in us as we grow and develop. Humanity is not a static thing. Evolution hasn't ended. Evolution is continuing. At every step some new thing comes in and not all of the arts came in at the same time.

Do you think the introduction of electronic visual records forebodes the end of cinema?
Definitely. The cinema now is a closed book. The new book is all the electronic media. People today who are five and ten and fifteen years old are not in cinema. The generation that today is thirty or so is still in cinema, but not those who are six and ten.

What do you think that it will be called when it is not cinema?
The new terms will develop. They will come.

Who in your life has been influential on you? Who are your muses?
Everybody. I'm one of those who cannot reduce favorite art to a favorite two or three painters, musicians or films. I like some for one period of my life and then one day I like Beethoven and I hate Mozart. Then I like Mozart. The next month I will hate Mozart and I will like Satie or John Cage. My taste is very wide, from folk music to post-John Cage. That applies to every art and they all influence me. They all give me pleasure, inspire me and give me ecstasy. They all change me slightly and therefore they all influence me slightly.

When you choose music for your films what happens?
When I was editing *Walden,* for instance, P. Adams Sitney says he used to come by the Chelsea Hotel and I had two TVs going, there was a portable radio and a record player too. I was listening to the radio and watching those images at the same time. And I kept recording, taping. I have hundreds and thousands of cassettes. Then, when I begin to edit I look and look and look at my footage. And I also have a tape recorder into which I speak at the same time. Sometimes I feel I should make some emphasis. Or I use music either to complicate or add another dimension, or to stress something for myself. I need that, more or less.

Haven't there been some changes here at the Archive recently?
Not changes: additions. There are two reasons. One is that the Essential Cinema collection is dying. We used to run the whole collection, that is 130 programs from beginning to end. This would take about two or three months. Now we've discovered that at least half of our prints are gone — faded or destroyed in the projection. Maybe more than half. To replace them is too costly, so our Essential Cinema programs are becoming fewer and fewer. So there are empty spaces in our schedule. At the same time we have money problems. When we bought this building it was in a shambles. We put one and a half million into renovation. We took $850,000 from the banks and we still owe the banks $375,000. On the first day of every month we have to pay $10,000 and this is what kills us. That's why we work with no salaries in order to pay the banks. Fabiano Canosa came and said that he could help us by doing some programming. We said, "Terrific!" Because this is the right time. We have space, we have the time and he knows certain areas of international cinema very well and knows the filmmakers. So he started his series. He made my life a little easier. I concentrate on the avant-garde and he concentrates on the international cinema. The avant-garde doesn't bring people and the international cinema that he programs brings people. So that helps financially, of course, not drastically, but it helps. On the other hand there is an irony here. From the beginning of the '60s, when we started the Film-Makers' Cooperative it was open for all. It's open to all, every filmmaker. Your card to the Co-op is your film. But Shirley Clarke, Emilio De Antonio and some other filmmakers had dreams to go to Hollywood, to reach many more people. They did not want to join the Co-op. They were looking for those mysterious distributors who would take their films and will eventually throw them across the country and they eventually, with those false dreams, destroyed themselves. But the Cooperative developed and grew. Later, these filmmakers, I mean, Shirley Clarke and others, they found out that in reality what they were making was still so different from what Hollywood and all the thousands of theatres are interested in, that they won't take their films. They were closer to us. It's a part of the New Cinema, so it's a different sensibility. Just look at *The Connection*. It's not Hollywood, it's still the Beat, the hippie, a different sensibility. So they failed. They came back to the Co-op 10 years later around 1970. Then a new generation, Sundance and all other independents came along and all the international independents. When we were in trouble, even when we bought this building and we desperately needed money and some of them had contacts, they ignored us completely. We stuck to it and did what we had to do. Now when they need

us and have no other place to go, they come to us and we say, "Okay, we'll help you. You didn't help us but we are nice, we'll help you. Here is a theatre for your films. We worked hard and we didn't sleep well. We worked every night wondering how we were going to pay those bills. We sweated, but here, we can help you." So we are helping other independents that are not avant-garde and really they don't even like avant-garde. Godard declared just a year ago in Paris that he hates the avant-garde. But, you see, we are not that type of people. We say, "We like all cinema," but they like only themselves and their own cinema. Each one for himself. We are here for the entire tree of cinema, for all of the branches and for all of them. I don't think they understand that. Still it's okay. Still we would like it if they would come and help us to pay those banks and free us. It's only $375,000.

Did you get this building in 1980?
We bought it in 1979.

It was an old courthouse. I remember you gave me a tour during the construction.
It was active until 1961, then closed. In 1967/68 for one year it was run by St. Mark's Church. They got a grant and had workshops here. In the basement here Jack Smith was developing his film *No President*. Right here in the basement.

---

1. Mekas notes in his diary on 11 November, 1959, "My realization that I was betrayed by the second version of *Shadows* was the last stone. It helped me realize that what I was talking about, what I really saw in the first version of Shadows, nobody else really saw: I was pursuing my own ideal, my own dream. They didn't know what they had: a blind man's improvisation which depended on chance accidents".

2. In 1963 Bruce Baillie founded The Canyon Cinema Cooperative in San Francisco. Modeled on the Film-Maker's Cooperative, the distribution catalogue contains many of the same films. Out of an original list proposed, only *Guns Of The Trees, Pull My Daisy* and the films of Gregory Markopoulos were included in the first Cooperative catalogue. *Shadows* and *Hallelujah The Hills* were distributed commercially.

3. During the shooting of *Guns Of The Trees* they were detained by the police numerous times on the grounds of being "beatniks". Also on the grounds of trespassing, spying and working without a permit.

4. The original committee at Anthology Film Archives to make choices for the Essential Cinema collection was: James Broughton, Ken Kelman, Peter Kubelka, Jonas Mekas and P. Adams Sitney.

5. *Film-Makers' Coop Catalogue.*

6. Director's notes.

Chapter Seven

Wholly Communion

1. 'A Few Poets Trying To Be Natural'

On Friday, 11 June, 1965 the International Poetry Incarnation transpired at the Royal Albert Hall, in London. The event was organized by John Esam, Dan and Jill Richter and the Poets' Cooperative, inspired — in part — by Allen Ginsberg's presence in London and his readings at the Institute of Contempory Art. The event began with Ginsberg chanting and playing finger cymbals, performing a Hindu mantra,[1] which was described, in a review published the following day by *The Times* newspaper, as a "heavily amplified incomprehensible song to the accompaniment of a bell-like instrument". Alexander Trocchi compèred the evening, which consisted of four hours' worth of readings and performances by Allen Ginsberg, Gregory Corso, Lawrence Ferlinghetti, Harry Fainlight, Adrian Mitchell, Michael Horovitz, Ernst Jandl, Christopher Logue, John Esam, Pete Brown, Anselm Hollo, George Macbeth, Simon Vinkenoog, Paulo Leonni, Daniel Richter, Spike Hawkins and Tom McGrath, as well as the playing of tapes of and by, William Burroughs. Poets who, although radically different in style, "showed their hatred of the narrow mind and heart and joined in celebration of God-as-total-consciousness".[3] Despite being organized in a matter of days, a press conference announcing the event the previous week guaranteed an estimated audience of 7,000 inside the venue, who had been invited to: "Come in fancy dress"; "Come with flowers," and "Come!". Many more were turned away at the door and, according to the press coverage the next day in *The Guardian*, those unable to enter were "clamoring to get in", with the event being described by many as the "biggest poetry-reading meeting in the English-speaking world".

Further, the event was viewed as the inaugural moment of the mass counterculture of the '60s; as Jeff Nuttall observed in *Bomb Culture*, the event was marked by a "frisson for us all to savor as there had been at the first Aldermaston and the Underground was suddenly there on the surface, in open ground with a following of thousands… […] 'London is in flames. The spirit of William Blake walks on the water of Thames. Sigma has exploded into a giant rose. Come and drink the dew.'".[4] While — according to Barry Miles' biography, *Ginsberg* — both the underground newspaper the *International Times* and the Arts Lab[5] "traced their origins to the Albert Hall event".[6]

Peter Whitehead filmed the events at the Albert Hall which would come to make up his film *Wholly Communion* on an NPR Eclair 16mm camera, borrowed from Louis Wolfers. One of the first 'silent' cameras available, the Eclair enabled Whitehead to shoot with the minimum amount of disturbance. However, while Whitehead was shooting the Eclair kept jamming, thus necessitating the hurried change of film, emptying and reloading the magazine, all on a camera with which Whitehead was unfamiliar. Fortuitously Whitehead told Wolfers that the event would be of interest and a curious Wolfers arrived midway through in order to watch the poets. When Wolfers saw the problems that Whitehead was having with the camera he helped in the 'un-jamming' and threading of the magazine, thus enabling the film to be changed more rapidly.

I don't want that sort of filth here. Would you send your teenage daughter to hear this sort of thing?
Comment reportedly made by the manager of the Royal Albert Hall.

Wholly Communion opens with images of a statue, behind which fast-moving clouds part to reveal bright sunlight. On the soundtrack is an edit of words and phrases about the 'sun' taken from various poets' performances. This cuts to a view of the outside of the Albert Hall, which is accompanied by Allen Ginsberg's incantation. As the chant progresses the film cuts to the interior of the ven-

International Poetry Incarnation

England! awake! awake! awake!
Jerusalem thy Sister calls!

And now the time returns again:
Our souls exult, & London's towers
Receive the Lamb of God to dwell
In England's green & pleasant bowers.

World declaration hot peace shower! Earth's grass is free! Cosmic poetry Visitation accidentally happening carnally! Spontaneous planet-chant Carnival! Mental Cosmonaut poet epiphany, immaculate supranational Poesy insemination!

Skullbody love-congress Annunciation,duende concordium, effendi tovarisch Illumination, Now! Sigmatic New Departures Residu of Better Books & Moving Times in obscenely New Directions! Soul revolution City Lights Olympian lamb-blast! Castalia centrum new consciousness hungry generation Movement roundhouse 42 beat apocalypse energy-triumph!

You are not alone!

Miraculous assumption! O Sacred Heart invisible insurrection! Albion! awake! awake! awake! O shameless bandwagon! Self evident for real naked come the Words! Global synthesis habitual for this Eternity! Nobody's Crazy Immortals Forever!

Spontaneous invocation which emerged from the collected poets at the Albert Memorial Press Conference one week before the International Poetry Incarnation at the Albert Hall, London.[2]

ue, with a brief edit of the assembled poets; finally the film cuts to Ginsberg, sitting on the low-level stage, singing and playing his miniature finger cymbals. The film then cuts to a series of brief extracts from performances by several of the poets: Ferlinghetti stands to read 'To Fuck Is To Love Again'; this is followed by Horovitz who reads 'For Modern Man'. Gregory Corso sits to read 'Mutation Of The Spirit'. Following Corso's introverted performance, the film cuts to Fainlight, reading his poem written while on LSD, 'The Spider'. This is interrupted by shouting from the audience and the camera spins around, zooming in to and across, the collected rows of seats, trying to find the source of the disturbance. At the end of Fainlight's reading Trocchi climbs on the stage and the microphone worn around Harry's neck picks up their brief altercation, as Trocchi tells Fainlight "You are not reading any more..." To a combination of shouts and cheers Fainlight asks to read another piece, to which Trocchi replies "Ladies and Gentlemen, hold on, hold on, this evening is an experiment and we're finding out what happens when you put five thousand people in a hall with a few poets trying to act naturally..." Fainlight is allowed to read a second poem: 'Larksong'. Mitchell reads his Vietnam poem 'To Whom It May Concern' and his two line 'Stunted Sonnet'. Logue reads his 'Chorus (After Sophocles)' and Trocchi reads from his novel *Cain's Book*. Following this Jandl performs his sound poem 'Schmerz Durch Reibung' and — aided by Horovitz and Pete Brown — 'Ode Auf N'. Finally Ginsberg — appearing to be drunk — takes the stage and reads a translation of Voznesensky's poem 'The Three Cornered Pear/America', ostensibly to Voznesensky who appears sitting in the audience. This is followed by a reading of his own poems 'The Change' and 'Who Be Kind To'. As the film ends and the titles roll, Ginsberg's voice is heard requesting the time and then declaring that he has "lost his poetry book".

The film owes at least part of its existence and style to the methods of cinema vérité and its American counterpart, direct cinema.[7] Like these modes of film production, *Wholly Communion* was made possible by technological advances which allowed for a single figure operating lightweight equipment, rather than demanding the complexities of an entire production crew. *Wholly Communion* also bears a superficial resemblance to the philosophy of the vérité tradition, which sought to "catch events while they are happening, rather than to question events that have happened in the past".[8] *Wholly Communion*, in part, attempts merely to present the events and alongside its aesthetic hand-held camera style, which incorporates zooms and sudden pans across performers or audience, signifies the vérité tradition.[9]

However, direct cinema, by definition, demands that the filmmaker assume a role of invisibility, the film must maintain a "stance of narrationless neutrality",[10] for the filmmaker to 'comment' or 'interpret' means the film can no longer said to be conveying 'truth'. Furthermore, the belief that specific technologies allow the filmmaker to avoid intention implies that such cinema can produce works which are eternally self-present, films which are totally unmediated, which conspire to a "metaphysics of presence and logocentrism".[11] Jacques Derrida has variously used the terms of differance, dissemination etc. to describe the endless deferral of self-presence manifested through all technologies of inscription (film, writing, etc.). Film can never create presence; the ontology of production technologies is such that they can only ever circumnavigate total immersion in an experience other than that of the film's production and its position as a product, yet it attempts to re-create the experience of 'being there' via the processes of cinematic technique. Such a cinema constructs a verisimilitude which fails to recognize the contradictions behind trying to create a direct vision. This cinema also fails to recognize that there is no single, homogenous 'truth of experience', the text is not hermetically deciphered but rather each viewer will maintain a different interpretation.

While Whitehead was able to use the lightweight equipment necessary to produce a vérité film, *Wholly Communion* never actually emerges as a 'pure' vérité text, despite the director's interest in the methods and technologies of vérité film production. Primarily this is because Whitehead — rather than attempting the impossible, the invisibility of the filmmaker — actively engages within his own interpretations of the poets and the relationship between performance, reading, writing and film. Thus Gregory Corso's introverted poem is shot from between two audience members who can be seen (although not heard) talking throughout the performance; furthermore, rather than maintain the shot which establishes Corso's status/role as an introverted outsider, the camera closes in on Corso's face, catching each twitch and nuance as he reads and thus making the poem even more personal. Jandl's sound poems are shot with an almost careless abandon, as the camera swings around, zooming in and out, mirroring the apparent chaos of the poems. This is further emphasized by a shot of the glaring lights during Jandl's piece, their burning intensity finding an aural parallel in the noises of the poems. Mitchell's condemnation of Vietnam is shot almost entirely from the front, in a medium close-up, the camera hardly moving. The sharp white of his suit contrasting with the inky blackness of the background forms a harsh chiaroscuro, emphasizing the bitterness of his

Ginsberg reading at the Royal Albert Hall

poem. Noticeably in the few, brief shots of the audience during Mitchell's reading, they are seen as silent and still, transfixed by and on, his performance. In contrast to Mitchell's reading, Fainlight's performance is filmed so as to emphasize his smallness, with the audience clearly visible before him and — as soon as shouts emerge from the audience — Fainlight's vulnerability is illustrated with a cut-away to a still photograph depicting the entire, crowded Albert Hall.

Wholly Communion must therefore be viewed as actively constructing images and interpretations. Each poet is presented in a contrasting style, further emphasizing the constructed nature of the film. Such a construction implies an active filmmaker, who seeks to master representation rather than 'merely catch the moment'. The film thus engages with the discourses of cinema vérité, but actively manipulates what is apparently random into an interpreted whole, Peter Whitehead has stated; "I'd like to think that with *Wholly Communion*, I tried to achieve a balance between the extent to which I disappear in the corner and just film what is going on and yet, nevertheless, you are aware of the creative eye of the director and so on".

Further, at 33 minutes, the length of the film precludes the presentation of entire poems for the most part and rather, presents extracts. This act of 'choice' once again reveals the active manipulation of the director. Whitehead also published a book to accompany the film. This contained not just an essay on the nature of the film's production, but also the full transcripts of the poems which were performed at the event. Together, the book and film both act as texts produced from — and through — the evening's events and can function independently, or together. Thus *Wholly Communion* (the film, the book) cannot be contained within superficial borders as either a book, or a film, but rather exists within a complex series of interconnections which emerged from the larger metatexts which circulate around the evening's events. *Wholly Communion* may be read as fulfilling the superficial function of the 'documentation' of an event of subcultural importance, but, it also serves as an attempt to explore the concept of documentary cinema as pertaining to an ontology of 'truth' or 'realism'. In place of this emphasis on the 'truth' *Wholly Communion* can be viewed as an attempt by Whitehead to add his signature to the event: "Any pretensions I had as cameraman about the objectivity of film, have, since making this movie, also been abandoned. Anyone seeing the film who thinks that at last they have seen the 'truth' about what DID happen, are deluded. They have seen the film that also 'happened' that night at the Albert Hall".[12]

2. An Interview With Peter Whitehead

How did you become involved in the event, were you invited to come in and film the event, or was it more a case of 'sneaking in' with a camera?
No, no. You want the whole story do you?

Yeah.
Okay, yeah. What had happened was that I already knew the poetry of these guys because I started to get *Evergreen Review* in '63, '64 something like that, I started getting *Evergreen Review* from America and that had Corso and Ferlinghetti and all these people in and then I heard that Ginsberg was coming to London. So I got very excited about it and wanted to take some photographs and went to see him in Better Books.[13] He gave a poetry reading in Better Books which was — I think — about two weeks before the actual event. [I] went down there and at that point I was just part of the audience, but I mean there was only about twenty people there, you know, Ginsberg was there, Bob Cobbing. Bob Cobbing ran Better Books, he was the British answer to Ernst Jandl, he was the sound poet and he was a pretty strong force in getting the thing going. He had the poetry reading in Better Books, I went along and said "can I take still photographs?" and he said "fine, yeah, no problem" and I stayed around talking afterwards. I met a guy called John Esam and it was at this event that they started talking about renting the Albert Hall, which sounded — of course — totally crazy at that moment. And I just sort of got dragged along with it, I said, "Well listen, Christ Almighty! if you are going to rent the Albert Hall..." and they said "yes, we're going to get Voznesensky in from Russia and..." I said, "You know, I'd like to film it." There was a girl called Barbara Rubin[14] there, who also said she was going to film it. They said "well, it looks as though Barbara's going to film it". So I said "Okay, well, you know, I'd like to film it if there is a possibility." Barbara was one of these people who got a Bolex and stuck one film in it, then reversed it, then stuck the film back in, then reversed it, then stuck the film back in and so finally it came out looking like minestrone soup. I think they ... at some point they cottoned on that it would be more fun to record it than allow Barbara to do her number. I was working as a newsreel cameraman then and had made a couple of documentaries — science documentaries — but they didn't really know me from Adam. And I said "Listen, I'd like to film it." And they said, "Well, what does it amount to?" and I said "Nothing. I'll just come, I've got an NPR silent camera, I'll just come and sit in the corner with everybody and film and se e what happens." They said "what about the sound?" I said "Not a problem, I'll just put a Nagra there." They said "Well okay, all right, it all sounds all right." Then I got in touch with Shaffer and they gave me £90 to buy the film, 45 minutes' worth of film.

Who were the people who gave you the money?
Friends of mine from Cambridge, you know Peter Shaffer, the playwright? Peter's brother: Brian Shaffer and his wife Elinor, they gave me the money. I went and bought five rolls of film — or — four rolls of film, about eleven minutes each. Of course not knowing what was going to happen, I just went along with a Nargra on one shoulder and a camera over the other. I just went in the backstage door and said "I'll be filming" and that was it. And I just recorded the event from crawling around — as you can see from the film — amongst the poets.

Did Barbara Rubin film it at all?
I don't know. I don't think she did. I haven't spoken to her since. But I don't know if you are interested in the story of the soundtrack, are you?

Yes.

[Laughs.] What happened was I stuck my Nagra out in the corner with the microphone out, on automatic record and I didn't even have it synced because I had this silent camera. I was walking around filming it. Anyway I got all these great images, processed them all, then transferred the sound, thinking, of course, [that] it would be perfectly decent — or decent enough — and there was almost no sound at all. I don't know what it was on the automatic thing [but it] had only picked up the audience, or something or other ... So I had no soundtrack. Nothing. I showed it to the guys at the Academy Cinema who wanted to see it and I said "it would be wonderful...". There was a soundtrack but it was so badly recorded that by the time you cranked it up, it sounded awful. So I virtually had no film at all and I was really pissed off by the whole thing. And then John Esam said "Well I just listened to the whole thing at the BBC yesterday." And I said, "what do you mean the BBC?" and he said "Well, we sold the rights to the BBC for a program. A radio program." I said "Where were they recording?" He said "They were up in the box and they recorded everything through the neck mics ... they've got an absolutely perfect recording". Well anyway we nicked a copy of the recordings and I transferred them all over. I then had to sync it all up, I had the job of cutting the image and cutting the sound and syncing every single word, but I had a perfect soundtrack, so in the end I married the soundtrack to the image. Otherwise there would have been no *Wholly Communion*.

How long did that take?

It certainly took a week, yeah, because you know, on an old Acmade editing machine, backwards and forwards clipping bits out. You can see in a couple of bits where it is not completely in sync, none of it was shot in sync you see, so I had to sync it all up and add bits of background sound. But it is part of the feeling of the film. What you feel, I think, from the film is that you are there. It is part of the whole crazy event.

One thing that I found interesting is that you have each poet performing — ostensibly — one poem, but they performed for longer than that?

Oh yeah. But I only had 45 minutes of film. I knew it was going on [for] three hours.

So what made you choose to film each one for a minute, rather than film Corso and Ginsberg in total or something. That was just the way you felt or...

God knows. But if you actually hear anybody talking about the event they will say that the great moments were this, this, this and this. And I got them all. Luck, or intuition? But, you see, when you film something and capture it you have to start filming beforehand. How on earth I did it I don't know. But — yeah — at some point I decided to do 'so much of so and so'. I think I waited each time to see if I liked the poem, I liked Ferlinghetti, [he] stood up and said, "To fuck is to love again" and everyone just howled and all the guys in the aisles ran off to phone the police. So, of course I started to film, but then — I think — on Ferlinghetti, the magazine jammed. There were lots of considerations. But when you think I had only 45 minutes and that was cut down finally to the finished film of 35 minutes, you'll realize I used every single inch that was usable. Somewhere there is actually six or seven minutes more of the Ginsberg [footage]. I have got the whole of the Ginsberg. I was keeping most of the film for Ginsberg, to be honest. Yeah, I kept on saying, "I must keep one roll for Ginsberg," because my primary interest had been Ginsberg. I had to edit it while I was going along, it was not like I could go along and shoot six hours of film and edit it afterwards, I was actually editing intuitively as I went along. Harry Fainlight, I suppose, did pretty well, because it became obviously such a dramatic moment and I then filmed a second poem which he read

Corso reading at the Royal Albert Hall

which was 'Larksong', but of course Harry is now dead so it is total history, it really is very valuable, probably the only film of Harry ever made, I don't know.

Why did the person from the audience just jump up and start shouting?
What happens is: Simon Vinkenoog is one of the poets who is meant to read, but didn't from what I can remember, he was totally stoned on mescaline. Now in the middle of Harry Fainlight's poem, which is called 'The Spider' and is an account of an LSD trip, Harry was waxing lyrical in the middle of re-creating his LSD trip and suddenly this howl came from somewhere — we didn't know where — someone was shouting. I didn't even know what the sound was, finally I figured it out it was 'love' that he was shouting: "Looovvve! Looovvve!" you see. He's shouting 'love', but number one, he is Dutch; number two, he's on mescaline. And this interrupts Harry's poem and of course he finds it then very difficult to get started again. Harry turns around and accuses Simon, who was a friend, you know, "You're a lovable idiot," you know, "Fucking hell! I want to carry on with the poem." But then the audience start to barrack and everything. I don't know why, quite. Half of them were saying, "Get on

with it. Read the poem," and others were shouting, "Enough! Enough!" Harry was reading the longest and most difficult poem, then insisted on finishing it — which was fair enough. But then, having had — I suppose — all this drama go on, he refused to sit down and wanted to read another poem and that was when Alex Trocchi was trying pull him down, saying, "Come on Harry, you have read enough — there is a lot of other people". But he was getting nasty about it and everybody then said, "Let him read! Let him read!" So he was allowed to read another poem, but even after that one he wanted to read another one.

On the film it looks as if he wants to explain it...

Yes, he wanted to explain it. And you don't explain poetry. You read poetry, you don't have to explain it. But poor Harry, he was on a trip too. Imagine a young guy who has never read poetry to more than six people in his life suddenly — this English guy who has always been in love with Allen Ginsberg and the Beat poets — suddenly he is part of this scene and there are seven thousand people in the Albert Hall all jumping up and down screaming at you. You want to grab as much time as you can, you can't blame the poor guy.

Ginsberg seems really wasted during that as well, rolling on the floor and pulling Harry when he gets off of the stage.

By the time he got going he was completely drunk. I have it on tape somewhere — I have some other bits and pieces where you hear him ... In fact when he first stands up he says [drunken voice], "Now I've got to circumnavigate all this lousy poetry". That's his first words. And by then he was pretty fed up, I think he was wrong because it was a great event, but then he got up and he livened up a bit. The first poem he read was the Voznesensky poem. I presume you know that Voznesensky wasn't allowed to read.

Why wasn't he allowed to read?

His embassy wouldn't let him read. He had come along to read the poem, but the Russian embassy said, "No". So what Ginsberg did then was read one of his poems for him/to him, which was very nice. And he read one of the poems that Voznesensky had written in New York at the press conference, about a press conference, so it was the American reaction to him, then him [to] the American ... I thought it was one of the best moments in the film. It was the very first thing he reads. Then he reads a poem of his own which is called 'The Change' — the long poem. But he was completely drunk at this stage, I think we were lucky to get him at all.

Why was he unhappy with the event?

Well, you know, when you look at my film which is 35 minutes, it is out of three and a half hours, I think, there was a load of rubbish which I didn't film. I decided not to film it. And again, maybe I'm being a bit pretentious to say it's a load of rubbish but there were a lot of English poets which I didn't think much of ... I filmed a weenie bit of Horovitz, a weenie bit of Christopher Logue and there was several other people who read I don't know anymore, I can't remember. But — I think — by the time Ginsberg got up to read we had had two and a half hours...

It was all getting a bit much then...

Yeah and for the audience it was great but for Ginsberg who was waiting to read, who knew all the poets and had heard them read before and the ones he hadn't heard were English poets he did not care tuppence for, I suppose he was just sitting there drinking, thinking, "When the hell am I going to get up and do it?". You were talking about Barbara Rubin, there is one shot in the film of Ginsberg lying down flat on his back and being sort of cradled by some female, that is Barbara Rubin, so she obviously didn't do any filming.

The vérité style of the film, was that a conscious decision to film it like that, or was it just the frantic-ness of having one camera and running around and trying to do everything?
It is all those things. I had at that time seen a couple of films from America, that were the original cinema vérité films. I had been fascinated by them. They were shot with a silent camera in a situation that was completely happening, okay? I was interested in that because I was working as an independent newsreel cameraman for Italian television in London. Now what happened was they never knew quite what they wanted, some guy would arrive and say, "The prime minister is doing this, can we film it?" I used to be working all the time with these independent producers who had no idea whatsoever of what they wanted and I would end up, of course, practically making films almost every day of my life. I'd just suddenly go off and I soon learned to make it in a certain style which is basically one camera and the zoom. You arrive in a situation and they'd say, "Well, listen, we want to establish London," and I'd say, "Well, how about a Parliament Square?" And they'd say, "Oh, great". You'd start on Big Ben, you'd pan down to the pigeons, whisk over to a Japanese tourist with a camera, you'd pan over to a London bus with the word London on it and bang! you've introduced the whole film. And I used to do this once or twice a week, this is how I would make money. And this is how I managed to get a camera and my own editing machine. And then, when I arrived there [the Albert Hall], part of the deal, if you like, [with the] poets was that I said, "I'll be invisible, I'll just be there with the camera on my shoulder, which is silent and I will not intrude" and all my films since then I have tried to maintain that. At least, I like to be — in a way — in the corner and nobody knows I am there.

In *Charlie Is My Darling*, which I made with the Rolling Stones, Joe de Moraes said it was the first road movie ever made, it certainly was in England. The first road movie made here. That is why Andrew Oldham[15] said I could do it, because he knew I could film in that particular style: completely out of the way, I'd sit in the corner with the camera, no extra lights, just a guy with the sound, a little rifle microphone. It was so new then, it was so exciting. We are so used to it now; it was so incredible. People didn't believe you could do it, they didn't believe you could film without lights; they didn't believe you could film without a tripod; they didn't believe you could film with a silent camera. The silent camera had only just been invented, I was using the first NPR Eclair camera in England when I made *Wholly Communion*. So the answer is the style, I was conscious of what I was doing, because I'd seen a couple of American films, the Maysles brothers![16] I thought they were fantastic, they were so exciting, because you really were in with the action and that is what I wanted to do and that is what I did with *Wholly Communion*.

And they went on to film the Rolling Stones, of course, the Stones at Altamont.[17]
That's right, they did that. In the meantime I had done *Charlie Is My Darling*, which was some time before the Bob Dylan one in England which is supposed to be the first one.[18] *Charlie Is My Darling* has not been recognized of course because it has never been released, it got stuck up with the Allen Klein, Andrew Oldham, Rolling Stones saga. But so ... yeah ... and of course when I was in the Albert Hall I had no choice but to film in that kind of a way. But I think it was the perfect situation for it. Why I quite like the film is the style changes with each of the poets: Corso is in there and it goes right in close between the two heads and it is so introverted. Then of course Ginsberg is mad and extroverted and there is the girl dancing, then of course there is the Ernst Jandl sound poetry. All kinds of chaos.

And the camera moves around him....

Yeah. I think this is why the film was recognized. It did very well at the time, because I think it was a film of an event that people wanted to see, but people did also think it was a new kind of film.

Okay, what about the question of your use of a vérité style and vérité ideas, where you are just observing, at what point then when you are editing do you choose what to edit, because that obviously implies a conscious decision?

Have you got the book of the thing? I published a book, I wrote at the time a one-page introduction about my involvement with it and I talk about that very thing as to what is objective and what is subjective and so on. I published the book because I had cut the poems. I published the book because I thought it was fair to the poets to publish the whole poem at least. But then of course I did make the point that I was making the decision of intruding, although I was trying to be non-intrusive, I was intruding. But the only real reason for that is that I only had 45 minutes of film. I only arrived with four rolls of film, so I had to edit.

Yeah, but you still had to edit out certain bits, I was just wondering what way...

Most of the stuff I edited out of the 45 minutes was out of focus, or falling over, or looking for something, or trying to find where the poet had gone to, because Allen Ginsberg pushed me over at one point for getting in his way. I suddenly thought, "What's happen[ing]?", he was yanking me down saying, "Get out of the fucking way. Bloody photographers!" or something similar. So there was not much I didn't use, I used everything that was remotely usable.

There are a couple of points also where you go to still photography...

Well once again I had to. I had to. I had to bring in a few stills. And I froze an image of course, on the Voznesensky. That is very important.

You cut to him in the audience.

The point is Ginsberg said, "Voznesensky, I'm reading his poem," and I thought, "Well shit! Yes," and I had swung over and by a miracle it landed on Voznesensky who was near me, but then I'd cut back to Ginsberg, so it was so quick, that when I came to edit the film I thought, "Well, you know, I need more of Voznesensky". So then I froze the image. So this is where all the devices, all the devices in it are necessary really to convey the meaning of what is going on.

What about the beginning of the film, because you mentioned a minute ago about the Italian television and the film's beginning is almost the same as that, when you open on the outside...

Yeah. On all the poets, a dead ringer. I had to, I went up and thought, "The Albert Hall. I've got to do a shot of the outside of the Albert Hall." Oh yeah, one of the reasons is they had a press conference there. The press conference had triggered it all off, that's why they had a big audience, the press conference was shown on the news, that's why 7,000 people turned up. They announced the International Peace Incarnation Poetry Incarnation Peace William Blake the whole thing and they had it on the steps of the Albert memorial. Now, I wasn't invited to that, which shows that I really wasn't considered to be part of it. From the moment that I left Better Books to the moment I arrived on the night to do it, I had no other contact with anybody. In fact I think I only rang two days before and said, "Is Barbara Rubin doing it?" And they said, "No" and I said, "Well listen I'd like to do it," and they rang me back and said, "Yeah". Anyway I heard the thing was on the

Ginsberg reading at the Royal Albert Hall

Albert Hall memorial — I shot it afterwards of course — obviously. And also I wanted a little bit more to introduce it with the mantra and when I went up to film the Albert Hall from the Albert memorial — of course there was all those figures of these poets, on the Albert Memorial, all the English poets — Donne, Shelley — all their little faces. So I just thought it was the obvious thing to do: just pan over from the Albert memorial with all the old poets, swinging over to the Albert Hall with all the new, modern Beat poets, whatever you want to call them.

And the lines about the sun?

And then — that was again — on the editing table, while doing it, I noticed that three different poets, the three Ginsberg, Corso and Ferlinghetti, all used the almost identical phrase, they each of them say: "sun, sun, sun" — three times ... and I thought, "Well perfect, start with the light which was outside, the white-stone faces of the poets, pan over then go into that darkness", because the whole aspect and ambience of the movie is the darkness isn't it? This dome, this womb. I chose to call it *Wholly Communion*. That was my title, not the name of the event. It was inside the womb, the church, it was this sort of religious experience. Then there was this incredible white light in some of their poems and I shot that somewhere else, that wasn't the Albert Memorial it was Hyde Park Corner, with this Greek charioteer, bringing the sun, whatever, the light fading in and out. And then of course right at the end of the film it fades into darkness and you hear Ginsberg saying on the soundtrack, "How am I going to finish this?" then you hear him saying...

"I've lost my poetry book".

And that is when the film has faded right down into darkness. So, start with the light, end with the dark. Outside, going inside, yeah, you know what I mean? These are just little devices that you do instinctively at the time, when you are putting it together.

I thought the end, ending on that line, "I've lost my poetry book" because it is like a move from poetry as literature, to poetry as performance and then, finally, poetry as film, you know?
Correct. And the fact that it was also in the book, because — in fact — the very last poem he read at the event was 'Who Be Kind To' and that was a very nice poem, I don't think there is any of that in the film because we only had parts of 'The Change'. That ('Who Be Kind To') was written in his notebook, one of his semi-diary notebook poems that I think he had written the night before. So when he said he lost his poetry book, it really was his diary in which he had written the night before a poem for the event and that ended the event. So that is why I thought that was a lovely line to end on. I think also I was touched by that, because Ginsberg was trapped in this drunken mess and then he went out (because he is very inward-looking a lot of the time), then suddenly he gets out and does this amazing extroverted thing, really projecting it out and the girl dances. And I know that feeling, because I am a bit of an introvert, but given the chance I get very extroverted, but afterwards I feel, Bang! Like I have been sucked out. Like I have been raped; you actually feel as if you have been stolen. And I feel sure that, when he came down and couldn't find his book and said, "I've lost my poetry book", I'm sure — my feeling was — this public event, reading poetry to people rather than publishing a book, must be for the poet — and certainly for Fainlight — had been a rape. Definitely been sucked out of themselves, when the poets become objects rather than subjects and I felt that Ginsberg's plaintive cry was not so much for the lost book but for the lost part of Ginsberg that had been sucked out in the previous hour. Which it is, he really gave a lot of himself, especially in a poem that was [in] a notebook.

There is another moment in the film, a really short flash, where — during Ginsberg's piece, with the woman dancing — where the film goes into negative, I just wondered why the film goes into negative?
There are two bits there, where — when I was editing it — I did decide to intrude, if you like. Did you notice there is one bit where it goes into darkness and out again? Well of course a lot of people think that is a mistake, you know. But it is very deliberate. I think — at the time — it was a bit out of focus, or I fell over or something again, or moved at some point ... then I noticed that what he was saying at that particular moment. He was talking about the spirit leaving the body, then he says; "Come back sweet spirit", or something like this, "To your only place".[19] So I thought that was very nice, going to darkness and then in fact — when he calls it back to the body — going to light again. There was an image of absence. That was all. Just this moment of absence, where the moment had entered into the spiritual plain. That moment I felt I could put in total darkness. And just after, I thought that was so brilliant and clever [laughs], that I ought to do something else as well ... No, what I think it was, I had — after all — shot a film about poets reading poetry and I was aware afterwards looking at it that it was all in slightly different styles in relationship to the different poets and it was my duty presumably in making the film to try to make the film, or the style of the film, meeting the subject half way — without being pretentious — how could I make the film slightly poetic? Which is probably why I did the bit in the beginning with the poets' faces and the dissolves and the light shining on ... you know, I just wanted to decorate it a bit. A bit of the roccoco [laughs]. So that's why I found the darkness was a nice touch, because at that point you suddenly become aware of the film. I wanted to remind people just at that moment — near the end of the movie — that, nevertheless, it was a film. Because actually from the minute it starts you are sucked into it, you don't really very often ... you're not thrown back into that Brechtian awareness of the film.

And that is reiterated by Ginsberg saying, "I've lost my poetry book".
And then it's ... yes. It's tied up at the very end. I felt quite happy with it in the end, in the sense that although it had been largely entirely subjective — and I had just been sitting there with my camera — when I came to edit it and put it together, I was able to, you know, put a little bit of my own stamp on it and make something out of it. There is no such thing as an objective film of course. No way. At least I was admitting to a few little poetic pretentions, which I just popped in here and there.

Which is of course exactly what they were doing; Beat poems are, in part, about 'real' life, but it is a single, self-centred view of 'real' life that is possible because it is from your own perspective.
I went on to make a film called *The Fall*, which is a two-hour film about the collapse of the protest movement in America, where I divided the film up into three parts. The first part of the film is the camera and the second part is the editing machine. The first part is image, the second part is word and the third part is where the soundtrack and the image and the word and the image come together. It is in fact editing machine plus ... I then — this was a couple of years later, 1968 when I made this — and I was very conscious by that stage of where you intrude into the concept of 'truth' or 'reality'. And you do so at every move, at every bloody move: from the camera, which way you point it, why you're there, what you're doing ... *The Fall* is totally about [that]. Although it is about the collapse of the protest movement in America and the occupation of Columbia University, it is very much about the question of: am I telling the truth?

Film is a voyeuristic medium, especially if you are sitting at the back of halls, or dressing rooms, or whatever — just watching everybody else.
Yes. You are the voyeur. And *The Fall* is totally about this whole question of being a voyeur or not. In fact I put myself in it and I have myself in it and I film myself being in it. Obviously the other side of the coin from being the voyeur is to be Narcissus and I even confront the question of my own narcissism. So I then put myself in the film and I actually talk, finally, to the camera, but the only point at which I am prepared to talk directly to the camera is where I am in a situation which I consider to be where the inner and the outer is equal, which is when I'm inside Columbia [University].[20]

One thing which is interesting is that watching *Wholly Communion* now — obviously it has become history — but was there a sense at the time of imminence, because if you research the period of the event, many people credit it as an influence; the Arts Lab, the *International Times*...
It did it [encouraged the birth of the counterculture]. It was the moment when a bunch of isolated people ... or the beginning of a little network was growing — people here, people here — becoming conscious of themselves in a certain kind of way, copying Beat ... you know, American painting certainly, American poetry ... various different people were doing things and suddenly overnight you were not just part of some lunatic fringe: 7,000 people turned up and supposedly 2,000 were turned away. Suddenly it wasn't just that it was a public event and 7,000 people came, it made everybody realize that there was far more people out there interested in what was going on than one had thought. It gave impetus and confidence to people, you could be cynical about it and say you know, you publish your little book of poems and you expect to sell fifty copies and you are very happy, then the next minute you hear 7,000 people have turned up and I suppose they

all started to think, "God! Wow! I'm going to sell 5,000 copies of my book of poems next week" [laughs]. You know, suddenly it became commercial.

You actually felt that at that time, that evening?
No, not in the evening, but in the course of time afterwards. Well, I don't know, for me I was landed with a film, I didn't have time to think about anything. I suddenly got this film and no soundtrack and I had to raise money ... I mean for the next two months of my life it was just a question of, you know, one had given birth to this bloody thing, it was keeping it alive. Suddenly it was dying because I had no soundtrack, then I got a soundtrack, then I had to get the money, then George Hoellering at the Academy [Cinema] wanted to show it, it had to be blown up to 35mm, then I had to get the money, then the NFFC were prepared to put up the money, but they wanted signatures from all the poets. I had to get signatures from all the poets and they didn't believe it possible, they laughed themselves silly...

Hadn't they all left the country by then?
Yeah! I had to go to Paris to get Corso, I had to write to Ginsberg in somewhere else ... I think I forged a few of them, because it was the National Film Finance Corporation who agreed to put up £1,000 to blow it up to 35mm.

But it was originally shot in 16mm. Where did you first show it?
The first showing was at the Mannheim Film Festival and it won the gold medal. I went to Mannheim, basically, with *Charlie Is My Darling*.

That was made at the same time?
Well, June, then in August I made *Charlie Is My Darling,* [so] I think the festival was in October or something. I arrived in Mannheim financed by the Rolling Stones, by Andrew Oldham, because I persuaded them that having made *Charlie Is My Darling* that because it was 'arty', an art movie, that it would be good to show it in a festival. Andrew was still sort of flexing his muscles a bit about the Stones, he wasn't sure if they should be making movies at all! So I arrived in Mannheim fully paid for my fare and hotel and everything, ringing up Andrew Oldham everyday saying, "Yeah, I think it's going to be all right, I think it's going to be okay". Then [laughs] *Wholly Communion* won the gold medal and *Charlie Is My Darling* didn't win anything. So I came creeping back and I had to ring up and say, "Well, I'm ever so sorry, but they liked *Charlie* a bit — not too much". People didn't like *Charlie Is My Darling* because they liked to think of the Rolling Stones as all dressed up in smart suits, earning a lot of money and driving around in Rolls Royces. I showed them to be very ordinary people who happened to be very good musicians, on the verge of something really interesting happening. But *Wholly Communion* was the film that won the prize, it's ironic, I was actually disappointed that *Wholly Communion* won because I found myself in an awkward position with the Stones' thing. But when I got back I realized it was good to have won the prize. Then it was shown at the Academy.

That was in Oxford Street?
Yeah. But I will tell you another story that's amusing. Okay, it won the gold medal at Mannheim, which is the first prize, right, so they then ring me up and say can they show it on German television? And I said, "Yeah, but how, do you want to do a German soundtrack...?" "No! No! It has won the gold medal we've rung up Channel One on German television, we've told them all about this film and they are prepared to show it next Monday night, there's a slot at eight o'clock on Channel One and they'll show it exactly as it is, the Gold Medal Win-

Harry Fainlight and Alexander Trocchi

ner at Mannheim." I said, "Well, that sounds very good," and they said, "£800" — which was almost paying the entire cost of a potential blow-up at this time. And they showed it on prime-time German TV, in English, with 'To fuck is to love again' and all this kind of stuff ... on German television. So of course I thought ... So I sent it to the BBC. Or at least I got Contemporary Films, who were distributing it at this time — the NFFC were only prepared to give me money if I had a distributor — and George Hoellering set up Charlie Cooper at Contemporary [Films], they were all a bit of a fucking cult ... not a cult, what's the word?

Clique?

Worse than that ... a cartel. Anyway, Charlie Cooper said, "Well okay, I'll send it to the BBC," and I said, "Well, if German TV is prepared to show it..." And we got a curt little letter back from the BBC — some guy had looked at it — saying: "Dear Mr. Cooper, Thank you very much for showing me *Wholly Communion*, the film of the International Poetry Reading. In my opinion it is the worst film I have ever seen in my life. Thank you." And it still has not been shown to this day on British television.

In England it was just shown at cinemas — independent cinemas....

I don't think it was ever shown after the Academy actually. I think it was shown with *Fists In The Pocket* by Belochio in a double bill, I think it was shown a couple of times later by Hoellering. I think it was shown in various universities and things like that, Charlie Cooper sent it around. But there wasn't really any other kind of distribution; there weren't any art cinemas, apart from London, in those days.

---

1. Allen Ginsberg had recently been in India and was returning to America, via Europe.

2. Various, 'International Poetry Incarnation', in Peter Whitehead, ed, *Wholly Communion*, Lorrimer Films Limited, 1965, p.9. Reproduced with the kind permission of Peter Whitehead & Lorrimer Films.

3. Alexis Lykiard, 'Introduction', in *Wholly Communion*, p.7.

4. Jeff Nuttall, *Bomb Culture*, p.193. Note sigma is a reference to Alexander Trocchi's *Project Sigma*, a proposed coalition between counterculture artists and thinkers in a synthesis of art and politics. Trocchi had become involved with the Situationist International while living in exile in Paris in the '50s and early '60s and much of *Project Sigma* was based on ideas originating with the Situationists, notably Trocchi's *Sigma: A Tactical Blue Print* and *The Invisible Insurrection Of A Million Minds*.

5. The Arts Lab (aka The Arts Laboratory) was started in 1966 by Jim Haynes. Located in London's Covent Garden, it was a multimedia designated space at which various events — including readings, performances, film screenings and happenings — transpired. Within months other similarly experimental spaces were running in other towns and cities.

6. Barry Miles, *Ginsberg: A Biography*, Viking, London, 1990, p.372.

7. The two terms indicate the minor cultural and philosophical differences between the filmmakers involved in the 'movement/s'. While some filmmakers (such as Edgar Morin) preferred the title cinema vérité, others (such as Mario Ruspoli) preferred the term 'direct cinema'.

8. Richard Meran Barsam, *Nonfiction Film: A Critical History*, George Allen & Unwin Ltd, London, 1974, p.249.

9. Whitehead's next film, *Charlie Is My Darling*, the documentary of the Rolling Stones' tour of Ireland when the band were on the verge of success, similarly engaged with cinema vérité, while his subsequent films — *Tonite Lets All Make Love In London* (1967) and *The Fall* (1969) — explore different strands of documentary filmmaking. Notably, however, Whitehead repeatedly engages with explorations of the complex network of relationships which exist between the filmmaker/subject/audience.

10. Michael Renov, 'Towards A Poetics Of Documentary', in Michael Renov, ed, *Theorizing Documentary*, AFI/Routledge, New York/London, 1993, p.201.

11. Jacques Derrida, *Of Grammatology*, John Hopkins' University Press, Baltimore and London, 1976 (1967), p.23.

12. Peter Whitehead, 'Notes On The Filming', in *Wholly Communion*, p.10.

13. Better Books, in London's Charing Cross Road, was owned by Tony Godwin. According to Jeff Nuttall's book *Bomb Culture*, the shop had "a wild mod decor and a succession of influential managers, Bill Butler, Miles, Bob Cobbing..." (p.192).

14. Barbara Rubin produced various underground films including *Cocks And Cunts* (1966) and *Christman On Earth* (1963), a two-reel, simultaneous projection designed so that the two images would be superimposed on top of each other. Shot in black and white, the film could also be projected through various coloured gels. Rubin was also responsible for organizing "what organization there was to the [original Park Avenue South located Filmmaker's] Co-op" and wanted "a brave, new, licentious world of film showings with freedom" (Joan Adler, 'On Location' in Stephen Dwoskin, *Film Is* ... The International Free Cinema, Peter Owen, London, 1975, p.15). Rubin was also responsible for introducing Andy Warhol to the Velvet Underground and collaborated with the Warhol Factory regulars on the production of various films. According to Allen Ginsberg, Rubin "dedicated her life to introducing geniuses to each other in the hope that they would collaborate to make great art that would change the world" (Ginsberg, quoted in Victor Bockris & Gerard Malanga, *Up-Tight: The Velvet Underground Story*, Omnibus Press, London, 1983).

15. Andrew Loog Oldham was the Rolling Stones' first manager.

16. The Maysles brothers (David and Albert) made several vérité films, including *Showman* (1963), *With Love From Truman: A Visit With Truman Capote* (1966) and *Salesman* (1969).

17. The Maysles' film of the Rolling Stones performance at the Altamont freeway was made in collaboration with Charlotte Zwerin. Entitled *Gimmie Shelter* (1970), the film focuses on the legendary 'death of the '60s' free concert at which Meredith Hunter was killed. This question was asked by Jack Hunter who was also present at the interview.

18. *Don't Look Back* (1966), by D.A. Pennebaker, which documents the 1965 Bob Dylan tour of England.

19. The actual line is: "Come, sweet lonely Spirit, back/to your bodies, come great God/back to your only image..." Allen Ginsberg, 'The Change', Kyoto-Tokyo Express, 18 July, 1963.

20. Focusing both on the occupation of New York's Columbia University by protesting students and on Whitehead's own role as a filmmaker in a foreign land, *The Fall* (1968) emphasises Whitehead's deconstruction of the documentary, with its emphasis on a quasi-Godard style self-reflexivity. The film repeatedly examines its own function and construction as a text which depicts events.

Chapter Eight

Hallucinations & Homecomings: Notes On Conrad Rooks' *Chappaqua*

Conrad Rooks was born on 15 December, 1934, in Kansas City, Missouri, the son of the president of the Avon cosmetics company. According to Rooks' biography his family were pioneers who landed and settled in Virginia in 1622, under a land grant issued by Charles II, before migrating westwards. During this journey west, the family often lived with the Native Americans and "it is from this deep root that Rooks has drawn his inspiration and love for America and the Indian".[1] As a child, Rooks was a regular at his local cinemas and later explained "Babysitters were hard to find during the war years, so my mother used to leave me in one of the three local cinemas for the afternoon. Sometimes I went to all three in a day. I saw all the Hollywood films of the early Forties. All the Bogarts, everything. And that sort of forced film culture stayed with me, so that from then on I always thought in terms of a story being told by the association of images".[2]

Rooks spent two years in the US Marines (1953–55), before travelling to New York in order to study television and film production. Two and a half years in television school taught Rooks various filmmaking skills, but when he left he was unable to find work. Finding himself unemployed, Rooks decided to form his own company and, with a friend, co-founded Exploit Films, a production company whose films were aimed at the increasingly popular 'nudie films' market. The company produced three films, which Rooks would remember as "just teases. Nothing sexy about them except the titles — *White Slavers, Girls Incorporated*, things like that".[3] Exploit Films ended abruptly when Rooks' partner vanished, taking with him both "the money and the girls", as Rooks would later comment. During this period Conrad Rooks would hang out in Greenwich Village where he met Harry Smith[4] and, according to legend, taught the young Andy Warhol how to load film into a camera.

> **There is a hiatus between blocks of association, rents as it were in the fabric of reality through which we glimpse the old myths that were here before the white man came, and will be after he is gone, a brief inglorious actor washed off the stage in the waters of silence. Rooks has brought to the screen the immediate experience of silent beauty conveyed in the Peyote vision — older Gods waiting impassively at the end of the line.**
> William Burroughs,
> *Chappaqua Press Book*

Rooks began to experiment with alcohol while in his teens and later with drugs, to which he became addicted. As a result of his father's sudden death in 1962 Conrad was "shocked into realizing the futility of an existence dependent on alcohol and drugs".[5] Rooks undertook a thirty-day sleep cure at a clinic in Zurich, Switzerland, in order to free himself from his addictions. The experiences of this cure informed the 'narrative' of his film *Chappaqua*, while the possibility of relapsing into drug addiction created an urgency which motivated Rooks' desire to produce the film, partly in order to avoid a possible regression. *Chappaqua* was financed, primarily, with Rooks' inheritance and money borrowed from his family and friends and the final budget was estimated at $450,000.

Chappaqua was 'written' (the film was largely 'improvised'; the 'writing' consisted of the final interpretation of the footage in the process of editing), produced and directed by Conrad Rooks over a three-year period; filming commenced in January 1964 and was completed in April 1966. The original conception for the film was based on a poem by Rooks called 'Chappaqua'. This poem focused on the process of maturing, the sadness surrounding the death of a loved one and leaving home. The title, 'Chappaqua', refers to the geographical community in upstate New York, where Rooks lived from the age of nine and — as stated in the film's narrative — Chappaqua also means "the sacred place of running water". Chappaqua was "where all the tribes came to bury their dead, the Indians are all gone, vanished. They are dead. But they did dance there." The title thus has multiple meanings that refer to both the town Chappaqua and also to the concepts of death and transition articulated in the Native American tradition. In many ways the film can also be read as an autobiographical poem concerning Rooks' own experiences.

Robert Frank became the director of photography, having been introduced to Rooks through Harry Smith. Frank's expertise as a cinematographer renowned for the creation of personal and improvised films enabled him to engage with the improvised nature of *Chappaqua*; "Frank realized that Rooks worked out of panic: panic contrived to realize the flow from his psyche which must give birth to the drama ... it was this innate fear which gave Rooks the power to create".[6] Conrad would film when he was inspired, sometimes shooting for 24 hours non-stop and travelling around the world to shoot sequences that only appear for a few minutes in the finished film (the locations included: France, Mexico, India, Ceylon and England, as well as 48 American states). Frank was also able to work with Rooks despite Rooks' notorious temperament, even though he was temporarily sacked from the production at one point, when Rooks "hired some character he met in a bar who didn't know his ass from a light meter".[7]

Rooks had become acquainted with William Burroughs via a correspondence, which began in 1960, one year before they met. Initially Rooks had wanted to produce a film of *Naked Lunch* and he purchased the film rights in 1963; however, the project proved impossible and was consequently abandoned. Nonetheless Rooks recognized Burroughs' potential as an actor and when he was producing *Chappaqua*, Rooks cast Burroughs as the personification of heroin addiction: Opium Jones. Burroughs also influenced Rooks' understanding of the film, making Rooks aware of the "new film language based on lines of association"[8] which occurred during the production of the film. Through Burroughs, Rooks met Ian Sommerville who worked on the film soundtrack, "charting 50 tracks of sound and corresponding these with the fixed image".[9]

The French actor Jean-Louis Barrault portrayed Doctor Benoit, having been introduced to Rooks in January 1965 by Eugene Shuftan, who was working as a consultant on the production. Barrault was initially unsure of committing himself to the production due to his schedule and commitments to the Theatre de France l'Odeon. However, Barrault shared Rooks' interest in improvisation, spontaneity and 'exorcism'. Barrault had shared an apartment with Antonin Artaud in the '30s and subsequently was familiar with Artaud's conception of a Theatre of Cruelty; as a consequence of this friendship, "when Rooks mentioned Peyote, Mexico and pyramids, Barrault grasped immediately the general direction of the film."[10] Due to their mutual interests Rooks was able to persuaded Barrault to appear in the film, telling him that he would only be required to commit himself to four days' work.

While shooting in Ceylon, Rooks met Swami Satchidananda — a disciple of Siva Ananda, the founder of the Divine Life Society — and became a devotee. The Swami appears in *Chappaqua* and is credited as the Guru. The composer Ravi Shankar, whom Rooks had befriended in 1959, appears in the film as the Sun God and also scored the film. Allen Ginsberg and Peter Orlovsky both make brief cameo appearances in the film, with Ginsberg credited as portraying the Messiah. Rooks cast the model Paula Pritchett, in her first acting role, as the Water Woman, while various other 'celebrities' appear in the film including Moondog, Ornette Coleman and Lower East Side anarchist band The Fugs (whose line up included the Beat poets and underground publishers Ed Sanders and Tuli Kupferberg). Finally Rooks played the lead role in *Chappaqua* as the junkie, alcoholic Russel Harwick, a thinly veiled autobiographical role.

The film opens with a diary text, describing the plight of the central protagonist Russell Harwick:

"I began this diary as a record of my experiences while suffering from alcoholism. I began drinking when I was 14 moderately at first on vacation from school amongst friends. By 15 I was suffering from delirium tremens (alcoholic fits). At 19 I found marijuana, hashish, cocaine or heroin kept me off alcohol. For a limited time my pattern became a nightmarish maze of shifting addiction — alcohol, then drugs. Finally I was introduced to hallucinogenic peyote, psilocybin and LSD 25. Under the influence of peyote I had a vision. I tried to forget it, returning to drink, but the memory haunted me..."

The film opens with Harwick indulging in a final night of alcoholic and narcotic debauchery in a New York nightclub. The following morning, while running past the reservoir in Central Park, Harwick sees Allen Ginsberg (The Messiah) and Peter Orlovsky chanting ("Hari Om...") and playing finger cymbals. Harwick sits down and briefly joins the two men in their mantra, before running off to catch a taxi for the airport. Harwick flies to France, where he has booked himself into a sanatorium, located within a chateau on the outskirts of Paris. On the way to the chateau, in the chauffeur-driven car, Harwick sits next to a wizened, cigarette-smoking, malevolent figure: Opium Jones.

As he is driven into the grounds of the chateau he is watched by two figures, one on each balcony. The first is Dr. Benoit; the second is the sinister figure of Opium Jones. In the sanatorium Benoit informs Harwick that he will undergo a progressive withdrawal from his addictions. As Benoit helps Harwick into his room the figure of Opium Jones appears. Harwick is questioned by Opium Jones on the history of his addiction; while describing his habit he collapses, screaming hysterically and begging for a fix. Opium Jones states: "No incoming calls" and shoots up Harwick, who hallucinates an apparition/figure, who is racing around the room on rollerskates.

During the withdrawal program Harwick makes numerous attempts to escape, but these become mere tableaux, during which he dances with his pursuers, or hides behind trees. When not trying to escape (if he really is), he describes his life and the nature of his addictions to Dr. Benoit. These moments of descriptive clarity are punctuated by flashbacks of Harwick's life, in *Chappaqua* and as a biker hanging out in New York. During his detoxification Harwick hallucinates wildly, seeing images from 'religious' rituals, including gatherings in India, a guru meditating and a druid at Stonehenge. Other hallucinations include Harwick shooting Burroughs and a midget in a Saint Valentine's Day Massacre pastiche, Harwick dressed as Opium Jones in an abattoir, memories/fantasies of a beautiful woman (including a sequence in which she 'finds' peyote) and a demonic figure running through the sanatorium.

At the film's close, a detoxified Harwick leaves the sanatorium, watched by Opium Jones who, tossing aside his cigarette in disgust, mutters; "an unworthy vessel obviously. I withdraw from the case". Harwick climbs into a helicopter and takes off from the chateau's grounds, he plays on a flute and shouts his farewells; "I'll see you in Chappaqua". He sees a figure, wearing a hospital gown, dancing on a balcony and points at it and laughs. The figure on the balcony is also Harwick. As the helicopter circles the building the mad, dancing figure climbs onto the roof of one of the château's spires and waves farewell.

Chappaqua primarily focuses on heroin and alcohol addiction; it repeatedly alludes to peyote and suggests that Harwick sought help because of a vision he had while taking peyote. In one sequence Harwick lies in bed and tells Dr. Benoit that "Peyote — all of this reason for me to come here, to this clinic, started with peyote. I — in the drug world, la monde de la drug — I came across a friend who had this peyote ... You eat it because you get high, euphoric and I ate this ... I ate a great amount of this. I had this fantastic vision ... [the film begins to illustrate this vision, with images of Aztec pyramids, a woman, sunlight and a deer, then cuts back to Harwick in bed talking to Dr. Benoit] ...here, inside [Harwick taps his forehead] I see a circle of yellow, a door of gold like an illumination. All the sound, everything outside of me stops. Then I went interior, inside. And in this vision it was like a tunnel, a long tunnel and I went through ... through this tunnel". As Harwick speaks the film depicts the sun rising, intercut with images of Ravi Shankar playing. The scene cuts back to the sanatorium and Benoit speaks; "This description of your vision is, for me, very exciting. But my grandfather was Descartes and I am built with logic". The Doctor thus draws attention to the primary difference constructed by the text's 'narrative': the difference between Eastern and Western cultures and philosophies. This sequence directly links the phantasmagoric trance induced by peyote with spiritual illumination, the narrative states that it was the taking of peyote that motivated Harwick, enabling him to understand he had to give up heroin and alcohol and this provided Harwick's initial motivation for his 'spiritual quest'.

The film maintains an ambiguity in its hallucinatory mise-en-scène and visual phantasmagoria and suggests that different drugs could have different effects. Burroughs has stated "the consciousness-expanding drugs act to increase awareness and the state of increased awareness can be a permanent acquisition. It is unfortunate that cannabis, which is certainly one of the safest of the hallucinogenic drugs, should be subject to the heaviest legal sanctions. Unquestionably, this drug is very useful for the artist, activating trains of associations that would otherwise be inaccessible ... Opiates, on the other hand ... have the effect of diminishing awareness of surroundings and bodily processes".[11]

Chappaqua is shot to emphasize the hallucinatory nature of Harwick's withdrawal and this emphasis on the hallucinatory in the text simultaneously emphasizes the 'expansion of consciousness' associated with 'spiritual enlightenment'. Harwick is not merely giving up an addiction to the debasing effects of alcohol and drugs, he is simultaneously undergoing a 'spiritual awakening', which owes its original impetus to the stimulating peyote vision. This is emphasized via a hallucinatory scene in which a 'demonic' figure runs through the hospital and appears to drown in a pool, while a beautiful woman appears and floats in the pool; as the vision ends Harwick apparently wakes under a translucent film and gasps for breath, as if he had been drowning or suffocating, but, crucially, he has survived, while the demonic figure appears to have been exorcised. As the *Chappaqua Press Book* makes clear, one central thematic of the film is the "transformation of the main character thru ritual magic and exorcism of the Evil Spirit" and Dr. Benoit is thus a character who is "the modern witch doctor, [a] psychoanalyst ... seeking to exorcise O-kee-pa the Evil Spirit — the black demon with spots in the film".[12] Addiction is thus constructed as the result of, or symbolized by, demonic possession. Addiction is shown to be, at least in part, the result of a lack of spirituality in Western materialist culture, "in order to sustain his creed contemporary man pays the price in a remarkable lack of introspection. He is blind to the fact that, with all his rationality and efficiency, he is possessed by 'powers' that are beyond his control, his gods and demons have not disappeared at all, they have merely got new names".[13] In William Burroughs' account of the film's themes he describes the character Russel Harwick as being "Western civilization poisoned by its own drugs and by a surfeit of images".[14] To counter the negative aspects of Western society, not only does Harwick cure his addiction, he also has visions of an Eastern spiritual guru, in the form of Swami Satchidananda. The Swami is seen meditating in Harwick's visions and in a later scene appears to be blessing Harwick.

Stylistically *Chappaqua* is a combination of colour, sepia and black and white images. The film is frequently characterized by multiple images. For example, footage depicting Harwick in the countryside/wilderness is superimposed with the bright lights of Times Square, or images of Ravi Shankar that are combined with footage of the rising sun. During the film's opening, which illustrates Harwick's drug 'freak out' and subsequent fleeing of the demonic nature of his addiction through New York, the image becomes optically manipulated, bleached into stark chiaroscuro. This combination of styles does not appear to have the traditionally ascribed black and white/colour breakdown which serves to delineate an opposition between reality/fantasy, rather the combination seems to have been constructed at random and thus draws attention to its manufactured state as both a film and as physical celluloid. This serves to continually throw the film's audience into a state of confusion and demand that they ask themselves at what point the film's verisimilitude is constructed. It also mirrors the loss of a 'coherence' of 'identity' experienced by Harwick in the face of his addiction. The deconstruction of the traditional binarism between colour film and black and white also serves to emphasize the constructed nature of 'reality' and to suggest that fantasy, rather than being the other of 'reality', is merely a different species of 'reality'.

The overall structure of the film appears to be randomly assembled, with the simple linear narrative framework (Harwick as junkie/Harwick enters the sanatorium to clean up/Harwick leaves) acting as a framework on which to explore and articulate other themes and concerns; Harwick's history, spirituality, fantasy, sexuality, hallucinations, etc. William Burroughs observes that the "selection of material is dictated by the logic of association ... a scene organically belongs just there. Rooks has created a new language, a language of juxtaposition, the scenes find their own position. [...] The film may be said to consist of material found rather than contrived".[15] This emphasis on the footage being 'found' and the autobiographical nature of the film, is further emphasized by *Chappaqua*'s narrative progression and shooting, which — in many ways — mirrored Rooks' personal growth; thus, for example, Swami Satchidananda becomes the Guru in the film, yet he only met Rooks once the film was already in production. The Swami thus appears within the film because — as Rooks has become a devotee — so it becomes important that Harwick too recognizes the value of a more spiritual existence. By utilizing Ravi Shankar in the narrative Rooks is also referring to his own 'spiritual journey'. When Rooks first met Shankar in 1959, Rooks was a drug addict and alcoholic; however Shankar told Rooks to express himself in film and stated that he would one day score a film by Rooks. Shankar assisted Rooks in his thirst for 'spiritual illumination' when, in January 1966, while shooting footage in India, Ravi Shankar took Rooks to the Kumbh Mehla, at Allahabad. Here they bathed in the Holy Ganges with nine million Hindus and Rooks decided to follow a traditional Indian way of life.

This emphasis on the production of the film as processive and on the protagonist's personal development as mirroring Rooks' own, enables the text to resist an interpretation as either 'fiction' or 'realism', but rather as both simultaneously. Indeed, as Rooks commented on the film's completion, "I guess it's true to say that *Chappaqua* just about wiped me out financially. But keeping the money would have killed me too. Making the film was the best therapy in the world for me. I'm completely through with drugs and I've not taken a drink in ten years. Therapeutically speaking you could say it was pretty successful. In other ways, though, I've been murdered by the industry".[16] The film thus emerged as a form of therapy through which Rooks was able to escape his drug addiction. The idea of film as a form of therapy also emerges within the 'narrative' of *Chappaqua*, when, at several points within the mise-en-scène, the film's crew emerge from the shadows, thus suggesting that the film represents an ongoing discourse of therapeutic articulation for Rooks. During the start of one scene a voice can be heard to say "roll it", before the camera spins across the room clearly shooting the assembled technicians, lights, etc. and the film crew can be seen in various other sequences within the film. Rooks is making a film, at least in part, for therapeutic purposes, hence the film crew are clearly present within Harwick's room in the chateau. During these moments of distanciation the audience is also jolted into an awareness of the film's constructed status, once again blurring the lines between 'reality' and 'fantasy' and drawing attention to the film's ongoing 'autobiographical' status: Rooks is both living and simultaneously experiencing his own life again, as Harwick. It is not surprising that Rooks would later state: "Making films has become an addiction for me, just as powerful as anything I've ever known. I'll do whatever is necessary to make them. The obstacles don't matter".[17]

When Conrad Rooks screened *Chappaqua* at the 1966 Venice Film Festival, it was awarded the Silver Lion. Following this initial success at the film festival, Universal acquired the distribution rights for the film, having assured Rooks that it would be promoted; however they "left it unshown on a shelf".[18] Rooks subsequently had to invest time and money to regain control of the film, with some estimates suggesting that he had to pay nearly as much as the original production costs in order to regain the rights to the film. This meant that, despite its obvious interest to a 'counterculture' audience, the film was never adequately distributed. This situation was worse in Britain, due to a blanket ban on films which, the censors argued, could 'encourage' drug use. *Chappaqua* was not released until 1968 and, even then, was only certified after John Trevelyan, the head of the BBFC (British Board of Film Classification), had obtained psychiatric advice to back up Rooks' claim that the film was an accurate portrayal of the results of drug use and the effects of withdrawal. *Chappaqua* became the first 'drug' film to gain a certificate following this ban and the text occupies an ambiguous middle ground between underground films and exploitation movies such as Roger Corman's *The Trip* (1967) and Arthur Dreifuss' *The Love-Ins* (1967), both of which were also banned[19]. *Chappaqua*'s ambiguous position is due partly to Rooks' complex relationship to the underground; employing Frank to shoot the film and casting 'underground' figures to appear in it, yet simultaneously enjoying the luxury of a (relatively) large budget and attempting distribution through a commercial corporation. Notably, Rooks' early experience in film was in the production of exploitation films and his relationship with the underground was fraught; for example, he was condemned by various underground critics such as Parker Tyler, who stated that the film lacked "true ideas and a true filmic imagination".[20] The problematic nature of Rooks' relationship with the 'counterculture' is further apparent in the film's narrative, which — while not condemning drugs — attempts to articulate a perspective against drug use, yet continually emphasizes the narcotic nature of cinema via the use of optical effects. This suggests that *Chappaqua*'s visual pleasure is in its presentation of 'psychedelic' effects and Tyler compares it to *The Trip*, suggesting that both films luxuriate in hallucinatory ephemera and invest in the illusionary while simultaneously recognizing the real as its other. Yet to read *Chappaqua* as an exploitation movie, fails to recognize the autobiographical nature of the text, much of which is articulated via the mise-en-scène, which far exceeds the aesthetic of the exploitation movie. Neither an underground film nor an exploitation movie, *Chappaqua* demands to be read as a personal film and as such it retains all of the different influences and traits of Rooks himself.

1.*Chappaqua* Press Book, author and publication details unknown.

2. Conrad Rooks cited in Conrad Rooks, *Siddhartha*, author and publication details unknown. Following *Chappaqua*, Rooks commenced work on a production of Hermann Hesse's *Siddhartha*. After four years' work the film was eventually completed in 1972. Following the completion of *Siddhartha*, Rooks travelled the world with his family, eventually settling in Thailand.

3. Conrad Rooks quoted in Philip Oakes, 'Rooks' Move', *Sunday Times*, 30 May, 1971.

4. Harry Smith was briefly employed to work on *Chappaqua* by Conrad Rooks and, according to Bill Breeze's 'In Memoriam, Harry Smith' (in Paola Igliori, ed, *American Magus: Harry Smith A Modern Alchemist*, Inanout Press, New York, 1996) Smith accompanied Rooks to Oklahoma in order to begin work on the film. However Harry Smith vanished on their arrival in Oklahoma, only to arrive hours later, with a group of Kiowa tribes people and "bushels of peyote" (p.9). When Rooks left, Smith elected to remain with the Kiowa. Note, however, that the use of superimposition in *Chappaqua* is clearly influenced by Smith's own superimpositional work, as manifested in *No.14 Late Superimpositions* (1964), which includes images of the Kiowa.

5. *Chappaqua Press Book.*

6. *Chappaqua Press Book*

7. Ted Morgan, *Literary Outlaw: The Life And Times Of William S. Burroughs*, Henry Holt and Company, New York, 1988, p413.

8. *Chappaqua Press Book.*

9. *Chappaqua Press Book.*

10. *Chappaqua Press Book.*

11. William Burroughs and Daniel Odier, *The Job, John Calder*, London, 1984 (1969), p133.

12. *Chappaqua Press Book.*

13. *Chappaqua Press Book.*

14. William Burroughs, untitled, in *Chappaqua Press Book.*

15. 'Untitled'.

16. Conrad Rooks quoted in 'Rooks' Move'.

17. Conrad Rooks quoted in 'Rooks' Move'.

18. Conrad Rooks, *Siddhartha.*

19. Steven Puchalski observes that *Chappaqua* "was the first full-blown entry into the Trip Sweepstakes" ('A History Of Hallucinogens In The Cinema', in *Slimetime: A Guide To Sleazy, Mindless, Movie Entertainment*, Critical Vision, Stockport, 1996, p188.). The trip movie was ostensibly a '60s 'sub-genre' that emerged from the psychedelic subculture and blossomed in exploitation movies such as *Hallucination Generation* (1967), *Blonde On A Bum Trip* (1968) and *Psych-Out* (1968) and eventually reached its commercial zenith in the success of the major studio production *Easy Rider* (1969), from Terry Southern's screenplay.

20. Parker Tyler, *Underground Film: A Critical History*, DaCapo Press, New York, 1995, (1969), p66.

Chapter Nine

An Interview With Allen Ginsberg

How do you perceive the relationship between the Beats and underground film?
There was a literary and artistic Beat Generation and there was an alliance, certainly between Robert Frank and Kerouac, as Kerouac wrote the preface to the American edition of *The Americans* — the book of photos. He [Frank] preferred Kerouac above the offered introduction of Walter Evans, which would have been quite honorific, but he wanted something more akin to his own spirit and he chose Kerouac. That was a conscious decision on his part. In fact, oddly enough, on my desk I have a photo of Robert Frank that I took. We taught together later, many years later, in 1984 and we still work together. He may do a video for me, for a rock and roll song I have [done] called 'The Ballad Of The Skeletons'. He may do an MTV music video for that. He has just done one for Patti Smith.[1] It's a song I wrote and performed at the Albert Hall last November with Paul McCartney, he's on the Mercury Records CD also, playing with me.

But anyway, many of the poets in New York, including Corso and Orlovsky and myself and some of the painters like Al Leslie and Larry Rivers and the painter Alice Neal — who is an old bohemian also — all participated in the film *Pull My Daisy*. So I don't know how you could separate Beat or underground there to the extent that that was one of the first improvised underground films. Then, as far as Jack Smith's films ... the first publisher of Burroughs' *Naked Lunch*, Irving Rosenthal, who was his editor at *Big Table Magazine*, which was condemned by the police following the episode of censorship of *Chicago Review* of which Rosenthal was editor ... Rosenthal then became editor of *Naked Lunch*, working at Grove Press and edited the American version and did a very beautiful job[2]. He wrote a book called *Sheeper*, which deals with Jack Smith, Herbert Hunke (who just died, by the way), William Burroughs and myself and many others and also was one of the chief actors, poseurs — so to speak — in the tableau vivant of *Flaming Creatures* — he's the bearded one — short, bearded fellow. I don't know if you would call him a Beat prose writer or not, but he certainly was involved with the production of one of the singular works of the Beat Generation.

Yeah.
And, of course we all knew each other. I think Jonas Mekas with the underground film felt that the entire business, in the inception at any rate, was between *Flaming Creatures, The Flower Thief* — from San Francisco...

Yeah
...was all under the general stereotyped category of Beat, yes, I suppose.

I always felt that *Flaming Creatures* was more camp...
Oh, it is.

I was wondering if camp can really be said to be Beat...
Well I don't know. First of all — as Burroughs once commented on the nature of art, whether it is social or solipsistic, "'Tis too starved an argument for my sword" — in the words of the Immortal Bard.[3] What kind of distinction is that? If Irving Rosenthal works with Jack Smith and if Jack Smith is a friend of mine does that mean that camp is not Beat, or Beat is not camp, that there is some fence between them?

I guess...
Are you proposing a chain link fence or something [between them]? Besides which there is plenty of camp in Burroughs and there is a bit of camp in Kerouac's *Mexico City Blues* poems

Ginsberg and Burroughs outside the Naropa Institute from The Life And Times of Allen Ginsberg

that are dedicated as camp to Gore Vidal. Everybody involved here, from Jack Smith to Irving Rosenthal to myself to Burroughs is gay, so what do you want?

Yes, but I was thinking about the emphasis — especially in current [Queer] theory on camp...[4]

Well, I don't know anything about current theory, that is just intellectual "blah! blah! blah! blah!" Basically, I mean when it comes to questions like that, trying to make so great a distinction and pigeonhole things separately like that it doesn't make sense, that is what I mean "blah! blah! blah! blah!" It's really a dehumanisation of character if you try and break it up like that, if it is either/or, it is an old Aristotelian stupidity: it's both! And neither! And no contradiction either.

One thing that is interesting, at least to me, about *Pull My Daisy* — and a lot of Beat writing — is the emphasis on reality, the 'vérité' aspect...
I'm not sure what you mean there, it is certainly characteristic of Robert Frank's photos and photography.

The emphasis on 'truth'; watching it one gets the impression that this was reflective of 'what was happening'...
Well it was! We were making it up on the spot, so naturally it was what was really happening. There is a slight hyperbole there, a slight exaggeration, like making believe I'm self-conscious in front of Alice Neal, there is a little acting in there, remember; when I'm blowing the air out of my mouth when I'm sitting down on the couch next to Alice Neal — as the preacher's wife or something. There is a little bit of acting there, the little cowboy scene where I am on the table shooting, that is just playfulness, you know?

Yeah.
However what is real is, effectively, we had a general synopsis from actual situations we had been in with Neal Cassady and his wife and family...

The events of '55.
Although we took the events out of context, there is quite a bit of hyperbole...

Sure, but what I noticed is the move from that [*Pull My Daisy*] to *Chappaqua*, with the emphasis on the spiritual and psychedelic aspect...
That was a particular thing of Conrad Rooks, who was a disciple of Swami Satchidananda (he is still alive, he is a very famous Swami. He was the disciple of Swami Shivananda, who Gary Snyder and I had visited in India, years before).

I'm interested in that move from the emphasis on 'real' events to the emphasis on the 'spiritual'...
But that is very much Conrad Rooks' take, he was the director, scriptwriter and filmmaker, so that is his thing. It doesn't mean a whole generation followed him around or something with a move ... I actually ... what year was that?

That was '66.
Yeah, but before that is another film — much more serious — by Robert Frank called *Me And My Brother*, that was shot between '64 and '66. Have you seen that? That featured Peter Orlovsky, the poet and his brothers who were in and out of mad houses. Originally we were going to make a film of 'Kaddish' — my poem — you know the poem?

Yes I do, the piece for your mother.
So I actually sat down — when I got back from India — in Robert's house and I wrote a whole script, scene by scene, I was broke and he paid me $20 a day to write a scene. So we finished that, but he couldn't raise money to make it. So he started filming around my house and around Peter Orlovsky's brothers — who were also in mental hospitals — and he completed

that and it is about an hour and a half [in length] and it is, I think, his major monumental work. That was mid-'60s, early '60s, completed in February '66, I think we were last shooting and that is — I think — a little before *Chappaqua*. Or maybe they are simultaneous in their shooting. But then, you know, he [Frank] has done a lot of little short videos over the years with Peter Orlovsky. The most recent was one hour continuous shooting with a high-refined video camera by Sony, and half of that is Peter Orlovsky and that was only a couple of years ago. He has done one video of me doing 'White Shroud', reading it to him for the first time in my house — that's a later poem, I don't know if you know that. And there is another one of Gregory Corso reading a poem called 'The Ass'. But there is a lot of little videos and films that he did over the years that we are in and out of. And he's taken photos for the back of my *Collected Poems* and other books. I have a new *Selected Poems* and his photo will be on the front cover ... So we've been working together — I talked to him yesterday — so it's a long, long relationship, I don't know if you could say it was Beat or not Beat ... it's an artists' relationship. Friends actually. He is my mentor as a photographer actually. I have several books and large shows in that direction. I don't know if you've seen any of them?

I've seen some of them...
I had a large show — 108 photos — during the Venice Biennale ... but anyway, so he [Frank] is a big influence on me and visa-versa I suppose. Kerouac [was] a big influence on him.

Yeah, right, because they spent a lot of time together, because they travelled to Florida together at one point.
Yeah. Then there is the relationship between ourselves and ... who was the hero of *The Flower Thief*?

Taylor Mead.
Taylor Mead. His writings are quite interesting. Kerouac liked Taylor Mead's writings, he wrote a blurb for *Memoirs Of An Amphetamine Youth* ... Taylor acted in Amiri Baraka's, LeRoi Jones' plays and Frank O'Hara's plays.[5]

That happened before he moved to Europe for a couple of years.
Yeah, but he's back here now and still doing that sort of thing. So there is a big intermixture of all that and the San Francisco scene of *The Flower Thief* is very much representative of that flower generation. And Taylor Mead, very much with his innocence a kind of Chaplinesque flower ... flower-power personage. A great title, *The Flower Thief*, very much representative of that ethos, or culture, in San Francisco at the time. Warhol, of course, is part of ... it's not Beat, but grows out of that same atmosphere too.

Because you were in a couple of Warhol's movies: *Couch* and *Fifty Fantastics And Fifty Personalities*.[6]
Couch! I've never seen *Couch*.

I thought that the part you were in was lost.
No, it exists. I think Gerard Malanga has a copy of it and also at the Museum — and they'll make me one. But it's not just me, it's me and Kerouac and Corso and Orlovsky on the couch all at once.

And Taylor?
Maybe Taylor — I don't know.

I was talking to Taylor about *Couch* and he said that it was all shot from behind and he kept on saying to Warhol "shoot from the front" and Warhol kept on saying "No. I only want to shoot from behind" or something.
No. No. No. It was from the front.

Really?
Yeah. Maybe another time, but I remember we were sitting around and talking and cavorting on the couch and a camera was just aimed at the couch.

Right.
I haven't seen the film, but that is my recollection.[7] But, you see, it [the underground] was all one scene with Jonas Mekas as a sort of captain, when there were new Warhol films we'd all come out for that and when they were seized we would do whatever we could legally and so forth. When *Flaming Creatures* was seized we all went to the court to try and defend it.

That was seized in 1964.
Yes. Around the same time the district attorney was cracking down on Lenny Bruce. A man named Richard Kuh, an infamous district attorney who also tried to stop *Naked Lunch* from being published and then ran for mayor and lost when people remembered his role as a censor.

When *The Subterraneans* was made into a film by MGM what was the reaction to it [among the Beats]?[8]
Everybody thought it was a betrayal by Hollywood, as usual. See, Kerouac had an agent who did not really guard his property properly, who didn't really take care of Kerouac. And they allowed them to do whatever they wanted, so the theme of the black girl with a white guy was completely changed...

Right, because she is white in the movie...
...because of the racism and she's made into a French girl, so the whole thing was a fraud, but not only thematically or ... as far as changing characters with the elimination of miscegenation, but also it is just stupid: bongo drums ... idiocy. Sterling Lord was Kerouac's agent and should have protected him from that kind of manipulation and didn't. He didn't really respect Kerouac and I don't think he ever did properly, because he let his books come out in the wrong order and in a way that was commercially and artistically demeaning, some of the best work like *The Subterraneans*, or *Maggie Cassidy*, [and] *Tristessa* in paperback, cheap paperback, rather than hard cover like real novels. But he's still his agent, posthumously.

A whole load of exploitation movies came out at that time all with the word 'Beat' in the title...
Yes, I think a guy named Albert Zugsmith stole the phrase 'Beat Generation' for a movie and copyrighted it [laughs].[9]

Because at one point that was going to be the title of *Pull My Daisy*.
I don't know, it might have been. Jack wrote a three-act play that has never been published, which is quite good.

Yes, *The Beat Generation Or The New Amaraean Church*; the last act formed the basis of *Pull*

Hollywood beatniks in The Subterraneans

***My Daisy;* I have seen some of that, Alfred Leslie showed me some of it.**
Did Leslie tell you what happened to the film? To the negatives and the out-takes?

Didn't they get burnt?
He [Leslie] very unwisely and rashly went and took the negatives and out-takes from the vault where they were and brought them home and then had a fire. You are never supposed to do that, take them out, you know, you are always supposed to have them on deposit in a vault, you are not supposed to take them out like that, it's quite rash. A lot of very beautiful footage was lost that way.

I know that him [Leslie] and Robert Frank don't talk anymore about it.
I don't think they do, no. Probably not. I think Leslie was probably … I don't know, it seems to me he was the one that acted rashly.

I know you were very good friends with Harry Smith.
Well, I took a number of photographs of him and the last several years of his life he was at Naropa Institute with us.

Yes. He lived with you for about eight months or something.
When he was indigent and on the Bowery. He was homeless.

Could you talk a little about your experiences with and knowledge of Harry Smith. What drew you to his work?
I met him in 1960, I'd heard a lot about him because I knew Jordan Belson, you know Jordan Belson's work?

I know the name...

Oh, he did abstract films, high on ether. Well [to return to Harry Smith's films], the *Heaven And Earth* movie is a fantastic dream, an enormously beautiful collage, making use of all the classical collage methods, with archetypal images that he cut out from anywhere or drew and it influenced my thinking and even my own artwork now. Also his music collection, you know about that?

Yeah. He documented a lot of music which would have otherwise been lost, folk songs and such.

Influenced not only Bob Dylan and Jerry Garcia, but everybody up to me in blues singing and folk music. And you know he got a Grammy for it, late in his life, the last year of his life. He had an enormous influence on music and musicians and on the folk music scene which was certainly part of the pre-Beat and Beat Generation and on Dylan and just on everybody. And then his film ... his film ... I heard a description by Jordan Belson in San Francisco and I recognized him from the description I was given when I saw him in the Five Spot in 1960 or so, listening to Thelonious Monk. We met and then after a while he took me up to his house to see his various movies. And I was amazed by his arrangement of symbols of Tibetan Buddhist material, because I had been interested in that all the way back then, with Kerouac and then ... I realized many of his connections were quite amazing, like Count Weleska who was a Tibetan Buddhist cognoscenti who had a store in New York with Buddhist icons and Takas and Harry had connections with the Guggenheim Museum of Non Objective Art — where I used to go when I was a kid — then he had connections with all the bebop people, he was friends with Thelonious Monk, the Baroness and all that. But also he was broke the whole time, so I brought a copy, a dark copy of [the] *Heaven And Earth* movie and brought it down to Jonas, who I had met in '58 because of *Pull My Daisy*, Jonas had never met him or heard of him and all of a sudden there was this genius with this enormously long hour-and-a-half *Heaven And Earth* movie. He recorded in the early '70s at the Chelsea Hotel all of my music and put out a Folkways album called *First Blues* of mine, then he also recorded Gregory Corso's early poetry and all of Peter Orlovsky's music, that has never been put out, but the tapes are there at the Smithsonian Institute, which bought up Folkways. So he did a tremendous contribution to American culture, but also to the entire culture, by making use of the materials of collage in a very unique way and influencing almost everybody.

He is so important, yet he is virtually unknown, almost totally unheard of...

Well that was his genius, to have created so much behind the scenes, almost anonymously, he was notoriously well known among the artistic community.

He always worked as an alchemist. It's the metaphor of the alchemist, controlling history from behind the scenes...

Right, right.

A lot of Beat films are of performances, like *Fried Shoes, Cooked Diamonds* and *Gang Of Souls*.[10]

I haven't seen much of *Gang Of Souls* ... that's much later. *Fried Shoes* was much later. That was around Naropa [Institute], that was an Italian film crew and an Italian guy that was interested in doing it, with a great Italian lady translator who was a friend of [William] Faulkner and Ezra Pound who came to Naropa because she admired Kerouac and my own poetry and was our own translator, Fernanda Pivano her name was.

Do you know what the first performance film was that you were all involved in?
What do you mean performance film?

Films of you reading, reciting poetry. Is there anything earlier than *Wholly Communion*?
There's *Wholly Communion*. Though maybe before that, or maybe at the same time as that there was *Don't Look Back* ... [11] Dylan is performing, you know, 'Subterranean Homesick Blues', performing and reading a poem ... I don't know if ... yes! 1965, I think it was, there were a whole group of films made that were broadcast on television, by Richard Moore, for a poetry conference in Berkeley, they were made during the poetry conference for showing on KPFA, which, I think ... KQED in Berkeley, Channel 13, the educational broadcasting system. And the out-takes and the originals, are at the San Francisco State College Poetry Archives and that includes recitations of poetry by Gary Snyder, maybe Philip Whalen, Michael McClure, myself, Robert Duncan, Charles Olson, many, many poets. The out-takes turned out to be quite good also, out-takes of Neal Cassady ... The entire Beat literary movement was based, to some extent, on Kerouac's estimate of bebop as an improvised, spontaneous, form.

The whole kind of 'blowing' thing ... the whole idea of improvisation as 'blowing' and that stuff...
Well, that's not a new thing, that's the basic method of poetic discourse for certain Buddhist cultures, like Tibetan and Japanese and Chinese, discourses. That's why at the Naropa Institute we have the Jack Kerouac School of Disembodied Poetics, because of the convergence of spontaneous mind manifestation of traditional Buddhist Eastern thought and the Western bohemian Beat version of literally spitting forth intelligence. Are you recording this?

Yeah.
Good, okay, so you've got the right terminologies.

Yeah. Thank you.
Okay. Good luck.

---

1. Robert Frank produced the video for Patti Smith's song 'Summer Cannibals' (1996).

2. Irving Rosenthal was the editor of the University of Chicago magazine, *Chicago Review*, which in 1958 published extracts from *Naked Lunch*. The University Dean — following an article in a local paper which attacked Rosenthal's editorial policy — asked to read the next issue, which contained a selection from *Naked Lunch*, alongside material by Jack Kerouac. The Dean banned the magazine and Rosenthal resigned and founded *Big Table Magazine*.

3. This is a reference to one of the first meetings of William Burroughs and Allen Ginsberg, at which Ginsberg was famously impressed that Burroughs was able to recite Shakespeare in a manner which both retained the Bard's meaning, yet simultaneously iterated Burroughs' own interpretation.

4. See the Jack Smith essay in this volume.

5. Mead appeared in LeRoi Jones' *The Baptism* and Frank O'Hara's *The General Returns From One Place To Another.*

6. Andy Warhol's *Couch* (1964) depicts Allen Ginsberg, Gregory Corso, Jack Kerouac, Peter Orlovsky, Gerard Malanga, Baby Jane Holzer, Amy Taubin, Billy Linich and Rufus Collins, amongst others. The protagonists sit/sprawl/laugh/dance/fuck/suck on a couch in the Factory. Two versions exist; one version is forty minutes long, the other is 24 hours. Warhol's *Fifty Fantastics And Fifty Personalities* (1965) includes folk singer Donovan, alongside poets Ed Sanders, Harry Fainlight, Peter Orlovsky and Ginsberg. The film "isolate(s) a single figure before the camera ... these portraits narrate the sitter's response to the process of being photographed" (David Jones 'The Producer As Author' in Michael O'Pray *Andy Warhol Film Factory*, BFI, 1989).

7. In Warhol and Hackett's *Popism: The Warhol Sixties* (Hutchinson & Co, Ltd, London, 1981, (1980) Warhol describes Taylor Mead's anger when: "I filmed a reel of Jack Kerouac, Allen Ginsberg, Gregory Corso and him on the couch at the Factory — that I did it from the side and you couldn't really see who was who — and then on top of that, we lost the reel" (p.240). Gerard Malanga: "...the only existing footage of Jack Kerouac, Allen Ginsberg and Gregory Corso occurs in the 1964 film, *Couch*, by Andy Warhol. The sequence... is one of 3 or 4 rolls, for which only one survives in the current version of the film. The remaining footage is either misplaced or lost, simply that Warhol had brought the rolls to his house and they've not turned up since. The sequence is approximately 3-minutes, shot at a nearly right angle from where they are seated. The lighting is of such poor quality as to obscure them in near total darkness." (Gerard Malanga, personal correspondence).

8. *The Subterraneans* (1960): "From the Jack Kerouac book that shocked conventional America" screamed the publicity. Directed by Ronald McDougall and starred George Peppard, Leslie Caron, Janice Rule and Roddy McDowall.

9. Albert Zugsmith produced Orson Welles' *A Touch Of Evil* (1958) and a string of low-budget exploitation movies including *High School Confidential* (1958), *Beat Generation* (aka *This Rebel Age*) (1959) and Russ Meyer vehicle *Fanny Hill: Memories Of A Woman Of Pleasure* (1964). Zugsmith also worked as producer/ director on various features including *The Female Animal* (1958), *College Confidential* (1960) and *Confessions Of An Opium Eater* (1962).

10. Constanzo Allione's *Fried Shoes, Cooked Diamonds: The Beats At Naropa Institute* (1978) depicts the central Beat writers and poets — including Ginsberg, Burroughs, Corso, Diane DiPrima, Amiri Baraka, Anne Waldman and Chogyam Trungpa Rinpoche, amongst others, at the Naropa Institute, in the early '70s. During the film the Beats discuss literature, philosophy and poetry and partake in an antinuclear demonstration at Rocky Flats. "Conversations and teachings and home scenes of myself and the poets, including singing, nakedness, meditation and readings" — Ginsberg. *Gang Of Souls* (1989) directed by Maria Beatty depicts various Beat poets, including Ginsberg, Burroughs and DiPrima.

11. The vérité Bob Dylan tour movie *Don't Look Back...* (1966), was directed by D.A. Pennebaker and includes brief footage of Ginsberg with Bob Dylan.

Part Two

The War Universe Of William S. Burroughs

Chapter Ten

Image Hoard

1. Cinematic Experiments & Collaborations: Balch/Burroughs/Gysin/Sommerville

The cut-up process was devised/discovered by Brion Gysin, in September, 1959, in room 15 at the Beat Hotel, 9 rue Git-le-Coeur, Paris. While preparing a mount for a drawing Gysin's sharp stanley knife cut through a mound of old papers. Through this apparently random event the written text was opened to the potentialities of montage and juxtaposition: "shift cut tangle word lines".[1] Cut-ups overturned the supremacy of the text, removing any notion of textual 'totality', instead following rhyzomic lines of flight. The technique was developed in the work not just of the resident Beat writers and poets, Gysin, William Burroughs, Sinclair Beiles and (the eventually reluctant) Gregory Corso, but also in the visionary applications and explorations of its radical philosophy, by Antony Balch and Ian Sommerville. Balch was the first filmmaker to collaborate with William Burroughs and the first to recognize the inherent cinematic potential for the cut-up.

Balch met Gysin at Jean-Claude de Feugas' flat at 10 Rue Git-le-Coeur and Gysin invited the young filmmaker across the road to the Beat Hotel. Balch had extensive experience in all areas of film — editing, print grading, cutting, lighting, etc. — having worked as a production assistant on various television commercials and, eventually, directing an advert for the pet food Kit-E-Kat: "That kind of filmmaking was a very good training ground, because you really did do everything".[2] In addition to making commercials Balch also subtitled films, including Alain Resnais' *L'Anée Dernière A Marienbad* (*Last Year At Marienbad*, 1961).

Balch also worked as a film distributor throughout the '60s and '70s and acted as a film programmer for two central London cinemas: the Jacey in Piccadilly and The Times in Baker Street. One of the first to reject the superficial nature of the divide between 'good' and 'bad' taste, Antony Balch was responsible for programming films ranging from European softcore porn, to the Surrealist films of Luis Buñuel, to Yoko Ono's *Fluxus* works. Similarly Balch distributed an eclectic combination of films, many of which were re-titled to appease the salacious desires of the movie-going public. These films included *Weird Weirdo aka Le Grand Ceremonial* (1968), *Heterosexual* aka *Juliette De Sade* (1969), *Doctor In The Nude* aka *Traitement De Choc* (1972), *When Girls Undress* aka *Matratzen-Tang* (1972) and *The Sexy Darlings* aka *Robinson Crusoe Und Seine Wilden Sklavinnen* (1971). Antony Balch also distributed such cult classics as Ted V. Mikels' *The Corpse Grinders* (1971) and Russ Meyer's *Supervixens* (1975), amongst others. One notable acquisition was Benjamin Christensen's groundbreaking *Häxan* (Sweden, 1921); having re-titled the film *Witchcraft Through The Ages*, Balch commissioned William Burroughs to narrate the film for its British release in the autumn of 1968. The text of the narration is an expanded text based upon the original sub-titles.

Following his meeting with Gysin and subsequent introduction to Burroughs and Sommerville, Balch began to work on several films with the residents of the Beat Hotel, completing three underground collaborative films and two exploitation feature films, before his death — from stomach cancer — on 6 April, 1980.

You see we are not just taking cuttings — we are stockpiling sophisticated weaponry.
William Burroughs,
Port Of Saints

Balch began producing his first short film in Paris, 1959, shooting on an old wartime 35mm De Vry camera. Balch would later describe the film as being "terribly pretentious: there was an old man, a would be ballet dancer and we got him dancing under the bridges of Paris; there was Jean-Claude de Feugas who appeared naked on a

Witchcraft Through The Ages *aka* Haxan

kind of funereal couch with candles all around; and then an old boyfriend making it with a girl on a lawn — it was very daring at the time".[3] When Balch saw the footage he realized that it "didn't amount to much"[4] and the film was never completed.

The first collaborative project to be cinematically released was *Towers Open Fire* (1963). Although this film was primarily a collaboration with William Burroughs, the film also credits Ian Sommerville, Brion Gysin and Michael Portman (the uncredited actors who play the members of the board are: David Jacobs, Bachoo Sen, Scottish Beat writer Alexander Trocchi, Liam O'Leary, Norman Warren, John Gillett and Andrew Rabanech). The film was shot in black and white, on a fifteen-year-old De Vry camera, with Balch hand-painting the celluloid for the last scene and was eleven minutes long. Filmed over a period of a year (from December 1962–63) in Paris, Gibraltar and London, *Towers Open Fire* is a cinematic interpretation of several of Burroughs' major themes. Despite some critical commentary to the contrary,[5] the film itself is not a cut-up, although it contains a short cut-up section within it, shot on a Seine quayside in Paris, which Balch copied in order to make it look older. However the film's structure is such that it resists easy interpretation. The film depicts the destruction of the stock market (via stock footage of the Crash of 1929, which was purchased by Balch from Pathe News) and the disintegration of the Board. A commando figure (Colonel Bradly) — portrayed by Burroughs in complete camouflage and wearing a gas mask — with an 'orgasm gun' (actually a ping-pong-ball firing toy, purchased from Hamley's toy shop) bursts into a room and destroys photographs of a family. These images of the breakdown of control are intercut with various other images of autonomous liberation. These include Balch masturbating (viewed from the waist up and shot at his mother's house, with Balch using his right hand to masturbate and his left to trigger the camera in order to film himself at orgasm); Burroughs' hands passing over old film canisters as if he were performing a magical ritual (the narration at this point emphasizes this, stating "Curse go back. Curse go back."); and Burroughs sitting in his fatigues armed with a tape recorder and radio. Other scenes show Burroughs watching the Dreamachine, tearing paper into strips and describing how to make a cut-up and staring at a caged bird in the Paris Zoo. At the film's end the Board's books and papers are blown away, down a country road. This is followed by a young man, portrayed by Burroughs' associate Michael Portman, who dances in the street, while vivid colours splash across the sky. Finally there is an optically manipulated image of Colonel Bradly climbing through a window.

The film's soundtrack is made up from a spoken word monologue delivered by Burroughs and various pieces of Arabic music. The soundtrack was recorded and assembled "on a Grundig in Gloucester Terrace, some of it was done in a recording theatre, some of it was Arab music and some was music from De Wolfe's music company".[6] The narration of *Towers Open Fire* consists of Burroughs assuming both the voices of control and of rebellion, opening with Burroughs stating "Kid what are you doing over there with the niggers and the apes? Why don't you straighten out and act like a white man?" (This opening narration is taken from the chapter 'Where You Belong', in the 1966 version of the novel *The Soft Machine*[7]) and ending with Burroughs ordering: "TOWERS OPEN FIRE!"[8] Burroughs' cut-up novel *Nova Express*[9] includes a section, similarly titled 'Towers Open Fire', which could almost be a reworking of the film, with its description of an attack on the Nova Guard and descriptions of "Installations shattered — Personnel decimated — Board Books destroyed — Electronic waves of resistance sweeping through mind screens of the earth — The message of Total Resistance on short wave of the world — This is war to extermination — Shift linguals — Cut word lines — Vibrate tourists — Free doorways — Photo falling — Word falling — Break through in grey room — Calling Partisans of all nations — Towers, open fire –"[10]

When the film was completed Balch sent it to the BBFC (British Board of Film Classification) who replied that the words 'fuck' and 'shit' should be cut from the dialogue for domestic release.

While in Paris, Balch had seen Tod Browning's masterpiece *Freaks* (1932) at the Cinémathequе, which had never been screened in England, having previously been considered as unsuitable for release. Through the filmmaker Kenneth Anger, Balch found out that the film rights were owned by Raymond Rohauer. Balch approached Rohauer and asked if he could distribute the film in England. Balch raised enough money to make a print of *Freaks* and opened the film in a program with *Towers Open Fire*, at the Paris Pullman cinema, in West London.[11]

Following its release, Antony Balch stated that *Towers Open Fire*

> "wasn't a total success, but it does have some good scenes in it. I knew Burroughs' and Gysin's work and I knew them, but some of the things they were saying hadn't really sunk in. Some of them had, some hadn't ... One or two scenes do work: the Stock Exchange crash is a gas, the dream machine [sic] shots are very beautiful, the boardroom is quite amusing. It was the British Film Institute boardroom, they let me shoot the scene there and they were all very nice, no complaints. I mostly regret that the pictures in the [B]oardbooks were drawn by me with a magic marker, hurriedly copying from the *Egyptian Book of the Dead* or some such. Those terrible drawings on the wall behind were all done by me at the last minute ... if Brion had been there, he could have drawn some great things".[12]

Antony Balch's next film was *Guerrilla Conditions* and consisted of footage from the period 1961–1965, depicting the daily lives of Burroughs and Gysin. The film was shot in and around the various hotels at which Burroughs and Gysin lived; the Beat Hotel, Paris, the Hotel Villa Muniria, Tangier, the Empress Hotel, London and the Chelsea Hotel, New York, as well as Burroughs' temporary New York loft home, at 210 Centre Street. The film was originally

From left to right: Burroughs, Gysin and Hamri in **Destroy All Rational Thought**

intended to be a 23-minute, silent documentary. The film was never completed and some of the footage was utilized in Balch's next film *The Cut Ups* (aka *Cut-Ups*, 1967).

In his book *Bomb Culture*, Jeff Nuttall describes a 1964 meeting with Burroughs and Balch, at a Hotel in Bayswater, London, during which they discussed film. This account describes both Balch and Burroughs as being "unimpressed with Jack Smith's *Flaming Creatures*",[13] but states that Balch was excited by a Stan Brakhage "birth film".[14] Nuttall describes Balch's and Burroughs' interest in the Brakhage film's subliminal effects: "the direct impact on the nerve, the dislocation, redirection of the neuropsychological complex".[15] This interest in the subliminal effects of film would be one of the thematics articulated in *The Cut Ups*.

The Cut Ups was the first film to recognize and utilize the cut-up and was completely constructed by cut-up. Just as Burroughs had developed a new form of 'literature' from cutting up text, Balch did the same with film. Balch cut all of the original material into four sections, then handed the footage over to a "lady who was employed to take a foot from each roll and join them up".[16] The editing was purely a mechanical task, most importantly "nobody was exercising any artistic judgment at all. The length of the shots (except for the last) [was] always a foot".[17] Balch's decision to produce *The Cut Ups* from foot-long segments of film was based on his recognition that the cuts should be made at the shortest length that an audience could take in an image; "a foot ... is long enough for people to see what's there, but not enough to examine it in detail".[18] Antony Balch would also occasionally vary the speed at which the film would be projected, screening it at both 16fps and at 24fps.

Among the images *The Cut Ups* depicts, is film of Burroughs — as a doctor — examining a teenage youth (Baby Zen), Burroughs standing on the subway and Burroughs exploring the cartography of the city, manifested via the streets of New York, Tangier and Paris. The film also shows Gysin at work: producing a massive roller painting and calligraphic writing. Gysin is also depicted creating a grid on which he writes the phrase "Guerilla conditions/army needs base/enemy cannot reach our area/poetry creation/myth..." before turning the page through 90 degrees and continuing to write over the previous text, producing a visual density of text which transforms into a calligraphic haze. *The Cut Ups* also contains footage of Ian Sommerville and the Dreamachine, amongst its image hoard. In some segments the footage is optically manipulated, using both superimposition and mirror effects, to create resonant fragmentations and multiplications of the image.

The voices of both Burroughs and Gysin dominate the soundtrack repeating permutations of the phrases/statements: "Yes/Hello/Look at this picture/Does it seem to be persisting?/Good/Thank you". The soundtrack was constructed by Ian Sommerville, Gysin and Burroughs and was based on a Scientology auditing test. The final edit of the film was twenty minutes and four seconds long and the audio tape supplied by Sommerville of the permutated phrases lasted exactly that, including the final phrase — "Thank you" — which closes the film. *The Cut Ups* opened in 1967 at the Cinephone in Oxford Street, London, where it played for two weeks. During the film's run Balch cut the film down to a shorter twelve minute version, which he preferred.[19]

The cut-up texts were produced by Burroughs to "make explicit a psychosensory process".[20] The cut-ups, in part, re-create the continual fragmentation of sensory experience that is commonplace. Cut-ups also serve as an attempt to circumnavigate the linear frame work of written texts, as Burroughs notes "writing is still confined in the sequential representational straitjacket of the novel".[21] The cut-ups were a challenge to the linear, textual construction/consumption, producing texts as a liberating device. Burroughs' books use the cut-up to open up the text for the reader, allowing language and images to emerge from the juxtaposition of words and to create a universe of possibilities. The cut-up texts also function as 'magical' texts, they attempted to expose the methodology of control and to destroy it; Burroughs has also suggested a prophetic quality in the cut-up texts. However, *The Cut Ups* functions antithetically to this and — rather than liberate the viewer — it forces the audience to watch a series of flashing images, with varying results. According to Balch "half the audience would love it and half would hate it, women would be sitting there with their heads in their hands having headaches".[22] In an article in *Sight And Sound* magazine, Balch confessed that he enjoyed watching members of the audience demanding refunds; "It shows we're really getting to them!"[23] Gysin reiterated this perspective in an interview in which he stated that the films were "still shockers when they're shown" [and that audiences] "yell and scream and jump up in their seats and are very affected by them".[24]

The Cut Ups was a radical cinematic experiment; primarily this was due to its renegotiation of the ontology of film. The process of viewing *The Cut Ups* is analogous to the process of viewing the Dreamachine; like the Dreamachine the film creates a rhythmic pattern of flickering light and images across the audience's retinas; as Ian Sommerville noted, "Flicker may play a part in cinematic experience ... Films ... impose external rhythms on the mind, altering the brain waves which are otherwise as individual as finger-prints".[25] *The Cut Ups* presented images which were simultaneously random, yet precise, with scenes structured according to lengths of celluloid rather than lengths of action or narrative. The only order imposed on the film is that which attempts to remove coherent, linear narrative structure. The film demands that an audience experience film differently: as pure light and motion, devoid of 'rational logic', conventional narrative and recognizable visual pleasure; instead *The Cut Ups* constructs the audience's relationship with film as one based on the aesthetic of pure speed, as images strobe past the audience's collective retina.

Following *The Cut Ups*, Balch collaborated with Burroughs on *Bill And Tony* aka *Who's Who* (1972).[26] The film was inspired by a Burroughs text entitled 'John And Joe' and by a series of performances by Gysin and Sommerville which transpired in Paris. These performances were manifested in the form of a series of projector experiments undertaken during the period 1960–1964, beginning when Gysin was involved with the sound poetry group Domaine Poetique. As Gysin told Terry Wilson: "There were theatrical performances

Top: prototype wild boys from Secrets Of Sex; *below: victim of control from* Horror Hospital

in which we used projected images in a way that they hadn't been used up until that time — and still haven't been used again ... I worked it out with Ian Sommerville as a technical help ... and a very great one ... and we did shows that persuaded other professional artists, like George Maciunas of Fluxus and people like that, who included it into the area of experimentation which they called Expanded Cinema".[27] These experiments included projecting images of one person's body onto another person and projecting images of Gysin's naked body onto his clothed body: "I would wear black, for example and then open the zipper and, uh, wearing a white tee shirt underneath I would be somebody else ... I would be another projected person, into which I could walk, or out of which I could walk".[28] One of these performances, which transpired at the American Centre in Paris in 1961, featured Brion's naked body being projected onto his clothed body and it was this performance that Balch would describe as one of the central motivations in producing *Bill And Tony*.

The film was shot in a small studio in the central London and has head shots (from the throat upwards) of Burroughs and Balch, filmed against a black background, reading from a Scientology auditing manual and from the *Freaks* script. Like Gysin's performance, the film was intended to be projected onto the faces of each reader; thus Burroughs would mutate into Balch and Balch into Burroughs. The film was not shot for release but as an experiment in creating "a real mask of light",[29] and for personal usage. The film — and the performances — were all experiments which radically challenged the concept of fixed identity, allowing the collaborators to use light in order to become one another.

In 1964[30] Brion Gysin and Antony Balch developed a script for a film based on *The Naked Lunch* (the script went through several revisions). It was written by Gysin, while Balch drew comprehensive storyboards. In May 1971 Balch, Burroughs and Gysin co-founded Friendly Films Ltd in order to produce a film of *The Naked Lunch* from Gysin's script, a musical which included six songs, some of which were later scored by Steve Lacy.

Gysin's script focuses on William Lee, a writer who is able to write his own reality and is fleeing New York for Neverzone following the shooting of two narcotics cops. On the way to Neverzone, Lee waits for his connection in Bugs Bar, here he witnesses a pop group using a gallows in their act, later he hides out at the EverHard steambath. Lee flies to Neverzone on Transvestite Airlines, where customs ignore his weapons and narcotics but question him about his manuscripts, asking him if they are for his personal use. Lee replies: "Yes. I make with the live word. I got an exclusive".[31] In Neverzone he hangs out in the Plaza, a "psychic cesspool through which swirls a mass of mangled humanity".[32] At a party in Sal's Rumpus Room, Lee meets Dr Benway and is taken to the Doctor's hospital (in the outline for the film Gysin noted that "Benway's outrageous routines are the funniest ever written and should be played by Groucho"[33]). Sal phones Benway and tells him to send his most sensitive patients to a screening/party of 'Gallows Girl' the Last Blue Movie, by A.J., which stimulates the audience into autoerotic suicide. Lee escapes from the clinic and — realizing he has written the movie — knows he must "un-write the damage".[34] As the gallows party catches fire, Lee "finds himself ... in Bugs Bar looking at a fire in an ashtray ... still waiting for his connection. When he tries to score from the Chinaman who is sweeping up the credit titles, the Chinaman looks up and shakes his head, saying: 'No Glot, Clome Fliday'".[35]

In order to gain the necessary experience in commercial film production to film *The Naked Lunch*, Balch directed two exploitation movies, the 'sex' film *Secrets Of Sex* (1969) and the horror movie *Horror Hospital* (1973), both of which were produced in collaboration with producer Richard Gordon.[36] *Secrets Of Sex* was originally to have been called either *Bizarre*, or *Eros Exploding*, however Balch decided on the name change following the nine minutes worth of cuts forced on the film by the BBFC's John Trevelyan.[37] The film has an episodic structure, with each vignette — which focus on the "war between the sexes" — being introduced by an Egyptian mummy. Balch manages to allude to various Burroughsian elements, including the sex war, symbolized by a confrontation between go-go dancing topless women and muscular machinegun-wielding young men, who appear almost as a late-'60s camp version of the *Wild Boys*. The film makes a further allusion to Burroughs in a section in which a woman captures dead men's souls and traps them in house plants. When she is finally killed her (male) assassin strangles her, while proclaiming death to all alien women, thus iterating a proposal suggested by Burroughs that women were in fact alien agents for an insect trust.[38] Amongst other references, *Secrets Of Sex* alludes to scientology, Jean Genet, *Nova Express* and even French situationist Guy Debord.

Horror Hospital featured Robin Askwith (who, the following year, became a British sex film icon in the *Confessions* series) as a music-biz failure, recuperating on a 'Hairy Holiday' at a Health Hotel, run by Pavlovian brain surgeon Dr Storm. The hotel is in actuality a front for Storm's experimental mind-control surgery on various "stupid adolescents". *Horror Hospital* punctuates its story with scenes of bloody violence, such as a midget who drags around a sack of severed heads, a lobotomized woman getting whipped and fucked and a Rolls Royce with a vicious spring-mounted blade that decapitates escapees. Balch's direction and script maintain a camp edge throughout and the film gained a cult following. However, unlike *Secrets Of Sex*, the film contained no direct Burroughs references.

These two films give some idea of the aesthetic sensibilities and the feature film making skills, that Balch would have employed had he directed *The Naked Lunch* from Gysin's script. Although the two films 'lack' the experimental and underground qualities of Balch's previous, collaborative films, they maintain a clarity of vision, style, velocity and humor which — when combined with the cinematic experiments of *Towers Open Fire*, *The Cut Ups* and *Bill And Tony* — could have made a success out of Gysin's script.

Brion Gysin's *Naked Lunch* screenplay was never produced, despite interest in the project as early as 1971. According to Ted Morgan's Burroughs biography *Literary Outlaw*, Mick Jagger was interested in acting in the film in 1971. However Jagger would not appear in the film if Balch was the director, because "he thought Balch was coming on to him sexually and in any case he didn't have a reputation as a director in the industry".[39] In April 1972, Terry Southern and Burroughs traveled to Hollywood in order to meet the producer Chuck Barris, who was interested in the *Naked Lunch* script. However, when their chauffeur-driven Daimler was switched for a two-seater with a driver it was apparent that Barris had changed his mind.[40]

Other Balch, Burroughs, Gysin and Sommerville footage — much of it unseen — was saved from destruction by Genesis P-Orridge following Balch's death in 1980. When P-Orridge obtained the reels of film he compiled a comprehensive index, noting every shot, its location and the protagonists in it. In this process P-Orridge was aided by Peter Christopherson, David Dawson, Akiko Hada and Terry Wilson, who "was able to identify many segments I was unsure of, like knowing which person was 'Baby Zen' ... and what Mikey Portman looked like, etc".[41] This footage — 28 cans of reels according to P-Orridge — formed the basis of three 'new' films.

The first of these was *Ghosts At Number 9* aka *Ghosts At Number 9 (Paris)* (1963/1967–1982). The title is a reference to the address of the Beat Hotel, Paris. *Ghosts At Number 9* utilizes a representative selection of largely unseen film from seventeen of the cans, which were labeled both *Guerrilla Conditions* and *Ghosts At Number 9*. The film consists of silent 35mm footage shot by Balch for *Guerrilla Conditions* and subsequently cut-up (assembled) and used in *The Cut Ups*, images such as: Gysin painting, Burroughs walking through New York's Chinatown, Dreamachine footage, Burroughs examining Baby Zen etc. *Ghosts At Number 9* also uses footage which was possibly intended as rehearsal versions of *Naked Lunch*, for example Burroughs packing his suitcase and vacating a hotel room[42] and Burroughs looking at a map — actually a Gysin painting — with 'the Captain'. *Ghosts At Number 9* also includes a section of visual experiments analogous to those performed in *Bill And Tony*, all of which were on a can which was marked Superimpositions. According to Genesis P-Orridge: "Brion confirmed what I thought, which was that *Bill And Tony* was primarily an experiment. It was to have been longer, with more superimpositions happening to blur everything further. Colour was prohibitively expensive so the two experimental sessions were never integrated as Antony Balch intended".[43] These experiments include superimpositions, primarily of Burroughs' face, which create a double exposure effect and mirror experiments which divide and transform the images into optical distortions. Other footage used in *Ghosts At Number 9* includes head/shoulder and torso shots of a youth masturbating (out of shot) and lying face down on a bed, close-up shots of Burroughs' hands and various footage of the dreamachine.

The soundtrack of *Ghosts At Number 9* utilizes a combination of Burroughs' readings from *Nova Express* and *The Revised Boy Scout Manual* amongst others and the Master Musicians of Joujouka. The soundtrack also includes various news reports of A-bomb tests, electronic drones, loops and trouble/riot noises, produced as an audio cut-up by P-Orridge: "I sat with my dozens of tapes by WSB/GYSIN/BALCH/SOMMERVILLE and picking out cassettes at random would fast forward and rewind them without monitoring, then hit play for a few seconds. Dumping fragments, cut-ups, of my sound archive onto the master. I even included a trip I made to a demolition derby in Lawrence, Kansas with Uncle Bill and James [Grauerholz]".[44]

The second of the three 'new' films was *William Buys A Parrot*. This two-minute, colour, 16mm film depicts William — in a white suit and black fedora — buying a parrot.[45] Burroughs sits at a table, upon which is the bird's cage and has a cigarette and a drink. The hand-held camera focuses on the 'parrot' in the foreground. The footage appears to have been shot in Tangier, although "Gysin interestingly suggested it was Gibraltar. I wondered if he meant a house in Tangier with a view of the Gibraltar straits".[46] P-Orridge added a soundtrack to the silent footage, made up from an industrial pulsing rhythm and a loop of Burroughs intoning: "Boys, school showers and swimming pools, full of them". The film was also screened at the Burroughs/Gysin themed Final Academy, at the B2 Gallery and Ritzy Cinema, both in London. He also notes that the film was, as far as he was aware, not intended to be a complete text, but became viewed as such following its screening as a vignette. A further film, named *Transmutations* by P-Orridge, also exists. This colour film depicts Gysin "painting a huge roller painting on canvas speeded up"[47] to a live soundtrack of the Master Musicians of Joujouka, recorded by P-Orridge, at the Commonwealth Institute, London. According to P-Orridge this film was transferred to a video loop for continuous exhibition at the B2 Gallery.

The film collaborations of Antony Balch, William Burroughs, Brion Gysin and Ian Sommerville, attempted to articulate a radical perspective through experimentation. The experiments in film were part of a larger series of experiments based on re-negotiating the nature of the experience and construction of reality. Stimulated by the cut-up process, they were attempting to "Show them the rigged wheel of Life-Time-Fortune. Storm The Reality Studio. And retake the universe".[48] Burroughs' cut-up trilogy, the films and the audio experiments, all explored — and attacked — the power of control, questioning the nature of 'perceived reality' through the cut-up process, (re)creating 'separate realities' and thus exposing existing 'truths' as constructions.

The films — both those produced during the '60s and those produced following Balch's death — exist beyond the traditionally ascribed borders and limits of cinema. Like Burroughs' and Gysin's cut-up texts, the films cut/edit/splice/jump/fold, beyond the traditionally ascribed limits of their own textuality, images repeat and juxtapose across the films, proliferating endlessly: *Guerrilla Conditions* becomes *The Cut Ups*, part of which is remixed as *Ghosts At Number 9*. The films — like the cut-up and permuted 'literatures', collages, photographs, scrapbooks and Dreamachine, all of which emerged from the Beat Hotel — are experiments in creating a Body Without Organs (BwO). Described by Deleuze and Guattari in *Anti-Oedipus*, the BwO "resist(s) linked, connected and interrupted flows, it sets up a counterflow of amorphous, undifferentiated fluid. In order to resist using words composed of articulated phonetic units, it utters only gasps and cries that are sheer unarticulated blocks of sound".[49] The BwO resists all forms of fascism, hierarchical order and structure and replaces the binary 'either/or' with the multiplicity 'either … or … or…', playing multiple permutations against the dualistic universe. Burroughs has repeatedly stated his opposition to the Aristotelian dualistic basis of Western philosophy — in texts such as *The Job, The Third Mind* et al., and this collection of texts challenges the fundamental elements of such logocentrism, by suggesting and exploring new possibilities.[50] These Beat Hotel generated texts function as a BwO, they attempt to create in the audience a perspective which rejects the stupefying, rigid and totalising effect of traditionally ascribed linear narratives in favour of the aleatory and fragmentary effect of creating a zone[51] which exists in/as a gap, a space in which possibilities are allowed to emerge.

2. An Interview With Brion Gysin (Paris, October 1983)

The following interview with Brion Gysin on the films Towers Open Fire *and* Cut Ups *was conducted by Arthur and Corinne Cantrill and published in* Cantrills Filmnotes #43/44, *February, 1984. It is reproduced here with the kind permission of Arthur and Corinne Cantrill.*[52]

What was the origin of the films?
History! Back in '59, I think, a very short time after *Naked Lunch* was published, we were living in the rue Git-le-Coeur there, next to the Place Saint Michel in the famous Beat Hotel and saying how interesting it would be to get in touch with somebody who was into films and that we would like to do something of the same sort. And in the very same street, a very short time after that, I met Antony Balch who was at a party, as a matter of fact. He was a young film distributor who was very interested in making films of his own. He had started a small one — I never saw it, he said it was too embarrassing ever to show. We just became very intimate friends and we started filming — just bits and pieces whenever he had some film. I've forgotten exactly what camera he had at the time, a Bolex, I suppose. And bits and pieces were filmed around that area of us just walking around, or in the rooms or whatnot. Then we went to Morocco, where I'd been living previously and then went back to live for an even longer time and he came there and William [Burroughs] came there too and we filmed a bit in Tangier. Then we next, I think, filmed in London and then afterwards in New York. So there are those four locales which are seen in the *Cut Ups* film, at any rate. The film that he made first was *Towers Open Fire* and that was partly filmed here in Paris at an exhibition where you see the Dreamachine whirling 'round. It was an exhibition called 'The Object' which was at the Musée des Arts Decoratifs in 1962, I think. But that film is more or less narrative really, in a way based on a text that William had written in Gibraltar where the towers were and the 'towers open fire' were those towers between Gibraltar and Spain on that part where the artificial frontier is. Antony had gone to Gibraltar (I was in Paris when he went down there) and saw William and was very impressed by this piece of text, so that's where the title comes from. William liked the atmosphere in Gibraltar very much, it was so inhuman. He used to go to a hotel which was right on the border, on the disputed and still-barricaded border between Spain and Gibraltar. A number of young friends took part in the film; particularly Ian Sommerville and Michael Portman is the young man sitting on the curb who does a funny little dance. Five of us were intimately connected with the making of the film. All the other people were just found or turned up or filmed in the streets, like the Chinaman in the telephone booth and things like that. And Antony was applying — though more particularly in the making of the *Cut Ups* film - the 'cut-up' technique where he simply took all the footage he had and handed it over to an editor, just telling her to set up four reels and put so many feet on each one in order — one, two, three, four and start again, the same number...

From each sequence...
Even the sequences are cut and parts of them appear on one or another reel.

So he was just cutting the footage up, so much on each reel and finally the four reels were joined together.
That's right, exactly.

Did Balch do the filming?
Yes, he did the filming.

And was his attitude to filming a casual one — was it one of many things he did, or was he very heavily interested in film?
He had been interested in film since his childhood. His mother was an actress who had begun as a singer, I think, in Cochrane's Reviews and claimed that, at the time of his birth, she lost her voice and never sang again. But she went on for many years being a stand-in for movie work and did little parts herself and was always connected in some way or another with the cinema, even in that sort of rather distant way. Whereas he, from the age of about ten, set up his mother's dining room as a cinema. He was the only child and later went away to boarding school, but before that he set up a movie program which, even during his absence, she had to show at exactly the hours that he indicated, every day, even if there was nobody there to see it. His mother had to put through the projector these films which he'd borrowed or rented and he ran a program with a bit of newsreel, a bit of everything just like a professional cinema. His ambition had always been to be an exhibitor, really; a distributor necessarily and he was very good at both of those. He was good enough to be employed by a couple, the Cohens, who had inherited a whole chain of cinemas in England which had started in the 1930s. They had five or six cinemas in London and some in the provinces, but they had two which didn't make any money and one was curiously enough right on Piccadilly Circus, a downstairs cinema called The Monsignor at one time, I don't know what it's called now and he took over the programming there and made a great success of it. They had another movie house which they gave him too, which was in Baker Street station, which he renamed The Times. So he managed both of those houses, doing everything: front of house, seeing that the cleaning ladies cleaned up and sharpening up the lady in the cash box and above all being up in the projection booth.

It's really strange that he was such a passionate exhibitor, distributor and filmmaker as well. His filmmaking is very accomplished.
I know and nobody ever heard of a distributor who made films, or a film director who distributed them, either, so there was a certain contradiction there which was inevitable, because that's the way he made money to buy the film stock and make the films that we made together.

Was he very engaged with the filmmaking, or was it a casual involvement?
He was very, very engaged with it. It was important for him. You can tell by the technical quality of the image itself — he was very concerned with all of that.

What was your role in this?
Where to begin? First of all, the cut-ups were my idea. I wrote a statement — if you've read any of the books that William Burroughs and I wrote together on the subject — *The Third Mind*, for example; pretty much everything is in there. After accidentally coming across the possibilities of putting together a text from cut-up pieces of newspaper and magazines which were by chance on my worktable (I had sliced through them while cutting a mount for a drawing), I put together some text to show him that painting was 75 years ahead of writing, that these methods which had been proposed in painting 'round the turn of the century, when the whole matter of painting was changed by throwing sand into paint, or later by the cubists, Braque first of all and then Picasso, cutting up pieces of newspaper and pasting them on to the canvas. Writing had simply never caught up, it was way, way

Brion Gysin

behind. And I wrote a text, which I then cut up and that's what the films are based on. In 'Cut-Ups Self-Explained' I wrote: [Brion Gysin reads from *The Third Mind*] "Writing is fifty years behind painting. I propose to apply the painters' techniques to writing; things as simple and immediate as collage or montage. Cut right through the pages of any book or newsprint … lengthwise, for example and shuffle the columns of text. Put them together at hazard and read the newly constituted message. Do it for yourself. Use any system which suggests itself to you…" Et cetera. When cut into three columns, which I named A, B and C — Antony, for the purposes of the film, took four 'columns', instead of three — I put together text A, C and B, which reads immediately: "Writing is fifty. I propose to apply ears behind painting. The painters' techniques as simple and use to writing; things immediate as collage through the pages or montage." … et cetera. The next one was: "Writing is fifty years behind painting. the painters' techniq I propose to aply ues to writing; things immedi-ate as collages." … et cetera. Each one has a different sort of resonance of the same original text. So it goes from text A plus C, B or text B plus C, A and that's the way the movies were made. This was written by William and me together in New York in 1964–65 and it took thirteen years to get itself printed. A Calder paperback is still available, in England.

In what other ways were you involved in the film, do you appear in it?
I am one of the actors and I made many suggestions for the places, they were picked out by me.

Did you leave the editing totally to Balch, or did any of you ever look in and suggest changes. I mean, were things looked at and you'd say, "well no…"?
No, no, that's called editing. There was no editing done at all on the movies, none.

So even he didn't watch what the professional editor was doing, he just gave her the instructions for assembly and left her to carry out the job.
Yes that's right.

The text for it, the sound of it; what was that?
Some of it was Moroccan music which had been recorded by me. Just the music in Morocco had kept me there for what is still more than a third of my life. I heard some music there in 1950 and I lived there for 23 years because of the musicians that I became associated with. Some of it is that. Some of it is the application of cut-up to material heard over the radio; you recognize lots of pieces which would have been recorded sound and that's about all, really. What else do you remember?

Who is doing the reading?
That's Burroughs and me. Burroughs' was the rather gravelly voice and mine the more tenor voice. It's he and I in *Cut Ups* who read a text which I proposed, taken directly from the Scientology classes that he was going to at the time. That's the "stop-change-start", all of that and that's just Burroughs and I, our two voices back and forth. I had been more-or-less kidnapped by some Scientologists and had had a very weird adventure with them, a lot of which is reflected in a book of mine called *The Process* (it's coming back into print, I hope, within the next six months or so. But it's still read a lot by anybody who can find a copy). And William had been interested enough to follow on and actually take the Scientology courses in London at that time. But the section: "Does this image seem to be persisting", et cetera, that is all taken from Scientology.

We assumed that was from some kind of eye text!
Well, indeed, it is supposed to be developing perception. It's been passed through the sieve of L. Ron Hubbard's semantics!

You are not still involved with Scientology?
Oh no, I never was involved at all. They claimed I was an operating Thetan.

I find the *Cut Ups* film more impressive and it's interesting that you say that *Towers Open Fire* was filmed first. That figures, it's as if *Towers* was an early work and the whole thing became much more perfected in *Cut Ups*, even though that one was finished first.
You see, I was absent — I was stuck in the Beat Hotel here in Paris and they were over in London making the first film and when I saw it I was very critical of *Towers Open Fire*.

In what way were you critical?
Well, I didn't think it really was a work — I didn't think it worked entirely. I'd given my pre-conceived ideas from which the whole thing had sprung, but I was not satisfied with it, so that's how we made the second one, with a little bit more money and more time.

So that was at your urging, basically; you wanted to get the idea perfected?
Right, yes.

Because film obviously lends itself to the cut-ups technique, it is usually cut and assembled, but normally towards a seamless, narrative flow...
Right, much more linear. That's what I felt and during all of that time — yes, perhaps even as early as that — I was writing a movie script from *Naked Lunch*, which has never been

produced, though the script still exists. And I wrote songs for it — it was like a musical film. It may one day still be, who knows?

In *Towers Open Fire*, there's that long monologue at the beginning about...
"White, white, white, as well as the eye can see..."

Yes and after that, is the film edited in that systematic cut-up way?
No, it's not and that's one of the reasons for my criticism.

From a cinematic point of view *Cut Ups* is a much more exciting film — very powerful with an interesting structure and formal qualities that are not there in *Towers Open Fire*. In *Cut Ups* everything came together more successfully.
Simply because the method that I proposed was mechanically imposed on the images that we had, so it produced this effect which is much more disturbing. Although the first one is preferred by some people. Even James [Grauerholz of William Burroughs' *Communications*], though I should not speak for him in his absence, but I think that he prefers *Towers Open Fire* because he speaks of it all the time as a "Burroughs vehicle". He sees it as *Towers Open Fire* starring William Burroughs.

Because Burroughs physically appears in it.
That's what I meant.

But there was never the possibility of continuing with filmmaking, or are there other films we don't know about?
Oh yes, there are three more. First — I'm not sure of the order in which they were made, because I wasn't always there. I was back in Morocco, sort of commuting between Tangier and London, so I wasn't present at the time *Bill And Tony* was made — it must have been made last: it was a very expensive one, 70mm, at my insistence. I was very swept away by the first 70mm I'd seen and I thought we should do that. But I wasn't actually there and didn't have anything to do with the way it took. But the soundtracks are reversed. They are synced to the lips, but it's Bill who says "I am Tony" and it's Tony who says "I am Bill". It's Tony's image speaking with Bill's voice. It's a short film, I don't remember how many minutes. It has a different purpose, as a matter of fact, than the others. Then with the idea of getting money together and the necessary experience to make *Naked Lunch*, Antony made a soft porn, which was too soft by the time it got made, called *Secrets Of Sex*. First of all he made that, I wrote some of it, not all; then he made *Horror Hospital* which was like one of those Hammer horror films — that would be early '70s. They immediately fell into the hands, on Tony's death, of his commercial associate who wasn't interested in the rest, at all. That's how so much nearly got thrown out completely, or lost.

And these three films...
Well, the two were made — the soft porno and the horror — were the two aspects of what experience he might need to make *Naked Lunch* and the idea was to get the Cohens to put up the money for it, which never really worked out, because they were really only interested in the fact that he'd made their movie houses financially successful, because he did it remarkably well. He bought the films for their cinemas — we used to travel together to the film festivals: Cannes, Venice, for example, and he would buy something for nothing — something that some Danish exhibitor came along with and couldn't sell, Antony would pick up and then he would re-cut the film — cut it to shreds, title it — and do the

whole front of house down there in Piccadilly, or else up at Baker Street and the films made money. And then we got crossed a little bit by the fact that I knew — I was more likely to know — stars; and he didn't want anybody to talk about other directors: he wanted to direct his films. And I had got to know four or five stars who were highly considered, but were not really bankable and never have been, like Mick Jagger for example. Mick is still not bankable today, although he is right here in Paris now, recording at the moment. His films were not a success — the one he made in Australia[53] was a complete flop. And I found four or five other stars — James Taylor the singer, who looks a lot like William and would have loved to do it, but he also is not considered bankable. Then Dennis Hopper, who we met in Venice at the time. Dennis was very hot on the idea for a while and after Antony's death Dennis did get into some kind of business arrangement where he gulped down most of the money trying to make a film, *The Last Words Of Dutch Schultz*, that text of William's. It's written as a movie script; it's about 1930s gangsters.

Do you still hope that *Naked Lunch* will be made?
I don't hope very much anymore. I mean, Iggy Pop, who's a good and crazy friend, is always saying ... but he's too unreliable! And not bankable either. The only person who is still interested and is getting more bankable by the minute is David Bowie, who I was with this summer. I have a date to see him in January about things like that. He would very much like to do something about it.

But these are actors...
I'm sure it's not the way you begin. What you do is find a director who has just made a film for some throwaway money that some big company has had to get rid of. Like Bertolucci made *[Last] Tango [In Paris*, 1972] here simply because they had so much money in France they wanted to just mop it up and they were horrified that he turned out a successful film. It wasn't their intention at all, it was a financial embarrassment to them.

To get back to *Cut Ups* and *Towers Open Fire* — when these films were finished, what happened to them then?
They were shown at the Academy movie house in Oxford Street and this movie house finally asked if we could please take them off the screen because they'd had such a high incidence of people forgetting really very strange things in the theatre. There were more ladies who had left their handbags or their pants or their umbrellas or their shoes — an extraordinary number of unbelievable objects that they had never seen left behind before.

What about here in Paris or in New York?
Never commercially.

I should have thought you would have had a really big following in America.
No, maybe sort of, not yet. Of course William's following has derived from his work, but also an enormous amount from having gone back to live in America.

While these films were made he was out of America.
We were just there on a visit, as it were. We were there from December '64 to September '65 and that wasn't long enough. In fact we were still filming — some of that where I'm dressed in a white suit and buying some unnamable service or something from William who then becomes a doctor and examines the boy — that was filmed in the Chelsea Hotel.

But weren't you disappointed that, having produced these films, they had such a limited exhibition?
I have been so often disappointed, that I have no more disappointment left. Not even a slice.

I take it, you were trying to get the films shown in cinemas. You never thought about the New York Cinematheque type of underground film screenings in the '60s?
No, the whole New York art establishment, including Jonas Mekas, didn't want us, right from the start. Because of *Naked Lunch*, particularly, not because of me, particularly, but really because of *Naked Lunch* and William. We arrived with a very heavy aura of reputation which nobody wanted to have anything to do with. They found it too heavy and I think they found it competitive. They were trying to be very heavy themselves — Mekas, Warhol. Up to this day I've never met Mekas or Warhol. William has had them, since, come to him very much nowadays. I don't know about Mekas at all, I don't think so. But Warhol and the others, brought to him by Bockris — you've seen his book: *William Burroughs — Report From The Bunker*, where you see William with every star of the day, including Blondie. Not Cassius Clay, but almost everybody else. Brought around by Bockris as part of a sort of program, when William moved into this bunker down there on the Bowery, which is an underground place where the light of day has never entered.

Apart from Jonas Mekas, who has his own empire, there should be more detached empires such as the Museum of Modern Art in New York which is supposed to be profoundly concerned with important films.
No, they were very much against us, too.

Why?
As I said, because our reputation was too heavy.

What do you mean by heavy?
Well, you know, William had shot his wife and he had published the most shocking book of its time.

I should have thought that the Museum of Modern Art was slightly above that sort of pettiness.
No, not at all. Quite the contrary. Their mentor at that time was Frank O'Hara, the painter and all of that gang had joined with previous establishments. Say, the music world was old Virgil Thomson — who is still with us somewhere or other. I've known Virgil for almost fifty years, but there's no love lost ever. Well, I found, oddly enough, that this number of *Performance* [magazine], that just hit my table from London, says that I'm "dangerous".[54] So they thought that both William and I were very dangerous. William, particularly dangerous. I don't know; it's just rubbed off on me.

They don't see the films as having a life of their own and an existence of their own...
They feel threatened, that's all.

So from this entire series of circumstances, the films have fallen out of view.
That's right. They were shown in New York to a general audience for the first time in December 1978 at the Nova Convention[55] which was around William's 65th birthday and people were just knocked over — blown out of their shoes.

What I don't understand is that in New York there is Grove Press who were distributing controversial films such as Genet's *Un Chant d'Amour* a long time ago.[56]
That's why they went out of business as publishers, because Barney Rosset there, made that great success with *I Am Curious (Yellow)*[57] which made a whole lot of money and so he thought he could become a great film man. That's the only reason he got interested in all of those. Then he spent the money making that rather unfortunate film with Buster Keaton on the Beckett story: *Film.*[58] So it was just at that time that we left. Actually he asked us to take that film to Europe in the plane when we left in September '65, so it would get to the Venice Film Festival or something like that. Then he practically went out of business as a publisher, because he lost so much money on all of those films.

But Grove Press did have an impressive list of films that they made available.
And never these two. They thought I had been a very bad influence on Burroughs, having introduced him to the technology of the cut-up and everything else, it had made him less saleable. So there was a certain amount of animosity.

So you were a villain within the publishing world.
I was a villain.

3. *Thee Films*: An Account By Genesis P-Orridge

Genesis P-Orridge was a founding member of the 'performance art' group Coum Transmissions (1969–1979), alongside Cosi Fanni Tutti and, later, Peter 'Sleazy' Christopherson. The group were notorious for their transgressive, boundary-breaking performances. In 1976 — assisted by electronics wizard Chris Carter — Coum Transmissions formed the industrial 'noise' band Throbbing Gristle (1976–1981, 2005-present).[59] Throbbing Gristle created/explored an aural aesthetic frequently (although not exclusively) defined via extreme noise and jarring splices of sound, randomly selected and presented, using the theories espoused by William Burroughs, Brion Gysin and Ian Sommerville of the cut-up, tape viruses and infra-sound. The musical results of these sonic experiments range from the tranquil to the confrontational. Throbbing Gristle also utilized Gysin's adaptation of Hassan I Sabbah's credo: "Nothing is true. Everything is permitted".

Genesis P-Orridge met William Burroughs in 1973, when Burroughs lived at 8 Duke Street, St James, London, having corresponded with him since 1971. Burroughs was instrumental in helping Coum Transmissions get an arts grant and offered P-Orridge a legal testimonial in 1976 when P-Orridge was prosecuted for sending "indecent" mail (a collage juxtaposing Buckingham Palace with photographs of buttocks). P-Orridge became acquainted with Brion Gysin's artwork through his friendship with Burroughs and, when P-Orridge was co-editing the encyclopedic volume *Contemporary Artists* (1974), he approached Gysin with the intention of including him in the book.

Through his friendships with both William Burroughs and Brion Gysin, P-Orridge became an archivist of the results of cut-up experiments and 'Beat Hotel' memorabilia. In 1981, Throbbing Gristle further disseminated Burroughs' material to the disillusioned 'punk' audience via organizing the release of an album of his tape experiments, *Nothing Here Now But The Recordings (1959–1980)*(IR0016), on their own Industrial Records label. At various performances by Throbbing Gristle — suitably named as 'disconcerts' — the band would perform alongside Antony Balch's *Towers Open Fire*. Throbbing Gristle's fourth album *Heathen Earth* was designed to facilitate dreamachine experimentation. Following the death of Antony Balch, P-Orridge became the custodian of the Balch/Burroughs/Gysin/Sommerville cinematic collaborations.

Genesis P-Orridge was originally approached with a series of questions concerning his — thus far undocumented — role in the saving, cataloguing, archiving and dissemination of the Balch/Burroughs/Gysin/Sommerville films; the following account proved to be his response. Where necessary this has been edited for clarity.

(Two Many) Ghosts At Number Twenty-Three/ Or Where They Came From

Almost as soon as William S. Burroughs' seminal opus *Naked Lunch* was lionized, first as a temporarily 'obscene and bogus' book and later as a permanently 'revered' literary classic, both he, Brion Gysin, Antony Balch and Ian Sommerville had conceived of it becoming an epic 'beatnik' movie.

> **E loved Brion very much.**
> Genesis P-Orridge.

All of them were in all kinds of cahoots together. Re-inventing and exploring with their constantly deepening experiments in deconstruction; writing; painting; sexuality; scientology; film; collage; audio tape; and, of course, neurobiology and pharmacology.

Incredibly, from the later 1950s onwards, Antony Balch had lugged a cumbersome, heavy and less than typical 'home-movie' camera around the beatnik world collating and editing many of these theoretical suggestions and illustrative scenarios. Dedicatedly working as if his logistical requirements were as immediate and portable as a Derek Jarman[60] Super-8 camera, Antony Balch filmed and developed as he went as much 35mm footage as he could afford. On his returns to London he would store these voluminous stacks of cans of raw material in his mother's home, his various offices and other rented storage spaces for future reference.

The result and legacy, with hindsight, is an incredibly significant and monumental celluloid archive. A body of documentary portraits and mementos that is truly unique. We have nothing else that is so revealing, so experimental, so influential or so critically vital in preserving such important 'Beat' figures and their unfolding, most radical ideas on film.

When Burroughs, Gysin, Balch and Sommerville were not all living in close proximity to each other in Tangier; or in the 'Beat Hotel' in Paris; or even later on in Duke Street, St. James, London; they would keep in touch with regular and occasionally irregular, letters and postcards.

Sifting through the hundreds of pages of correspondence between these four renegade literary musketeers covering 1962–1975 in particular, it becomes clear that an extension of all their collaborations and 'cut-ups' into a radicalised, expanded configuration of film seemed inevitable and essential to them all. They return again and again to discussing variations of use and non-formal application of the film material they had already shot on Antony Balch's 35mm movie camera and the appropriate heuristic soundtracks to accompany all this.

They all, at various times during this fertile period, proposed and counter-proposed all kinds of ideas for their 'films'. These included integrating 'found' gay pornography and Moroccan kitsch feature films; symmetry tests and superimpositions; split screens edited to non-linear formulae and the anarchic symphonics of Ian Sommerville's taped realisations of Gysin and Burroughs' minimalist audio permutations.

Parallel to all these positive and exciting considerations they also, of course, speculated on the possible repressive legal ramifications relating to explicit and implied homosexuality and drug use being included.

Antony Balch and his nomadic friends had a couple of different interchangeable titles for this morass of unresolved imagery and invocation. Sometimes it was referred to as *Guerrilla Conditions* and sometimes as *Ghosts At Number 9*. There is no evidence in any letters, statements, or interviews to suggest that these names were any more than working titles.

Ghosts At Number 9 refers of course to 9 rue Git-le-Coeur, Paris. The 'Beat Hotel'. I was once told that 'Git Le Coeur' means 'lying heart' but I might be misinformed. This scattered pile of primarily 35mm film cans was and still is also known as *Guerrilla Conditions*, a title I myself personally favour as it seems more open-ended and anything unashamedly unspecific curries such favour in my book.

During 1980 Antony Balch was dying of cancer. I was seeing Brion Gysin more and more regularly in Paris and corresponding with him. I kept insisting to both Brion and William that whilst I understood their books and other more traditional works were becoming more academically respected and assimilated, there was another aspect of their works and collaborations far more inspiring and culturally nourishing for a new neo-hip younger audience.

For this generation weaned on television, radio and records and that read books less and less, this was undoubtedly the legendary and underexposed cut-up experiments with tape and film. The ideas, the recordings and the films. In contemporary, accelerating media terms these

Top: Master Musicians of Joujouka; below: Genesis P-Orridge and William Burroughs at The Final Academy

manuals of possibility and artistic perception were increasingly and more obviously, imbued with far more longevity and clearly more highly significant in terms of social implication.

I felt firmly convinced that William Burroughs should seriously consider releasing a sample anthology on record of his mythical tape-recorder cut-up experiments. A persuasive and personal pet project, which in fact I am glad to confirm, did indeed come to fruition under my guidance upon Throbbing Gristle's own Industrial Records label under the haunting title, *Nothing Here Now But The Recordings*.

I was not the only transmedia activist that believed the time for a total re-appraisal and anthropological adventure was right. More and more people were referring to and understood the creative and social implications of Brion Gysin's seminally surreal cut-ups. In the area of alternative musics we, Throbbing Gristle and Psychic TV and others allies like Cabaret Voltaire and 23 Skidoo had taken what we felt we understood from various essays and other texts, in *The Job* and *The Third Mind* in particular and had tried to integrate these ideas directly into live and recorded sound, film and video performances and artifacts.

This upsurge in new groups fully versed in cut-up applications combined with these dialogues I had whilst trying to persuade William to finally make public these recorded researches, inevitably (it seems with hindsight) led me to conceive of a hyper-event: The Final Academy.[61]

The Final Academy would be an all-encompassing festival and celebratory series of events and exhibitions centred around the influence and heritage of Burroughs, Gysin and Balch. I soon shared the rudiments of this altruistic and optimistic idea with my friend David Dawson who ran his cutting edge B2 Gallery to great effect in Wapping, London.

David Dawson was unequivocally marvellous. He immediately saw the contemporary relevance and strength of such a spectacle and was also the person who knew enough about arts funding, event logistics, commercial sponsorship and media manipulation and more crucially had the appropriate establishment contacts to really make it happen.

Whilst David devoted himself to working up more completely The Final Academy concept and its realisation with me, I also continued in my conversations and letters to persuade William and Brion that the cut-ups and films were a set of ideas whose time and mass media application had truly come, with The Final Academy as the vehicle of vindication.

As I recall, what happened next was remarkable. Here is my version of the mythical salvage of the films. The title *Thee Films* came simply from only knowing there was something and referring endlessly to it as 'the films'.

How Do You Hold A Tin Can By Both Its Tales?

I got a phone message out of the blue during 1980 from Brion Gysin in Paris. He said I must phone him straight back as soon as I got his message because it was an emergency. This was unlike Brion, so I did immediately return his call. He told me that Antony had just died. Terry Wilson had called Brion in something of a panic. Apparently Antony shared an office with someone in Soho, London, from where he had been distributing *Horror Hospital*, a film he'd made; he also distributed Russ Meyer films and a few other sexploitation movies. Several stacks of dented and rusty film cans that were Antony's were stored in a corner in this tiny office. The primary tenant of the office hadn't received any rent for a while from Antony. Of course, he was dead! Somehow Terry had discovered that this very day this person was going to throw the film cans in their entirety into a builder's skip outside the front door unless someone came and claimed them. It was clear to this person that they had no obvious commercial value.

I asked Brion what he felt I should do? He told me very kindly and with sincerity, "I have spoken with William and everyone [which I took to mean Delta Balch at least]; we have all agreed that if you can still save them then you should have them. It's obvious that you know exactly what to do with them and that you're the best person to have them. Whatever is there is yours to use as you please." He went on to explain that from my many nagging and imploring attempts to explain to him and William the significance in a contemporary context, it was obviously me who cared the most about this material. Had the archival and editing mentality to assemble and promote it, and the popular culture access to finally get these experiments the acclamation they deserved. I promised him, in a solemn oath, that I would do everything in my power to bring these films to public attention. That if I had to do it I would make sure somehow one day they would be available on video to the public, just like books so that anyone who was interested in the ideas and how the experiments and cut-ups really looked could actually see and hear them. I promised that I would do everything in my power to keep these films safe; I promised to try and ensure that Antony got full credit for his persistent and significant contribution to underground film. I explained I was living on the dole at the time so I didn't know how exactly I would accomplish all this yet, but that the first vital task was to save the films.

I don't recall if Brion then gave me the address where the film cans were, or if he got me to call Terry. I feel I remember Brion telling me, but it makes more sense that I would have called Terry.

I had no money, of course. But I did have my dole check to cash. So I literally ran to the nearest post office. Collected my dole money. Ran home. It was by now mid-afternoon and the deadline for the dumping of these films was 5:00pm when the office was going to close. I decided that the only thing I could do was get a taxi from 50 Beck Road, Hackney in East London, where I lived in a licensed squat, into the West End. So what could I do except sacrifice my week's rent and food money and hail a black cab. I just hoped it was big enough to load all these films into.

When I got to the office in a little narrow street there was scaffolding outside. Lots of dust and cements bags and, 'lo and behold', there was even the potentially offending skip! Renovations were obviously in progress, which may have contributed to the frantic timing of this cultural crisis. It was very surreal going up some very narrow, winding stairs into a tiny office. I said I was there to collect the Antony Balch "stuff".

A very malodorous man gave me a filthy look. He was fat, out of breath, with those ill-fitting trousers that reveal the grossly compelling sickly pink bum crack no matter how many times they are hitched up. All visible hand and neck areas were a fertile meadow of misdirected pubic hair. The pale blue psychotic eyes of a man who would nail a client's hands to the floor for a tardy debt dismissed me with disconcerting unpleasantness. Not your typical 'beatnik' aficionado, I thought.

He pointed to the legendary piles of film cans. Truly covered in dust, rusting, bent. Taped shut so long ago the tape disintegrated into slivers of crackling yellow at the merest touch. Phew! I was in time. And no, they were not in a toilet.[62] Though perhaps, given the large human turd I had found defecated by meaninglessness into this constricted space, in a hyperreal sense, I guess they were.

I don't suppose you've lugged much old 35mm film in cans. But actually it's heavy. Just like big books. Luckily for me the taxi driver was friendly. He helped me carry the treasure trove downstairs to the pavement and using a small trolley he had in his cab next to the driver's side, we loaded up and drove away from where we had parked, with the meter running, next to the ominous skip.

Needless to say, I called Brion when I got home to give him the good news. He told me that William had been pleased I was saving what I could and fully supported my being the new proactive custodian of these films.

Never Let A Shoe String Become A Hamstring

There were 28 cans of reels of 35mm film. Almost all were black and white. There were three that were actually 35mm colour negatives that had never ever been printed. Not even by Antony Balch. So at first nobody had any idea what was on those.

After these surviving cans of film were entrusted into my possession I was curious to see what they actually were of course! As soon as I could scrounge together enough money I rented a professional film editing deck with an operator. One of those giant old machines as large as a table that as you spool through the reels allows you to see the images in a tiny scratchy screen. Derek Jarman helped me find a cheap place through his contacts.

Then came the archaeological process. I sat for days, sometimes with Derek Jarman visiting, or David Dawson and laboriously hand wrote a meticulous list of every single scene, every single edit section, in every single decaying can by noting as best I could a verbal description of what seemed to be happening visually.

Although, through my friendship with William and Brion I had become pretty familiar with the period documented and its primary players, there were a few glaring blanks in my abilities to distinguish between shots of young men masturbating and so on. Terry Wilson generously agreed to come in and sit through many repetitive hours of film in order to identify as many specific locales and people as possible. His arcane knowledge of such matters was encyclopaedic and invaluable.

There now remained only the mystery of the colour negative reels to solve. Derek Jarman in particular, given his obvious alchemical and painterly concerns with colour in film, was very excited to know more about how these looked and whether they constituted yet another entirely forgotten and 'lost' film project in its own right, or whether they were more of the same.

Luckily enough a solution to this problem presented itself to us all later in February 1983 during The Final Academy. Another incredibly important and significant milestone event in the greater re-appreciation of the beatniks that is also curiously omitted until now from all official biographies dealing with the main protagonists' careers and lives. Most peculiar! Most peculiar.

David Dawson, who co-curated with myself, assisted by Roger Ely, managed to get [the television channel] BBC2 to agree to screen the *Burroughs* [aka *Burroughs: The Movie*] documentary by Howard Brookner as a part of The Final Academy celebrations.

Howard was flown over to London. We were loaned an editing suite by the BBC. I agreed to assist him through the editing. So I sat for hours with him, helping and advising, as did others involved.

There were various chunks of information and voice-over in his documentary film that didn't have correlative images yet, so I naturally suggested that sections previously unseen by anyone from *Ghosts At Number 9* and *Guerrilla Conditions* could be put in these gaps to add a unique new historical depth and completeness. In return for this loan I asked for no money, just a simple acknowledgment for my contribution in the credits at the end of this program and any and all future releases of the film in any format in perpetuity. This clause was formally agreed in a contract dated 18 February, 1983, and signed by Howard Brookner, Alan Yentob of the BBC and myself.

I was given this credit when the documentary was broadcast. I believe it was at the end of *The Final Academy Documents,* issued by Factory/Ikon video later. When it was agreed to license/transfer the production to Mystic Fire in New York, I believe my name was removed. Certainly I do not believe I get any credit any more. I have no idea why my contribution was erased. I believe the documentary would never have got finished if David Dawson hadn't set up for the BBC to pay to finish it, or if I hadn't supplied footage and supervision.

My fee from the BBC was that they would at their own expense transfer the colour negatives to high quality video master positive so that I could see what was on these reels. In fact, when the colour negatives were transferred to U-Matic video the content turned out to be mainly more of the same. Though I did later discover a small reel of 16mm colour film which showed William Burroughs apparently buying a parrot from someone. I thought in Tangier, but Brion Gysin interestingly suggested it was Gibraltar. I wonder if he meant a house in Tangier with a view of the Gibraltar Straits. I found this film in a black plastic trash bag that Delta Balch gave me one day as I was leaving her home. She said the trash was to be thrown out from Antony's room but she wanted me to have it as per Brion's instructions. I had become friendly with Delta through meetings at the October Gallery where she attended events such as my showings of the films and Brion's paintings etc. I named this film *William Buys A Parrot* simply to identify it later.

The only extant print of *Bill And Tony* was also included in all these reels and rediscovered by my endeavours. Two [35mm] viewing copies of *Towers Open Fire* and two of *The Cut-Ups* were also included. Plus a good copy of *Witchcraft Through The Ages*. The film [*Witchcraft Through The Ages*] is dross though. Redeemed only by the voice-over and even then more for completeness and novelty than anything else. Though this period of time is — is — when William was synthesizing his theories of magick. Cutting out enemy images from photos, re-pasting them. Playing trouble tapes outside restaurants fallen into disfavor etc and which is a topic I discussed with William at length during 1971 when we first became friendly. So, I can only speculate on the significance, or synchronicity of his involvement in this project. There's a definite ironic completeness for sure. I always thought an audio only of this voice-over would save the awful experience of having to watch this film to hear William!

That both William and Brion told me at that time that the films and all rights to them were to all intents and purposes now mine is supported by various correspondences we had thereafter. Not just my being asked permission to include them in *Burroughs* and my credit to that effect; but also in letters asking for loans of them for events William was taking part in the USA later and so on.

Personally, I always saw myself as a volunteer custodian 'taking care' of the films. Publicising the films. Respecting the films. And preserving them for posterity. Once they were out there and re-appreciated both in terms of importance and historical chronology I had kept my promise to Brion (and William). I feel I always did everything I could to ensure they were safe.

I had no sentimental attachment to them. Except perhaps *William Buys A Parrot* which was previously unknown. I felt I had to a degree, invented the film by suggesting it was a complete piece in and of itself.

This particular can was, as I said, in a trash bag that Delta Balch gave me. It would not have existed a day longer either. I feel I gave birth to it in an obscure way.

A little later, the October Gallery in Holborn staged an exhibition of the paintings of Brion Gysin, from 11 March, 1981–4 April, 1981. The curators of the October Gallery had become friends of mine and had always been enthusiastic about William Burroughs and Brion Gysin (indeed Brion introduced ME to them). I organized screenings of *Towers Open Fire, The Cut Ups* and *William Buys A Parrot* as well as *Terminus* by Psychic TV as part of this event.

The Rest Before The Storm (Wherein All That Is Trash Turns To Gold)

I had already been invited to have afternoon tea with Delta at her home and received the trash bag. Apart from the 16mm film cans it contained there was voluminous correspondence between Burroughs/Gysin/Sommerville and Balch. Also there were audio cassettes of William and Brion Gysin and Antony Balch reading out loud the *Naked Lunch* film treatment that Brion had written. The large folders of the camera shooting instructions were also in there. As was a copy of the *Naked Lunch* script. Plus postcards, legal letters regarding trying to sell and realize the movie etc.

I told Delta that this was an overwhelming gift. She said she wanted me to have all of it because she felt she trusted me and that I would honor her son's memory as best I could. She had "always told him that those homosexual writers would destroy him!"

Nevertheless I insisted that I at least give Delta a token payment for legal reasons. Then she had sold me, a collector archivist, various materials owned by her and that would be a legitimate transaction that should remove the risk of later contention or dispute. She agreed and handwrote me a receipt for one hundred pounds sterling. She was fully aware that this was not necessarily a market value. She explained she did not want Burroughs or Gysin to "get their hands on it". Though she kept all of Brion's paintings, 26 at least, "because she liked them". She was a very proper and charming woman, and I could only respect each and every one of her decisions. She felt the loss of her son terribly. I liked her very much.

Thee Films As Material And Immaterial Ping Pong

To my knowledge, pretty much none of this stuff had been seen or bothered with for years. By anyone. Not even Antony, William, or Brion. Throbbing Gristle used to hire a copy of *Towers Open Fire* from an obscure film distributor in Surrey (I think). This took a lot of research on our part to find it in their catalogue. I believe it was Terry Wilson who finally gave me a lead during one of our first meetings.

Before The Final Academy I had been dubbing a few copies of VHS videos of the films and selling them mail order to occasional enthusiasts who discovered I had them. A few went to arts festivals, film festivals, art galleries and TV station researchers. I xeroxed the covers and copied them at home on two domestic machines. Later I dubbed them professionally at a Pakistani supermarket that also dubbed Hindi movies.

I saw this as stage one in the strategy of honoring my promises to Brion and Delta in particular. I was given to understand by William personally that I had his blessing too. It was never many copies. Probably less than fifty in all.

I guess these are now Limited Edition collector's items. But it is drudge work even for a fan like myself. Of course we proselytized the films via live disconcerts too. Showing them during, before or after Throbbing Gristle and/or Psychic TV gigs. I think this had a wider, deeper impact.

From the time I received into my hands these films and other raw materials, I proselytized them as best I could. Screening them in Holland at film festivals, in Hamburg for Klaus Maeck and in London. Also organizing their being shown at other Arts Centres and Festivals, either on film or video. I also got them, or bits, shown on TV a few times. All of which was intended to advertise positively their existence and cultural importance. I believe I succeeded. I also licensed them to various small video labels to get them out to a new, younger public, as inspiration and confirmation of contemporary attitudes and trends in film and video. I think their significance increases with time. Just as I believed it did with the audio cut-up recordings I worked so hard to salvage, index and then release as *Nothing Here Now But The Recordings*.

After The Final Academy, Ikon Video — a sub-group of Factory Records — negotiated with me, for the historical movies and with William and John Giorno for their reading performances to release a deluxe collector's edition — on 11 June, 1984 — called *The Final Academy Documents*, in a red box on two VHS videos with four postcards enclosed.

Later I became friends with the proprietors of Mystic Fire Video (in particular William Breeze who ironically, all these years later is now viola player with Psychic TV). I facilitated the initial stages of their release in the USA of *Thee Films*. Although the title was changed and Burroughs, rather than Antony, received pre-eminent crediting, I suppose for marketing reasons. I believe I still got a thank you on the cover.

At this point I felt I had succeeded pretty well in the task I had set myself for Brion and Antony. The films were now commercially available. Critically acclaimed and reassessed. The Burroughs documentary was also commercially released. Though my part and David Dawson's part were conspicuous in their absence.

I felt very strongly that I had given my word to everyone that this material could and should be made available as essential historically in some form. I feel to this day that I kept my word and did a good job of representing the material and preserving it for posterity.

I must make it clear that it soon became obvious to me that I was taking on this burden for love of Brion and respect for Delta. I never met Antony, but I think, I hope, his incredible work will continue to be more thoroughly appreciated and respected. He deserves it too and I am honored to have had a chance to play my part in all that.[63]

Lost Where The Agents Of Control Turn *The Final Academy* Into The Final Movie

I had been quite deeply involved in an underground movie in Germany called *Decoder*, helping with theories and ideas as well as appearing in a cameo role (typecast of course). As many of Brion and William's more interesting ideas relating to cut-ups were central to the plot Klaus Maeck asked me if I thought Burroughs might be interested in appearing too. I said possibly, I would do what I could to help persuade him. It transpired that whilst he was in London, after we flew him in for the Final Academy, William did indeed shoot a cameo role as a shop proprietor selling cassette recorder parts to the 'hero' played by Mufti [F.M. Einheit] of Einstürzende Neubauten.

I literally hired Derek Jarman as my cameraperson for the whole period of The Final Academy. Whenever he could Derek accompanied me to events, dinners, filming for *Decoder*, etc.

He shot plastic carrier bags full of Super-8 film for me on the strict understanding it all belonged to me later for a film I would construct. In fact, as a bonus fee for Derek helping me out I agreed later to let him use a small section of this movie. It was of William in Tottenham Court Road outside the shop location with various fans and passers-by. Very slowed down. It was titled *Pirates* (aka *Pirate Tape* aka *Pirate Tape William S. Burroughs*, 1982) and I did the soundtrack for it as a further thankyou to Derek.

The rest of this film footage was still in bags in my archive in Brighton when Scotland Yard raided it in 1991. They took all the film of William Burroughs, Brion Gysin, at The Final Academy filmed by Derek Jarman and myself. Produced by myself. They took DAT tapes that were parts of the soundtrack. It remains lost.[64]

It was, of course called *Thee Final Academy*.

Later in the 1980s sold cans to WSB/Miles.

Washed my hands of them.

4. Ongoing Guerilla Conditions

On 2 October, 1999 at London's Horse Hospital newly unearthed footage shot by Antony Balch was screened under the title *Ongoing Guerrilla Conditions* — essentially featuring unedited and unassembled footage from the aborted *Guerrilla Conditions* project. The exhibition of the footage was coordinated by the Islamic Diggers (aka Joe Ambrose and Frank Rynne), who were previously responsible for the 1992 event 'The Here To Go Show' in Dublin, which celebrated the work of Gysin and Burroughs, in literature, films and artwork. Drawing upon the archives of Terry Wilson and Felicity Mason, the event included the exhibition of paintings by Gysin, film screenings and performances by the Master Musicians of Joujouka and was subsequently documented in the 1995 film *Destroy All Rational Thought*.

Ongoing Guerrilla Conditions featured several images and sequences that were familiar from both *The Cut-Ups* and *Ghosts At Number 9*. However, additional scenes are also apparent in this footage, including sequences involving a running street chase and a brawling group of young men.

The silent footage was accompanied by a soundtrack supplied by the Islamic Diggers:

> "...a live DJ soundscape around the footage while looking at it, so the noise has never been the same two nights running. But the soundscape is deeply informed by the work we've been doing for years, especially in the areas of Joujouka, Burroughs, Gysin, panic music. A lot of the recordings of Joujouka and Gnoua which we use were recorded in Morocco by Frank Rynne. A lot of the other beats, samples and loops arise from our own archive. We've done a lot of work with dreamachines, cut-ups, sonic experiments. And we use the voices of pals like Lydia Lunch, etc. We try to create a soundscape which takes on board the ideology shared by Balch, Burroughs and Gysin, the essential trio who created this footage, while also reflecting the environments in which they did their experiments. You might have some Chet Baker, maybe him singing "Let's Get Lost" or "Funny Valentine", or Maureen Tucker representing the New York sound of white noise punk guitar attack, the slick hip hop of Rawkus, percussion from Gnoua or Cameroon, electricity, a Sufi choir from Fez, our own Islamic Diggers tracks".[65]

According to Joe Ambrose, the footage presented as *Ongoing Guerrilla Conditions* came from various sources including author Terry Wilson, who was given footage by Antony Balch. Terry Wilson, states Ambrose, "saw a great deal of Balch when he was terminally ill. More of it was rescued from the rubbish bins into which Delta Balch threw it".[66] The footage had remained unscreened because, as Ambrose states, Balch "essentially left his film company affairs in chaos".[67]

Also screened as part of the same event by the Islamic Diggers was *Three Minute Movie*, which was ostensibly designed as an advert for Burroughs' books. The Islamic Diggers rediscovered Balch's *Three Minute Movie*

> "after spending a long period of time, a few years, going through various little piles of the Brion Gysin archive. We then stuck it together, which was easy enough when we finally got our hands on the whole lot of it and created a soundtrack. The original soundtrack has disappeared though I think we're hot on the trail of it. We put together our thing for it using Joujouka and Gnoua samples. The people who assisted us in reassembling *Three Minute Movie* were the Irish graffiti painter China White and Marek Pytel, a London filmmaker".[68]

Joe Ambrose believes that *Three Minute Movie* was "originally intended [by Balch] to be shown in between a double bill of Fellini movies in Soho'".[69] Although it is uncertain as

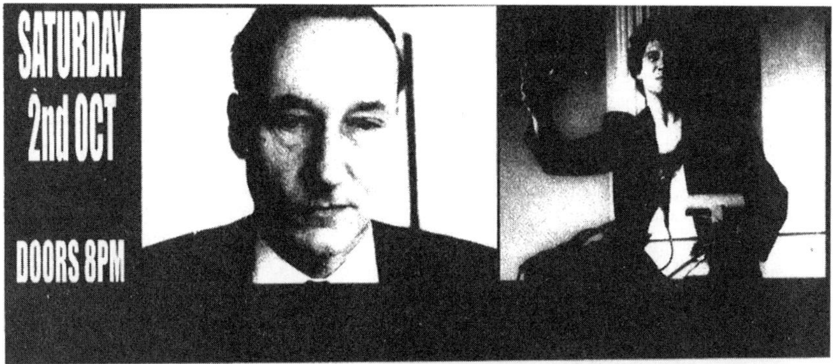

ONGOING GUERILLA CONDITIONS **ANTONY BALCH & WILLIAM BURROUGHS**

A rare and previously unseen, reel-by-reel, unique insight into the working practices of Burroughs and his coterie sees the brilliant *PRIMITIVE VISUAL SAVAGERY* of Antony Balch come into its own.

LIVE SOUNDTRACK & DJ SET FROM ISLAMIC DIGGERS!!!!

***Poster for world premiere of* Ongoing Guerilla Conditions**

to whether this ever transpired, it would certainly appear to have been exactly the kind of tactic in which Balch would have enjoyed engaging.

The archival searches of artists such as the Islamic Diggers means that other footage may also be rediscovered. Burroughs, Gysin and Balch affiliate Terry Wilson still possesses footage in his archive that has yet to be catalogued; while much of it may be prints of the known Balch movies, Wilson does not rule out the possibility that among the bags of footage he has there may be out-takes and alternative shots from the Balch movies.

---

1. William Burroughs in *Towers Open Fire*.

2. 'Antony Balch Interview', in *Cinema Rising*, #1, April, 1972.

3. 'Antony Balch Interview'.

4. 'Antony Balch Interview'.

5. On the film's 'release' at least one critic stated "William Burroughs ... applies his technique of apparently arbitrary juxtaposition of things ... to an eleven minute film" (Isabel Quigly, *The Spectator*, 21st June, 1963), while John Coleman described the film as "a massively indulgent chain of non-sequiturs" (*New Statesman*, 21st June, 1963)

6. Antony Balch Interview'.

7. Burroughs revised *The Soft Machine* three times: the first version was published by Olympia Press, Paris, in 1961, the second by Grove Press, New York, in 1966, and the third by Calder and Boyars, London, in 1968.

8. The entire narrative of *Towers Open Fire* was reproduced under the title 'Towers Open Fire!' in *Film*, #37, Autumn 1963.

9. Burroughs' other cut-up works include: the collaborative *Minutes To Go* (1960), written/compiled with Brion Gysin, Sinclair Beiles and Gregory Corso — who would almost immediately recant, claiming that his poetic 'muse' should not be cut up; *Time* (1965) a cut-up version of *Time* magazine; *So Who Owns Death TV?* (1967) a collaboration with Claude Pelieu and Carl Weissner; and *The Dead Star* (1969), amongst others. Burroughs also experimented with the self-explanatory fold-in method, in sections of *The Soft Machine* and *The Ticket That Exploded*.

10. William Burroughs, *Nova Express*, in *The Soft Machine, Nova Express, The Wild Boys, Three Novels* by William Burroughs, A Black Cat Book, Grove Press Inc, New York, 1980 (1964), p.62/63.

11. Antony Balch also arranged the first British screening of Sam Fuller's classic *Shock Corridor* (1963).

12. 'Antony Balch Interview'.

13. Jeff Nuttall, *Bomb Culture,* MacGibbon & Kee Ltd, London, 1968, p.155.

14. *Bomb Culture,* p.155. Note that the title is unspecified in Nuttall's text, although the film was almost certainly *Window Water Baby Moving* (1959) which depicts the birth of Brakhage's daughter.

15. *Bomb Culture,* p.155–156.

16. 'Antony Balch Interview'.

17. 'Antony Balch Interview'.

18. 'Antony Balch Interview'.

19. Genesis P. Orridge states that, according to Brion Gysin, there was originally a third feature-length version (one and a half hours) which was screened at events by the sound poet group Domain Poetique.

20. William Burroughs, quoted in Conrad Knickerbocker, 'Interview with William S. Burroughs' in *William S. Burroughs and Brion Gysin, The Third Mind,* John Calder Ltd, London, 1979 (1978), p.4.

21. William Burroughs 'The Fall Of Art' in *The Adding Machine: Collected Essays,* John Calder, London, 1985, p.62.

22. 'Antony Balch Interview'.

23. Antony Balch quoted in *Sight And Sound, Vol 38, #2,* Spring 1969,

24. Brion Gysin quoted in Jon Savage, 'Brion Gysin Interview', in V.Vale & Andrea Juno, eds, *William S. Burroughs, Brion Gysin, Throbbing Gristle: Re/Search #4/5,* San Francisco, 1982, p.55. This view is further iterated in the interview when Jon Savage states that he saw the films at a 'disconcert' by industrial music group Throbbing Gristle and that "people were actually completely flipped out and the whole concert ended up in a huge fight. The whole evening was very, very charged ... I felt, not as a result (but pretty damn nearly) of seeing those 2 films first, in a combination with all of that" (p.56).

25. Ian Sommerville, 'Flicker', in Paul Cecil, ed, *Flickers Of The Dreamachine,* Codex, Hove, 1996, p.10.

26. The film has been dated — by the British film Institute — as being produced by Balch and Burroughs in 1972, although it should be recognized that the film was almost certainly produced before this date. Balch is known to have discussed the project in 1970, in the *Cinema Rising* interview, which transpired on 19 December, 1970, but remained unpublished for two years. Due to the 'home movie' nature of the text any accurate dating is impossible. To further confuse matters Brion Gysin repeatedly stated that the film was shot on 70mm, while Antony Balch stated that it was filmed on 35mm. When Genesis P. Orridge saved Balch's films following his death in 1980, only one copy of the film was found among Balch's archive and this was a 35mm print.

27. Brion Gysin quoted in Brion Gysin/Terry Wilson, 'Planet R-101. Here To Go — Brion Gysin In Conversation With Terry Wilson', in Breger, Udo, ed, *Soft Need #17 — Brion Gysin Special,* Expanded Media Editions, Basel-Paris, October, 1977, p.101.

28. 'Planet R-101. Here To Go — Brion Gysin In Conversation With Terry Wilson', p.101.

29. William Burroughs, cited in Barry Miles, *William Burroughs: El Hombre Invisible,* Virgin Books, London, 1993 (1992), p.165.

30. This date has been suggested by Chris Rodley in his essay 'So Deep In My Heart That You're Really A Part Of Me' in Ira Silverberg, ed, *Everything Is Permitted: The Making Of Naked Lunch,* Grafton, London, 1992.

31. Brion Gysin, 'Naked Lunch: Brion Gysin Screenplay' in *The Final Academy: Statements Of A Kind,* catalogue compiled by The Final Academy, David Dawson, Roger Ely and Genesis P.Orridge, 1982, p.17.

32. 'Naked Lunch: Brion Gysin Screenplay', p.17.

33. Naked Lunch: Brion Gysin Screenplay', p.17.

34. 'Naked Lunch: Brion Gysin Screenplay', p.17.

35. 'Naked Lunch: Brion Gysin Screenplay', p.17.

36. Gordon went on to produce the alien-impregnation horror film *Inseminoid* (1980) amongst others.

37. *Secrets Of Sex* has been released — un-cut — on video in European countries under the title *Bizarre,* according to David McGillivray's *Doing Rude Things: The History Of The British Sex Film,* 1957–1981, (Sun Tavern Fields, London, 1992, p.105).

38. In Barry Miles' *El Hombre Invisible,* Allen Ginsberg is quoted as saying that, during his 1961 visit to Burroughs in Tangiers, Burroughs asked him: "'Who are you an agent for?' ... [because] he assumed that everybody was an agent at that point. Not necessarily for the government at all; an agent for a

giant trust of insects from another galaxy actually. Women were suspect as being agents and Burroughs thought that maybe you had to exterminate all the women, or get rid of them one way or another." (p.140/141).

39. Ted Morgan, *Literary Outlaw: The Life And Times Of William S. Burroughs,* Henry Holt & Company, New York, 1988, p.453.

40. Ted Morgan also states that, in 1977, Elliott Gould was interested in obtaining the rights and subsequently appearing in, *The Last Words Of Dutch Schultz* (1975), Burroughs' text/film script inspired by the official transcript of Schultz's last words. Burroughs also wrote a film treatment in 1980 called *Blade Runner (A Movie),* note that this has nothing to do with the film of the same name directed by Ridley Scott. Also in 1977 Jacques Stern took a year long option on *Junky* and paid Terry Southern to write a script. The film was going to be directed by — and star — Dennis Hopper. Unfortunately the project began to flounder, despite the suggestion that various stars were interested in the film (including both David Bowie and Jack Nicholson). When the option ran out the following year nothing had been completed.

41. Genesis P-Orridge, personal correspondence.

42. That this footage represents an early version/try out of *Naked Lunch* would seem likely, given that photographs of this sequence are used to illustrate an extract from Brion Gysin's screenplay, titled 'Naked Lunch: Fragment of a Scenario' reproduced in the collaborative book *The Third Mind.* Further, in Genesis P.Orridge's notes on the contents of the footage on the rescued reels, he describes the shot as: Can One, shot #11; "WSB acting end *Naked Lunch* in Tangier (after shooting cops) packing his case".

43. Genesis P-Orridge, personal correspondence.

44. Genesis P-Orridge, personal correspondence.

45. In fact the bird is a cockatoo — or "Kokatoo" as William Burroughs refers to it in his correspondence with Antony Balch.

46. Genesis P-Orridge, personal correspondence.

47. Genesis P-Orridge, personal correspondence.

48. *Nova Express,* p.56.

49. Gilles Deleuze and Felix Guattari, *Anti-Oedipus; Capitalism And Schizophrenia,* vol 1, University of Minnesota Press, Minneapolis, 1992, (1972/1977), p.9.

50. In Deleuze and Guattari's *A Thousand Plateaus: Capitalism And Schizophrenia,* vol 2, (Athlone, London, 1988), they suggest that Burroughs' work ultimately fails to become a BwO, primarily because while it acknowledges fragmentation, the texts never fully escape from a higher unity. Deleuze would repeatedly utilize Burroughs in his later work, finally recognizing him as the prophet of Control society.

51. Burroughs' Interzone in *Naked Lunch,* Gysin's Neverzone in the screenplay of *Naked Lunch.*

52. The original version of this interview opened with the following paragraph: "As reported in our last issue (page 12) the Balch/Gysin/Burroughs films *Towers Open Fire* and *Cut Ups* were shown at the Anzart-In-Hobart Convention in 1983. We were astonished at the importance of these films and puzzled by their omission from avant-garde film histories. Henri Chopin provided us with an introduction and while we were in Paris last October we contacted Brion Gysin who kindly agreed to an interview which follows."

53. *Ned Kelly* (Tony Richardson, 1970).

54. This is a reference to a review, which states; "Gysin is a dangerous and very useful man in that, like a few others — Cage and Maclow — he knows how to make a text work and is pushing that area of operation further and further out. Why isn't more of this man's work available?" (Ken Hollings, 'Short Reviews', in *Performance: The Review Of Live Art, #26,* October/November 1983, p.6.)

55. The Nova Convention ran from November 30th–December 2nd, 1978. Primarily events took place at the Entermedia Theatre, New York, on 2nd Avenue and 12th Street. The Nova Convention was inspired by Sylvère Lotringer, who suggested organizing a 'Burroughs homage' to John Giorno, who discussed the idea with Burroughs' assistant James Grauerholz. The ensuing event was — according to Ted Morgan's *Literary Outlaw: The Life And Times Of William S. Burroughs* — a high point in the 'punk' movement and the 'counterculture' in general. The event featured performances and lectures/debates from, amongst others, Allen Ginsberg, John Cage, Ed Sanders, Frank Zappa, Patti Smith, Brion Gysin, Timothy Leary and Robert Anton Wilson.

56. Barney Rosset obtained Grove Press in 1951 for $3,000 as an 'ailing concern'. His radical vision transformed it into the publishing house responsible for publishing many 'notorious' books; D.H. Lawrence's *Lady Chatterly's Lover* (1957), Henry Miller's *Tropic Of Cancer* (1961) and William Burroughs'

Naked Lunch (1962). Rosset's desire to liberate the word from censorship meant that he had to fight expensive court cases for each of these books (including more than sixty cases for Miller's book).

57. In 1966 Grove Press took over the film distribution for Amos Vogel's *Cinema 16*. Rosset added Vilgot Sjoman's *I Am Curious (Yellow)* (1968) to the Grove distribution lists and once again was faced with defending an artist from censorship.

58. Alan Schneider directed *Film* (1965), which was written by Samuel Beckett; it received a Diploma di Meito at the Venice Film festival in 1965.

59. Throbbing Gristle was one of the first industrial bands, alongside groups/performers such as Cabaret Voltaire, 23 Skidoo, SPK, Monte Cazazza and Non, all of whom were equally interested in/influenced by the Burroughs/Sommerville/Gysin sonic experiments.

60. Derek Jarman (1942–1994) was the filmmaker, artist, magician and gardener responsible for a variety of films from Super-8 experimental films such as *A Journey To Avebury* (1972) and *In The Shadow Of The Sun* (1974) and feature-length films such as *Sebastiane* (1975), *Jubilee* (1977), *The Last Of England* (1987), *The Garden* (1990) and *Blue* (1993).

61. In 1982, curator David Dawson, performer Roger Ely and Genesis P-Orridge collaborated on organizing *The Final Academy*, a four-day program of events, running from 29 September to the 2 October, at the Ritzy Cinema, London, which celebrated the work of William Burroughs. This event included performances and readings from Burroughs, Brion Gysin, John Giorno, Terry Wilson and Jeff Nuttall, amongst others, as well as screenings of Antony Balch's films. On 4th October a Final Academy evening was held at the Hacienda, Manchester. A double video of the event, *The Final Academy Documents*, featuring readings by William Burroughs and John Giorno (filmed at the Hacienda) and the films *Towers Open Fire* and *Ghosts At Number 9*, was released by Ikon Video and Psychic Television.

62. This is a reference to the rumor that Genesis P-Orridge saved the films from a lavatory.

63. The following is a brief summery of the material P-Orridge saved from both Antony Balch's office and Delta Balch's house:

Film/s

1 large can 35mm black and white negative, 17 large cans of 35mm black and white prints. Silent, 2 projector prints of *Towers Open Fire*, 35mm, with sound, 1 incomplete print of *Towers Open Fire* (possibly a grading copy), 1 viewing print of *Towers Open Fire* (16mm, black and white, with sound), 1 viewing print of *Bill And Tony*, 35mm colour with sound, 2 reels (18 inch) 16mm *Witchcraft Through The Ages*, viewing print, 2 viewing prints of *The Cut-Ups*, black and white, 16mm with sound, 1 viewing print *William Buys A Parrot*, 16mm, colour, silent.

The 18 cans of miscellaneous footage contained the material intended for *Guerrilla Conditions* and *Ghosts At Number 9* and much of it was subsequently released as *Ghosts At Number 9 (Paris)*. Note, however, that the footage found in can number 8 was on three reels. The first of these reels became *William Buys A Parrot* and the second became *Transmutations*.

Film Treatments And Scripts

Naked Lunch Film Treatment: four volume, 14″ x 12″ spiral bound files, containing Balch's hand-drawn and felt-tip pen colored, storyboards, for feature-length film version of *Naked Lunch*. *Horror Hotel*, script by Antony Balch. Untitled and unpublished Brion Gysin screenplay.

64. Following the demise of Throbbing Gristle, on 23 June, 1981, P-Orridge co-founded Psychic TV which released a series of albums varying from avant-garde noise to pop and the Temple of Psychic Youth, a Wild Boys-inspired libertarian magical group who experimented with the ritual possibilities of sexuality. Some of these magical experiments/performance art events were documented on the video *Thee First Transmission* (1981). In 1991, following an evangelical Christian fundamentalist accusation of Satanism against the Temple of Psychic Youth broadcast on the television documentary strand *Dispatches*, the police raided P-Orridge's home, seizing his archive and forcing P-Orridge into exile (for a full account of the case see Simon Dwyer, 'From Atavism To Zyklon B: An Interview With Genesis P-Orridge' in Simon Dwyer, ed, *Rapid Eye 1*, Creation Books: London, 1995 [1993, 1989]).

65. Joe Ambrose, personal correspondence.

66. Joe Ambrose, personal correspondence.

67. Joe Ambrose, personal correspondence.

68. Joe Ambrose, personal correspondence.

69. Joe Ambrose, personal correspondence.

Chapter Eleven

Cut-Up/Burroughs/Punk/Cut-Up

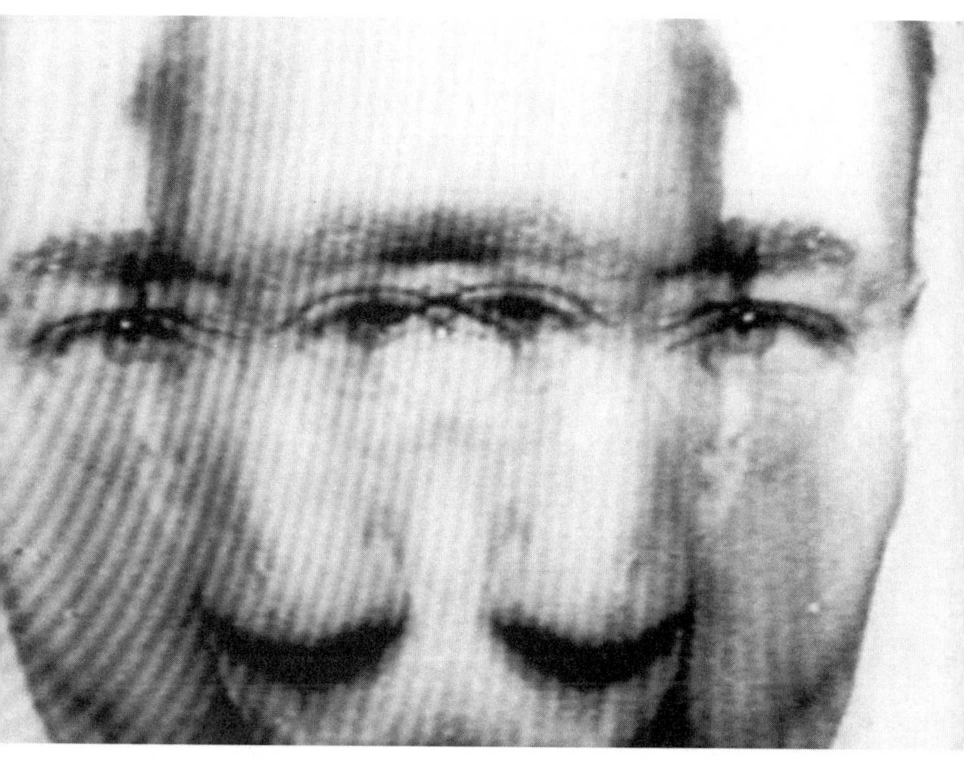

1. Electronic Revolutionaries

William Burroughs' literature always attempts to precipitate change, to galvanize multiple potentialities and is marked by a clear antipathy towards various manifestations of Control. Burroughs' work repeatedly plays the celebratory libertarian-anarchism implied by Hassan I Sabbah's reported last words: "Nothing Is True — Everything Is Permitted", against Control. One aspect of Burroughs' armory against Control, alongside weapons ranging from home-made guns to Deadly Orgone Radiation, is the tape recorder, a machine that, as Burroughs has suggested in various essays and interviews, could be utilized as a magical tool, a viral device and a sound weapon.[1]

The inherent possibilities of the tape recorder were first recognized by Brion Gysin, who, while living at the Beat Hotel in 1959, began exploring the use of cut-up recordings. Burroughs initially assisted Gysin in these experiments and in 1960, while living in the Empress Hotel in London, commenced his own tape recorder experiments. Burroughs was assisted in these experiments by Ian Sommerville, a mathematician and scientist, who also assisted Gysin in the designing of the dreamachine. The experiments conducted by Burroughs and Sommerville explored the cutting up of music, street noise, voices, as well as attempts to record sub-vocal speech and the physical manipulation of the tape during recording, playback and re-recording. Together Burroughs and Sommerville would push the tape recorder experiments to the limits in order to fully understand and examine the potential of the machines as tools for both Control and insurrection, as Burroughs stated, "We weren't thinking about art, we were thinking about alterations and the, shall we say, the potentialities of the tape recorder for altering additions and how they were undoubtedly being used for this purpose by official agencies".[2] The tape recorder experiments and other projects such as the development of the dreamachine, should not be understood purely in aesthetic terms, but also as scientific explorations analogical to Dr Wilhelm Reich's orgone accumulator and the Church of Scientology's E-Meter.[3] Sommerville is credited for his knowledgeable assistance in these experiments in Burroughs' cut-up novels *The Ticket That Exploded* and *Nova Express*, in which he appears as the 'Subliminal Kid'.

The results of the tape recorder experiments appear as tactics utilized by the protagonists in several of Burroughs' 'novels'. However it is through such incendiary non-fiction[4] texts as 'The Invisible Generation',[5] 'Electronic Revolution' and *The Revised Boy Scout Manual* that Burroughs details and suggests ways in which tape recorders and other information technologies, can be utilized as a weapon against Control. In 1966, in 'The Invisible Generation', Burroughs wrote "anyone with a tape recorder controlling the sound trackcan influence and create events". In the essay 'Electronic Revolution', William Burroughs suggests that the tape recorder could become a weapon which could be used to; "spread rumors ... with carefully prepared recordings",[6] or discredit opponents via editing together their prerecorded speeches with various random noises such as animal squeals before playing the tape back among crowds of people. Burroughs also suggests that the tape player could be used as a "front line weapon to produce and escalate riots";[7] as he wryly observes, "recorded police whistles will draw cops. Recorded gunshots and their guns are out".[8] Burroughs observes that a team of demonstrators armed with tapes

> There should be more riots and more violence. Young people in the West have been lied to, sold out and betrayed. Best thing they can do is take the place apart before they are destroyed in a nuclear war.
> William Burroughs

Decoder *lobby card*

could wreck havoc on the forces of law and order, by playing a combination of pre-recorded riot noises and footage gathered on the day: "cut/ups on the tape recorder can be used as a weapon".[9] Burroughs also speculates that a virus could be caused in somebody via cutting up a recording of a virus sufferer with a recording of the healthy subject.

Decoder, written by Klaus Maeck and directed by Muscha, with Maeck, Volker Schaefer and Trini Trimpop, owed its inspiration to this aspect of Burroughs' work. *Decoder* focuses on the sonic experiments of a disillusioned 'noise-freak' FM, played by FM Einheit (aka Mufti) of the 'experimental' musical group Einstürzende Neubauten.[10] FM is experimenting with white noise and infra-sound, recording the daily noises around him and mixing them in his home studio. FM wants to know: "the connection between these dumb-faced and contented people, gorging themselves on one hamburger after another and the monotonously happy muzak constantly oozing out of the speakers… " From his studio window FM watches the frantic movements of the streets. After having a dream in which he sees his partner, Christiana (Christiane Felscherinow aka Christiane F.), walking in a post-apocalyptic landscape with a figure of an old man, dressed in shabby coat and trilby and hearing the clipped tones of Burroughs' voice from his own cut-up tape recorder experiments, he awakes and immediately begins to experiment in his studio with his recordings of fast-food restaurant (H. Burgers) Muzak, a form of audio valium. A second dream depicts FM entering a small shop; when the shopkeeper (William Burroughs) asks him what he wants he replies "Nothing special" and, appearing uncertain of what he is doing or looking for, FM knocks over a box of electrical diodes. The shopkeeper, who has been carefully dismantling a cassette recorder, jumps up, strides over to FM and states: "You start from zero preconceptions — you want 'nothing special' — here it is". The shopkeeper gives him the dismantled machine.

While out walking and recording noises, FM enters an abandoned warehouse, inside he watches as a number of people drum repetitively on various pieces of percussion. Small fires burn in trash cans scattered throughout the building. As FM watches he is seen by the percussionists, who drag him into an inner chamber. Here FM is seduced by the flashing lights of a dreamachine, while Burroughs' voice asks "Is this machine recording?" Then a guru figure (credited as Höhepriester and played by Genesis P-Orridge) questions FM's presence in the building, asking if the tape player was being used to trigger a virus. FM explains his reason for recording and Höhepriester tells FM "Information is guarded like a bank and we have to rob this bank". FM explains that he wants to utilize sound as a weapon.

FM begins to use his tape experiments as a form of anti-muzak, replacing the artificially soothing muzak of H. Burger restaurants with his own tapes, which — instead of inspiring placid catatonic consumption — create nausea and violence among the restaurant's patrons. The insurrection caused by FM's anti-muzak and infra-sound tapes increases, leading to large-scale riots triggered off by punks holding tape players blasting out FM's tapes. In response to the growing defiance the Muzak Corporation coerce reluctant hit man Jager (Bill Rice) to kill FM. Jager, however, has fallen in love with peepshow model Christiana on one of his many visits to the "sleazy sin city" of the Reeperbahn, initially unaware that she is FM's girlfriend. Finally Jager — who is tired of being the lackey of the Muzak Corporation — recognizes that Christiana loves FM and is killed by a speeding truck. Maeck describes it, "In the end he knew he had to finish the job. He was in love with Christiane and then he realized Mufti, who he should find and kill, is her boyfriend. So he says, 'OK. I'll finish the job in my own interests' but he couldn't do it in the end… "[11]

Decoder's presentation of the ominous Muzak Corporation is reminiscent of Burroughs' conception of Control and the 'Board', as they appear in Balch's and Burroughs' collaborative film *Towers Open Fire*. Further, the ubiquitous nature of Control is emphasized by the repeated use of video and television monitors in the film. In Jager's office one wall is dominated by screens which repeatedly depict FM's actions, as well as those of the rioters and — at the film's climax when Jager refuses to act upon his murderous orders — he too becomes an image on a screen: rendered as a pure image to be observed.

Decoder *lobby card*

The television screen is also a recurring motif in the film, repeatedly used as a symbol of cultural colonization and control; thus, during a sequence in a bar, the television in the background becomes progressively more domineering, until it all but drowns out the German protagonists with its Anglo-American voices. In another scene FM goes to an amusement arcade in order to record the sounds of the computer games, these screens too reflect a cultural colonization by a foreign power, as the images of computer graphics are edited with images of American military strength. As FM states, when Christiana doubts his claims that sound can be used to control people, "The Americans started to play around with sound fifty years ago — that's how they won the war!" However, like the tape player which can create anti-muzak, television does not have to be purely repressive and after each of the dream sequences, which firmly position Burroughs as FM's inspiration, the camera pulls back, revealing the last fading seconds of the dream transpiring on television sets positioned near the slumbering FM.

Decoder also constructs a series of thematic oppositions, which — rather than maintaining a fixed polarity throughout the film — slide. Thus in the relationship between FM and Christiana, FM is initially identified with sound, while Christiana is identified with sight (as the object of the gaze in the peepshow). FM is further identified with science and technology, (via his continual tape experiments) while Christiana is identified with the magical and organic. She is repeatedly presented playing with her pet frogs and in one sequence is identified as magical by reciting the witches' speech from Shakespeare's *Macbeth*. Yet these polarities do not remain static, but are repeatedly re-negotiated; thus in one sequence Christiana and FM are talking to one another on the phone, both wearing blindfolds, as the camera pulls back it becomes apparent that both protagonists are in the same room. The narrative emphasizes that the blindfolds are Christiana's idea and not FM's and that they are her reaction to the scopophilic nature of her work and society in general (a society which is typified by Jager, for whom watching is both his job and his major sexual pleasure). Further FM's first dream occurs directly after Christiana's *Macbeth* recital and thus identifies the Burroughs' figure as manifesting both a scientific and magical quality. These oppositions are further emphasized by the film's lighting, which washes characters in neon tones of blue, red or green depending on the nature of the scene.

Stylistically *Decoder* bears a superficial resemblance to the New York-based para- punk/No Wave cinema of the late '70s. This is, in part, due to *Decoder*'s use of Johanna Heer, the Austrian/American cinematographer who had previously worked on Amos Poe's *Subway Riders* (1981). *Decoder* also echoes the para-punk films of Beth and Scott B and especially their films *Black Box* (1978) and *The Offenders* (1979), via its narrative emphasis on the omnipotent and oppressive nature of Control and the opportunities presented by 'punk' subculture for renegotiating and transgressing the hierarchy of the social order. Like the New York para-punk filmmakers and the underground film scene in general, *Decoder* casts 'underground'/'counterculture' performers and musicians in its central roles. It should be noted that the only 'professional' actor to appear in *Decoder* is Bill Rice, an American actor who emerged primarily through his work in para-punk films such as *Subway Riders* and *G-Man* (1978).

However, where *Decoder* radically departs from the American para-punk text is in the methods of its production. The New York para-punk films were shot on nonexistent budgets, primarily on sync-sound super 8 and originally screened in nightclubs and bars such as CBGBs and Max's Kansas City, alongside performances by bands, performers and poets. By social and economic necessity the para-punk films were rapidly produced, being scripted, cast, shot, edited and screened in a matter of weeks and sometimes days. As such the films, in common with punk, shared an aesthetic of immediacy, existing as statements of political, socio-sexual and artistic urgency. In contrast to the poverty of American para-punk filmmaking, the production of *Decoder* was aided via various filmmaking grants and 'enjoyed' the relative luxury of being produced in West Germany, a country in which it was recognized that film "constitutes an autonomous art form" and thus "deserves similar subsidy on the part of the state as is enjoyed by other forms of education and expressive art forms".[12] Further, film funding in Germany, as with many European countries, is viewed as an investment in and articulation of, a 'national culture'.[13] Thus, while *Decoder* is similar to the American underground and para-punk films, with its broadly contra political perspective, it equally belongs to a tradition of European avant-garde and art cinema, which has benefited from state investment to encourage the manifestation of a nation's culture on an international scale.[14]

Decoder presents a uniquely political interpretation of Burroughs' work and — via the use of Burroughs in the film's dream sequences — directly attributes the narrative's central concerns to Burroughs' tape recorder experiments. Burroughs only appears in the film for a short time during the electronic-shop sequence (shot with the assistance of Peter Christopherson during Burroughs' stay in London for *The Final Academy* events which transpired in 1982), yet via the repeated use of his distinctive voice and the use of the dreamachine, Burroughs remains a powerful figure clearly present in the margins of the text.

Maeck also directed and produced the short film *Commissioner Of Sewers* (1991), a documentary which focuses on William Burroughs during his 1986 visit to Germany. The film utilises footage of Burroughs reading in Berlin, on 9 May, 1986, from selected texts including *Naked Lunch, The Place Of Dead Roads* and *The Western Lands* against various backgrounds, which were added during post-production; the dreamachine, text, photographs of Burroughs and reproductions of his paintings. Alongside this performance footage Maeck utilizes extracts of Burroughs' appearances from *Towers Open Fire, Decoder* and Gus Van Sant's *Thanksgiving Prayer*, as well as footage of the author walking around Berlin Zoo. *Commissioner Of Sewers* also features an interview with Burroughs by German author Jurgen Ploog, recorded the day after the performance. The film's soundtrack includes Burroughs singing an old German 'schlager'.

2. An Interview With Klaus Maeck

What other films and work were you engaged with prior to *Decoder*?

My first film was a ten-minute experiment on 16mm, with a group of young students at some kind of youth hostel program, called *Dream*. That was made around 1976 and was about the only film education I had. In 1979 I opened the first punk store in Hamburg, which became more of a punk hangout than a store. I had a cheap super 8 camera and we shoplifted enough film material to be able to shoot our little movie called *Amok* - a'Koma' film production. No dialogues, the music explained everything; German punk and 'avant-garde' tunes, some English classics and Throbbing Gristle. Elements from *Clockwork Orange*, punk attitudes and the almighty power of television were the themes.

In the same year we did ... *Und Sie Wissen Nicht, Was Sie Tun Sollen* (*...And They Don't Know What They Should Do*), the title is very similar to the German title to the famous James Dean film, the one with the car race [*Rebel Without A Cause*]. The film showed punks in the quarter. In the end we added television footage of the busts of the German RAF[15] leaders, as they were led into prison. About a year later, in 1979 or 1980, the police cleaned up the punk quarter. Indeed one review in a good German daily paper helped a lot towards getting funding for the next project which I started to plan, or write about, in 1981/82. The working title was *Burger Krieg (Burger War)*. The German word Burger stands for civil, so the title also means civil war ... eventually the title changed to *Decoder*.

I wondered how you began to script *Decoder* and also what attracted you to Burroughs' work and these ideas in particular?

Well ... I forgot to tell you about another experiment I did around 1977. I was totally inspired and excited by Burroughs' cut-up idea, so a friend and I collected Super- 8 material to actually take Burroughs' idea literally. We cut the films into very small pieces, mostly only two to five frames and glued them together in a different order, 'accidentally', according to 'chance'. The result was a film where you saw hardly anything, you could not catch what it was about, but there were some images which stuck in your mind. Not many friends were as excited as we were and I have no idea where that film is today, although I would love to see it again.

So anyway, I have named the main inspiration. I wanted to realize Burroughs' ideas and the techniques which he described in the 'Electronic Revolution' and in *The Revised Boy Scout Manual* and in *The Job*. These were my favourite books. I tried to read Burroughs' novels, but I got into them much later. I did not understand much of his own results, but I wanted to use these techniques. I didn't like Burroughs' as a writer or an artist, I liked him as a revolutionary. Being involved in political work in the '70s showed me that I never really felt comfortable in these circles; the legal approach to organizing groups and demonstrations, spreading information via leaflets and magazines was boring and did not agitate too many new folks. And it was getting more and more dangerous in a time when the militant factions like Movement 2nd June and RAF etc. grew, becoming more and more active. And so did the pressure from the police and state. The other option was going underground, but I was scared of prison. I always missed a fun aspect in all political circles. The subtitle of my freak magazine *Cooly Lully Revue*, which was produced in 1976/77, was "magazine for the radical joy of life".

My approach became different, especially when I left my political friends when they hated punk for being fascistic. And I loved Johnny Rotten for his revolution in show business (and I still do). I was convinced that the only valuable political work must use the enemy's techniques. From the 'Foreword' of the *Decoder Handbook*: "It's all about subliminal manipulation, through words, pictures and sound. It is the task of the pirates to understand these techniques and use them in their own interest. To spread information is the task of all media. Media is power. And nowadays (1984!) the biggest revolutions happen at the market for electronic media. To spread information is also our task. And we should learn in time to use our video and tape recorders as weapons. The fun will come by itself."

Being in the music business and participating in the punk and new wave explosion I became more interested in music. Muzak was one thing I found. Subliminal music to influence people's moods, to make them function better, or buy more. So my conclusion was similar to that of 'bands' like Throbbing Gristle; by turning around the motivation, by cutting up the sounds, by distorting them etc. one should be able to provoke different reactions. Make people puke instead of feeling well, make people disobey instead of following, provoke riots.

The new burger chains spreading in Germany, being a part of the decadent imperialistic American culture, were a good target for this subversive war — described in Burroughs' manuals. One of our original ideas was to actually use low, low bass frequencies in some scenes so that the viewer in the cinema should feel uncomfortable — to feel the movie! (again Burroughs' instruction for using infra-sound).

How did you go about casting the movie?

From the beginning of writing the script, in 1981, I involved characters I was living and working with. FM Einheit from Einstürzende Neubauten was the ideal anti-hero, scrambling music in his underground laboratory, as in real life (Neubauten were my second favourites, after the Sex Pistols). To make a story I needed personal relationships and I asked Christiane F. who lived in our 'commune' at the time. Only a few people knew it was the famous junkie girl who got rich early by the licensing of her book *Children From Station Zoo*. She had left Berlin where everybody knew her by now and where it was hard for her to stay clean, as she was in those days. We lived in the middle of Hamburg's red light district St. Pauli, full of peepshows ... so there was the clue. She played two persons: one in public, being looked at through holes and for money and the other a very private person, who preferred to live with animals (frogs) instead of men. It was hard for her to find real friends, real love, in both the film and in real life, since many people were only after her money. The story came from there...

Well and we needed a bad guy. An agent, not from the state or police, but from a big private corporation, like Muzak Corp, or H-Burger, as we called the burger chain (H, of course, stood for heroin in those days). And to make an exciting story we needed dubious characters, confusion ... the agent was more interested in his personal obsessions than in his job. Well, in the end our story became so confused that nobody could really understand what was going on — unless he studied the film carefully. That is also due to the fact that 'we' in the beginning were two writers. After the first 'draft' I presented the script to Trini Trimpop who had done one film before and knew about possibilities for financial support from local film institutions. We worked on the script together for a second version. Soon Trini introduced another friend of his who was good at dialogues and additional levels. Getting more and more convinced that we could realize the film, finally Muscha joined the team to direct the movie.[16]

How did you get the funds to finance the movie?

The first money we were promised was from Hamburg's Film Funds. I remember that one member of the jury of five was to become Hamburg's Burgermeister (chief of the local country and city government) later. However, they liked the script and gave 250,000 DM — which was about half of the budget we needed. The money was only to be paid when we were able to get the funding for the other half. So we tried in Trini and Muscha's county and received additional funding of 100,000 DM. Finally, the Berlin based Kuratorium Junger Deutscher Film gave 50,000 DM. What sounds so easy now took a lot of time — each time we had to manufacture a dozen scripts including calculations, illustrations, crew and actor proposals and each time we had to wait another three months for a decision.

When we had the 400,000 DM after one year (one year after the script was finished, although we kept changing and adding scenes) we decided to go ahead and start shooting. It was getting urgent since there was a unique chance to get Burroughs involved. I had written a letter to him explaining the script based on his ideas and asked him to participate. I had already met him, my first contact with him was in 1980 when I visited him in Lawrence (where he still lives) to interview him for a German magazine. Well, he answered, saying that he would be open to participate whenever it would not involve too much time. And then this event in London came along — The Final Academy — organized by Genesis P-Orridge and others. I also had been in touch with Genesis and we organized a time to shoot one afternoon — we had exactly one hour! The location was a small store for electrical appliances in Tottenham Court Road. The video camera was operated by 'Sleazy' Peter Christopherson, also from Throbbing Gristle and early Psychic TV. We soon realized that Burroughs was not too good at repeating any lines or movement so we told him to stick to the old tape player we gave him to dismantle. While we were shooting, changing angles etc. he just kept on dismantling this machine and I think he enjoyed it. I also remember not being too happy about the performance of our two actors (Burroughs and FM Einheit), but what can you do in one hour?

Having finished, Burroughs left the store with a little gift for his participation — a bottle of vodka. In front of the store waited his two assistants and a few more people. One of them was filming through the window, while we worked, with his super 8 camera. Much later I learned that this was Derek Jarman, who used this footage for his film *The Pirate Tape* (1982). You can catch pictures of a very young Klaus Maeck in there. Nice little film, I like it.

The film appears to have really contrasting scenes, using red and blue light to delineate various characters. How did that idea come about?

At some point in the preparation of the movie we decided to work with Johanna Heer as the director of photography. We liked her last film, a New York underground movie called *Subway Riders*, which also starred Bill Rice. And we wanted him too, we loved his face and expression. There was no other choice for our agent. Asked to participate by Johanna he was happy to come to Hamburg for one month. The actual shooting of the movie took place in December 1982 in Hamburg.

We liked the extreme use of lighting by Johanna in her earlier films and gave her all freedom to do what she would like. She chose the obvious colors for the different characters, so Bill Rice always appears bathed in blue light, Christiane always in red. I am not the person to go into this too much, since I never really liked this idea too much. It was okay for the time, it was 'new wave'. Muscha was responsible for 'style' and sometimes he exaggerated.

How did the film production work, given that you were working as part of a group?

The relationship between the four of us? You could call it perfect teamwork. You could also call it organized chaos. None of us was a professional and most of the things that we did, we did for the first time. From script-writing to budget calculations, from getting the necessary documents to work in the streets to set decoration, from continuity to wardrobe, finally the long process of editing and adding sound — we did all of this ourselves and I never again learned so much about filmmaking.

I can still laugh about our naivety; until the first day of shooting we did not decide who was actually going to direct the movie. But quickly we learned that teamwork has its limit. Although any director needs good assistance there has to be one responsible person to decide. So the rest of us ended up as co-directors for Muscha, since he was the loudest and most secure in directing people.

Those four weeks of shooting were very intense. Including the main actors there was always about twenty people working, day or night, always close together, working hard. In these four weeks almost everybody had at least one 'breakdown' — where he could not stand it any more, when he wanted to drop out. But I think that is quite normal for such an intensive teamwork. Paradoxically having worked at such a thing once, you get addicted to making films. Well, I felt that at the time. It can change your life! Well, it actually did; Johanna married the sound man a little later and the camera assistant fell in love with FM Einheit's wife, who left him.

Can you talk a little about what happened when you began to shoot in Berlin...?
Probably the most exciting footage we recorded was in Berlin when President Reagan visited. We knew that there would be riots, it was a popular game at that time. We went there with one 16mm camera and one U-Matic video camera, which were set up safely on balconies. And we were in the middle of the action with three more Super-8 cameras. The game was to provoke the police. The political scene in Berlin was big and the police did not have many chances, we knew and it was fun. Whenever the police were going to another area, we had time to think of something new to get them back into action. We placed 'tape terrorists' — friends holding tape recorders — to get footage for our film wherever the action was. So the members of Einstürzende Neubauten were helping us too. Too bad that in the film our footage looks like archive footage from television, because we had to use video and blown-up Super-8 material which both obviously look different in a 16mm movie.

The best story of all is that we were more than surprised that our script became true before we even started. When we came to Berlin we realized that there were actually tapes spread around, distributed around the political circles, with the instruction to make further copies and then play them all at the same time, from Walkmans, from personal equipment in the homes through open windows etc. — and it worked!! At 11.00am you heard helicopters and shootings, although there were none. You heard Jimi Hendrix and some German political band. The police had heard of this action and confiscated a lot of tape recorders the night before — as weapons! Too bad I never heard of such an action again, although I am sure that so many exciting incidents could be provoked by that. Today the technology is so much better and smaller you could do even better!

So, as you can guess from all this background, yes I was fascinated by the 'guerrilla' aspect of Burroughs' work. I was interested to see whether it was possible to fight for your interests not on the streets, but from inside the system, through cultural media, like literature, film and sound. I realized what strange effects the combination of these media can have. Burroughs' films with Antony Balch presented experiments from the '60s and here we were in the '80s not having progressed too much in that field.

One of my favourite movies was — and still is — *Themroc* (Claude Faraldo, 1972) with Michel Piccoli, a French film. There is no dialogue at all in this film, only the sounds which surround you, so these sounds and gestures and mimicry become much more important. In this film, Piccoli becomes bored to death by his factory job and drops out, stops speaking, passing through crowds with an animal-like roaring voice — in the end he catches a cop to fry him on his self-made grill.

The editing of *Decoder* took almost one year, due to time and money shortage. We had to work at night, at weekends. For the music we were proud to work with Dave Ball, who had been in Soft Cell, Genesis P-Orridge and FM Einheit. Almost every single sound in the movie had to be amplified by the adding of artificial sounds which was fun to do. But remember, this was all handcrafted, there were no computers involved then. We ended up with various layers of sound tapes, all being put at the correct points by hand...

We will never know if the decision to wait for the 1984 Berlin Film Festival for the première screening was the right decision. Most critics did not like the film, they did not understand its background and meaning. We got bad reviews in Germany and so we were not able to find a distribution company. The film was shown at several European festivals, but was not screened in Germany until 1986 — another trick helped. Again we applied for funding, this time for the distribution. We found a small Berlin-based distributor who was able to get it into the cinemas by employing me as a kind of 'product manager' from the fund money. So I got a small salary for organizing the first and only tour through Germany. The film is still distributed today, but has no more than five to ten screenings per year, with hardly any income.

However, there is an exception; in Milan, Italy, a political/subcultural group named their magazine after the movie and by now they should have about twenty issues of *Decoder* published (in Italian only). After getting more into publishing they started to translate the Re/Search books about Industrial Culture, William Burroughs and other issues.[17] Today they run a small publishing company doing their own books and working for the famous Italian publisher Feltrinelli. The film *Decoder* is shown in their squatted 'social centres' quite often. The last time I was invited to present and talk about my films was in April, 1996, when more than 300 people came to see the movie. Around the same time they released it on video. At that event some guy walked up to tell me that *Decoder* was his first movie he saw and that it changed his life! See what you can do with film!

One of the central scenes in many ways is the telephone scene between Mufti and Christiane, where they are both talking to each other on the phone and the camera eventually pulls back and you can see that they are in the same room. I was really fascinated by that and wondered if you could tell me how the scene came about and also — given the film's emphasis on electronic forms of communication — what are your opinions of electronic communication, do you think that technologies like the telephone 'mediate' communication? I mean, it seems even more interesting given Burroughs' writings on the nature of language and the word...

If you ask me details like why we made the telephone scene between FM Einheit and Christiane I feel uncomfortable explaining, because it is a visual abstraction, or an instrument to create a character. One aspect is that Christiane doesn't like to be stared at, she wants to hide. She loves it when her boyfriend (played by FM) speaks to her through the telephone, if 'he is in her ear'. No face: no view. Hearing is feeling. Hearing the pure word, with no image to distract the mind.

Or is it a hint that we even use technical devices to communicate when we don't need to, when we could communicate in person? There are many 'hints', many details in the movie, which nowadays can be interpreted as a wise prophecy and so it might be it is nothing other than one transcription of zeitgeist at the time.

Decoder seems to me to be the only Burroughs-influenced film that actually focuses on that side of his work, the entire underground technological thing, with the ensuing riots and the tape-machines as weapons idea. Decoder seems almost to be unique in approaching Burroughs from a very political perspective; why do you think that is?

Why is there no other political approach to Burroughs in films? I don't know and I would love to see more of that. Although I have often heard the reaction that Burroughs' ideas are too '60s or '70s and are outdated. I do believe that so much more is there to learn from him. So many things that he described, analyzed and prophesied came true. Cut-ups are as common in films as they are in commercials, or as they are in modern music. And now, what can we do with the Internet?

How did the *Commissioner Of Sewers* film come about?

In 1986 I moved from Hamburg to Berlin. After being bankrupt with my punk store and independent record distribution, since the major companies came along and joined in, I was living on welfare. Now I had a new job in a small film distribution company, working on *Decoder* for three months, when I heard that William Burroughs was invited to read in Bremen. I contacted him and invited him to read in Berlin on the same trip. It was his last public reading in Germany. I booked a cinema with 350 seats — we wanted to present *Decoder* as another premiere. Nobody knew how many people would show up. I think there were so many that more than 100 did not get inside. However, we were prepared to film his reading with two cameras and in front of a blue screen. The reading was at 10.00pm, which was late for the old man. He went to sleep a little in advance and we had to wake him up at 9.30pm. First thing he asked for was a big joint and totally stoned he entered the stage. But his reading was fantastic and so was the reaction.

Why did the film take so long to produce, from the actual performance to the finished video?

It took me five years before I could edit the material — again due to money shortages. A professional video-editing suite is very expensive and I had to wait for a better chance. In 1991, living in Hamburg again, I met my co-producer who offered me the use of his studio for nothing, if he got 50 percent of all future income. "Fair deal" I thought and I doubt he will ever see the amount of money which I would have had to pay.

How did the visual effects come about, those colourful backgrounds while William Burroughs is reading? They're interesting because they remove the performance from any kind of 'real' context, from the 'vérité' nature of most of the performance films that Burroughs — and the Beats in general — have appeared in. The effects also go back to what I was saying earlier about mediated communications, about using technology to rewire speech.

My idea from the beginning was to illustrate his reading with background material. Well, I had time enough to collect that over the years. We used footage done in the Berlin Zoo while he was visiting (incidentally, the zoo was the only tourist attraction he wanted to go to visit. The same happened years later when he stayed in Hamburg to work on *Black Rider*[18]). Then there was some of my video-8 footage, shot during another visit to his home in Lawrence, Kansas, in 1990. And some excerpts from his own experimental movies, etc. Then images of the words typed onto a typewriter; these were words from book pages etc.

This was still not enough and I added another level by putting on some music, in order to create an atmosphere. Who wants to watch a reading? To serve all senses I wanted to involve all possible layers of word, image and sound — especially since the mixture of all creates something new, sometimes surprising. You put music to an image and it starts to live. You put an image to music and it starts to move. You put another image on top and it creates meaning, another life.

It is too bad I only had ten days to edit this movie, because parts of it are really just experiments which could have been more perfect, more sophisticated. As with *Decoder* I know what I would do differently today. But then again, *Commissioner Of Sewers* is a time document, nicely illustrated to ease the access to this brilliant man.

Be aware that for Germans it is not always easy to understand his American accent, even if you do speak English. And so many people here do not understand his humour, which is what makes him so funny and lovable.

What are your plans for the future, do you see yourself making more films?
By studying Burroughs' work, his books and his paintings, I got much more interested in art (and in the art of living). I am still interested in experimenting with all media and with different approaches, the most exciting results I still find in the interzones, in various crossovers of art and culture; between the lines.

I keep on writing, although not much of it is published yet, although there may be a first book of mine published in Italy soon. I keep on filming every few years, whenever there is a chance. And I started painting, much to my surprise I am more fascinated by it than I ever imagined. But I have my daytime job which fills most of my time. In 1988 I founded a music publishing company called Freibank, with my partner Mark Chung. When he split from Einstürzende Neubauten I also took over the management of the band, which is still going after 16 years. They were the first band we published, we soon started working for others such as Nick Cave and Diamanda Galas. Over the years the spectrum widened and nowadays we work with many artists and bands and we became one of Germany's most attractive independent publishers. This keeps me busy, too busy to write new scripts or novels, too busy to make films. But my time will come again.

---

1. Various books by William Burroughs' ranging from *The Wild Boys, Port Of Saints* and *Painting And Guns,* among others, reveal his interest in weaponry and tactics.

2. Burroughs, quoted in Barry Miles, *William Burroughs: El Hombre Invisible,* Virgin Books: London, 1993 (1992), p.160.

3. Burroughs' interest in and dissemination of, the 'fringe' areas of science is discussed at length in Simon Strong's essay "Burroughs: A Biological Mistake?" in Paul Cecil, ed, *A William Burroughs' Birthday Book,* Temple Press, Brighton, 1994.

4. The dualism of 'fiction' and 'non-fiction' is, of course, redundant when dealing with these texts, a more appropriate terminology would be 'slipstream', as these Burroughs' texts frequently dance between routines, cut-ups, political philosophy and scientific methodology.

5. William Burroughs, 'The Invisible Generation', in William Burroughs with Daniel Odier, *The Job: Topical Writings And Interviews,* John Calder, London, 1969/1984, p.162.

6. William Burroughs, 'Electronic Revolution', in *Ah Pook Is Here And Other Texts,* John Calder, London, 1979, p.125.

7. 'Electronic Revolution', p.125

8. 'Electronic Revolution', p.126

9. 'Electronic Revolution', p.125

10. Einstürzende Neubauten (1980–present day) are Germany's most famous avant-garde musicians/ experimentalists, who have experimented with the very limits of sound and music, exploring the use of non-instruments. The group is notorious for utilizing the percussive potentialities of 'scrap'-metal, but have experimented widely with the very rhythms and sounds which define the modern world, ranging from concrete bridges, heartbeats and drills to burning oil. In the studio the band experiment with the very recording process itself, mixing, remixing and cutting/up their music, via a direct engagement with the musical potentialities of electricity and the mixing desk itself.

11. Klaus Maeck, cited in 'KM: Interview' By Tom Vague and Manuella Rickers. Hamburg, October, 1984, in *Vague [The 20th Century And How To Leave It]*, Psychic Terrorism Annual, No 16/17, 1988, (1984), p.87.

12. Burckhard Dreher, *Filmforderung In Der Bundersrepublick*, Deutsches Institut fur Wirtschaftsforschung, Sonderheft III: Berlin 1976, p.45, cited in Thomas Elsaesser, *New German Cinema: A History*, Rutgers University Press, New Brunswick, 1989, p.28.

13. It would be naive to assume that film merely articulates a nation's culture; it also contributes to a construction of the national culture and identity.

14. State investment in film via grants, tax relief and subsidies clearly encourages independent (non-Hollywood) filmmakers, however it should be noted that this funding, although beneficial, is not substantial.

15. The Red Army Faction, one of '70s Germany's infamous terrorist left-wing organizations.

16. Trini and Muscha made the debut film with *Humanes Toten* (1979).

17. *ReSearch* is the San Francisco based subcultural journal, issues have included *The Industrial Culture Handbook* (which focused on Burroughs-influenced performers such as Throbbing Gristle, Cabaret Voltaire, SPK and Non) and *William Burroughs/Throbbing Gristle*, which included extracts from Burroughs' *Revised Boy Scout Manual*, as well as interviews with both Burroughs and Brion Gysin.

18. *Black Rider* was a theatre piece directed by Robert Wilson and featuring William Burroughs and Tom Waits.

Chapter Twelve

David Cronenberg's *Naked Lunch*

The Canadian filmmaker David Cronenberg is best known for his 'biological-horror' films: *Shivers* (aka *They Came From Within* aka *The Parasite Murders*, 1975); *Rabid* (1976); *The Brood* (1979); *Scanners* (1980); *Videodrome* (1982); *The Dead Zone* (1983); *The Fly* (1986); and *Dead Ringers* (1988). Cronenberg's films — while primarily identified in the media as 'generic' — exist beyond the traditional boundaries of either science fiction or horror texts. They are predominantly characterized by their visceral imagery of bodies undergoing metamorphoses and transmuting into something 'other'; in all of these films the transformation comes from within the protagonists and is frequently the result of science, rather than an alien or supernatural 'other'. These transformations are usually manifested on the bodies of the protagonists (although in *Scanners, The Dead Zone* and *Dead Ringers* the transformations occur on a psychical/psychological level) and include: a woman possessing a vampiric armpit phallus in *Rabid*; a vagina-like slit opening on a male character's abdomen in *Videodrome;* and a total genetic immersion with an insect in *The Fly*. Unlike conventional horror texts, however, the fragmentation and dissolution of the traditionally ascribed borders of the body are presented with an ambivalence that verges on the clinical.

Cronenberg has frequently stated that his major influences were not filmmakers,[1] but the authors William Burroughs and Vladimir Nabokov, both of whom appealed to him because of their status as 'alien' outsiders (Burroughs as an addict, homosexual, criminal, magician and outlaw, while Nabokov was a literal outsider, having emigrated to America from Russia, and further Nabokov's novel *Lolita* dealt with sexual transgression).

The films that Cronenberg has produced are clearly influenced by Burroughs' literary mise-en-scène and are frequently concerned with the same themes: physical and sexual mutation, disease, psychic powers, mind control, scientific developments and transformation. Cronenberg's apparently ambivalent stance may also be viewed as an echo of Burroughs' ability to distance himself and observe with an anthropologist's eye. Both men are concerned with looking at the 'naked lunch', at the "frozen moment when everybody sees what is on the end of every fork".[2] Both figures have been subject to censorship for their desire to explore and depict that which is considered to be taboo by dominant culture as part of their art. Burroughs' work utilizes descriptions of drug use, disease, violence and homosexuality (which as Cronenberg has suggested may be read in *Naked Lunch* as a veil under which lies a larger polymorphously perverse sexuality). While Cronenberg's work is characterized by the visual spectacle of the body as it enters a zone of transformation/s, both Burroughs and Cronenberg have been repeatedly asking (variations of) the question: "Which came first, the intestine or the tapeworm?"[3] Burroughs and Cronenberg both use science — and science fiction — as devices with which to examine and attack, contemporary society; as the cyberpunk author William Gibson has stated: "What Burroughs was doing with plot and language and the science fiction motifs I saw in other writers was literally mind-expanding. I saw this crazy outlaw character who seemed to have picked up science fiction and gone after society with it, the way some old guy might grab a beer opener and start waving it around".[4]

Although it appears that I am within a genre and represent that genre, I feel that I am an undercover agent for something else quite, quite different.
David Cronenberg

You weren't meant to see this.
Joan Lee in *Naked Lunch*

David Cronenberg frequently stated his interest in the potentialities in producing a film of the (famously) 'unfilmable' *Naked Lunch* — unfilmable because of the cost involved in making a literal version of the book, as well as its explicit sexual transgression — and this was realized when Cronenberg scripted and directed *Naked Lunch* in

Naked Lunch

1991. It should be noted, however, that while Cro nenberg's script recognizes the radicalism of *Naked Lunch*, the demands of dominant modes of cinematic production — unlike the underground — does not allow for the process of film to be exposed and deconstructed. Thus while part of Burroughs' work engages with the very processes of writing, the film *Naked Lunch* circumnavigates a similar exploration of its production as film in favour of a literalism of Burroughs' metaphors of writing.

David Cronenberg's *Naked Lunch* uses William Burroughs' novel as a starting point in creating an intertext. In his adaptation of *Naked Lunch*, David Cronenberg builds a 'narrative' around William Burroughs' alter ego William (Bill) Lee (Lee was Burroughs' mother's maiden name). The alter ego emerged from Burroughs' own work, firstly as the author of *Junkie* (aka *Junky*, 1953) and then as a protagonist in *Naked Lunch* and *Nova Express*, amongst others. The film utilizes aspects of Burroughs-biographica, such as Burroughs' shooting of his 'wife' Joan Vollmer, an act which Burroughs perceives as being central in his becoming a writer[5] and the figures of Hank and Martin, both of whom clearly resemble versions of Kerouac and Ginsberg (although they are designed to be merely 'signifiers' of Lee's literary/Beat Generation friends).

This biographical material is cut with scenes inspired by the short story 'Exterminator',[6] characters and routines from *Naked Lunch* — some of which are delivered as verbal routines within the film — and conspiracies from the cut-up trilogy. The narcotic fragmentation suggested in the metanarrative in and around the writing of *Naked Lunch* becomes mirrored by the film's disregard for the division between reality/fantasy, as William Lee (Peter Weller) slides, unannounced, between hallucination and consensus reality. The film's basic narrative concerns William Lee's accidental killing of his wife, Joan and subsequent fleeing into the hallucinatory world of Interzone, where he becomes an active agent and writes endless reports, dictated by mutant insect typewriters. These reports become the source of William Lee's book, *Naked Lunch*. Notably, David Cronenberg's *Naked Lunch* — in common with Brion Gysin's previous, unfilmed script — focuses on the author/writer as a narrative device in which to incorporate the multiplicity of worlds manifested within Burroughs' original. Cronenberg uses the emphasis on writing to introduce the textuality of the novel and also as a device with which he can break down the divide between William Lee's 'interior' psyche and 'external' events. The audience are presented with the spectacle of Lee writing, Lee reciting routines, Lee living/experiencing his writing as reality and Lee's fantasies, all of these receive an equal presentation; there is no clear break in the narrative or mise-en-scène to suggest fantasy/reality. In doing this the traditionally ascribed boundary between the mind of the writer and the writer's world and between the realm of the imaginary and the real, is crossed and re-crossed, thus challenging the audiences' conception of both the experience of writing and of the construction of reality: William Lee writes his own reality, as Burroughs has stated "the purpose of writing is to make it happen"[7] and "we are not setting out to explore static pre-existing data. We are setting out to create new worlds, new beings, new modes of consciousness".[8]

In part, Cronenberg's *Naked Lunch* is not Burroughs' *Naked Lunch*, but is a film by which the director attempts to place his signature under Burroughs, Cronenberg stated: "In my delirium I thought that should Burroughs die while I was writing the script for *Naked Lunch*, I would just keep on writing beyond the script, just write Burroughs' next book for him, his next several books..."[9] Cronenberg did not attempt to create a film from Burroughs' *Naked Lunch*, but instead cooked "up a new/old naked lunch for the cinema".[10] Cronenberg's script replaces the heroin of the original text with bug powder, in order to explore addiction and its metaphors without risking potential condemnation from self-imposed moral guardians. By introducing bug powder, Cronenberg is also able to emphasize the relationship between William Lee and the various insects and conspiracies, manifested within the film. Cronenberg also introduced a female character in the form of Joan Lee/Joan Frost (both of whom are portrayed by the same actress, Judy Davis and both of whom are shot). This introduction of the female figure acts as a device by which Lee's flight and writing could be illustrated, but also — by repeating the shooting of Joan — his continual trauma could be manifested. With the introduction of Joan Frost, Lee's homosexuality is rendered ambiguous and Cronenberg suffered criticism from the gay press for this decision, although Burroughs reportedly told him "it's your movie, do whatever you want".[11]

The engagement with textuality present in Burroughs' work — from the 'random' assemblage of *Naked Lunch* from a whole trunk-load of material,[12] to the cut-ups — repeatedly raises questions about the limits and borders of art, the traditionally ascribed boundaries of which are repeatedly exceeded by Burroughs' work, as words, passages, scenes, characters and ideas shift in/through/across texts/books/paintings/scrapbooks/films. Cronenberg's *Naked Lunch* is merely another combination of these themes, juxtaposed/cut-up/assembled/re-read and transformed into film; as Allen Ginsberg states in the dedication which opens the book *Howl*: "[To] William Seward Burroughs, author of *Naked Lunch*, an endless novel which will drive everybody mad".[13] Burroughs' writing, with its repetitions of character, scene and cross-references, is in many ways one piece of work.[14] Further, material left out and edited from Burroughs' texts is equally a part of his oeuvre. "The Burroughs machine, systematic and repetitive, simultaneously disconnecting and reconnecting ... eventually escapes from the control of its manipulator; it does so in that it makes it possible to lay down a foundation of an unlimited number of books that end by reproducing themselves..."[15]

Cronenberg's film can be viewed as a further area of Burroughs' extensive textual zone. Cronenberg may have written the script but the film was 'created' by both figures; as Cronenberg has stated "I was forced to ... fuse my own sensibility with Burroughs and create a third thing that neither he nor I would have done on his own".[16] The film was written by Cronenberg-as-Burroughs connecting and rewiring texts and films and re-negotiating the terrain. The film exists as a new cartography of the familiar terrain of Burroughs' *Naked Lunch*; as Cronenberg has suggested, the film has "more of me in it than ... William ... I think of it as the product of a dream I would have about Burroughs and his book, a dream to which I bring my own obsessions and idiosyncrasies".[17]

---

1. It should be noted that despite claiming no direct influence from other filmmakers, Cronenberg was involved with underground film in his native Canada and was one of the co-founders of the Toronto Film Co-op (alongside Bob Fothergill, Iain Ewing and Ivan Reitman). In Chris Rodley's *Cronenberg On Cronenberg* (Faber and Faber, London, 1992), Cronenberg states that the independence of the underground film scene in America was an inspiration to the marginalized Canadian filmmakers: "You'd sit and watch underground movies, which were whacky and stupid and bad and dumb and great to watch ... It was very exciting. Your film could be one of those and you were part of it." (p.15). Further, according to Rodley, "the Balch-Burroughs collaborations, which prefigured certain elements of the New York underground film movement, were of great interest to a young Cronenberg in the sixties" (Chris Rodley, 'So Deep In My Heart That You're Really A Part Of Me' in Silverberg, Ira, ed, *Everything Is Permitted, The Making Of Naked Lunch*, Grafton, London, 1992, p.112).

2. William Burroughs, *The Naked Lunch*, John Calder, London, 1982 (1959), p.1.

3. William Burroughs, in Chris Rodley, *The Making Of Naked Lunch*, South Bank Show, 1991.

4. William Gibson, quoted in Larry McCaffery, 'An Interview With William Gibson', in Larry McCaffery, ed, *Storming The Reality Studio: A Casebook Of Cyberpunk And Postmodern Science Fiction*, Duke University Press, Durham & London, 1991, p.278. Notably, David Cronenberg was approached in 1983 to direct *Total Recall*, a script which is based on a short story by '60s avant-garde science fiction author Philip K. Dick: 'We Can Remember It For You Wholesale', although the project was finally directed by Paul Verhoven (*Total Recall*, 1988). More recently Cronenberg has directed the film *Crash* (1996), which is based on J.G. Ballard's groundbreaking novel of sexual transgression, *Crash*. Both Philip K. Dick and J.G. Ballard emerged as 'new wave science fiction' writers in the '60s, a group of authors who were engaged in using science fiction motifs as a way in which to question and challenge society's norms and assumptions and both writers experimented — although to a far lesser extent than Burroughs — with literary forms. The 'new wave science fiction' writers frequently published their work in the magazines *New Worlds* and the (Burroughs-named) *Interzone*.

5. In the 'Introduction' to his novel *Queer*, (Pan Books, London, 1986 [1985]). Burroughs writes: "I am forced to the appalling conclusion that I would never have become a writer but for Joan's death and to a realization of the extent to which this event has motivated and formulated my writing. I live with the constant threat of possession and a constant need to escape from possession, from Control. So the death of Joan brought me in contact with the invader, the Ugly Spirit, and manoeuvred me into a lifelong struggle, in which I have had no choice except to write my way out." (p.18)

6. Published in the collection *Exterminator!*, John Calder, London, 1984 (1973).

7. William Burroughs, 'The Fall Of Art' in *The Adding Machine: Collected Essays*, John Calder, London, 1985, p.61.

8. William Burroughs, 'On Coincidence' in *The Adding Machine: Collected Essays*, p.102.

9. David Cronenberg, 'Introduction' in Ira Silverberg, ed, *Everything Is Permitted, The Making of Naked Lunch*, Grafton, London, 1992, p.17.

10. 'Introduction' in *Everything Is Permitted*, p.17.

11. David Cronenberg cited in Karen Jaehne, 'David Cronenberg On William Burroughs Dead Ringers Do Naked Lunch', in *Film Quarterly, vol. 45, #3*, 1992, p.5.

12. Burroughs, Sinclair Beiles and Brion Gysin assembled *Naked Lunch* for publication by Maurice Girodias's Olympia Press, Paris. The vast hoard of material and routines from which it was assembled was also used — alongside cut-up material — in other Burroughs books, such as *The Soft Machine* (1961), *Nova Express* (1964) and *Interzone* (1989).

13. Allen Ginsberg, *Collected Poems, 1947–1980*, Penguin Books, London, 1987 (1985), p.802.

14. Not only was material from the *Naked Lunch* routines used in the subsequent trilogy, but also William Burroughs describes the "overflow" ('An Interview With William Burroughs' by Allen Ginsberg, in *William Burroughs, The Soft Machine/Nova Express/The Wild Boys: Three Novels By* (Grove Press Inc, New York, 1980 (1961/1964/1969)) from *The Wild Boys* (1969) as being the source of his books *Exterminator!* (1973) and

Port Of Saints (1973/1975/1980). Burroughs also rewrote and re-edited various books, including *The Soft Machine, Port Of Saints* and *The Last Words Of Dutch Schultz* (1970/1975), while variations on routines were published by various small press publishers.

15. Gerard-Georges Lemaire, '23 Stitches Taken By Gerard-Georges Lemaire And 2 Points Of Order By Brion Gysin' in *William Burroughs and Brion Gysin, The Third Mind,* John Calder, London, 1979 (1978), p.17.

16. *Cronenberg On Cronenberg,* p.162. This statement echoes the concept of the Third Mind — introduced by Burroughs and Gysin to describe the third, higher sensibility, a superior mind, which emerges during collaborations. However, whilst Burroughs and Gysin believe in an animistic universe, Cronenberg does not: "Burroughs believes in things like possession in a medieval sense and in things that I don't endorse." (David Cronenberg cited in Karen Jaehne, *David Cronenberg On William Burroughs Dead Ringers Do Naked Lunch,* p.3–4).

17. David Cronenberg cited in *David Cronenberg On William Burroughs Dead Ringers Do Naked Lunch,* p.2.

Chapter Thirteen

Burroughs Animated

William Burroughs' experimental style, use of material drawn from dreams, religious texts and genre fiction, alongside the sexual themes, invariably makes literal adaptations of his work difficult. Cronenberg's *Naked Lunch* uses various modelling and special effects in order to bring various creatures from Burroughs' menagerie to life, most notably the Mugwumps, however the narrative emphasis is still broadly linear. Invariably some elements of the unique Burroughs' world are neglected by live action cinema rooted in dominant forms of storytelling. In contrast animation offers filmmakers an opportunity to engage more literally with the Burroughsian universe.

Ah Pook Is Here (1994) is a six-minute animated experimental short that draws on material presented in Burroughs' short story of the same name and material from *Interzone*. Opening with a field of stars accompanied by William Burroughs' brittle narration: "when I become death, death is the seed from which I grow". From the distant stars a spinning vortex emerges around which buzz numbers. The vortex fills the image and the audience pass through into a negative world where the stars are black and the vastness of space luminous white. Order is reversed and nothing is as it should be.

In the distance a cold, black planet appears, a small rotating world complete with its own moon. As the film continues it becomes apparent that the world is barren, scattered with detritus and dead trees, this is a post apocalyptic trumascape. Burroughs' voice continues detailing the gods and goddesses of the Mayan universe, describing the numerous deities that form the ancient pantheon "Itzama, spirit of early mist and showers. Ixtaub, goddess of ropes and snares..." As each is described they are manifest as transforming and mutating dirigibles, bombs, falling stars and the rockets more commonly associated with long ancient science fiction narratives. Finally: "Ah Pook, the destroyer".

Sitting in a dead and leafless tree, viewing the black moon through a telescope sits Ah Pook in silhouette, as the camera moves towards the God of Death the shadow vanishes, revealing an entity that resembles a combination of bloated fat male human torso and plucked raw turkey; this is Ah Pook.

The figure sits up and becomes both subject and narrator, speaking with Burroughs' voice, its flapping red lipless beak-like mouth asks "Hiroshima... Who really gave that order?" Simultaneously the entity inhales smoke from a hookah. Describing the bombing of the Japanese city the film cuts to present the view through the telescope as a pair of glasses are liquidised in the heat and flash from the blast of the bomb named Little Boy.

The reply, also voiced by Burroughs, comes from what may be the desolate god's alter ego that materialises to explain the order was given by "Control. The Ugly American, the instrument of Control." The entity, which flaps its dirty-red wings and hovers around Ah Pook's bloated flesh, explains the Control's need for time and the addictive cycle of Control, time and death. As the exchange continues, Ah Pook rolls onto his back on the thin branch, his tiny meatless legs kicking the forlorn atmosphere. The revelation: "Death needs time for what it kills to grow in, for Ah Pook's sake." It starts to rain. Muttering "you stupid vulgar, greedy, ugly American death sucker" the god climbs down from the tree and enters a cave on the planet's garbage strewn surface.

Inside he starts to explain the nature of rule and finally to the form of rule where no decision is made and rulers reached power through "surrender of self" and are "rulers by accident, inept, frightened pilots at the controls of a vast machine they can not understand calling in experts to tell them which buttons to push". While explaining this the entity checks the shells in a double barrelled shotgun, positions it in its mouth and pulls the trigger. A flash of light and red,

Love! What is it? Most natural painkiller what there is. Love.
William Burroughs

William Burroughs in Commissioner of Sewers

then back to the vast blackness of space. As the credits roll, Burroughs sings 'Falling In Love Again' accompanied by a solitary piano.

Directed by Philip Hunt, the short film captures both the grim comic nature and bleakness of the perspective that characterises much of Burroughs' work. The last god driven to suicide by the lack of human imagination, by the surrender of self, by Control. A myriad of themes from across Burroughs' work can be seen at play in *Ah Pook Is Here*: the nature of Control, desire and need and the use of animation enables the filmmakers to visually realise these.

The mise-en-scène, with its barren landscape and decomposing planet, floating in the dead gulf of a collapsed alternative universe, maintains a nightmarish quality. Ah Pook, with his bloated cadaverous body recalls the most nightmarish aspects of the flesh. The God becoming another figure in the Burroughs pantheon.

The Junky's Christmas (Nick Donkin 1993) combines footage of William Burroughs at his home in Lawrence with an animated version of the short story of the same name, published in *Interzone*. It opens with Burroughs looking at a Christmas Tree, before walking to a bookshelf and selecting a volume and lifting it down, framing Burroughs as storyteller. To a soundtrack of angelic harmonies he watches a pet cat play under the tree, then he begins to read from the volume. The film cuts to animation as the author begins to tell the story of Danny.

Shot using clay models and stop-frame animation, in black and white, the short film follows the petty criminal and junky as he is released from jail on Christmas Day. Broke and destitute Danny needs to find a fix, a drink and a room. But, when he finally gets his small dirty room and a gram of heroin, his junk fix has to wait, sobbing and groaning is coming from the next room.

Danny goes to check on his neighbour and finds a young man with kidney stones clutching his abdomen in agony. Used to faking kidney stones in order to get a fix, Danny laughs, recognizing the irony of the situation, before giving the boy his own fix. Returning to his room, Danny suffers the pangs of withdrawal. But then, as he starts to face the inevitable cold turkey paroxysms, a heavenly choir can be heard on the soundtrack and Danny floats into the air above his bed. Fragments of gold cascade through his psyche, the only colour in the film, as he realises: "for Christ's sake ... I must have scored for the immaculate fix". The miracle of the season told Burroughs style.

The film cuts back to the author reading his book. He closes it, tired old eyes appearing melancholy with faded memory. Then, pulling himself to his feet, Burroughs walks from his lounge to his dining room. Here a feast is spread across a table and his friends are gathered around. Burroughs joins them, raises his glass and delivers the yuletide toast: "a merry Christmas to all of you, to one and all I wish a merry Christmas".

Unlike *Ah Pook Is Here, The Junky's Christmas* tells a human story of generosity. The animation, rather than being fantastic, emphasis the expressions and appearances of the protagonists, from the contorted brows of the desperate drug addicts to the anuran face of a wealthy southerner, a frequent manifestation of the Ugly American in Burroughs' work. The exaggerated forms and shapes of animation are used to emphasis the humanism of the story, presenting a different side of the author's work; compassion.

Appendix

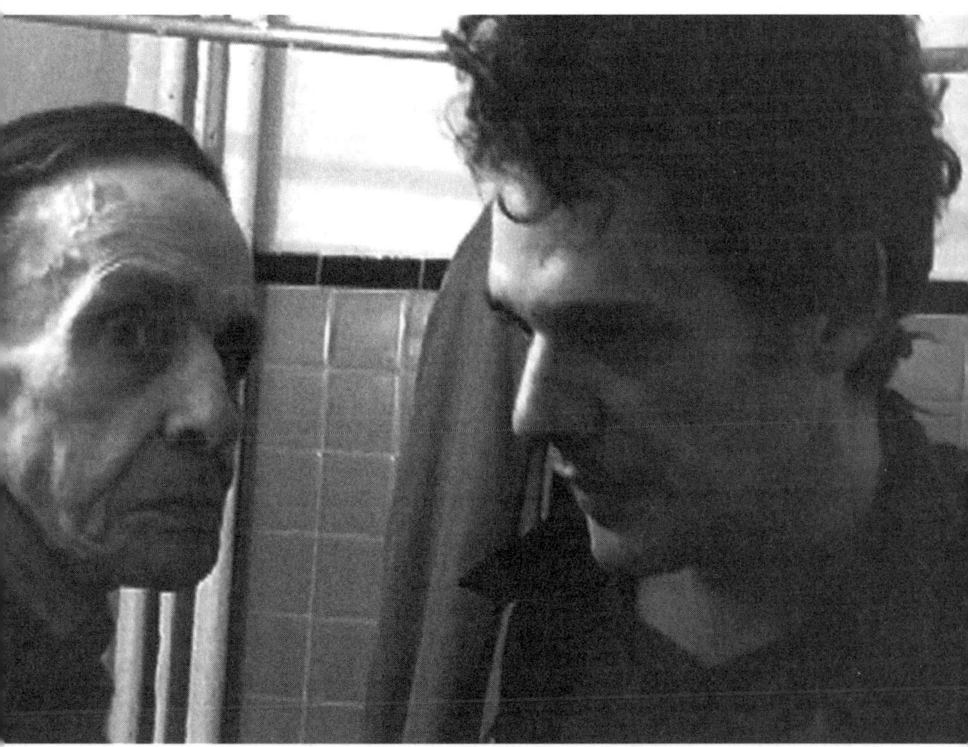

1. Mainstream/Hollywood & Beat Culture

Only three Beat novels have thus far been produced as films: *The Subterraneans* (1960), *Heart Beat* (1979) and *Naked Lunch* (1991 — discussed elsewhere). The first film, *The Subterraneans*, based on Jack Kerouac's novel, was directed by Ranald MacDougall and starred Leslie Caron, George Peppard and Roddy McDowall. This film has more in common with the Beat-themed exploitation movies than Kerouac's original text; with its images of 'wild' beatniks, 'jazz', 'bohemia' and so forth, the film invests heavily in cliché, at the expense of the original narrative. The film is further removed from the original text by its censoring of the theme of miscegenation. The location is similarly transformed from New York to San Francisco's North Beach. The original poster had a series of subtitles, including such classics as "I'm Leo: Why can't I love two people and three people and four? I want to love everyone!" and "I painted all the beautiful things I knew ... and the police said they were wicked..." The jazz soundtrack includes songs called 'Coffee Time' and 'Look Ma, No Clothes'.

The second Hollywood adaptation of a Beat text was John Byrum's *Heart Beat* (1979). Based on an early version of Carolyn Cassady's autobiography entitled *Heart Beat* (subsequently published as *Off The Road* (1990)), the film casts Sissy Spacek as Carolyn Cassady, Nick Nolte as Neal Cassady, John Heard as Jack Kerouac and Ray Sharkey as Ira Streiker (a figure based on Allen Ginsberg — who did not want to be named in the film due to various aspects of 'his' character's behaviour). The film details their lives and relationships from the '40s to the '60s. The film counterpoints the complex web of extended love affairs between Carolyn, Neal and Jack with the absurd caricatures of suburban normality Bob and Betty Bandix.

While few Beat novels have made the transition to film, the awareness of the Beats in relation to the emergent counterculture has grown. Whilst in the final stages of completing the first edition of this book, both Allen Ginsberg and William Burroughs died while Gregory Corso died in 2001. Beat has been relegated to history. Those inspired by it, or allied to it, are still producing work, but the original gesture of Kerouac, Ginsberg, Corso and the begrudging (non) affiliate Burroughs must be seen as having finally come to a close. Even as this has happened, however, interest in the literary, sociopolitical, artistic and cinematic gestures made by the Beats has increased. New editions of the classic Beat texts are available, while affiliated books are increasingly emerging onto the market and more obscure Beat titles are slowly re-emerging into the public conscious.

It is the mythology surrounding the lives of the Beats that informs Gary Walkow's film *Beat* (2000), which received a limited theatrical and video release. This feature-length film, set to a predictably brooding jazz score, is a loose biographical account of the relationships between Joan Vollmer (played by Courtney Love) and the emerging writers William Burroughs (Kiefer Sutherland) and Allen Ginsberg (Ron Livingston) and their colleague Lucien Carr (Norman Reedus). The film follows Joan's relationships to these figures from the initial stages of the friendship, which developed in the late '40s through to her death in 1951. The film locates its narrative through two deaths: the self-defensive killing of stalker David Kammerer by Lucien Carr in 1944 and William Burroughs' accidental shooting of Joan Vollmer.

There are techniques in film which are at times similar to dreams, but as I said Hollywood is not at its best when it deals with dream material.
William Burroughs

The film opens with a brief sequence set in New York,

in which Joan and a group of friends are purchasing a case full of benzedrine inhalers. The early scenes of the film focus on the stalking of Carr by Kammerer. Contrary to William Burroughs' advice, Carr uses and abuses Kammerer's obsessive friendship, but rejects his sexual advances. When the volatile Kammerer attacks Carr, he is forced to defend himself and kills his stalker. The film jumps to Mexico City, 1951 and life for the Burroughs' family in Mexico.

Here *Beat* follows the daily routine of the Burroughs/Vollmer family, focusing on Joan's drinking and William's addiction and the largely unsupervised play of the two children. William leaves Joan and the children to travel to Guatemala with Lee, a young man who is the object of his desire. This relationship is repeatedly marred by sexual frustration and emotional manipulation — as the young man will only engage in sex with Burroughs twice a week — and its central theme of unrequited desire mirrors the relationship between Joan and William.

Whilst Burroughs is traveling through the rainforests in search of Mayan ruins and tolerating Lee's apparently willful ignorance, Allen Ginsberg and Lucien Carr, who has recently been released from prison, visit Joan. The three friends leave on a road trip to visit a nearby volcano that has just started to erupt. On the journey Joan and Lucien flirt and discuss their relationships and Carr's crime. Carr believes he finally lost Joan to William while he was imprisoned. During this journey Ginsberg and Carr both debate William Burroughs' treatment of Joan Vollmer — at one point describing him as a 'psychic vampire'.

After the road trip the two friends depart for America, leaving Joan in Mexico City where she waits for William's return. As Ginsberg and Carr journey homeward they realize that they should have brought Joan and her children back to the United States with them. Meanwhile in Mexico City, William returns from his trip south to find a dejected and depressed Joan who informs him that he has missed his friends' visit.

A few days later, William, in need of money, is selling a gun. In a display of his shooting prowess he takes aim at a glass balanced on Joan's head and unwittingly kills her. In New York, hearing the news, Carr breaks down and begins to cry.

The final credits interchange subsequent biographical data with quotes from William Burroughs' introduction to *Queer*, correspondence between Joan and various friends and Ginsberg's references to the Mexican journey taken from 'Howl'.

In *Beat* the audience is presented with a thorough interpretation of the complex socio-sexual dynamics of the Beats' early friendships and Burroughs' emerging homosexuality. The apparent biographical roots of *Beat* are clear and notably Herbert Huncke is credited with being the historical advisor on the movie. The film also uses both Burroughs' *Queer* and Ginsberg's work as sources for the narrative.

Notably, however, given the factual basis for the film, several crucial details have been changed. According to Barry Miles' *William Burroughs: El Hombre Invisible*, Joan Vollmer was away during the summer of 1944, during which the Carr/Kammerer incident occurred. William Burroughs went to Ecuador and not Guatemala and his colleague was Lewis Marker and not Lee. Further, the relationship between Vollmer and Carr is purely speculative. These small changes are presumably to enable the economy of storytelling; however, they also play on the hype surrounding the Beats' imagined decadence.

Beat also presents Joan as a writer and she is repeatedly presented writing a manuscript; however the film notes in its end sequence that no book by Joan was ever published and only a few letters are believed to survive. The literary influence of Joan on the Beats in the film is also emphasised in a sequence set in New York. Here she is depicted locating the story in the newspaper that contains the immortal lines 'and the hippos were boiled in their tanks', a sentence that would, of course, form the basis for an early unpublished literary collaboration between William Burroughs and Jack Kerouac. To some extent then, *Beat* comments — albeit in a barely perceptible fashion — on the occlusion of women within the literary ranks of the Beats and the viewer cannot help but wonder exactly what Joan was writing throughout the film.

Beat captures the milieu of these writers early in their lives and does so without resorting to the more melodramatic overtones of *Heart Beat,* which dealt with many of the same questions: sexual liberation, writing and an alternative approach to existence. However, the film serves to create a mythology as much as re-create historical accuracy and as such is frustrating to those in the audience already versed in literary history.

2. Notes On Gus Van Sant

The independent film director Gus Van Sant has — in part — become the logical heir to the Beats in film. His films *Mala Noche* (1985), *Drugstore Cowboy* (1989), *My Own Private Idaho* (1991) and *Even Cowgirls Get The Blues* (1993) all reveal an interest in America — and the vastness of the American landscape — which is similar to that manifested in Jack Kerouac's writing. Like Kerouac, Van Sant recognizes the seductive, vertiginous romance of travel and his characters are frequently motivated by the need to travel in/through America (through the Pacific North West in *Drugstore Cowboy*, from Portland to Idaho — and even Italy — in *My Own Private Idaho* and to Dakota in *Even Cowgirls Get The Blues*). The cinematography in each of these films emphasises the beauty of the American countryside — specifically the North and Midwest.

Gus Van Sant became interested in film production while studying at the Rhode Island School of Design, where he was a student from 1971–1975. One of the first films he directed after leaving college was the ten-minute *The Discipline Of D.E.* (aka *The Discipline Of Do Easy*, 1977) which was adapted from the William Burroughs short story of the same name and published in the collection *Exterminator!* The film gained some attention at the 1977 New York Film Festival. In 1985 Van Sant directed his debut feature film *Mala Noche* on a budget of $25,000, which he obtained from his savings from working in an advertising agency. The black and white film was based on a novella by the gay, Portland Beat author Walt Curtis. Set in Portland, the film depicts a gay store clerk's sexual obsession with a Mexican immigrant. *Mala Noche* won the LA Film Critics' Award as the best independent feature in 1987.

The success of *Mala Noche* enabled Gus Van Sant to raise the budget for his next film project: *Drugstore Cowboy*. Based on an unpublished 'autobiographical' novel by convicted felon James Fogle, who, at the time of the film's release, was incarcerated at the Washington State Penitentiary, the film — which is set in 1971 — depicts a gang of addicts who rob pharmacies and hospitals in order to obtain drugs. The gang consists of Bob Hughes (Matt Dillon) and his wife Dianne Hughes (Kelly Lynch), who lead a younger couple, Rick and Nadine (James Le Gros and Heather Graham). The two couples live in various cheap apartments together as an extended family, until they are forced onto the road. While hiding out at a motel, Nadine — whose naiveté makes her the frequent target of Bob's frustrations — overdoses and dies. Bob, believing this to be the inaugural event in a seven-year hex, caused by Nadine's leaving a hat on her bed, decides to clean up. Returning to Portland he signs on for rehabilitation where he meets Tom the Priest (William Burroughs). One evening Bob — having given up drugs — is visited by Dianne, who is now leading the gang; she invites him to join them, but he declines. Dianne leaves Bob a bag of drugs, which he passes on to a thankful Tom. Returning to his apartment Bob is beaten and eventually shot by two hoodlums who think he still has the narcotics. On the way to the hospital the police question him, repeatedly asking who shot him, all Bob can repeat is "the hat".

Drugstore Cowboy is located in the milieu of the alienated, rebellious edges of American society, which are — in part — the same edges that the Beats engaged in their relationships with hustlers and petty thieves, in and around Times Square in the '40s and '50s. Van Sant's film never moralizes about the protagonists' drug usage or robberies, but rather marks them as outsiders, in the form of the classic, existential anti-hero — a fact that is emphasized by the usage of the word 'cowboy' in the film's title. As Cindy Fuchs has observed, *Drugstore Cowboy* is "less about drugs than it is about an American obsession with individualism in the face of failed myths and mediated pleasures".[1] In part the film announces its relationship with its topic and with the Beats, via its usage of Burroughs. The character portrayed by Burroughs was originally named Bob Murphy in the script, but following a discussion with Van Sant, the character's name was changed to Tom the Priest (the Priest is a reference to the Burroughs short story 'The Priest They Called Him', published in *Exterminator!*). According to Barry Miles' *El Hombre Invisible,* James Grauerholz wrote the script for Burroughs' role because Van Sant was too busy working on the film. In his cameo role Burroughs describes the imminence and danger of the growth of a worldwide police force and the war on drugs: "Narcotics have been systematically scapegoated and demonized. The idea that anyone can use drugs and escape a horrible fate is anathema to these idiots. I predict in the near future right-wingers will use drug hysteria as a pretext to set up an international police apparatus ... I'm an old man, I may not live to see the final solution of the drug problem."

Following *Drugstore Cowboy,* William Burroughs and Gus Van Sant collaborated on *A Thanksgiving Prayer* (aka *Thank You America,* 1990). The film was designed to be a promo for Burroughs' Island Records album Dead City Radio. The short film depicts Burroughs reading his cynical prayer, mixed with footage depicting 20th century American history. In 1997 Van Sant made a similar promo for Ginsberg's song 'Ballard Of The Skeletons'

Gus Van Sant's following feature film, *My Own Private Idaho,* was also set amongst the disenfranchised outsiders, although, rather than junkies, the film focuses on a group of teenage hustlers, living — and surviving — on their wits. In his script-writing for *My Own Private Idaho* Van Sant utilized, in part, an adaptation of the cut-up method of Burroughs and Brion Gysin, juxtaposing sections of three screenplays together to create the final script, which utilized text based on Shakespeare's *Henry IV;* a script called *My Own Private Idaho* about two Chicanos; and sections from a previously unused script called *In A Blue Funk,* which focused on the same characters as the finished film. Van Sant originally intended to cast the film with street kids — thinking the budget would only be $50,000 — however the success of *Drugstore Cowboy* enabled Van Sant to cast River Phoenix as the narcoleptic hustler Mike and Keanu Reeves as his friend Scott. *My Own Private Idaho* follows the two friends as they search for Mike's mother. Scott, however, eventually rejects Mike, marries and comes into his inheritance. Mike, without his companion, has nobody to look out for him and as the film ends he collapses into a narcoleptic trance by a deserted roadside. As he lies unconscious a car pulls up and the driver picks up the sleeping boy and carries him into the car...

Van Sant locates the narrative of these early feature films amongst the outsiders and the alienated, of American society. These outsiders — homosexual, or junkie, or criminal — are presented as living in complex social structures that enable them to survive without the traditional bonds of the phallocentric Oedipal family structure (for example, the web of relationships between the couples in *Drugstore Cowboy* and the extended street family around the hustlers in *My Own Private Idaho*). The films thus present a radical alternative to the majority of dominant films, by suggesting that relationships can exist outside of traditionally ascribed structures.

In his mise-en-scène, Gus Van Sant presents images that are reminiscent of avant-garde cinema and surrealism. For example, during Bob's opiate haze, following a robbery in *Drugstore Cowboy,* there is a close-up of Bob's face, over which superimposed images — presumably those on which his stoned mind is focused — slowly tumble/float across the image: a hat, a cow, etc. As Michael O'Pray has observed, these stylisations may be viewed as homage to Antony Balch's *Towers Open Fire.* While in *My Own Private Idaho,* Van Sant uses more directly surreal images, such as a house that falls from the sky at the film's opening. This surrealism is reiterated via the emphasis on Mike's repeated narcoleptic episodes. Van Sant's films also use 'home movie' segments, which serve to emphasis the personal nature of his films, as well as drawing attention to the construction of cinematic verisimilitude. These segments act as moments that draw attention to the various conventions and gazes of film and camera in a manner analogous to the Beats' emphasis on the various possibilities of the written word. This is especially true in *Drugstore Cowboy*, where the narration and home-movie-style sections that open and close the film serve to create a more intimate relationship between the audience and the film's protagonists.

3. Shocking Beatniks & Beatsploitation

Following the craze and success, of the Juvenile Delinquent genre manifested in films such as *The Wild One* (1954), *Blackboard Jungle* (1955), *Rebel Without A Cause* (1955) and a wealth of similar rock and roll, drag racing and gang war movies, exploitation producers sought out the next 'youth' subculture with which to shock and titillate their audiences. The beatniks provided filmmakers with a ready-made subculture to incorporate into a series of exploitation movies. The representation of beatniks allowed filmmakers to appropriate and parody, a collective mainstream fantasy version of 'beatnik culture' manifested via the lifestyle and accoutrements of the goatee beard-wearing 'dropout': bongo drums, poetry, jazz, parties, weird slang, existential angst, artistic pretentious, drugs and, to a lesser extent, their beliefs in Buddhism, communism and free love. The themes associated with the beatniks in the public eye would also guarantee a salacious audience, anxious to witness — and vicariously enjoy — the exploits of the 'bizarre new youth culture', as long as they were granted the salve of moralistic tongue clicking by the film's closing credits. These beatnik-themed exploitation movies were ostensibly a reworking/sub-genre of the classic juvenile delinquent movie and the beatnik genre would soon evolve into the beach party movie, the biker movie and the hippie/LSD movie. Nevertheless, they remain an interesting cycle of thus far neglected exploitation movies. The following is merely a selection of these films.

The Beat Generation (aka *This Rebel Age*, 1959), was directed by Charles Haas and produced by Albert Zugsmith. The film's cast includes Zugsmith regular Mamie Van Doren, as well as Steve Cochran and Jackie Coogan and cameos from Louis Armstrong as himself and Vampira as a beatnik poetess. The film is ostensibly a crime film; detective Dave Culloran pursues a psychopathic rapist against a Coffee House/beatnik backdrop.

Roger Corman produced and directed *A Bucket Of Blood* (1959), a comedy-cum-horror film transpiring in the beatnik milieu. Shot over five days, the film follows Walter Paisley (played by Corman regular Dick Miller) as he waits on various beatniks in The Yellow Door coffee house and wishes he could be as cool as they are. Walter tries and fails to be a sculptor, until accidentally killing a cat and covering it in clay — and naming it 'Dead Cat' — to critical acclaim. As his fame increases amongst the critics and the beatniks he wants to impress, Walter is forced to repeat his artistic success, but instead of using felines he begins to use people. The film is a Corman classic, with its combination of comedy-gore-horror narrative, beatnik jokes (incredibly absurd 'hep' dialogue such as the girl who asks Walter to "take me away to some cool blue place and gas me", weird/pretentious art and artists, 'folk' music and lame beatnik poetry, etc.

Gene Fowler Jr directed *The Rebel Set* (aka *Beatsville*, 1959), a crime film located within the beatnik milieu. *The Rebel Set* followed a group of beatniks led by Coffeehouse proprietor Edward Platt, as they rob a million dollars from a train.

In England, Edmond T. Greville directed *Beat Girl* (aka *Wild For Kicks*, 1959), in which Gillian Hills plays Jennifer, a young art student whose father and stepmother 'don't understand her.' Jennifer rebels, first by hanging out at a coffee shop, going to hear folk and jazz music, then by becoming increasingly involved with a sleazy Soho club, run by Kenny (Christopher Lee). Finally Jennifer becomes 'wild for kicks' — stripping at a party, driving fast and playing chicken by lying prone on railway tracks in front of an oncoming high-speed train. The film is notable for its brief appearances by Oliver Reed and Adam Faith.

Edward A. Mann directed *Hallucination Generation* (aka *Hallucination* aka *The Drifters*, 1966), the adverts read: "Tonight you are invited to a 'pill party', you will experience every jolt ... every jar of a Psychedelic Circus ... The Beatniks ... Sickniks ... and Acid-Heads ...

and you will witness their ecstasies, their agonies and their bizarre activities ... You will be hurled into their debauched dreams and frenzied fantasies! LSD! DOPE! HORSE!" The film follows a group of drugged-out American beatniks in Spain, as they get stoned and break the law; it has been accurately described by Steven Puchalski as "one of the lamest"[2] drug movies ever.

Other films depicting 'beatniks', or located within the Beat milieu, include: *La Notte Brava* (aka *Night Heat* aka *On Any Street* aka *Bad Girl's Don't Cry* aka *Les Garcons*, directed by Mauro Bolognini, 1959) an Italian French co-production, scripted by Pier Paolo Pasolini, which focuses on a group of Roman beatnik adolescents; the Canadian production *A Cool Sound From Hell* (aka *The Young And The Beat*, 1959), directed by Sidney J. Furie, a melodrama which follows a 'beatnik' drug dealer; the English *Design For Loving* (aka *Fashion For Loving*, Godfrey Grayson, 1962), a comedy drama focusing on a beatnik fashion model; Jack O'Connell's *Greenwich Village Story* (aka *They Love As They Please*, 1963) which follows a young writer and his ballet-dancing girlfriend, set against the beatnik background of New York's Greenwich Village; *Il Marito E Mio E L'Ammazzo Quando Mi Pare* (aka *Drop Dead, My Love*, Pasquale Festa Campanile, 1967) about a woman who wants to murder her husband, who is forty years older than her, in order to marry a young beatnik; and *What's So Bad About Feeling Good?* (George Seaton, 1968), "about a group of beatniks whose lives are changed by a strange virus".[3]

While this genre of exploitation movies died a death with the 'end' of beatniks and the birth of hippie/biker movies, it is briefly alluded to in John Waters' *Hairspray* (1988), which pays an affectionate tribute to the genre, with a brief cameo from Pia Zadora as a 'Howl'-reading, hair-ironing beatnik, living on the 'wrong side' of Baltimore.

4. Notes On Charles Bukowski

Although not expressly identified as a Beat writer, Charles Bukowski has come to be identified in the popular imagination with the Beats. Born in Andernach, Germany in 1920, Bukowski's family moved to America in 1922. Bukowski grew up in Los Angeles and spent much of his life working in a variety of dead end jobs, drinking large quantities of alcohol, playing the horses and writing. He produced a string of books: novels (*Post Office* (1971), *Factotum* (1975), *Women* (1978), *Ham On Rye* (1982) and *Hollywood* (1984)); short stories (*Notes Of A Dirty Old Man* (1969), *Erections, Ejaculations, Exhibitions And General Tales Of Ordinary Madness* (1972), subsequently reprinted as a two-volume paperback: *The Most Beautiful Woman In Town And Other Stories* (1983) and *Tales Of Ordinary Madness* (1983), *South Of No North* (1973) and *Hot Water Music* (1983)); and more than forty volumes of poetry (including: *Flower, Fist And Bestial Wail* (1959), *Longshot Poems For Broke Players* (1961), *The Genius Of The Crowd* (1966), *The Flower Lover* (1966), *At Terror Street And Agony Way* (1968), *The Days Run Away Like Wild Horses Over The Hills* (1969), *Legs Hips And Behind* (1979) and *War All the Time: Poems 1981–1984* (1984). Like the work of the Beats, these books share a recognition and celebration of the outsider, who exists at the margins of society and often are based on autobiographical — or quasi-autobiographical experiences. Bukowski like Allen Ginsberg, Jack Kerouac and William Burroughs was influenced by writers such as Antonin Artaud and Louis Ferdinand Celine. Bukowski also shared the literary freedom that existed as a direct result of the Beats' battles with censorship and — like Allen Ginsberg, Gregory Corso, William Burroughs, Jack Kerouac, Diane DiPrima, Ed Sanders, Carl Solomon and Neal Cassady — Bukowski was published by Lawrence Ferlinghetti's City Lights Books, of San Francisco (in addition to John Martin's Black Sparrow, of Los Angeles). He was also included in a collective volume of poetry with Philip Lamantia and Harold Norse. In common with the Beat poets, Bukowski performed his poetry (although more begrudgingly), reading at bars and colleges and experimented with the style of poetic form.

Where Charles Bukowski differed from the Beats was in his cynicism — which occasionally bordered on the nihilistic. While the central Beat writers explored mysticism, magic and the occult, Bukowski celebrated the godless void. While the university-educated Beats gathered at coffee houses, Bukowski worked manual jobs — including twelve years spent as a clerk at the Post Office — and drank in bars. While the Beats were identifying as a 'group' and supporting each other, Bukowski's self-perception was as a man alone, who did not seek the companionship of a group identity: "a grouping of another 'in' type of thing. this is the way death begins. a kind of glorious personal death, but no good, anyhow".[4] Despite this cynicism, Bukowski contributed a regular column, called 'Notes Of A Dirty Old Man', to the weekly *Open City*, a publication which emerged from the Los Angeles underground press in the late '60s, and later, in the *Los Angeles Free Press*. While the Beats were becoming recognized in America, Bukowski remained largely unknown until the early '70s, but enjoyed a massive cult following in Europe. The strength of this European interest in Bukowski has

> The only thing that amounts to a writer is the next line you're going to write down. All past things don't mean shit. If you can't write that next line, you as a person are dead. It's only the next line, this line that's coming as the typewriter spins, that's the magic, that's the roaring, that's the beauty. It's the only thing that beats death.
> Charles Bukowski

Charles Bukowski

meant that two of the film adaptations of his work have been produced by European film companies, while the third was directed by a European.

Despite the fact that Charles Bukowski did not like film and stated that: "It's embarrassing to see a movie, I feel gypped, sitting there with all these people",[5] several films have been produced based on Bukowski's stories.

In 1981 Marco Ferreri directed *Storie Di Ordinaria Follia* (aka *Tales Of Ordinary Madness* aka *Conte De La Folie Ordinaire* aka *C'Etait La Plus Belle Fille De La Ville*), an Italian/French co-production based on Bukowski's *Erections, Ejaculations, Exhibitions And General Tales Of Ordinary Madness*. The film follows the alcoholic poet Charles Serking (Ben Gazzara) as he wanders aimlessly from one sordid sexual event to the next. The film opens with Serking spending a night with a twelve-year-old girl, before travelling back to Los Angeles. Here he fights with Vicky (Tanya Lopert), his ex-wife, who lives in the same run-down apartments as Serking, before meeting and having violent sex with Vera (Susan Tyrrell). Vera accuses Serking of rape and informs the police, who arrest him.

Serking is released the following day and goes to a bar where he meets nihilistic/masochistic prostitute Cass (Ornella Muti), who pierces her cheeks. Serking and Cass enter into a fragmented relationship, which is broken when Serking's alcoholism lands him in hospital. On leaving hospital, Serking discovers that Cass has attempted suicide and takes her to the beach where they make love. Cass then returns to Serking's apartment and using a large safety pin, pierces her vagina closed. Serking travels to New York, but returns to find that Cass has killed herself. When he goes to visit her corpse he embraces it and is ejected from the funeral home. Returning to his boarding house, he meets a young girl, who undresses for him.

Bukowski was not involved with the production of the film and he hated the finished results. The film is a singular failure, primarily because it ignores the eternal loneliness of the Bukowski's 'characters' and the sensitivity to the 'human condition' that informs most of his work, in favour of the depiction of sex and alcoholism.

Dominique Deruddere directed *Crazy Love* (aka *Love Is A Dog From Hell* aka *L'Amour Est Un Chien De L'Enfer*, 1987; note that the American title, *Love Is A Dog From Hell,* comes from a collection of poems published by Black Sparrow Press in 1977). Based on Charles Bukowski's short story 'The Copulating Mermaid Of Venice' and sections of *Ham On Rye,* the film was funded, in part, by the Ministries of Culture of the Flemish and French Communities. The film depicts Harry Voss in three periods of his life, each of which is marked by a combination of desire, lust and loneliness. In the first section of the film, set in 1955, a twelve-year-old Voss (Geert Hunaerts) fantasizes about the ideal of romantic love, symbolized for Voss by a photograph, which he has stolen from a cinema lobby, of an actress playing a princess. Unfortunately Voss discovers the illusion of such fantasies when, encouraged by an older — although equally naive — friend, he attempts to make love to a sleeping, drunken older woman, although flees in terror when she awakes. Disillusioned, the twelve-year-old is shown how to masturbate by his friend.

The second section of the film depicts a nineteen-year-old, acne-covered Harry (Josse De Pauw), who is cajoled by his friend into attending his graduation party. After a few calming drinks Harry attends the dance, but is too embarrassed by his acne to approach the object of his desire Lisa Velani (An Van Essche). Harry enters the bathroom and carefully wraps his entire head in toilet paper, then — his disfiguring acne thus hidden — approaches Lisa and the two dance.

The third — and final — section of the film depicts an adult Harry, who with his friend Bill (Amid Chakir) steals a bottle of whisky and drunkenly roams the streets. Seeing an ambulance parked in a deserted street, the two men open up its back door to investigate and find a body inside. They steal the body and take it back to Harry's low-rent room. The corpse is that of a beautiful young woman and — while Bill, now feeling remorseful, suggests burying the corpse — Harry makes love to her. Taking the corpse to the beach, Harry demands that Bill perform a wedding ceremony, then Harry and his true love enter the sea...

Crazy Love was Deruddere's first feature film and is undoubtedly the most successful adaptation of Bukowski, primarily because the script (by Deruddere and Marc Didden) maintains a perspective which is similar to that manifested in Bukowski's writing. The film captures Bukowski's tenderness — especially in its depiction of Harry as a child — as well as his 'sleazy-ness' and maintains a balance between the two elements so that, in the last segment, Harry's lovemaking with the corpse becomes an act of warmth and humanity, rather than deviance. Notably, Deruddere cast the same actress — Florence Beliard — to play both the corpse and the princess of the young Harry's cinematic fantasies, thus emphasizing the genuinely romantic nature of Harry's actions. When asked about his opinion of the finished film Bukowski stated: "I liked *Crazy Love*. As I told Deruddere, 'You made me look better than I am.' He over-sensitized me. But it came out nicely and much of it was actually me".[6]

The only film based on Charles Bukowski's work, with which he was directly involved, was *Barfly* (1987), an American production made by Cannon Films and Francis Ford Coppola's Zoetrope Studios and directed by Barbet Schroeder (although, according to Bukowski, Sean Penn wanted Dennis Hopper to direct the film). Schroeder first became aware of Bukowski's work while he was directing *Koko Le Gorille Qui Parle* (aka *Koko The Gorilla*, 1978) and perceived a kinship in the figure of Bukowski.

In 1979 Schroeder paid Charles Bukowski $20,000 to write a screenplay — a powerful incentive for Bukowski who at the time was "living in a dive and just barely getting by"[7] — and promised the writer that he would not change the screenplay at all without prior consultation. Bukowski stated that: "Barbet just showed up one day. Said he wanted to make a film about my life. He kinda talked me into it. I was very reluctant, because I don't like film. I don't like actors, I don't like directors, I don't like Hollywood. I just don't like it. He laid a little cash on the table — not a great deal, but some. So I typed it out".[8]

Bukowski refused to examine or study other screenplays in order to understand the technique and wrote the screenplay for *Barfly* by gut instinct. The screenplay was based on Bukowski's own experiences during his twenties when he was a barfly in Philadelphia and Los Angeles:

> "I drank and I fought. My means of existence ... I don't know how I ever made it. The drinks were free, people brought me drinks. I was more or less the bar entertainer, the clown. ... There were characters in there. There was ugliness, there was dullness and stupidity. But there was also a certain gleeful high pitch you could feel there. ...We had a roaring time. And we'd be sitting there, eight guys. And suddenly somebody would make a statement, a sentence. And it would glue everything we were doing together. It would fit the outside world in — just a flick of a thing, then we'd smile and go back to our drinking. Say nothing. It was an honorable place, with a high sense of honor and it was intelligent. Those minds were quick. But given up on life. They weren't in it, but they knew something".[9]

Barfly took Schroeder seven years to produce — primarily because of trouble raising the necessary budget — but was eventually shot (by *Paris, Texas* cameraman Robby Muller) over a six-week period and edited in four weeks, in order that it was ready to be premiered at the Cannes Film Festival, in May 1987. *Barfly* opens with writer and drunkard, Henry Chinaski (Mickey Rourke) getting beaten senseless by Eddie, the barman of The Golden Horn. The film then follows Henry as he meets Wanda Wilcox (Faye Dunaway) and begins a stormy drunken relationship with her. Wanda soon prostitutes herself with Chinaski's nemesis, the barman Eddie, to earn the rent, while Henry becomes involved with the literary editor Tully Sorenson (Alice Krige). Tully pays Henry for his latest short story and hopes to be able to help him. Henry — who does not wish to be redeemed — cashes Tully's cheque, picks up Wanda and goes to the bar, where he buys everybody drinks. Tully enters the bar and is chased out by Wanda. Henry drunkenly challenges Eddie to a brawl in the street behind the bar.

What all three of these Bukowski films have in common is that their overall structure is broadly cyclic: *Storie Di Ordinaria Follia* opens and closes with Ben fascinated by the (myth of) 'virginal innocence' of teenage girls, *Crazy Love* begins and ends with the same actress portraying both of Harry's fantasy figures (the princess and the corpse) and *Barfly* begins and ends with Henry being beaten senseless by the bartender, in the lot behind the Golden Horn. The cyclic structure of each of these texts suggests that the events that have transpired will be repeated, endlessly, by their protagonists; this repetition is mirrored, in part, in Bukowski's books, which repeat similar themes in and across texts.

During the seven-year period that preceded the production of *Barfly*, frustrated by the endless delays, Barbet Schroeder began to take a video camera to Bukowski's house and shot Bukowski's drunken monologues. Bukowski acquiesced and let Schroeder film him because he had "a guilt complex ... I never thought Barbet would get *Barfly* off the ground".[10] The ensuing footage was collected onto a video and released under the title *Charles Bukowski Tapes*.

In 1990, Christine Choy and Renee Tajima produced a documentary portrait of the Madison Hotel, in downtown Los Angeles. The short film, *Best Hotel On Skid Row*, was narrated — although not scripted — by Charles Bukowski. In 1995, a live video, entitled *Bukowski At Bellevue*, depicting Bukowski reading was released.

5. Affiliated Works

Although Charles Bukowski is the 'post-Beat' author whose work has proved most popular with filmmakers, several other authors who have been affiliated — either by friendship, by shared publishers, by stylistic similarity to Beat Generation authors and/or by fighting censorship battles — have also had their work filmed.

Hubert Selby Jr's groundbreaking novel *Last Exit To Brooklyn* was filmed by West German director Ulrich Edel as *Letzte Ausfahrt Brooklyn* (*Last Exit To Brooklyn*, 1989). Selby, like Bukowski, was never expressly identified as a Beat writer, or a member of the Beat Generation; however, he was published in the final issue of the journal *The Black Mountain Review* (#7, 1957), which was edited by Allen Ginsberg and Robert Creeley and focused on the Beat Generation and the San Francisco Renaissance. The issue also included contributions from William Burroughs, Gregory Corso, Allen Ginsberg, Jack Kerouac, Gary Snyder and Philip Whalen. *Last Exit To Brooklyn* was published by Grove Press, thanks — in part — to LeRoi Jones, who assisted Selby in getting a literary agent.

Invariably *Letzte Ausfahrt Brooklyn* loses the experimental tone of the book and collapses the fragmented narratives into a cohesive whole. The film also tones down the violence of the book, especially in the gang rape of Tralala — removing the savage violence of the book. Nevertheless, overall the film maintains a trajectory that is broadly similar to the original source.

Selby's 1978 novel *Requiem For A Dream* was filmed in 2000. Directed by Darren Aronofsky and starring Ellen Burstyn and Jared Leto, *Requiem For A Dream* is a harrowing study of addiction (to both illegal drugs and prescription medications) and the film retains the visceral power as Selby's original novel. Although Selby remains only an affiliate rather than a core Beat writer, it is worth noting that this film shows exactly what can be achieved in transforming an edgy, 'difficult' novel into a film.

Beat associate Terry Southern co-wrote the film scripts for Stanley Kubrick's *Dr Strangelove* (1963), Tony Richardson's *The Loved One* (1965), Roger Vadim's *Barbarella* (1967), Dennis Hopper's *Easy Rider* (1969) and Aram Avakian's *End Of The Road* (1969). Southern's own novel became the source for Joie McGrath's *The Magic Christian* (1969) and his collaborative novel (with Mason Hoffenberg) became the source for Christian Marquand's *Candy* (1968).

The comedian Lenny Bruce, who was affiliated to the Beat Generation by his desire to challenge the norms of a society he could only ever view as hypocritical and obscene, by his endless fights against censorship, by his fierce intellect and by the frequently improvised nature of his stand-up routines, has also been the source of several films. A film of Bruce delivering a comedy routine which details part of his trial for obscenity is caught in John Magnuson's *Lenny Bruce Performance Film* (1968). *Lenny Bruce Without Tears* (Fred Baker, 1972) presents a portrait of the comedian, using a combination of performance, archive footage and narration. The film includes appearances from Paul Krassner, Kenneth Tynan and Steve Allen, amongst others. Lenny Bruce also directed, scripted and voiced an original cartoon *Thank You Masked Man*, produced by John Magnuson and Bruce. With the animation directed by Jeff Hale, the short film is a vicious satire of the mythology of the red-blooded all-American hero, using the archetypal figure of the Lone Ranger as its template. In 1974 Bob Fosse directed *Lenny*, a biographical portrait of Lenny Bruce, based on the stage play by Julian Barry. The film starred Dustin Hoffman as Bruce and Valerie Perrine as his wife Honey.

William Burroughs' longstanding literary associate in Tangier, Paul Bowles, had his novel *The Sheltering Sky* produced as a film in 1990. *The Sheltering Sky* was produced by Jeremy

Thomas (who also worked with Cronenberg on the film *Naked Lunch*), directed by Bernardo Bertolucci and starred John Malkovich and Debra Winger.

Ken Kesey wrote two novels in the early '60s: *One Flew Over The Cuckoo's Nest* (1962) and *Sometimes A Great Notion* (1966) and before he 'gave up' writing in 1964 to cross America from California to New York in the psychedelic painted, 1939 International Harvester 'Furthur' school bus driven by Neal Cassady and the Merry Pranksters. This trip — fueled by LSD and optimism — took in visits to the Beats — Burroughs, Ginsberg and Kerouac (who, legend has it, was upset by the Merry Pranksters' usage of a Stars and Stripes flag for a couch cover and carefully folded it up) — by the new generation of the underground. *Sometimes A Great Notion* was the source for the film *Never Give An Inch* (aka *Sometimes A Great Notion*, 1971), which was directed by Paul Newman — following the departure of the original director Richard A. Colla — who also starred alongside Henry Fonda in the film. Kesey's first cult novel *One Flew Over The Cuckoo's Nest* was made into a film directed by Milos Forman and starring Jack Nicholson, Louise Fletcher, Will Sampson and Brad Dourif; it was released to critical acclaim in 1975.

Another text that owes much of its style to the Beats is Hunter S. Thompson's autobiographical account *Fear And Loathing In Las Vegas*, which, after an awkward and complex gestation, was finally realized on film by director Terry Gilliam in 1997. Once again, this reveals exactly how a cinematic adaptation of an 'unfilmable' modern novel can be successfully produced.

6. Beats On Film

The following list details appearances by the central Beat writers in film and video and the major Beat documentaries. While the key figures of the Beat movement have regularly appeared on television these appearances are excluded from this list, except in cases where the program has been constructed around a single Beat figure. Note that while every effort has been made to ensure that this list is complete, other works may exist and this is especially true of videos documenting live performances.

Beat Documentaries

Cain's Film (Jamie Wadhawan, 1969) presents a biographical portrait of Scottish Beat connection and Sigma mastermind Alexander Trocchi. The film details the central aspects surrounding Trocchi's phenomenological study of addiction, *Cain's Book* (described by Burroughs as a "real classic, a real milestone"), including details on the book's banning for its drug references. The film includes commentaries from William Burroughs, Ronald Laing, Jim Haynes and Felix Topoloski and is shot in part at the Arts Lab.

Burroughs: The Movie (Howard Brookner, 1983), an indepth documentary of William Burroughs, including footage of the Nova Convention and extracts from *Thee Films*, alongside interviews with Burroughs, Ginsberg, Herbert Huncke, Lucien Carr, Brion Gysin, James Grauerholz and William's son, William (Billy) Burroughs III, amongst others. The film primarily follows a biographical trajectory and includes footage of William Burroughs demonstrating his extensive defensive armoury (steel cobra, knife, gun, blow gun etc.). Other memorable sequences include Burroughs and Ginsberg arm in arm describing their old routines and Burroughs meeting the artist Francis Bacon. One scene juxtaposes Burroughs reading a Dr Benway routine from the 'Hospital' section of *Naked Lunch*, with footage depicting the hilarious/gore sequence in all of its lurid and bloody detail, in a white walled toilet/operating theatre, with Burroughs as Dr Benway and Jackie Curtis making a cameo as the Nurse. This brief sequence offers a tantalizing glimpse at the possibilities inherent in making a film from Brion Gysin's screenplay.

There have been numerous documentaries focusing on Kerouac, these include *Jack Kerouac's America* (aka *Kerouac* aka *Kerouac, The Movie*, John Antonelli, 1984), *Kerouac* (aka *What Happened To Kerouac?* Richard Lerner and Lewis MacAdams, 1986) and *Jack Kerouac's Road — A Franco-American Odyssey* (Hermenegilde Chiasson, 1987). Commonly these films feature interviews with Kerouac's friends and associates: Allen Ginsberg, William Burroughs, Lawrence Ferlinghetti, Michael McClure, Carolyn Cassady, Herbert Huncke, Joyce Johnson and John Clellon Holmes, alongside archive footage of Kerouac on *The Steve Allen Plymouth Show*. Kerouac also examines the author's later years with footage of the older, conservative Kerouac arguing with Ed Sanders and William Buckley on *Firing Line*. Jack Coulter appears in docu-drama reconstructions as Kerouac in *Jack Kerouac's America*.

The Life And Times Of Allen Ginsberg (Jerry Aronson, 1986), a biographical documentary, including interviews with Allen Ginsberg, William Burroughs, Timothy Leary, Ken Kesey, Norman Mailer, Abbie Hoffman, Amiri Baraka and Joan Baez, amongst others. Alongside interviews the film utilizes archival footage and photographs, in order to contextualize Ginsberg's work. The film also depicts Ginsberg reading from 'Howl' and 'Kaddish'.

The Beat Generation — An American Dream (Janet Forman, 1987), a documentary about the personalities behind the Beat Generation, includes interviews with William Burroughs, Allen Ginsberg, Amiri Baraka and David Amram, amongst others. The film also utilizes archive footage of Jack Kerouac and Thelonious Monk.

A Moveable Feast: Profiles Of Contemporary American Authors — Allen Ginsberg (Bruce Berger, 1991), a short profile of Ginsberg, includes footage of Ginsberg reading.

No More To Say And Nothing To Weep For (Colin Still, 1997), subtitled 'An Elegy For Allen Ginsberg, 1926–1997, and produced for Channel 4 television, England, this hour-long film offers a brief overview of Ginsberg's life, with appearances from Gelek Rinpoche, Gary Snyder, Robert Creeley, Bob Rosenthal, Ed Sanders, Lawrence Ferlinghetti, Ann Charters, Ann Waldman. Philip Glass and others. This is cut with a variety of archive footage of Ginsberg — including some home movies. The final section of the film focuses on Ginsberg's relationship with Tibetan Buddhism and the question of death in his work and includes moving footage of Ginsberg performing his song 'Father Death'. The last scenes in the film depict Ginsberg on his deathbed, while Peter Orlovsky describes his final moments. Finally Patti Smith delivers a brief elegy.

Steen Moller Rasmussen and Lars Movin's Danish documentary *Words Of Advice: William Burroughs On the Road* premiered in 2007. Opening with Burroughs reading in Denmark, the film follows the author's journeys to the end of the road in Lawrence, Kansas. Alongside previously unseen footage of Burroughs, there are interviews with his friends in Lawrence, who offer an insight into Burroughs' later years.

'Performance' Films

Most of the films and videos in which the Beats appear are documentaries of performances and/or singular special events; this 'oeuvre' includes Peter Whitehead's *Wholly Communion* (discussed elsewhere).

The 'genre' also includes Iain Sinclair's and Robert Klinker's *Ah! Sunflower* (1967) a documentary of Allen Ginsberg's visit to the Dialectics of Liberation Conference, which transpired at the Roundhouse, London (produced for WDR TV, in Germany). While this film focuses on the Beats in '60s London, both Constanzo Allione's *Fried Shoes, Cooked Diamonds, The Beats At Naropa* (1978) and Robert Frank's *This Song For Jack* (1983) document the friendships, discussions, readings, meditations and activities at the Jack Kerouac School of Disembodied Poetics at Naropa Institute, Boulder, Colorado.

Castelporziano, Ostia Dei Poeti (aka *Lunatics, Lovers And Poets* andrea Andermann, 1981), is an Italian production featuring various poets — including Allen Ginsberg and William Burroughs — gathering and reading poetry on the beach where Pier Paolo Pasolini was killed.

Poetry In Motion (Ron Mann, 1982), a documentary, featuring poetry readings from Allen Ginsberg, William Burroughs, Amiri Baraka, Ed Sanders, Anne Waldman, Robert Creeley, Jim Carroll and Charles Bukowski.

West Coast, Beat And Beyond (Chris Felver, 1984), features readings by Allen Ginsberg, Lawrence Ferlinghetti, Jack Kerouac and Ken Kesey, amongst others.

A video of the 1983 Final Academy event in Manchester, entitled *The Final Academy Documents* (1984) was released by Ikon Video. This included footage of readings by both William Burroughs and John Giorno, alongside Antony Balch's *Towers Open Fire* and the previously unavailable *Ghosts At Number 9 (Paris)*. This has subsequently been made available on DVD.

John Giorno's Giorno Poetry Systems have issued a series of video's featuring Beat — and related — writers, artists, musicians and performers. This series includes: *It's Clean It Just Looks Dirty* (directot unknown,198?), Maria Beatty's *Gang Of Souls* (1989) and *Old Habits Die Hard* (directot unknown,198?).

Michael McClure and ex-Doors keyboardist Ray Manzarek's collaborative performance is documented in Sheldon Rochlin's and Maxine Harris's *Love Lion* aka *Love Lion: Performance With Words And Music By Michael McClure And Ray Manzarek* (1991).

Gregory Corso improvised a piece on American History in the short *Gregory Corso Reads From The U.S Constitution And Bill Of Rights* (James Rasin and Jerry Poynton, 1992). Jerry Poynton also directed the short video *New Orleans, 1938* (1995) depicting Edgar Oliver reading Huncke's short story of the same name.

In addition to these films, Allen Ginsberg briefly appears in D.A. Pennebaker's *Don't Look Back* (1966), a cinema vérité documentary following the then Beat-affiliated folk singer Bob Dylan on his 1965 tour of Britain. Bob Dylan went on to direct a film of his 1966 tour with The Hawks. The resulting film, which was co-directed with Howard Alk and photographed by D.A. Pennebaker, was released in 1972 as *Eat The Document*. Bob Dylan also directed *Renaldo & Clara* (aka *Renaldo And Clara*, 1977). This film is part documentary of Bob Dylan's Rolling Thunder Tour and part-improvised sketches based upon the lyrics of Dylan's songs and the experiences of the '60s and '70s and includes an appearance by Ginsberg in a role credited as 'the Father'. Ginsberg also appears in video artists Nam June Paik and Shigeko Kubota's *Allan 'n' Allen's Complaint* (1982).

William Burroughs can be seen dancing with Laurie Anderson in *Home Of The Brave* (Laurie Anderson, 1986), which documents the performance artist, musician and filmmakers, live show as constructed for her 1984 'Mister Heartbreak' tour.

Beat Appearances

Many of the following films feature the Beats as specific figures, who — when utilized within a text — act as signifiers for and often representatives of, large cultural and/or sociopolitical metanarrative/s. It should be noted that, while both William Burroughs and Allen Ginsberg are called upon to discuss, or represent, questions of sexuality and homosexuality, it is predominantly Ginsberg who appears in films focusing on the anti-war/protest movement.

Dynamite Chicken (Ernest Pintoff, 1971); described as a 'multimedia mosaic', this film edits together various footage as a comment on media, including Allen Ginsberg, Tuli Kupferberg, Lenny Bruce, Leonard Cohen, Joan Baez, Yoko Ono, et al.

Breathing Together: Revolution Of The Electric Family (Morley Markson, 1971); this film explores American militants against the background of the electronic age and includes a re-enactment of the Chicago trials. The film features an appearance by Allen Ginsberg.

Marihuana Marihuana (Jamie Wadhawan, 1972) follows Alexander Trocchi and Simon Vinkenoog as they travel to Amsterdam to meet The Lowlands Weed Company, a company formed by Kees Hoekert and Robert Jasper Kronfeldt, one of the founders of the Dutch 'anarchist' group the Provos.

Underground And Emigrants (Rosa von Praunheim, 1976); an interview-based documentary on the underground theatre and arts scene in New York, this film includes an interview with William Burroughs, amongst others.

The War At Home (Glenn Silber and Barry Alexander Brown, 1979); a film which locates the Vietnam war within the specific socio-geographic context of Madison, Wisconsin and follows the effects of the war on the townspeople and the university. The film includes footage of the aerial bombardment of Vietnam, student protests and extracts from interviews with various politicians and demonstrators, including Allen Ginsberg.

Beeldenstorm (aka *Iconoclasm* aka *A Storm Of Images*, Johan van der Keuken, 1982); produced in the Netherlands, this montage film includes footage of Allen Ginsberg.

Growing Up In America (Morley Markson, 1988), a documentary examining the central figures associated with the '60s 'youth revolt' — often depicted via archive footage — and following these figures to the present. The figures discuss their lives and how they would change them given the chance. Those interviewed include Allen Ginsberg, Abbie Hoffman, Jerry Rubin and Timothy Leary, amongst others.

Heavy Petting (Obie Benz, 1989), a documentary about sexuality in the 1950s which includes interviews with Allen Ginsberg, William Burroughs and Abbie Hoffman, amongst others. These interviews are intercut with various examples of related archive material, ranging from sex and health documentaries to clips from '50s television and film.

As actors, the Beats have appeared in a wide variety of films, predominantly those by either underground or independent filmmakers. William Burroughs has had most 'success' as an actor appearing in a string of films, including Gus Van Sant's *Drugstore Cowboy* (1989) and *Even Cowgirls Get The Blues* (1993). In Michael Almereyda's *Twister* (1988[11]) Burroughs appears — in a role credited as 'Man in Barn' — alongside cult actors Harry Dean Stanton, Crispin Glover and Suzy Amis. In 1989 Burroughs appeared in Howard Brookner's *Bloodhounds On Broadway*. David Blair's *Wax, Or The Discovery Of Television Among The Bees* (1992) combines stock and original footage which is carefully juxtaposed and manipulated via digital technologies and features a cameo by Burroughs as James 'Hive' Maker — a photographer who wants to photograph life after death.

Both Burroughs and Ginsberg appear in Robin Spry's *Prologue* (1967), in scenes shot at the Democratic Convention in Chicago. Jacob Burckhardt's *It Don't Pay To Be An Honest Citizen* (1985) follows a young filmmaker, who after being mugged, vows to get back his stolen film and features appearances by both Burroughs and Ginsberg.

Allen Ginsberg and Peter Orlovsky appear in cameos as themselves, naked and chanting, in John Palmer and David Weisman's *Ciao! Manhattan* (1972). The cast is predominantly made up from (one time) Warhol associates, including Edie Sedgewick — who plays the lead role Susan — as well as Paul America, Brigid Polk, Viva and Jane Holzer. *Ciao! Manhattan* follows Susan in the amphetamine haze of late '60s New York in a portrait of glamor and addiction that has been described as documentary. Notably, Edie Sedgewick died three months after the film was completed.

Gregory Corso appeared in Rachel Amodeo's indictment of homelessness, *What About Me?* (1993), appearing alongside such underground notables as Richard Edson, Rockets Redglare, Nick Zedd, Tommy Turner and Johnny Thunders.

The following films are of related interest.

The Dream Machine (1983); a collaborative piece by Derek Jarman, John Maybury, Cerith Wyn-Evans and Michael Kostiff, funded by the Arts Council of Ireland, this work features four short filmic 'dreams' inspired by the dreamachine.

Harry Smith has increasingly been recognized for his various cultural roles and in 2006 Rani Singh completed *The Old Weird America*. Focused primarily on Smith's role as a musicologist, the film features both archival performances of music from the Anthology of American Folk Music and contemporary reinterpretations of these classic folk songs by a variety of musicians including Sonic Youth, Nick Cave and Beck. The film contextualises Harry Smith's *Anthology* with interviews with Allen Ginsberg amongst others.

2007 saw the release of Mary Jordan's feature length Jack Smith documentary *Jack Smith and the Destruction of Atlantis*.

7. Herbert Hunke

A central influence on the Beat writers, Herbert Huncke has been the subject of one feature length documentary, Laki Vazakas's *Huncke And Louis* (1999). The film depicts the relationship between the writer and Louis Cartwright from 1993 until 1996. Vazakas met Huncke in the late '80s and became a close friend of the outlaw author. The film emerged from the director's fascination with the "long, tumultuous friendship between Huncke and Louis".[12]

While the director was familiar with Huncke's role as "Virgilian guide to the Beats"[13] he was "more interested in how Herbert and Louis became family to each other, how they managed to stay close, how they survived. I was interested in how they were getting by, day-to-day".[14]

Given complete access to their lives, the film combines conversations with Huncke and various associates alongside cinema vérité style footage of Huncke's daily life: "I was close with both men"[15] Laki recalls "and they gradually grew accustomed to my camera. Huncke once told me that my camera 'was incidental to our friendship'".[16]

Huncke And Louis opens with Huncke holding court at the Cafe Nico and Ann Charters talking about Beat culture but rapidly moves to a story of survival against insurmountable odds — poverty, homelessness, sickness and addiction — and the importance of companionship and love, as the film progresses it becomes clear that this friendship is fraught with pain and sorrow.

The film took six years to shoot and edit, documenting the often painful turns that the two men's relationship takes, yet amongst the gathering darkness brought on by Louis's self-destructive desires there emerge moments of quiet tenderness. Huncke's "shadowy"[17] status, even amongst those audiences familiar with the Beats, means that the film retains an underground status, and as Vazakas observes "Response to the film has been varied. Many artists and writers seem to connect with the uncompromising qualities of *Herbert And Louis* and of the filmmaking. When I've shown the film at colleges, some students seem horrified by the sight of a senior citizen taking prodigious quantities of drugs".[18]

Huncke And Louis is especially interesting because it is not simply a documentary about Huncke's life, it does not feature archive footage. Instead *Huncke And Louis* is, in the spirit of the Beat literature, a presentation of a period of life mediated through an artistic process.

Joe Ambrose filmed Herbert Huncke in conversation with writer Spencer Kansa at the Bayswater Hotel, London, in 1995. The footage was then used in Ambrose's short film *Herbert Huncke U.S. Junkie* (2000). In the movie Huncke discusses numerous topics, including his relationship with Jack Kerouac and William Burroughs. When it was first screened, the soundtrack of Huncke's voiced was mixed with live percussion performed by Islamic Diggers and musician Daniel Figgis. As Ambrose notes, "For the purposes of that occasion and by way of whimsy, we called ourselves The Master Musicians of Dublin".[19]

---

1. Cindy Fuchs, 'Drugstore Cowboy' in *Cineaste, vol xviii, #1,* 1990, p.43.

2. Steven Puchalski, *Slimetime: A Guide To Sleazy, Mindless, Movie Entertainment,* Critical Vision, Stockport, 1996, p.189.

3. British Film Institute, *Film Index International,* 1993–1995.

4. Charles Bukowski, *Tales Of Ordinary Madness,* City Lights Books, San Francisco, 1983, p.178.

5. Charles Bukowski, quoted in Chris Hodenfield 'Gin-Soaked Boy' in *Film Comment, vol 23, #4,* July/August 1987, p.54. Note that Bukowski did like the following films: Milos Forman's Ken Kesey adaptation *One Flew Over The Cuckoo Nest* (1975), David Lynch's *Eraserhead* (1976) and *Elephant Man* (1980) and Mike

Nichols' *Who's Afraid Of Virginia Woolf?* (1966). Bukowski also enjoyed the films of Akira Kurosawa (director of films such as *Shichinin No Samurai* (1954), *Kumonosu-Jo* (1957) and *Kagemusha* (1980)), for their battle scenes.

6. Charles Bukowski quoted in Kevin Ring 'Outsider Looking Out' in *Beat Scene, #11*, p.10.

7. Charles Bukowski quoted in 'Gin-Soaked Boy', p.57.

8. Charles Bukowski quoted in 'Gin-Soaked Boy', p.56.

9. Charles Bukowski quoted in 'Gin-Soaked Boy', p.57–58.

10. Charles Bukowski quoted in 'Gin-Soaked Boy', p.58.

11. This film has been variously dated as 1988, 1989 and 1990. 1988 emerges from Carole Zucker's essay on Crispin Glover's acting in *Twister*; 'The Concept Of "Excess" In Film Acting: Notes Toward An Understanding Of Non-Naturalistic Performance', in *Post-Script, Vol 12, #2*.

12. Laki Vazakas, personal correspondence.

13. Laki Vazakas, personal correspondence.

14. Laki Vazakas, personal correspondence.

15. Laki Vazakas, personal correspondence.

16. Laki Vazakas, personal correspondence.

17. Laki Vazakas, personal correspondence.

18. Laki Vazakas, personal correspondence.

19. Joe Ambrose, personal correspondence.

Bibliography

Note: Where possible full references have been given, although the nature of some archives precludes complete details.

Adler, Joan; 'On Location', in Dwoskin, Stephen, *Film Is... The International Free Cinema*, Overlook Press, Woodstock, 1975.

Arthur, Paul; 'Routines Of Emancipation: Alternative Cinema In The Ideology And Politics Of The Sixties' in James, David E., ed, *To Free The Cinema: Jonas Mekas And The New York Underground*, Princetown University Press, Princetown/Oxford, 1992.

Babuscio, Jack; 'Camp And The Gay Sensibility' in Dyer, Richard, ed, *Gays And Film*, British Film Institute, London, 1977.

Barsam, Richard Meran; *Nonfiction Film: A Critical History*, George Allen & Unwin Ltd, London, 1974.

Battock, Gregory, ed; *The New American Cinema: A Critical Anthology*, E.P. Dutton & Co, Inc, New York, 1967.

Bockris, Victor and Malanga, Gerard; *Up-Tight: The Velvet Underground Story*, Omnibus Press, London, 1983.

Brecht, Stefan; *Queer Theatre. The Original Theatre Of The City Of New York. From The Mid-60s To The Mid-70s*, Suhrkamp Verlag, Frankfurt am Main, 1978.

Breger, Udo, ed; *Soft Need #17 — Brion Gysin Special*, Expanded Media Editions, Basel–Paris, October, 1977.

Bukowski, Charles; *Tales Of Ordinary Madness*, City Lights Books, San Francisco, 1983.

Bukowski, Charles; *The Most Beautiful Woman In Town And Other Stories*, City Lights Books, San Francisco, 1983.

Bukowski, Charles; *Notes Of A Dirty Old Man*, City Lights Books, San Francisco, 1973.

Burroughs, William; 'Electronic Revolution', in *Ah Pook Is Here And Other Texts*, John Calder, London, 1979.

Burroughs, William; *The Naked Lunch*, John Calder, London, 1982, (1959).

Burroughs, William; *The Soft Machine/Nova Express/The Wild Boys: Three Novels By...* Grove Press Inc, New York, 1980 (1961/1964/1969).

Burroughs, William; 'Towers Open Fire!' in *Film*, #37, Autumn 1963.

Burroughs, William; *Port Of Saints*, Blue Wind Press, Berkeley, 1980.

Burroughs, William; *The Adding Machine: Collected Essays*, John Calder, London, 1985.

Burroughs, William; *Queer*, Picador, London, 1986, (1985).

Burroughs, William; *The Western Lands*, Picador, London, 1988, (1987).

Burroughs, William; *Exterminator!*, John Calder, London, 1984, (1974).

Burroughs, William; *The Burroughs File*, City Lights Books, San Francisco, 1984.

Burroughs, William; *Painting And Guns*, Hanuman Books Ltd, Madras–New York, 1992.

Burroughs, William; 'Introduction' in Silverberg, Ira, ed, *Everything Is Permitted, The Making Of Naked Lunch*, Grafton, London, 1992.

Burroughs, William and Gysin, Brion; *The Third Mind*, John Calder, London, 1979, (1978).

Burroughs, William, with Odier, Daniel; *The Job: Topical Writings And Interviews*, John Calder, London, 1969/1984.

Cantrill, Arthur and Corinne; 'Harry Smith Interview', in *Cantrills Film Notes, #19*, October 1974.

Carney, Ray; 'Complex Characters', and 'Unfinished Business', in *Film Culture*, vol 25, #3, May/June 1989.

Carney, Ray; *The Films Of John Cassavetes: Pragmatism, Modernism, And The Movies*, Cambridge University Press, Cambridge, 1994.

Carney, Ray; 'Escape Velocity: Notes On Beat Film', in Phillips, Lisa, ed, *Beat Culture And The New America: 1950–1965*, Whitney Museum of American Art, New York, Flammarion, Paris, 1995.

Carney, Ray, guest ed; *Post Script: Essays And Films In The Humanities*, 'Special Issue: John Cassavetes', vol 11, #2, Winter 1992.

Cassady, Carolyn; *Off The Road: My Years With Cassady, Kerouac, And Ginsberg*, Penguin Books, London, 1991 (1990).

Cassady, Neal; *The First Third And Other Writings: Revised & Expanded Edition*, City Lights Books, San Francisco, 1991 (1971).

Cecil, Paul, ed; *William Burroughs Birthday Book*, Temple Press, Brighton, 1994.

Cecil, Paul, ed; *Flickers Of The Dreamachine*, Codex, Hove, 1996.

Clarke, Shirley and De Hirsch, Storm; 'A Conversation' in *Film Culture*, *#46*, Autumn 1967 ("published belatedly" October 1968).

Deleuze, Gilles; *Nietzsche And Philosophy,* trans. Hugh Tomlinson, Columbia University Press, New York, 1983, (1962).
Deleuze, Gilles & Guattari, Felix; *Anti-Oedipus: Capitalism And Schizophrenia, vol 1,* University of Minnesota Press, Minneapolis, 1983, (1972).
Deleuze, Gilles & Guattari, Felix; *A Thousand Plateaus: Capitalism And Schizophrenia, vol 2,* Athlone, London, 1988.
Derrida, Jacques; *Of Grammatology,* John Hopkins University Press, Baltimore and London, 1976, (1967).
Dollimore, Jonathan; *Sexual Dissidence: Augustine To Wilde, Freud To Foucault,* Clarendon Press, Oxford, 1992, (1991).
Drew, Wayne, ed; *David Cronenberg: BFI Dossier Number 21,* British Film Institute, London, 1984.
Dwoskin, Stephen; *Film Is... The International Free Cinema,* Overlook Press, Woodstock, 1975.
Dwyer, Simon, ed; *Rapid Eye No. 1,* Creation Books, London, 1995, (1993, 1989).
Dyer, Richard, ed; *Gays And Film,* British Film Institute 1977.
Dyer, Richard; 'Believing In Fairies: The Author And The Homosexual' in *Fuss,* Diana, ed; *Inside/Out: Lesbian Theories, Gay Theories,* Routledge, London, 1991.
Elsaesser, Thomas; *New German Cinema: A History,* Rutgers University Press, New Brunswick, 1989.
Ely, Roger, compiler; *The Final Academy: Statements Of A Kind,* The Final Academy Catalogue, 1982.
Emery, Prudence and Silverberg, Ira; 'Production History: Notes And Scenes From The Making Of The Film' in Silverberg, Ira, ed, *Everything Is Permitted, The Making Of Naked Lunch,* Grafton, London, 1992.
Frank, Robert; *The Americans,* Cornerhouse, Manchester, 1993, (1957).
Fuchs, Cindy; 'Drugstore Cowboy', *Cineaste,* vol xviii, #1, 1990.
Fuss, Diana, ed; *Inside/Out: Lesbian Theories, Gay Theories,* Routledge, London, 1991.
Gever, Martha, Greyson, John & Parmar, Praibha, eds; *Queer Looks: Perspectives On Lesbian And Gay Film And Video,* Routledge, London, 1993.
Ginsberg, Allen; *Journals: Early Fifties, Early Sixties,* Grove Press, Inc, New York, 1978.
Ginsberg, Allen; *Collected Poems, 1947–1980,* Penguin Books, London, 1987, (1985).
Ginsberg, Allen, et al; 'International Poetry Incarnation' in Whitehead, Peter, ed, *Wholly Communion,* Lorrimer Films, London, 1965.
Glicksman, Marlaine; 'Highway 61 Revisited', *Film Comment, vol 23, #4.*
Gow, Gordon; 'Witchcraft Through The Ages', (review), *Films And Filming, vol 15, #5,* February 1969.
Grant, Barry Keith, ed; *Planks Of Reason, Essays On The Horror Film,* Scarecrow Press, Inc, Metuchen, N.J and London, 1984.
Gysin, Brion; 'Collaborators Antony Balch, Ian Sommerville' in Ely, Roger, compiler, *The Final Academy: Statements Of A Kind,* The Final Academy Catalogue, 1982.
Gysin, Brion; 'Dreamachine' in Cecil, Paul, ed, *Flickers Of The Dreamachine,* Codex, Hove, 1996.
Gysin, Brion and Wilson, Terry; 'Planet R101. Here To Go. Brion Gysin In Conversation With Terry Wilson. June 1976, Paris', in Breger, Udo, ed, *Soft Need # 17 – Brion Gysin Special,* Expanded Media Editions, Basel–Paris, October, 1977.
Hoberman, J.; 'The Forest And The Trees', in David E. Williams, ed, *To Free The Cinema: Jonas Mekas And The New York Underground,* Princetown University Press, Princetown/Oxford, 1992.
Hoberman, J.; 'On The Burroughs Bandwagon', *Première,* January 1992.
Hoberman, J.; 'Introduction', in Parker Tyler, *Underground Film: A Critical History,* Da Capo Press, New York 1995, (1969).
Hoberman, J.; (untitled review of *The Flower Thief*), *Village Voice,* 14th November, 1995.
Hodenfield, Chris; 'Gin-Soaked Boy', in *Film Comment,* vol 23, #4, July/August, 1987.
Hollings, Ken; 'Short Reviews', in *Performance: The Review Of Live Art, #26,* October/ November 1983.
Holmes, John Clellon; 'The Philosophy Of The Beat Generation', in Honan, Park, ed, *The Beats: An Anthology Of 'Beat' Writing,* J.M. Dent & Sons, Ltd, London, 1987.
Home, Stewart, ed; *What Is Situationism? A Reader,* AK Press, Edinburgh, 1996.
Honan, Park ed; *The Beats: An Anthology Of 'Beat' Writing,* J.M. Dent and Sons Ltd, London, 1987.
Huncke, Herbert; *The Evening Sun Turned Crimson,* Cherry Valley, Cherry Valley, 1980.
Huncke, Herbert; *Guilty Of Everything,* Hanuman Books, New York–Madras, 1991.
Igliori, Paola; *American Magus: Harry Smith A Modern Alchemist,* Inanout Press, New York, 1996.
Indiana, Gary; 'Burroughs', in Silverberg, Ira, ed, *Everything Is Permitted, The Making Of Naked Lunch,* Grafton, London, 1992.
Jaehne, Karen; 'David Cronenberg On William Burroughs: Dead Ringers Do Naked Lunch', in *Film Quarterly,* vol 45, #3, 1992.
James, David E; *A Critical Cinema 2: Interviews With Independent Filmmakers,* University of California Press, 1992.
James, David E, ed; *To Free The Cinema: Jonas Mekas And The New York Underground,* Princetown University, 1992.

Johnson, Joyce; *Minor Characters,* Picador, London, 1983.
Johnson, Kenneth Rayner; 'The Secret Language Of Alchemy', in Simon Dwyer, ed, *Rapid Eye 1,* Creation Books, London, 1995, (1989, 1993).
Katzman, Lisa; 'Moment By Moment', in *Film Comment,* vol 25, #3, May/June 1989.
Kelman, Ken; 'Smith Myth' in P. Adams Sitney, ed, *Film Culture, An Anthology,* Secker and Warburg, London, 1971, (1970).
Kerouac, Jack; *The Beat Generation Or The New Amaraean Church,* Act Three, unpublished.
Kerouac, Jack; *On The Road,* Penguin Books, London, 1991, (1957).
Kerouac, Jack; *The Dharma Bums,* Flamingo/Harper Collins, London, 1994, (1958).
Kerouac, Jack; 'Introduction', in Frank, Robert, *The Americans,* Cornerhouse, Manchester, 1993, (1957).
Kerouac, Jack; *Lonesome Traveller,* Granada Publishing Ltd, London, 1982, (1962).
Kerouac, Jack; *Desolation Angels,* Mayflower, 1968, (1960).
Luebering, J.E.; 'Urban Pirates And Anti-Tapes, Maeck To Introduce Midwestern Premier Of His Decoder', (publication unknown), 30 March, 1995.
Lykiard, Alexis; 'Introduction' in Whitehead, Peter, ed, *Wholly Communion*, Lorrimer Films, London, 1965.
McColgen, Gary; 'The Superstar: An Interview With Mario Montez', in *Film Culture,* #45, Summer 1967.
McGillivary, David; *Doing Rude Things: The History Of The British Sex Film,* 1957–1981, Sun Tavern Fields, London, 1992.
McKenzie, James; 'An Interview With Allen Ginsberg', in Knight, Arthur Winfield and Knight, Kit, eds, *The Beat Journey, vol 8,* The Unspeakable Visions Of The Individual, 1978.
Malanga, Gerard; 'Interview With Jack Smith', in *Film Culture,* #45, Summer 1967.
Mead, Taylor; 'The Movies Are A Revolution', in *Film Culture,* #29, Summer 1963.
Mead, Taylor; Son Of Andy Warhol, unpublished.
Mekas, Jonas; 'Notes On The New American Cinema', in P. Adams Sitney, ed, *Film Culture, An Anthology,* Secker and Warburg, London, 1971, (1970).
Mekas, Jonas; 'New York Letter: Towards A Spontaneous Cinema', in *Sight And Sound,* vol 28, #3 & 4 (double issue), Summer/Autumn, 1959.
Mekas, Jonas; 'Appendix: The Independent Film Award', in P. Adams Sitney, ed, *Film Culture, An Anthology,* Secker and Warburg, London, 1971, (1970).
Miles, Barry; *Ginsberg: A Biography,* Viking, London, 1990.
Miles, Barry; *William Burroughs: El Hombre Invisible,* Virgin Books, London, 1993, (1992).
Morgan, Ted; *Literary Outlaw: The Life And Times Of William S. Burroughs,* Henry Holt and Company, New York, 1988.
New American Cinema Group, Inc; *Film-makers' Cooperative Catalogue #7,* New York, 1989 .
Nicosia, Gerald; *Memory Babe: A Critical Biography Of Jack Kerouac,* Grove Press, Inc, New York, 1983.
Nuttall, Jeff; *Bomb Culture,* MacGibbon & Kee, London, 1968.
Oakes, Philip; 'Rooks' Move', *Sunday Times,* 30 May, 1971.
Phillips, Lisa, ed; *Beat Culture And The New America: 1950–1965,* Whitney Museum of American Art, New York, Flammarion, Paris, 1995.
Philips, Lisa; 'Beat Culture: America Revisited', in Phillips, Lisa, ed, *Beat Culture And The New America: 1950–1965,* Whitney Museum of American Art, New York, Flammarion, Paris, 1995.
P-Orridge, Genesis; *Muzak – A Concept In Human Engineering,* May, 1983.
Puchalski, Steven; *Slimetime: A Guide To Sleazy, Mindless, Movie Entertainment,* Critical Vision, Stockport, 1996.
Rayns, Tony; 'Pull My Daisy' (review), *Monthly Film Bulletin,* vol 41, #480, January 1974.
Renan, Sheldon; *The Underground Film: An Introduction To Its Development In America,* Studio Vista, London, 1968 (1967).
Renov, Michael, ed; *Theorizing Documentary,* AFI/Routledge, NYC, London, 1993.
Renov, Michael; 'Towards A Poetics Of Documentary', in Renov, Michael, ed, *Theorizing Documentary,* AFI/Routledge, NYC, London, 1993.
Rice, Ron; 'Diaries, Notebooks, Scripts, Letters, Documents', in *Film Culture, #39,* Winter 1965.
Rodley, Chris; 'So Deep in My Heart That You're Really A Part Of Me', in Silverberg, Ira, ed, *Everything Is Permitted, The Making Of Naked Lunch,* Grafton, London, 1992.
Rodley, Chris, ed; *Cronenberg On Cronenberg,* Faber and Faber, London, 1992.
Rosenthal, Alan; *The New Documentary In Action: A Casebook In Film Making,* University of California Press, Berkeley & Los Angeles, 1971.
Rosenthal, Irving; *Sheeper,* Grove Press, Inc, New York, 1967.
Sargeant, Jack; *Deathtripping: The Extreme Underground,* Soft Skull, New York, 2007, (1995).
Schaub, Martin; 'Robert Frank, Or: The Subject Matter Is The Photographer Himself', in *Dox,* #3, Autumn, 1994.

Schaffner, Heide; 'The Prophet', in *The Kenyon Collegian,* 6 April, 1995.
Sharpley, Anne; 'Where Is This Man Heading? The Elusive Mr. Burroughs Grants A Rare Interview', in *Evening Standard,* 1963.
Shaviro, Steven; *The Cinematic Body, Theory Out Of Bounds,* vol 2, University of Minnesota Press, Minneapolis/London, 1993.
Silverberg, Ira, ed; *Everything Is Permitted, The Making Of Naked Lunch,* Grafton, London, 1992.
Sitney, P. Adams; *Essential Film,* NYU Press, New York, 1975.
Sitney, P. Adams, ed; *Film Culture Reader,* Praeger Publishers, New York, 1970 (reprinted as *Film Culture, An Anthology,* Secker and Warburg, London, 1971).
Sitney, P. Adams, ed; *Film Culture, An Anthology,* Secker and Warburg, London, 1971, (1970).
Sitney, P. Adams; *Visionary Film: The American Avant-Garde,* Oxford University Press, NYC, 1974.
Smith, Jack; 'Rehersal For The Destruction Of Atlantis', in *Film Culture,* #40, Spring 1966.
Solnit, Rebecca; 'Heretical Constellations: Notes On California, 1946–61', in Phillips, Lisa, ed, *Beat Culture And The New America: 1950–1965,* Whitney Museum of American Art, New York, Flammarion, Paris, 1995.
Sommerville, Ian; 'Flicker', in Cecil, Paul, ed, *Flickers Of The Dreamachine,* Codex, Hove, 1996.
Sontag, Susan; 'Jack Smith's Flaming Creatures' in Battock, Gregory, ed, T*he New American Cinema: A Critical Anthology,* E.P. Dutton & Co, Inc, New York, 1967.
Stein, Rikki, with Gysin, Brion, Breger, Udo, Briskin, Jerry; 'Hamri – Send Up With Your Shadows' in Breger, Udo, ed, *Soft Need # 17 – Brion Gysin Special,* Expanded Media Editions, Basel–Paris, October, 1977.
Stevenson, Jack; *Desperate Visions #1: Camp America,* Creation Books, London, 1996.
Strong, Simon; 'Burroughs: A Biological Mistake?', in Cecil, Paul, ed, *William Burroughs' Birthday Book,* Temple Press, Brighton, 1994.
Tallmer, Jerry; 'Introduction', in *Pull My Daisy – Text Ad-libbed By Jack Kerouac, For The Film By Robert Frank And Alfred Leslie,* Grove Press, Inc, New York, Evergreen Books Ltd, London, 1961.
Tartaglia, Jerry; 'The Gay Sensibility In American Avant Garde Film' in *Millennium Film Journal.*
Thom, Albie; *Polemics For A New Cinema,* Wild & Wooley Press, Sydney, 1978.
Tyler, Parker; 'For Shadows, Against Pull My Daisy', in *Film Culture,* #24, Spring 1962.
Tyler, Parker; *Underground Film: A Critical History,* DaCapo Press, New York, 1995, (1969).
Vague, Tom and Rickers, Manuella; 'Klaus Maeck: Interview By..., Hamburg, October, 1984', in Vague, Tom, ed, *Vague [The 20th Century And How To Leave It],* Psychic Terrorism Annual, #16/17, 1988 (1984).
Vale. V, and Juno, Andrea, eds; *Re/Search 4/5, William S. Burroughs, Brion Gysin, Throbbing Gristle,* ReSearch, San Francisco, 1982.
Vogel, Amos; *Film As Subversive Art,* Weindenfold & Nicolson: London, 1974.
Watson, Steven; 'Chronology', in Phillips, Lisa, ed, *Beat Culture And The New America: 1950–1965,* Whitney Museum of American Art, New York, Flammarion, Paris, 1995.
Warhol, Andy; *From A To B And Back Again,* Picador, London, 1978.
Warhol, Andy and Hackett, Pat; *Popism: The Warhol '60s,* Hutchinson & Co Ltd, London, 1981.
Weldon, Michael, with Beesley, Charles, Martin, Bob, and Fitton, Akira; *The Psychotronic Encyclopedia Of Film,* Plexus, London, 1989 (1983).
West, Phil; 'Decoder', (review), no other details available.
Whitehead, Peter, ed; *Wholly Communion,* Lorrimer Films, London, 1965.
Whitehead, Peter; 'Notes On The Filming', in Whitehead, Peter, ed, *Wholly Communion,* Lorrimer Films, London, 1965.
Wilson, David; 'Chappaqua', (review), *Monthly Film Bulletin,* vol 37, #433, February, 1970.
Wilson, Terry; *Here To Go,* Creation Books, London, 2001.
Young, Allen and Ginsberg, Allen; *Gay Sunshine Interview,* Grey Fox Press, Bolinas, 1974.
Young, Colin and Bachmann, Gideon; 'New Wave – or Gesture?', *Film Quarterly,* vol 14, #3, Spring 1991.
Zedd, Nick; *Bleed: Part One,* Hanuman Books, New York–Madras, 1992.
Zucker, Carole; 'The Concept Of "Excess" In Film Acting: Notes Toward An Understanding Of Non-Naturalistic Performance', *Post-Script,* vol 12, #2.
Author Unknown; *Chappaqua Press Book,* photocopy, no other details.
Author Unknown; *Conrad Rooks' Siddhartha,* microfiche, no other details.
Author Unknown; 'The Times Diary: Honest Drug Film Beats Ban...', *The Times,* 20 January, 1968.

CD ROM

British Film Institute, *Film Index International,* 1993–1995.

Index Of Films

M

N

O

P

Q

R

S

Picture Credits

The front cover and frontispiece shows Allen Ginsberg in *Wholly Communion* and is reproduced courtesy of Peter Whitehead.

p.15 Allen Ginsberg chanting in *Chappaqua*.
p.17 *Pull My Daisy*
p.55 Shooting *Shadows*
p.69 Taylor Mead in *The Flower Thief*
p.91 Harry Smith's *Early Abstractions*
p.101 Jack Smith's *Flaming Creatures*
p.111 Phoebe Neville in *Cup/Saucer/Two Dancers/Radio*
p.125 Peter Whitehead
p.143 *Chappaqua*
p.151 Allen Ginsberg in *Fifty Fantastics and Fifty Personalities*
p.161 The Virus Board in *Towers Open Fire*
p.163 William Burroughs in *Ghosts At Number 9*
p.195 William Burroughs in *Commissioner Of Sewers*
p.209 Cronenberg, Burroughs and Weller
p.215 William Burroughs in *Commissioner Of Sewers*
p.219 Herbert Hunke in *Hunke And Louis*

p.29 & p.33 courtesy Alfred Leslie; p.91 & p.97 courtesy Harry Smith Archives & Anthology Film Archives; p.93 courtesy Harry Smith Archives; p.101, p.103, p.105, p.107, p.151 BFI, p.111 & p.117 courtesy Jonas Mekas; p.113 courtesy Stephen Shore; p.125 & p.133 courtesy Peter Whitehead; p.129, p.137 & p.141 courtesy David Larcher; p.153, p.161, p.163, p.167, p.229 courtesy Screen Edge & Cherry Red Films; p.165 courtesy Jack Stevenson; p.175 & p.183 (bottom) courtesy Genesis P-Orridge; p.183 (top) courtesy Frank Rynne; p.191 courtesy *Horse Hospital*; p.197, p.199 courtesy Klaus Maeck; p.195, p.215, p.217 courtesy Klaus Maeck & Screen Edge; p.219 courtesy Laki Vazakas.

While every effort has been made to locate copyright holders this has not been possible in every case. Many of these photos were designated for publicity and it is in this spirit that they are reproduced here.

Film Sources

The Final Academy Documents (including *Towers Open Fire* and *Ghosts At Number 9*) and *Thee Films* (including *William Buys a Parrot, Towers Open Fire, The Cut-Ups, Bill & Tony* and *Ghosts At Number 9*) are available on DVD via Cherry Red www.cherryred.co.uk

Joe Ambrose & Frank Rynne *Destroy All Rational Thought*, Klaus Maeck *Commissioner Of Sewers* and *Bukowski At Bellevue* are available on DVD via www.screenedge.com

Laki Vazakas *Hunke And Louis* is available via beatnow@gmail.com

Additional Information

Harry Smith www.harrysmitharchives.com
Master Musicians of Joujouka www.joujouka.net
Anthology Film Archives www.anthologyfilmrchives.com
Dreamachines and related subjects can be found at www.brainwashed.com
Throbbing Gristle www.throbbing-gristle.com
Information correct at time of publication.

Jack Sargeant is the author of numerous books on underground film and culture including *Deathtripping: The Extreme Underground*, also published by Soft Skull, and *Suture*. In addition he has co-edited *No Focus: Punk On Film* and *Lost Highways*. He has written introductions to Joe Coleman's *The Book Of Joe* and Lydia Lunch's *The Gun Is Loaded*, amongst others. He has written essays on topics as diverse as drugs and film, erotic depilation, amputee fetishism, and car-crash pop songs. Sargeant has also edited numerous true crime books. His work often appears in high-brow journals, academic books and low-brow magazines; he doesn't see the difference. He currently lives in the Antipodes.

Tessa Hughes-Freeland is a writer and filmmaker who lives in NYC. Her articles have appeared in numerous pop culture magazines and her films have been screened internationally in a wide range of venues, from museums to seedy bars.

Stephanie Watson is based in the UK and is a writer on film and cultural studies.

Arthur and Corinne Cantrill are filmmakers and writers whose journal *Cantrills Filmnotes* remains definitive. For information on obtaining copies, or purchasing a complete run of issues, see: http://www.sca.unimelb.edu.au/staff/arthur/